TIDES AMONG
NATIONS

TIDES AMONG
NATIONS

by Karl W. Deutsch

THE FREE PRESS
A Division of Macmillan Publishing Co., Inc.
NEW YORK

Collier Macmillan Publishers
LONDON

The Free Press
A Division of Macmillan Publishing Co., Inc.
866 Third Avenue, New York, N.Y. 10022

Collier Macmillan Canada, Ltd.

Library of Congress Catalog Card Number: 78-57053

Printed in the United States of America

-printing number

1 2 3 4 5 6 7 8 9 10

Library of Congress Cataloging in Publication Data

Deutsch, Karl Wolfgang
    Tides among nations.

    Includes bibliographical references and index.
    1. International relations. 2. Nationalism.
3. International organization. I. Title.
JX1395.D46   301.5'92   78-57053
ISBN 0-02-907300-6

To Rupert Emerson
Great Teacher, Scholar, Friend

Contents

Introduction   1

I.   Overviews and Orientation

Chapter 1.
The Growth of Nations   13
Chapter 2.
The Trend of European Nationalism: The Language Aspect   35
Chapter 3.
Nationalistic Intolerance and Economic Interest   44
Chapter 4.
Race Discrimination Among and Within Nations   65
Chapter 5.
Social Mobilization and Political Development   90

II.   Problems of Integration: National and International

Chapter 6.
Problems of Nation-Building and National Development   133
Chapter 7.
The Propensity to International Transactions   144
Chapter 8.
Shifts in the Balance of International
Communication Flows   153
Chapter 9.
A Generalized Concept of Effective Distance
and Political Development (with Walter Isard)   171

III.   Integration: Some Recent and Contemporary Cases

Chapter 10.
Large and Small States in Regional Integration   179

Chapter 11.
Symbols of Political Community   199
Chapter 12.
Problems of Central European Integration:
A View in 1954   217
Chapter 13.
Toward Western European Integration:
An Interim Assessment in 1962   234
Chapter 14.
Arms Control and Western European Integration:
Some Prospects in 1966   249
Chapter 15.
National Integration: A Summary of Some Concepts
and Research Approaches   269

IV   **Perspectives**

Chapter 16.
Nation and World   297
Chapter 17.
Limited Growth and Continuing Inequality:
Some World Political Effects   315
Chapter 18.
Some Prospects for Today's Industrial Countries   328

Index   335

Introduction

The tides of the sea rise and fall on the rocky coasts of New England and Canada, as they do at Britanny and elsewhere around the world. At some places, their ups and downs are gentle and barely discernible; at others they show terrifying power. Under certain conditions—when there is a new moon, when sun, moon and earth are lined up so as to add their gravitational attraction, and when a storm has occurred far out at sea, and when a strong onshore wind is blowing—the tide becomes a riptide, flooding the country far inland and causing vast destruction. And while the tides wax and wane, they also have cumulative effects as time goes on. They may change the outlines of a coast, adding some land at one place, sweeping it away at another; and over a very long period of time, they will even change the rotational speed of our entire planet, slowing it down by their friction.

There are tides among nations too. Their powers rise and fall; their states grow stronger or break down; small states or peoples may merge into larger ones, or small nations may secede from larger empires or federations. There may be riptides among nations—vast torrents of change in politics, economics, and culture, sweeping away old structures and creating new ones. And there may be cumulative effects in the changing fortunes of nations, adding up in time to changes in the fate of humanity and in the quality of human life.

Like all images, the image of the tides fits only imperfectly, and indeed to a very limited extent. Tides in nature have existed for millions of years; but modern nations and modern nationalism have existed mainly since the sixteenth and seventeenth centuries in parts of Western Europe, and they are much younger in most of Asia, Africa, Latin America, and Oceania. Tides of the sea are caused by natural forces, but people make their own history—within the limits of their circumstances, but still in important part by their own decisions.

The argument need not be belabored further. If the image of the tides will have drawn attention to the changing fate of peoples and nations within the context of the larger changes of world history and human development, it will have served its task.

THE THEME OF THIS BOOK

In their essence, the essays in this book deal with a single theme. They are concerned with the interlinked questions of nationalism and internationalism, war and peace. Those questions can be posed and attacked in many different ways, but for the sake of human survival they cannot be ignored.

Before World War I, most students of world politics believed that both nationalism and war would predominate forever in the affairs of humanity. A minority of scholarly writers, along with many adherents of the international labor movement and other groups aiming at political and social change, believed on the contrary that both war and nationalism would soon be overcome by evolution or abolished by concerted human effort. Much of the subsequent discussion of international affairs has been dominated by the contest between those two perspectives.

After World War I the second group of views, envisioning a non-nationalistic and warless world, came to prevail among the backers of the League of Nations. The first view, seeing nationalism and war as basic and perpetual, was soon revived with the rise of fascist movements and regimes in Italy, Germany, Japan, and other countries in the 1920s and 1930s. With their defeat in World War II, the hopes for a world of internationalism and peace rose to ascendancy again, spurring the founding and growth of the United Nations. They later receded, in part, with the setbacks of that organization and with the changing fortunes of the cold war and the armaments competition that followed.

At the start of the 1970s—two generations after 1914—the contest between the two broad views of world politics still seemed undecided, at least in the court of general political opinion. So far as the evidence of research and social science is concerned, however, its weight suggests that the argument was based on a badly posed question: Both contending views, it now appears, are wrong.

War still must be abolished during the next thirty years—at least in its large-scale, all-out form—or else it will destroy humankind. But nationalism cannot be abolished for two or three more generations, and probably not for a century; and for part of that time it may still increase in many countries, and among many ethnic and racial groups. One of the life-and-death questions of world politics in our time thus comes down to this: How can we understand nationalism and the growth of nations, and how can we keep the peace in a nationalistic world? How can we maintain this peace long enough to tide us over the dangerous decades and generations before us, until the conditions are created in which the age of nationalism can be ended—the conditions in which war will join incest, cannibalism, and chattel slavery on the list of deep-rooted social practices and institutions which the people of the world have overcome?

The papers collected in this volume address themselves to the various aspects of this common theme. They illustrate some of the developments in the thought of one man who started out as a student of nationalism in the late 1930s and who has pursued this topic since that time. They also illustrate the development of the topic itself since the great pioneering studies of such historians as Hans Kohn, Carlton Hayes, and Arnold J. Toynbee, and such students of government as Sir Ernest Barker, Rupert Emerson, and Quincy Wright.

Finally, they illustrate some of the changes in political science during the last thirty years. Retaining a principal concern for historical and descriptive analysis, political scientists have moved increasingly toward a more systematic comparative approach, toward the use of explicit theories and models, including those in mathematical form, and toward the use of verifiable quantitative data. We are still interested in the quality of events, in the answer to the questions: What is this event like? What does it resemble? But we increasingly also ask the quantitative questions: How large is this event or this process? How widely will it spread? How fast is this change occurring? Is it larger or smaller than the trends that oppose it? How soon is it likely to reach a critical level? We are still far from able to answer those questions satisfactorily, but we have gone some way toward that goal. And we cannot afford to stop trying.

Some of the approaches and detours in the search are illustrated in the chapters of this book. The papers on which they are based were written at different times between 1940 and 1974. (Their publication dates were often, but not always, one or two years after the time of actual writing.) The earlier papers, written between 1940 and 1951, largely stressed historical evidence, and sometimes economic analysis in general terms. Most of the papers of the 1950s and 1960s stressed quantitative evidence; and they often were aimed at reaching some quantitative conclusion.

More important than the shift in emphasis, however, was the continuing unity of the two concerns. The historical analyses dealt with the quantitative rise or decline of some political practices or social processes, and the quantitative studies aimed at gathering evidence for the persistence or change of some quality of political and social life. The two approaches are, in my view, interdependent and in the long run inseparable if the study of politics is to develop as a social science—that is, as verifiable knowledge which people can share.

DEVELOPMENT OF NATIONALISM

Part I of this book deals mainly with the development of peoples, states, and national societies and political systems. It views nationalism mainly from within the nation, but it notes that nationalistic ideas and practices in many countries share striking similarities. The nationalist's assertion that his ethnic group, racial group, or people is unique is itself one of the most uniform aspects of modern politics.

The first three chapters in the first part deal mainly with general historical and economic patterns. Chapter 1 traces in broad outline the process of the growth of nations. Additional work of mine will be found in my book *Nationalism and Social Communication.* Important recent contributions to this topic have been made by Jorge Dominguez, *Social Mobilization, Traditional Political Participation and Government Response in Early 19th Century South America* (Ph.D. dissertation, Harvard University, 1972); Paul J. Werbos, *Beyond Regression: New Tools for Prediction and Analysis in the Behavioral Sciences* (Ph.D. dissertation, Harvard University, 1974); and Douglas A. Hibbs, Jr., *Mass Political Violence* (New York, Wiley, 1973).

Chapter 2 examines in somewhat greater detail the rise of nations in Europe, in particular the rise of national languages in that part of the world, with the inference that what happened in Europe before 1914 and 1939 might well continue there during the middle third and perhaps the last third of this century, and that in the decades ahead it might find its parallels throughout much of the rest of the world.

Chapter 3, written in 1940–44, then examines some of the economic aspects of nationalism and race discrimination, not only among sovereign states but also within them, with particular regard to such matters as housing and real estate, employment and promotion, business opportunities, social contacts, and the transmission of property. Chapter 4 extends the argument to race relations and to their more recent changes in the United States.[1] Both chapters specifically deal with the notion of some writers that nationalism is economically irrational and show this idea to be false. The basic economic argument behind that notion rested on unrealistic assumptions of pure competition and on an ignorance of— or disdain for—the more modern economic theory of monopolistic competition. The latter analysis shows that nationalism and race discrimination are economically rational and profitable for many social groups and for long periods of time. Those who are rewarded by such discriminatory practices include many real estate interests and real estate agents, important parts of the financial community, many employers of labor, and to a lesser but significant degree, many clerks and other incumbents of lower-middle-class positions, many skilled workers and other favored labor groups, and many consumers of goods and services produced by the cheaper labor of the groups that have been successfully subjected to discrimination.

The resistance to reducing such linguistic, ethnic, or race discrimination is thus not solely psychological. Discriminatory habits and institutions are widely supported by significant economic rewards to important social groups. Meanwhile, the general social costs of such discrimination—beyond the obvious costs borne by its victims—often remain hidden and are so widely scattered throughout the whole of society that they rarely give rise to resistance by any group that is not itself directly and massively hit by them. Persons and groups trying to abolish discrimination must reckon with these resistances and with the widespread predisposition toward apathy. Starting from those realities, they can then seek alliances and strategies to change them.

A point not developed in Chapters 3 and 4 but implied in their agrument is

[1] George W. Shephard, Jr., and Tilden J. Lemelle, eds., *Race Among Nations: A Conceptual Approach* (Boston: D.C. Heath, 1970).

that, to a lesser but perhaps not insignificant degree, conditions of monopolistic competition may be present in most or all market processes, including the restricted market processes in socialist countries, such as their "markets" for employment and promotion. If so, then some conomic forces may tend to reward formal or informal linguistic, ethnic, or race discrimination in the public sectors of welfare states such as Britain, Canada, or Belgium, and they may do so even in such communist-ruled planned economies as the Soviet Union, Czechoslovakia, Yugoslavia, or the Chinese Peoples' Republic. To the extent that discrimination is being reduced in those countries or has actually been abolished there, this has been accomplished not merely by the automatic implications of a large public sector or of a socialist economy but also—to a crucial degree—by a deliberate political and moral effort. If such efforts were to slacken, or if they should be abandoned, linguistic, ethnic, and race discrimination might well revive in the public sectors of Western-style welfare states, as well as in some of the bureaucratic socialist countries at their present level of development.

In Chapters 3 and 4 an argument is presented that racial, linguistic, or national discrimination is related to monopolies and monopolistic practices by individuals and groups. Monopolistic behavior, in turn, tends to be related to the absence of change—to stability and stagnation. But most of human history in the long run is the history of change, and of radical change at that. From this fact arise the questions at the heart of Chapter 5. What have the great changes of modern history—the spread of the commercial and industrial revolutions, the rise of big cities, mass communications, mass literacy, and mass politics—done to the relations of the world's different nationalities, language groups, and races? What have they done to the separateness or unity of countries and regions? What have they done to the stability of privileged peoples, elites, and governments? Which of these changes are still continuing, and which are likely to prove irreversible? How far and how fast have they been moving until now, and what further speeds and scopes of such changes may be expected?

Chapter 5 examines data from nineteen developing countries from this point of view. Written originally in 1960 and 1961, its data were limited by what figures were then available. It was continued in many aspects by the Yale and Harvard data programs and by the first *World Handbook of Political and Social Indicators.*[2] The effects of social mobilization on the political development of particular countries has been studied since then in a number of special monographs, including John T. McAlister, *Revolution in Vietnam* (New York: Random House, 1969); Michael C. Hudson, *The Precarious Republic: Political Modernization in Lebanon* (New York: Random House, 1968); Hugh W. Stephens, *The Political Transformation of Tanganyika 1920-67* (New York: Praeger, 1968); William J. Foltz, *From French West Africa to The Mali Federa-*

[2] Bruce M. Russett, H. R. Alker, Jr., K. W. Deutsch, and H. D. Lasswell, *World Handbook of Political and Social Indicators* (New Haven: Yale University Press, 1964); Richard L. Merritt and S. Rokkan, eds., *Comparing Nations: The Use of Quantitative Data in Cross National Research* (New Haven: Yale University Press, 1966).

tion (New Haven: Yale University Press, 1964); and Dorothy Hess Guyot, *The Political Impact of the Japanese Occupation of Burma* (Ph.D. thesis, Yale University, 1966, typescript). Relevant additional work is being carried on by such younger scholars as Eldon C. Kenworthy on Latin America and William Irvin on Canada. More recent data on a worldwide basis is available in Charles L. Taylor and Michael C. Hudson, *World Handbook of Political and Social Indicators, 2nd ed.* (New Haven: Yale University Press, 1972). A summary estimate of the average speeds of social mobilization and of linguistic assimilation, on the basis of data available up to 1967, is given in Chapter 16 of the present volume. A new work, provisionally entitled *Berlin Handbook of World Political and Social Indicators*, on data from the 1970s, is being prepared again under the leadership of Professor Charles L. Taylor, in the International Institute for Comparative Social Research at the Science Center Berlin (West).

CONCEPTS OF INTEGRATION: NATIONAL AND INTERNATIONAL

Part II deals with the integration of smaller regions and populations into larger national units. It treats such integration as a social process that occurs largely by evolution and is not readily susceptible to manipulation by design. Chapter 6 discusses the notion of "nation-building," of creating "nations by design."[3] Such designs have often seemed to fit the convenience of some powerful advanced nation more than they fit the actual conditions of life among the developing African, Asian, or Caribbean countries concerned.

What actually constitutes a country, and what makes a nation? One important element—though not, of course, the only one—is the higher propensity to carry on various social, economic, and political transactions within a national system, in contrast to markedly lower levels of transactions across its boundaries. Chapter 7 explores those differential propensities and proposes a rough scale by which one could measure the levels of intranational and international integration which a population may have reached at some particular time and place. Chapter 8 then focuses from the same standpoint on a particular class of transactions, the flows of local, intranational and international mail communications, their relative proportions, and the changes in these over time. The flow of mail is viewed as an indicator of a wide variety of human relations—social, cultural, and economic. The same method of analysis is applicable to other classes of transactions. An analysis of this type can indicate whether the population of any particular country has become more or less preoccupied with affairs within its own borders, in contrast to affairs across or outside them. It can suggest whether the world as a whole has become relatively more or less "international." The data examined in Chapter 7 offer evidence that in terms of postal communi-

[3] See Arnold Rifkin, ed., *Nations by Design* (New York: Doubleday, 1968).

cations many countries, and the world as a whole, were becoming more international between 1890 and 1913, but the opposite trend prevailed from 1913 to 1951, and perhaps beyond.

Many kinds of transactions decline with geographic distance, or with some power of it. It is thus often possible to predict the flow of such transactions between two populations, P and Q, over the intervening distance D, from the formula $PQ/_Dk$ where k is that power of the distance giving the best fit. From such a formula, however, a virtual (as opposed to geographical) distance between any two populations can be computed for any class of transactions. Thus a generalized concept of distance can be developed. The differences in these virtual distances between the same populations, but in regard to different transactions, can then be applied to the exploration of possible processes of integration or disintegration between them. Chapter 9, which was written jointly with Walter Isard, explores some aspects and limits of this approach.

INTEGRATION: SOME RECENT AND CONTEMPORARY CASES

Part III of the book deals with recent and contemporary problems. Some of the experiences of the medieval and modern Swiss cantons are then compared in Chapter 10 with those of the American colonies on their way to becoming the United States in the eighteenth century, and with the experiences of the Italian and German states in the nineteenth century in their process of uniting into the large modern states, respectively, of Italy and Germany. In all those cases, larger and more highly developed political units made a distinct contribution as core areas in the process of integration. What the larger units did—Bern and Zurich; Virginia, Massachusetts, Pennsylvania, and New York; Prussia and Bavaria; Piedmont and Tuscany—depended to a large extent on their own domestic political structures and processes, and only secondarily on international processes and on initiatives and actions of smaller states. What smaller political units could achieve was to promote policies of integration that corresponded also to the internal dynamics of their larger partners and were acceptable to the governments, public opinion, and major interest groups of the larger units. From this analysis, first presented publicly in 1955, it followed that in the process of West European integration, too, the initiatives and policies of Belgium and the Netherlands would have only limited effects—in contrast to the more sanguine publicity they then received—and that the real development of European integration would not be as fast as a part of the press, and later the Treaty of Rome in 1957, envisaged, but would be much slower, confined to those steps that the leaders and voters of France and the German Federal Republic would be willing to accept in each period. As of 1978, when these words are being written, that more cautious prognosis seems to have proved realistic.

More thorough studies of pairs of countries, oscillating between almost-

integration and reaffirmations of national sovereignty, have been written by
Bruce Russett for the United States and Britain and by Peter Katzenstein for
Prussia-Germany and Austria.[4]

Chapter 11 treats the role of political symbols of community, along with some
of the inferences one can draw from them about changes in the mutual relations
among states, in particular among their elites and governments, over a period of
several decades.

A more qualitative analysis over a much longer time span is offered for the
region of East-Central Europe in Chapter 12. At its core are the questions:
When and why do people wish to change the scale of their political community?
When they live in large states or empires, why do some people long for secession
and the forming of a smaller state "of their own," and why, when they live in
small sovereign states, do so many people dream of integration into a larger
political union? Among those who now live under Communist regimes, is the
same discontent with the size of their currently existing states continuing, as it
did under the monarchies and republics of the preceding century and a half?

Chapters 13 and 14 present assessments of the state and prospects of Western
European integration, based on evidence from the late 1950s and the mid-1960s,
respectively. Each appraisal was reached by using a multiplicity of data, and each
was a good deal more reserved than the sanguine predictions of many other
writers at each time, without losing sight of the much more limited but real
progress that was being made.[5] Finally, chapter 15, written in 1974–76, tries
to sum up a general theory of political integration as it has developed in the
course of my work.

SOME PROSPECTS FOR THE FUTURE

The book concludes with Part IV, which contains three chapters on perspectives for the future. Chapter 16 deals with the past and prospective relationships
between nation states and the interdependent system of world politics. It
discusses the prospect that during the next half-century world politics may
become in some aspects more similar to domestic politics, and that some international counterparts to intranational welfare policies and income taxes may
have to be found and accepted.

Chapter 17 then reexamines the prospects of world politics in the light of

[4]Bruce M. Russett, *Community and Contention: Britain and America in The Twentieth
Century* (Cambridge, Mass.: MIT Press, 1963), and Peter J. Katzenstein, *Disjoined Partners:
Austria and Germany since 1815* (Berkeley: University of California Press, 1976).

[5]For fuller data, see K. W. Deutsch, L. J. Edinger, R. C. Macridis, and R. L. Merritt,
France, Germany and the Western Alliance (New York: Scribners, 1967); R. L. Merritt
and D. J. Puchala, eds., *Western European Perspectives on International Affairs: Public
Opinion Studies and Evaluations* (New York: Praeger, 1967); and, for an important recent
contribution, R. Inglehart, *The Silent Revolution: Changing Values and Political Styles
Among Western Publics* (Princeton, N.J.: Princeton University Press, 1977).

some recent images of limited world resources and limited or stagnant economic growth. It concludes that among persons and groups who view each other as aliens, coldly and with fear and envy, prospects of scarcity may turn into incitements to hostility and hate, and eventually into doctrines of war and civil war. Among persons and groups linked to each other by feelings of solidarity, sympathy, and mutual identification, on the contrary, perceptions of scarcity may lead to the voluntary acceptance of shared sacrifices, a more profound sense of community, and eventually the practices and institutions needed to sustain it. The timing of the shift from growth perspectives to prospects of some eventual slowing down of gross quantitative economic increases may, therefore, prove to be crucial.

The justice of many of the claims of the poorer countries and peoples of the world cannot be denied. Their hesitant steps toward self-help and cooperation and their continuing pressure on the rich countries cannot be stopped. In the long run—the next thirty to fifty years—the present distribution of economic resources probably will have to undergo some changes in their favor. For the age of nationalism, in which we are still living, may leave us with this lesson: On our small planet, there is no substitute for human solidarity.

The last chapter deals with the anticipated challenges and burdens that lie directly ahead. They are looked upon here as mainly challenges and burdens for the world's highly industrialized countries, which among them control approximately four-fifths of the productive machinery of the world, while four-fifths of humanity have among them only about one-fifth of the world's productive machinery and one-fifth of the world's income. By A.D. 2010 the world's population may well have risen to between 7 and 8 billion people, and all of them will have to eat. Equipping them to produce enough to feed themselves will be expensive, but equipping them to kill is already cheap today, and the progress of nuclear physics will make it cheaper tomorrow. We in the highly industrialized countries have a great deal of responsibility for the outcome, because we control most of the world's productive equipment, and in case of nuclear war we would be just as mortal as poorer people are. Our cities and our lives would be at stake side by side with theirs.

There are ways to avoid such a future of despair and mutual suicide. There is hope that the earth can become once again a home for all of its people, but the decisions between one kind of future and another most often will be decisions of politics. The tides among nations need not be left to blind processes of fate. By our decisions and our persevering action we can turn them into tides of life.

I | *Overviews and Orientation*

1 | The Growth of Nations

In its original version, this essay attempted a provisional summary and overview of the results of the first twelve years of my studies of nationalism and the conditions for its rise, decline, or changes in social and political content. My approach at that time owed much to four sources: the theory of communication and control, known as cybernetics, developed by Norbert Wiener; the notion of worldwide "fundamental democratization" of the sociologist Karl Mannheim; the stress on logical empiricism, reproducible quantitative evidence, and the operational approach, developed by Philip Frank, Otto Neurath, P. W. Bridgman, and the movement for the Unity of Science; and the open-minded humanistic, historical, and analytic approach of a great teacher and scholar, Rupert Emerson. There seemed to be no need to exhibit all this underlying philosophical and methodological structure in a paper first read to historians, but it was present and at work, as it has been in my later studies.

The substance of this chapter was read at the annual meeting of the American Historical Association at New York, December 1951; it subsequently appeared in print in *World Politics*. It is the latter version that is given here, with one brief interpolation: The transition to a world in which the majority of its population will no longer be employed mainly in agriculture, foreseen in 1951, is now in 1977 actually taking place. Before the end of the 1970s, it now seems likely, a world historical watershed will have been crossed.

At many places and times, tribes have merged to form peoples; and peoples have grown into nations. Some nations founded empires; and empires have broken up again into segments whose populations later attempted again to form larger units. In certain respects, this sequence appears to describe a general process found in much of history. This process shows a number of patterns which seem to recur, and which to a limited extent seem to be comparable among different regions, periods, and cultures.

From Karl W. Deutsch, "The Growth of Nations: Some Recurrent Patterns of Political and Social Integration," *World Politics* 5, no. 2 (January 1953): 168–195. Copyright © 1953 by Princeton University Press. Reprinted by permission of Princeton University Press.

Such recurrent patterns of integration, like other relative uniformities in history, raise the problem of the comparability or uniqueness of historical events. Yet the search for such relative uniformities in politics and history is essential to the pursuit of knowledge in these fields. No historical or political analysis can be written without the use of general concepts in which some notions of uniformity are necessarily implied.[1] Indeed, such recurrent patterns offer a background of similarities against which differences can stand out, and against which investigators can evaluate the specific and perhaps unique aspects of each particular case of national or supra-national integration.

At the same time, the study of the growth of nations may reveal cumulative change. It may suggest that the present period is unique in respect to both the extent of nationalism and the potentialities for supra-national organization. To the student of contemporary politics, it may further suggest specific problems of research and policy in the on-going process of social and political integration on the national as well as the international level.

Before discussing the recurrent problems of national integration, it may be well to note the use of a few terms. For the purposes of our discussion, a distinction is made between a *society*, which is defined as a group of persons who have learned to work together, and a *community*, which is defined as a group of persons who are able to communicate information to each other effectively over a wide range of topics.[2] A similar distinction is adopted between a *country*, which denotes a geographic area of greater economic interdependence and thus a multiple market for goods and services, and a *people*, which is a group of persons with complementary communications habits. A *nation* is then a people which has gained control over some institutions of social coercion, leading eventually to a full-fledged *nation-state;* and *nationalism* is the preference for the competitive interest of this nation and its members over those of all outsiders in a world of social mobility and economic competition, dominated by the values of wealth, power, and prestige, so that the goals of personal security and group

[1] The alternative views that all history is random, or that all important historical events are unique, involve grave philosphic difficulties. Historians who criticize the search for certain historical uniformities by their colleagues use in effect other uniformities which they prefer. Similar considerations apply to much of the debate about uniformities in other fields of social science. All knowledge involves the matching of patterns, and thus requires at least some similarities between some aspects of the events or processes studied. It thus requires some degree of relative uniformity among the processes to be investigated, in order to enable each science to proceed beyond the relatively simple and the relatively uniform to the recognition and study of those situations which are relatively complex and unique. Simplicity and uniformity, in this view, are not sweeping metaphysical assumptions about all aspects of all processes. They are properties of those aspects of processes which were first selected for investigation, or first investigated with success. With the growth of each science, this concern with the simple and the uniform reveals itself as a steppingstone to the study of more difficult matters. Cf. H. T. Pledge, *Science Since 1500,* New York, 1947, which superseded, in this respect, the view of E. A. Burtt, *The Metaphysical Foundations of Modern Physical Science,* London, 1932, and J. H. Randall, Jr., *The Making of the Modern Mind,* 2nd ed., Boston, 1940, pp. 227–29.

[2] Cf. K. W. Deutsch, *Nationalism and Social Communication,* Cambridge, Mass., 1953.

identification appear bound up with the group's attainment of these values.[3]

While peoples are found at almost any period in history, nationalism and nations have occurred during only a few periods. A nation is the result of the transformation of a people, or of several ethnic elements, in the process of social mobilization. Thus far, however, the processes of social mobilization and communication have at no time included all people. The "universal states" listed by A. J. Toynbee as stages in the disintegration of particular civilizations[4] were superficial short-cuts, rather than solutions to the problem of the unity of all people.

Periods of "universal states" have left behind them, however, a number of widespread languages, such as Latin, Greek, or Arabic; and a measure of cultural assimilation among certain social groups such as the nobility, town population, or the clergy of some "universal church."[5] The results have somewhat resembled a *layer-cake pattern*, with a high degree of cultural assimilation and participation in extended social communication among the top layers of society; a lesser degree on the intermediate levels; and little or no assimilation or participation among the mass of the population at the bottom.[6]

In several parts of the world, the cycle—from local isolation to "universal" empire and back to a new age of localism[7]—has been traversed more than once. Yet the cycle has usually shown a net gain, in the sense that there has been a gain in man's technological and scientific command over nature,[8] and that some of the most important cultural, intellectual, moral, and spiritual traditions of the earlier civilization have tended to survive that civilization in which they arose, and continue, often as a "universal church" or religion, to influence the development of new peoples and new regions.[9]

[3]*Ibid.;* and "Nationalism and the Social Scientists," in L. Bryson, *et al.*, eds., *Foundations of World Organization: A Political and Cultural Appraisal,* New York, 1952, pp. 9–20, 447–68. For other studies in this field, cf. now K. W. Deutsch and R. L. Merritt, *Nationalism and National Development, An Interdisciplinary Bibliography 1935–1965,* Cambridge, Mass., 1970.

[4]A. J. Toynbee, *A Study of History,* London, 1939, iv, pp. 2–3.

[5]For examples of such limited assimilation during and after the expanding phase of certain civilizations or universal states, see *ibid.,* Vols. i–iv, *passim,* and the appendix of "Lingue Franche" in Vol. v, pp. 483–526. Cf. also A. C. Woolner, *Languages in History and Politics,* London, 1938, and H. A. Innis, *Empire and Communication,* Oxford, 1950, and *The Bias of Communications,* Toronto, 1952. On particular languages, see Woolner, *op. cit.,* pp. 109–48, 156–67; H. A. R. Gibb, *The Arabs,* Oxford, 1940; George Antonius, *The Arab Awakening,* Philadelphia, 1939, p. 16; P. K. Hitti, *History of Syria Including Lebanon and Palestine,* New York, 1951, pp. 483–89.

[6]Cf. Royal Institute of International Affairs, *Nationalism,* London, 1939, p. 9; A. P. Usher, *Economic History of England,* Boston, 1920, pp. 20–21.

[7]For a discussion of the changes of linguistic disintegration following upon the dissolution of a universal empire, see Ramón Menéndez Pidal, *Castilla, la tradición, el idioma,* Buenos Aires, 1945, pp. 191–194.

[8]For the Graeco-Roman and medieval civilizations, this point has been stressed by Gordon Childe, *What Happened in History,* Harmondsworth, Eng., Penguin Books, 1950, pp. 279–82.

[9]A. J. Toynbee, *op. cit.,* v, p. 79, and *passim.*

As a result, much of world history has consisted of recurrent "feudal ages" in various parts of the world, though such periods in most cases were "feudal" only in the loose sense of the word. They were characterized by intense localism and dispersion of agriculture and settlement, as well as of military and judicial power, and by sharp distinctions between the class of scattered power-holders and the mass of the peasant population. At the same time, these "feudal" periods were marked by a certain universalism of political and cultural traditions, by memories of a past universal state, or by the knowledge of a highly developed civilization in some other area.[10] Such unifying memories or traditions were no mere disembodied thoughts: they were carried and disseminated by the institutions of organized churches and monastic orders, by a thin but far-flung network of trade relations and routes of pilgrimage, and sometimes by the movement and resettlement of small numbers of persons with special skills, industrial or military, over considerable distances.

From the point of view of nationality, all these were variations of the common layer-cake pattern. Assimilation to a common standard among the upper classes might be feeble, as during the "dark ages" in Western Europe; it might be somewhat more strongly developed, as among the European nobility at the time of the Crusades; or it might be almost complete, as in a universal state, as it had been in that of Imperial Rome. In any case, it would touch the masses of the people in the villages only indirectly and slowly. And even where it did touch and assimilate them in the course of centuries, there their continued passivity and lack of direct participation in affairs of wider import seemed to make it irrelevant for long periods of time whether the underlying population in the villages had been assimilated at least imperfectly to a common standard as in Italy, or whether they had remained as sharply differentiated as Czechs and Germans in Bohemia, or as Malays and Chinese in Malaya.[11] Only when this relatively passive population was mobilized in the processes of economic growth and political organization, did its cultural and social characteristics acquire in each case a new and crucial importance in the process of nation-building.

The processes of partial social mobilization and of nation-building have been recurrent phenomena in history, at least in certain general characteristics. What uniformities can we find in this growth of nations in the past? And in what ways is our own age different in respect to the growth of nations from any age that has gone before?

---

[10] A Conference on Feudalism was held on October 31 and Nobember 1, 1950, at Princeton University under the auspices of the Committee on Uniformities of the American Council of Learned Societies. For the point made in the text, see the papers submitted to the Conference and the abridged report on its proceedings issued by the Council (Washington, D.C., multigraphed). See now R. Coulborn, ed., *Feudalism in History,* Princeton, 1956.

[11] Cf. Elizabeth Wiskemann, *Czechs and Germans,* London, 1938; Victor Purcell, *The Chinese in Malaya,* London, 1948; Rupert Emerson, L. A. Mills, and V. Thompson, *Government and Nationalism in Southeast Asia,* New York, 1942.

SOME POSSIBLE SPECIFIC UNIFORMITIES

Uniformities which have been found in the growth of nations include the following:

1. The shift from subsistence agriculture to *exchange economies.*
2. The social mobilization of rural populations in *core areas* of denser settlement and more intensive exchange.
3. The growth of *towns,* and the growth of social mobility within them, and between town and country.
4. The growth of *basic communication grids,* linking important rivers, towns, and trade routes in a flow of transport, travel, and migration.
5. The differential accumulation and *concentration of capital* and skills, and sometimes of social institutions, and their *"lift pump" effect* on other areas and populations, with the successive entry of different social strata into the nationalistic phase.
6. The rise of the concept of *"interest"* for both individuals and groups in unequal but fluid situations, and the growth of *individual self-awareness* and awareness of one's predispositions to join a particular group united by language and communications habits.
7. The awakening of *ethnic awareness* and the acceptance of *national symbols,* intentional or unintentional.
8. The merging of ethnic awareness with attempts at *political compulsion,* and in some cases the attempt to transform one's own people into a privileged class to which members of other peoples are subordinated.

Some of these similarities may be discussed briefly.

The Shift to Exchange Economies

The shift from subsistence agriculture to an exchange economy seems to have characterized all cases of wider national integration which I have been able to find. Where the exchange economy came to embrace the bulk of the population and to bring many of them into direct contact with each other in the interchange of a wider variety of goods and services, there we find a tendency to "national" or at least regional, linguistic, and cultural "awakening," provided only that sufficiently large numbers of individuals enter the exchange economy and its more intensive communication *faster* than they can be assimilated to another "alien" language or culture.

Where these shifts take place, the ethnic and in part the linguistic situation becomes, as it were, loosened or softened, and capable of settling again into new and different molds. The awakening of the Slavic population of the Balkans, and the rise of regions of greater intensity of trade and exchange around which the revived Serbian and Bulgarian languages and nationalities were constituted, may perhaps serve as illustrations.[12]

Further Social Mobilization
and Integration in Core Areas

The shift to an economy and culture based on wider interchange takes place at different times and different rates of speed in different regions. The result is often the existence of more "advanced" regions side by side with more "undeveloped" ones. The former are then often in a position to function as centers of cultural and economic attraction for some of the populations of the latter, and thus to become nuclei of further integration. The "when" is thus often as important and sometimes more important than the "where," and the processes of social mobilization and partial integration are truly historical in the sense that each step depends to a significant extent on the outcome of the step that went before.

Political geographers have sought to identify *core areas* around which larger states were organized successfully in the course of history. Characteristic features of such core areas are unusual fertility of soil, permitting a dense agricultural population and providing a food surplus to maintain additional numbers in non-agricultural pursuits; geographic features facilitating military defense of the area; and a nodal position at an intersection of major transportation routes. Classic examples of such core areas are the Ile de France and the Paris basin, or the location of London.[13]

It should be noted that the density that makes a core area is one of traffic and communication rather than mere numbers of passive villagers densely settled on the soil. Thus the dense population of the Nile valley seems to have been less effective as a wider center of integration than the sparse population of the Arab territories beyond Mecca and Medina, who more than compensated for their smaller numbers by their proportionately far greater mobility, activity, and traffic.

The theory of core areas, however, cannot account for the persistence of some

---

[12] By the end of the [eighteenth] century many village notables (*knez*) began to come into contact as hog exporters with foreign lands, especially with the supply services of the Austrian armies. Among this class the leaders of the Serbian uprising of 1804 were found . . . [who] started the movement for Serbian independence and beyond that for Southern Slav unification . . ." (Hans Kohn, *The Idea of Nationalism,* New York, 1944, p. 549). Cf. also S. Mladenov, *Die Geschichte der Bulgarischen Sprache,* Berlin, 1929; Alfred Fischel, *Der Panslawismus bis zum Weltkrieg,* Stuttgart, 1919. For some general social and political aspects of the shift to an exchange economy, see Karl Polanyi, *The Great Transformation,* New York, 1944.

[13] For core areas and population clusters, see D. Whittlesey, *The Earth and the State,* New York, 1939, pp. 11–12, 142–52; and Preston James, *Latin America,* New York, 1942, pp. 4–8. For the nodal location of London, see Sir Halford Mackinder, *Britain and the British Seas,* New York, 1902.

states and the failure of others. What counts for more may well be what happens within each core area, and perhaps particularly what happens in its towns.

The Growth of Towns, Mobility, and Ties Between Town and Country

There is no developed nation, it appears, without towns which have or have had a period of considerable growth, of mobility within the towns, and of increasing ties of social mobility, communication, and multiple economic exchange between town and country.

There have been towns, of course, where one or more of these conditions did not exist, and to that extent national development has been incomplete, absent, halted, or retarded. On the other hand, to the extent that there was such growing mobility and communication within towns and between town and country, national development was accelerated.

The Growth of Basic Communication Grids

Most nations do not seem to have grown from single centers. Many nations have had several capitals and have shifted their central regions several times in the course of their history. Even the classical example of growth around one center, France, has long had two capital cities, Paris and Orléans; and some significant phases of the unification of the French language took place at the Champagne fairs and along the trade routes leading through that region—not to mention the role of the North-South routes and connections in helping the North to consolidate its victory over separatist and Albigensian elements in the Midi during the religious wars of the thirteenth century.[14]

A more extreme case, Germany, has no single core that could be easily identified,[15] and it seems more helpful to think of Germany as essentially a grid of routes of traffic, communication, and migration. The basis of this grid is a pattern in the shape of the capital letter E, in which the back and the bottom strokes are formed by the valleys of the Rhine and the Upper Danube between Cologne, Basel, and Passau, while the middle stroke is formed by the river Main and the routes going eastward from Mainz to Frankfurt and beyond, and the top stroke is formed by the routes following the *Börde*, the strip of fertile and easily traversable land from Wesel on the Rhine to Magdeburg on the Elbe.

To this basic pattern which was already established well before A.D. 1000,

[14]Whittlesey, *op. cit.*, pp. 138–39, 151. Cf. W. Von Wartburg, *Evolution et structure de la langue francaise*, Leipzig, 1934, and *Les origines des peuples romans*, Paris, 1941.
[15]This is illustrated by the divergent views of such writers as Whittlesey, *op. cit.*, pp. 166–70; Josef Nadler, *Das stammhafte Gefüge des deutschen Volkes*, Munich, 1934. pp. 104–9; Theodor Frings, *et al.*, *Kulturräume and Kulturströmungen im mitteldeutschen Osten*, Halle, 1936, p. 312.

there were then added the North-South routes from Augsburg and Munich to Nuremberg and Bamberg and northward to Brunswick, or northeastward to Leipzig and Halle or Meissen and Dresden. These routes became important chiefly during and after the twelfth century, and the Frankfurt-Leipzig and Nuremberg-Leipzig connections gained steadily in importance through the sixteenth century. All these northeastward and eastward communication lines were tied together once more by the river Elbe, which cuts them all, and all of them, when prolonged across the Elbe, came to a common focus in the region of Berlin, near the narrowest part of the North German plain between the Bohemian mountain massif and the North Sea. From Berlin these routes fanned out again southeastward into Silesia and northeastward to East Prussia and the German cities on the coast of the Baltic countries. The succession of language centers, the shift of the centers of printing, publishing, and journalism, the migrations of merchants, nobles, and settlers all followed the main lines of this grid, or a very few minor routes which form secondary parts of the same basic pattern.[16]

The same notion of a basic grid seems to be applicable to the unification of China, Russia, Switzerland, Canada, and the United States.[17] It would be interesting to investigate the relationship of such a grid to the incomplete unification and more recent separations of the areas that now comprise India, Pakistan, and Bangla Desh.

It is not suggested that a grid in itself can make a nation. Also necessary, as a rule, are a minimum of cultural compatibility and, in many cases, sufficient similarity between spoken dialects to permit the emergence of a common language for large sections of the population. The cultural and linguistic data in themselves are given by history, of course, at each stage of the process. Yet we know how much of a difference in language or culture has been bridged successfully in the emergence of such nations as the Swiss, the British, or the Canadians, provided that enough tangible and intangible rewards and opportunities were present, ranging from greater wealth, security, freedom, and prestige to the subtler attractions of new common symbols, dreams, and ways of life.

[16] Adequate references to this summary would amount to a separate chapter. In addition to the works cited in the preceding note, see e.g. Ludwig Salomon, *Geschichte des deutschen Zeitungewesens,* I, Oldenburg-Leipzig, 1906, pp. 10–17, and *passim;* Gerhard Lüdtke and Lutz Mackensen, *Deutscher Kulturatlas,* 5 vols., Berlin, 1928–36.

[17] Cf., on China, G. B. Cressey, *The Geographic Foundations of China,* New York, 1934; Percy M. Roxby, "China as an Entity: The Comparison with Europe," *Geography,* XIX, No. 1 (1934), pp. 1–20; John de Francis, *Nationalism and Language in China,* Princeton, N.J., 1950; etc. On Russia, see Robert Kerner, *The Urge to the Sea: The Role of Rivers, Portages, Ostrogs, Monasteries and Furs,* Berkeley, Calif., 1942; V. O. Kluchevskii, *A History of Russia,* Vol. 1, New York, 1911; J. W. Thompson, *Economic and Social History of the Middle Ages, A.D. 300–1300,* New York 1931. On Switzerland, see Aloys Schulte, *Geschichte des mittelalterlichen Handels und Verkehrs zwischen Westdeutschland und Italien,* Vol. 1, Leipzig, 1900; Lüdtke und Mackensen, *op. cit.;* Hans Nabholz, *Geschichte der Schweiz,* Vol. I, Zurich, 1932; C. Englert-Faye, *Vom Mythus zur Idee der Schweiz,* Zurich, 1940; Richard Weiss, *Volkskunde der Schweiz,* Zurich, 1946.

The Differential Concentration of Capital,
Skills, and Social Institutions

A major factor in national differences and national pride today are the differences in the general standard of living. To some extent such differences tend to cut across the differences between social classes; there is a social, moral, or traditional component in what is considered "bare subsistence" in a given community, or in what counts as "luxury" in another; and a significant part of what is considered the poor population in a relatively wealthy community may be appreciably better off in terms of physical goods and services than even many of the relatively well-off members of a poor or economically backward people. This difference between the generally prevailing standards of wealth, comfort, and opportunity among different regions or peoples has sometimes been called the *Kulturgefälle* ("the drop in the level of culture") by German writers who have employed this concept to bolster claims to German supremacy or exclusiveness vis-à-vis the populations of Eastern Europe and the Balkans.

Behind the differences in the standards of living lie differences in levels of productivity and in the supply of factors of production, that is, in the material means to pursue any one of a wide range of conceivable ends regardless of the difference in importance assigned to some of these ends relative to others in some particular culture. These differences in productivity may involve geographic factors such as soils, water supplies, forests, mineral deposits, and the absence of obstacles to transportation. All such geographic factors, however, depend on specific technologies to give them significance. Every concentration of natural resources requires, therefore, a concentration of productive skills and knowledge if people are even to know how to use them; and resources as well as skills require a concentration of invested *capital* if they are to be used in fact.

It should be clear that, as technology progresses, the relative importance of the man-made factors of production, such as capital and skills, has tended to increase relative to the importance of the few natural facilities which once were the only ones that more primitive technologies could exploit. There is reason to believe that present-day differences in living standards are due far less to differences in natural factors of production, and far more to differences in the supply of skilled labor, schools, housing, and machinery.

Particular peoples and nations may then tend to crystallize, as it were, around particular concentrations of capital and technology, or of particular social institutions which offer individuals greater opportunities for the pursuit of the goods or factors which they have learned to desire.

Thus we find in very different parts of the world the growth of peoples around specific social institutions or specific concentrations of economic opportunity. The combination of trade routes, cities, Alpine passes, and peasant freedom did much for the integration of the Swiss people; and so perhaps did the combination of dikes, fertile land, fishing, trade, and cities for the Dutch and Flemish peoples. The growth of the Bulgarian tobacco industry in the late nineteenth century may have had a somewhat comparable effect on the Bulgarianization of some of the populations of the "Bulgarian-Macedonian border;[18] and there may have been similar relations between the growth of the American tobacco trade and the British loyalties of Glasgow merchants at the beginning of the eighteenth century;[19] and again between the growth of the nineteenth-century cotton trade and the emergence of a set of separate cultural and political loyalties among the populations of the "Cotton Kingdom" in the South in the United States.[20] Elsewhere we find the emergence of distinct peoples not so much around specific economic opportunities but rather around a combination of material opportunities with a new and distinctive way of life. Thus the Cossacks on the Russian-Tartar border and the Sikhs in the areas of Hindu-Moslem conflict in India each unite individuals into a people by offering them more freedom and dignity through a life of martial valor in a situation where such valor is rewarded.

The effects of differential standards of living and of productivity operated long before the Industrial Revolution, but they were increased by its coming. Where large economic or industrial developments have taken place, they have had a "lift-pump" effect on the underlying populations. They have induced migrations of populations to the regions of settlement, employment, and opportunity, and put these newcomers into intensive economic and political contact with the locally predominant peoples, and with each other. This physical, political, and economic contact had one of two cultural and linguistic consequences: either it led to national assimilation, or, if national assimilation to the dominant group could not keep pace with the growing need for some wider group membership for the newcomer, then the "lift-pump" effect would tend to lead eventually to a new growth of nationalism among the newly mobilized populations. Eventually, it might result in the assimilation of some previously separate groups, not to the still-dominant minority, but to the "awakening" bulk of the population.

This rebellious nationalism of the newly mobilized population rejects the language or culture of the dominant nationality. Yet it shares many of its values and it desires to share or acquire its wealth and opportunities. The motives for this secessionist nationalism are thus to a significant extent the same motives that would lead, under different circumstances, to national assimilation. Nationalism and assimilation are, therefore, ambivalent in the economic as well as in the psychological sense. The same wealth and prestige are pursued by either method: in national assimilation they are to be attained through sharing, while in national resistance they are to be attained by power.

Both national assimilation and national resurgence thus respond in a "lift-

---

[18] Cf. Hermann Wendel, *Makedonien und der Friede*, Munich, 1919.
[19] Cf. Andrew Dewar Gibb, *Scottish Empire*, Glasgow-London, 1937.
[20] Cf., e.g., William E. Dodd, *The Cotton Kingdom: A Chronicle of the Old South*, New Haven, Conn., 1919.

pump" situation to the power of the "pump." The intensity and appeal of nationalism in a world of sharply differentiated income and living standards perhaps may tend to be *inversely proportional to the barriers to mobility between regions and classes,* and *directly proportional to the barriers against cultural assimilation, and to the extent of the economic and prestige differences between classes, cultures, and regions.*

Seen in this light, the rise of nationalism and the growth of nations have some semi-automatic features, even though they have other features which are by no means automatic. As the distribution of scarce rewards is made unequal by economic or historic processes; as people learn to desire the same kinds of rewards; as they fail to be assimilated to the language and culture of the dominant group; and as they succeed in becoming assimilated with other individuals and groups who possess cultural and language habits more compatible with their own—as all these processes go on, situations conducive to nationalism are created without anyone's deliberate intention.

The Concept of Self-Interest and
The Experience of Self-Awareness

The concept of a nation is bound up with that of a national interest. Already the non-national or proto-national institutions of the city-state and the princely state imply the notion of group interests and interests of state, and all these notions of national, state, or city interests imply in turn the interests of individuals. But this concept of individuals with interests has itself gained its present importance only gradually in the course of certain developments of history.[21] Even today different regions and civilizations ascribe to it different degrees of significance, and it may lose again in the future much of its present importance.

At bottom the notion of interest perhaps implies a situation in which men are pitted against each other in a competitive situation in which some of them can improve or even maintain their positions only at the expense of others. The word "interest" denotes then the ensemble of individuals' chances for improving or maintaining their position against all competitors, and thus, indirectly, the amount and effectiveness of disposition of their resources applicable to the competitive situation in which they find themselves. Such competitive situations may be relatively vague and unpredictable, or they may be formalized and hence in part predictable to a more or less high degree. The more predictable they are, the more easily can they be recognized as competitive by the participants. Among the most highly formalized competitive situations are games.[22] Most real-life situations tend to differ from formalized games in their far greater

---

[21] Cf. Charles A. Beard, *The Idea of the National Interest,* New York, 1934, pp. 22-25. I am indebted to Professor Hans Kohn for valuable suggestions on this point.

[22] Cf. John von Neumann and Oscar Morgenstern, *The Theory of Games and Economic Behavior,* Princeton, N.J., 1944.

range of possibilities for changes in the rules and even in the very units of the
competition—a difference immortalized by Lewis Carroll in Alice's croquet game
in Wonderland.

Nevertheless, there is perhaps one characteristic similarity between games and
competitive social or economic situations, and that is the distinction between
objectively "rational" behavior, i.e. behavior rewarded by the intrinsic rules of
the game, or the "logic of the situation," as against subjectively convenient
behavior, i.e. behavior that is most probable because of the previously acquired
personal memories and habits of the players. Most individuals and groups learn
only to a limited extent from playing games, regardless of experience; much of
their behavior may remain an experience of their previously acquired and slow-
changing personalities or habits, rather than of any strategy objectively conducive
to winning.

Actual performance in a competitive situation is thus a series of compromises
between acting out one's character and "playing the game," but if one learns
enough to be able to stay in the game at all, the continued experiences of the
cues and rewards which the game offers may lead to cumulative learning of new
habits and thus to modifications of character in the direction of the traits rewarded by the game.

Markets and power contests resemble such "games." They reward certain
kinds of behavior on the part of the players; and they may teach them certain
patterns of habits and values. The simplest result of this process has been stated
vigorously by Ruth Benedict: a highly competitive culture, such as modern
Western civilization, has often tended to elevate to positions of power and prestige individuals with such markedly aggressive and competitive behavior that
other cultures might at times even doubt their sanity.[23]

The late Professor Joseph Schumpeter has suggested almost the opposite
observation: according to his view, the competitive games of the free market and
of laissez-faire industrialism have functioned very well in Western society, but in
the course of the decades and generations since the Industrial Revolution these
competitive economic institutions have inculcated something like a psychological
revulsion from competition and insecurity among the people who grew up to
live under them. Competitive institutions, according to Schumpeter, unwittingly
have taught people a non-competitive and even anti-competitive set of desires
and behavior norms which center on security: the continued operation of such
institutions is gradually becoming impossible due to the state of mind which
they have engendered, and which already has led to the widespread replacement
of laissez-faire private enterprise by various institutions of socialism or the
"welfare state."[24]

These seemingly contradictory observations perhaps illuminate two sides of
the same reality. As people leave the relative security of villages and folk cultures

[23] Ruth Benedict, *Patterns of Culture*, New York, Penguin-Mentor Books, 1946, p. 256.
[24] Joseph Schumpeter, *Capitalism, Socialism, and Democracy*, 2nd ed., New York, 1947.

for the mobility and uncertainty of travel, towns, and markets, and for the competition of wealth-getting, politics, and warfare, they may find greater opportunities and rewards for aggressiveness and self-assertion; and at the same time they may come to feel more poignantly the loneliness, the loss of security, and the loss of context and meaning in their lives which the transition to the new ways of life entails.

Nationalism is one peculiar response to this double challenge of opportunity and insecurity, of loneliness and power. People discover sooner or later that they can advance their interests in the competitive game of politics and economics by forming coalitions, and that they stand to gain the firmer these coalitions can be made, provided only that they have been made with individuals and groups who have to offer in this game the largest amount of assets and the least amount of liabilities. To form the firmest possible connections with the most promising group of competitors would seem to be sound long-run strategy. With which group such firm connections can be formed is by no means arbitrary: in politics and economics such coalitions will depend to a significant degree on social communication and on the culture patterns, personality structures, and communications habits of the participants. Their chances of success will thus depend to some degree on the links that make a people, the ties of nationality. Machiavelli's advice to princes to rely on soldiers native to their kingdom was sound: a policy along these lines became the basis of the military power of the rulers of Brandenburg-Prussia in the century that followed, with results that were to lead eventually to the emergence of a German nation-state.[25] The victory of the ethnic Turkish elements over the largely Slavic-speaking Janissaries in the struggle for the control of the Imperial Ottoman Court in the seventeenth century, and the emergence of the ethnic Turkish elements in the reform of the Ottoman Empire after 1908, and again in the salvaging of a much reduced Turkish state after 1918, may be other cases in point.[26]

Organization along ethnic or national lines is by no means the only type of alignment which may be tried in the competitive game. Yet of all these probable patterns of organization, ethnic or national alignments often combine the greatest strength and resilience with the greatest adaptability to a competitive world. So long as competitive institutions continue to prevail, nationalism can mobilize more people and organize them more firmly than can many competing types of organization. The potential rewards of nationalism then grow in proportion to the potential resources of wealth and power to which members of a particular people have, or can gain, access on preferred terms.

To develop thus the economic, intellectual, and military resources of a territory and a population, *and to knit them together in an ever tighter network of communication and complementarity based on the ever broader and more thorough participation of the masses of the populace*—all this is sound power politics; and

[25] Cf. Sidney B. Fay, *The Rise of Brandenburg-Prussia, 1640-1786*, New York, 1937, pp. 52-53.
[26] Cf. A. J. Toynbee, *Op. cit.*, v, pp. 486, 518-19.

those who carry out such policies tend to be rewarded by the long-run outcome of this contest.

What may fit the necessities of the competitive game may also fit some inner needs of its participants. Ages of social mobilization, of rapid changes in the traditional social contexts, tend to be ages of increasing self-doubt and self-awareness for the individuals who live in them. The questions: Who am I? Whom do I resemble? In whom can I trust?—are asked with a new urgency, and need more than a traditional answer.

As people seek answers to these questions they must try to take stock of themselves, of their memories, their preferences, and their habits, of the specific images and indeed of the specific words in which they were conveyed and in which they are now stored in their minds. As old cultural or religious patterns, beliefs, and ceremonies become questionable, self-searching must lead back to the childhood memories and the mother tongue, in terms of which so many experiences have been acquired, and out of which, in a sense, people's characters and personalities have been built up. When people seek for themselves, they thus may come to find their nationality; and when they seek the community of their fellows, they may discover once again the connection between ethnic nationality and the capacity for fellowship. Instances of this process can be found even in antiquity: it is well known that Socrates enjoined upon his pupils the imperative, "Know thyself," and that Socrates' pupil, Plato, proposed that all Greeks should henceforth cease to plunder or enslave their fellow Greeks, but should rather do these things to the barbarians.[27]

The phase of self-doubt and self-survey may end in conversion to a new religion or ideology, perhaps even one complete with a new language and traditions, such as was once the case in the matter of conversion to Islam, and sometimes to the Arab language; or in deliberate assimilation to a new nationality, as in many cases of emigration overseas, or in deliberate assimilation even in one's original country to the language and traditions one has now chosen to accept (e.g. Indians learning to speak Spanish and accepting Peruvian or Mexican national loyalties). In any case, the phase of self-doubt and self-appraisal tends to be followed by a phase of decision and of conscious or even deliberate identification with a group; and with the loosening of the ties of religion or status that group is likely to be a group delimited at least in part along national lines, in terms of habits of language and communication.

Our hypothesis finds some confirmation in a well-known pattern in the history of nationalism and the biographies of nationalist leaders. Many emotionally, culturally, and politically sensitive individuals react to a sojourn abroad, i.e. away from their native region or culture, with a far stronger assertion of nationalism and of allegiance to their own language, culture, and people. This precipitating crisis in the lives of many nationalists has been dubbed the *Fremd-*

27" . . . our citizens should . . . deal with foreigners as Greeks now deal with one another." Plato, *Republic*, v, 469–70, trans., Cornford, New York, 1945, p. 174. Cf. also Glenn R. Morrow, *Plato's Law of Slavery in Its Relation to Greek Law*, Urbana, Ill., 1935.

heitserlebnis ("the experience of strangeness"), and it has been described repeatedly in the literature of nationalism.[28]

From Group Awareness to the Nation-State

Individual awareness of one's language and people may appear to be a matter of personal psychology, even though there are social situations which make such awareness more probable. Group awareness, on the other hand, seems clearly a matter of social institutions. Some secondary symbols are attached to some aspects of group life and are repeated and disseminated over and over again by an organization or institution, often for a purpose that has nothing to do with nationality, or which might even be opposed to it. After a time, the institution may change or disappear, the organized repetition of the symbols may cease—but if there were enough of a primary reality capable of being symbolized, *and if there had been going on that basic process of social mobilization* which has been described earlier, then the results of the dissemination of those symbols may well prove irreversible. A stream of memories has been started that is partly self-regenerating, and so long as the foundations for the ethnic group exist, and social mobilization and communication continue to weld its members together, national group awareness may be there to stay. It can hardly be expected to give way to a wider supra-national allegiance until a basis for the appeal of wider symbols has again developed in the realm of objective fact, in experiences at least as real, as frequent in the daily life of individuals, and as relevant to their personal concerns, to their language, their communications, and their thoughts, as were those experiences which provided the basis for the awareness of nationality.

Given these underlying conditions, symbols and institutions of group awareness may be produced quite unintentionally. A process of social mobilization may even transform the function of existing symbols or institutions so as to turn them into agencies of group awareness, regardless of their original purposes. Thus nationalism was promoted sometimes by a supra-national church. Early medieval church provinces, such as Gallia and Anglia,[29] could not in themselves produce the unity of France or England, but they contributed to it, in conjunction with the other factors discussed earlier in this paper. The names of patron saints of provinces and regions, such as St. Stephen for Hungary, St. Wenceslas for Bohemia, St. Patrick for Ireland, or the Virgin of Czenstochowa for Poland, turned into patriotic battle cries.

Similar nationalistic effects might follow upon dynastic accidents, passing

[28]Cf. Kohn, *op. cit.,* pp. 98, 601 (Petrarch); p. 127 (Machiavelli); pp. 239, 659 (Rousseau); p. 294 (Jefferson). On the problem of individual self-awareness and identification with groups, cf. also Chr. Bay, I. Gullåvg, H. Ofstad, and H. Toenessen, *Nationalism: A Study of Identification with People and Power: I. Problems and Theoretical Framework,* Oslo, Institute of Social Research, 1950, mimeographed.

[29]*Nationalism,* a report by a study group of the members of the Royal Institute of International Affairs, (London, 1939), p. 11, with reference to G. C. Coulton "Nationalism in the Middle Ages," *Cambridge Historical Journal,* V, No. 1 (1935), pp. 15-40.

combinations of territories by the fortunes of war, inheritance, or marriage, but these nationalistic effects themselves were by no means accidental. Almost every territory in Europe has been combined at some time or other with almost every one of its neighbors, but only certain of these combinations have endured and kindled the loyalties and imaginations of their peoples. The combinations which endured in fact or sentiment were those which were reinforced by other elements in the process of social mobilization and integration, and they would themselves in turn strengthen this process by adding to it political memories, symbols, grievances, and "historic rights."

The same considerations hold for the long-range effects of earlier administrative divisions in some empire or kingdom of the past. Even then, most administrators would pay some attention to population clusters, transport, and communication lines in laying out their districts. Yet many long-standing administrative divisions or provinces have disappeared without giving rise to corresponding peoples or nations. Uruguayan nationalism destroyed the unity of the Old Spanish Viceroyalty of the River Plate, despite the occasional attempts of Argentine governments to revive its memories; and neither the memories of the Spanish Viceroyalty of Nueva Granada nor Bolívar's short-lived vision of Gran Colombia have kept together the different economies and peoples of Venezuela, Colombia, Panama, and Ecuador.[30]

Even symbols of insult may serve this organizing function, if the other conditions for national awakening are given. The term *les gueux*—"the beggars"—once applied to insurgent Netherlanders by their Spanish rulers, became a term of honor in Dutch history. The memory of the convicts transported to Australia in the early days of her settlement has been transformed by a contemporary poet into a blazing symbol of Australian nationalism.[31]

Reinforcing the impact of these symbols there appear the institutions of modern economic life and of the modern state, all of which require more direct communication with large numbers of peasants, artisans, taxpayers, or conscripts than was the case before. In the eighteenth century, Austrian officers were taught Czech, so as to command better their Czech-speaking soldiers, and the revival of the teaching of the Czech language followed. Landowners in Wales and Scotland, interested in raising the productive skills of the population on their estates, founded societies to study the resources, languages, and cultures of their regions, and made the century of the "agricultural revolution" also the century of the "discovery" of the works of "Ossian."[32]

No growth of nationalism was foreseen or desired in many of these cases, any more than in the more recent use of the Indonesian language by the Japanese in

[30] Cf., e.g., J. Fred Rippy, *Historic Evolution of Hispanic America,* 3rd ed., New York, 1945. On the limited significance of administrative divisions in the last-named country, see George Blanksten, *Ecuador: Constitutions and Caudillos,* Berkeley, Calif., 1951.

[31] Sheila Sibley, "Ballade of the Convict's Daughter," in *Jindyworobak Anthology,* Melbourne, 1945; reprinted in A. C. Garnett, *Freedom and Planning in Australia,* Madison, Wis., 1949, pp. 243–44.

[32] Cf., e.g., the data in Kohn, *op. cit.,* pp. 236, 352, 464, 637, etc.

the administration of the Dutch Indies during World War II, or in the compilation of grammars and dictionaries of Hausa and other African languages by colonial administrators. Yet the growth of nationalism was facilitated by the consequences of these acts.

Once the process of group consciousness has started, however, there appear also the deliberate pioneers and leaders of national awakening. There appear grammarians who reduce the popular speech to writing; purifiers of language; collectors of folk epics, tales, and songs; the first poets and writers in the revised vernacular; and the antiquarians and historians who discover ancient documents and literary treasures—some genuine, some forged, but all of them tokens of national greatness.

Side by side with the awakeners of national pride and fashioners of symbols appear the first organizers. There arise the first social circles and literary societies where the formerly despised native language is read or spoken. There follow the first benevolent societies, fraternal orders, credit cooperatives, and all the devices of mutual credit, support, or insurance, which now begin to collect the financial resources of the awakening nationality. There appear the organizers of the first schools, singing societies, athletic organizations, agricultural colleges, which herald the array of all the organizations for cultural, physical, and technological improvement which characterize every full-fledged modern nation.

Together with all this activity we find the gradual acceptance, or the deliberate proposal, of national symbols, of national colors, flags, animals, and flowers, of anthems, marches, and patriotic songs, from the "Rule Britannia" and the "Marseillaise" of the eighteenth century to the *"Nkosi sikelel i Africa"*—"God Save Africa"—of today's nationalist South African Negroes.[33] How all these symbols, maps, anthems, flags, and flag-salutes are then taught and impressed upon the populations and their children by informal group pressure and the media of mass communication as well as by all the coercive powers of the state and its system of compulsory public education—this is a story that has been told often and well by students of these late stages of the nation-building process.[34]

What does this process accomplish, and what does it aim at? When a nation has been built up, and when it has been reinforced finally by the full compulsive power of the state, then four things have been accomplished.

1. A relatively large community of human beings has been brought into existence who can communicate effectively with each other, and who have command over sufficient economic resources to maintain themselves and to transmit this ability for mutual communication to their children as well. In other words, there has been brought into being a large, comprehensive, and very stable

---

[33] Detailed documentation here would be unnecessary. On the Swiss symbols, see Englert-Faye, *op. cit.* For a novelist's description of the singing of the black anthem in South Africa, cf. Alan Paton, *Cry the Beloved Country: A Story of Comfort in Desolation,* New York, 1948.

[34] Cf. Carlton H. Hayes, *Essays on Nationalism,* New York, 1926, and *The Historical Evolution of Modern Nationalism,* New York, 1931; F. L. Schuman, *International Politics,* 3rd ed., New York, 1941, pp. 300–65.

human network of communication, capable of maintaining, reproducing, and further developing its channels.

2. There has been both an effective accumulation of economic resources and a sufficient social mobilization of manpower to permit the social division of labor necessary for this process and to permit its continuation.

3. There has been a social accumulation and integration of memories and symbols and of individual and social facilities for their preservation, transmission, and recombination, corresponding to the level of mobilization and integration of material and human resources, or even pointing beyond it.

4. There has been at least some development of the capacity to redirect, reallocate, or form a new combination of economic, social, and human resources as well as of symbols and items of knowledge, habit, or thought—that is to say, of the capacity to learn. Some of the social *learning capacity* is developed invisibly in the minds of individuals; some of it can be observed in the habits and patterns of culture prevailing among them; some of it finally is embodied in tangible facilities and specific institutions. Together, all these constitute the community's capacity to produce and accept new knowledge or new goals, and to take the corresponding action.

On all four counts, it should be evident, the nation represents a more effective organization than the supra-national but largely passive layer-cake society or the feudal or tribal localisms that preceded it.

On all these counts, there may be considerable contrasts between different nations. The social models accepted for imitation, the established institutions, the economic practices, and the methods of compulsion within each nation are all intimately connected with the cultural traditions and leading social classes currently prevailing there. Whether a leading class of business people or farmers or wage earners will prove more hospitable to accumulation of resources and to efficient dynamic innovation in their use may depend not merely on the general outlook to be found prevailing in each particular stratum, but also—and perhaps sometimes crucially—on the particular cultural goals and traditions which have become accepted by that particular class in that particular nation.[35] Yet, the impression remains that even the worst-led nation represents, relative to its numbers of population, a greater amount of social communication facilities, of economic resources, and of social learning capacity than any pattern of ethnic or social organization preceding it.

Where does this process aim? The nation has been valued as a means of social advancement. In a world of extreme differences between living standards,

---

[35] For some problems of conservative aristocratic leadership in undeveloped nations, cf., for the Arabs, the writings of H. A. R. Gibb; for an example from Tibet, Nicholas Mansergh, "The Asian Conference, 1947," in *The Commonwealth and the Nations*, London, 1948, pp. 115-16; and for Southeast Asia, Cora Du Bois, *Social Forces in Southeast Asia*, Minneapolis, Minn., 1949, pp. 33-36, 59. On the contrast, e.g., between French and American business investment policies, cf. David S. Landes, "French Entrepreneurship and Industrial Growth in the Nineteenth Century," *Journal of Economic History*, IX (May 1949), pp. 45-61.

individuals and groups have tended to use the nation as an instrument to improve their own standards relative to those of their neighbors. The intrinsic bias of this process has been, where the opportunity offered itself, to produce in the temporarily most successful nation a sociological pattern reminiscent of a *mushroom cloud.* The stem of this social mushroom was formed by the "national solidarity" between the poorest and the lower-middle strata of the nation; the poorest strata, both rural and urban, however, tended to be somewhat less in relative numbers, and offered their members greater chances for "vertical mobility" than was the case in other less "successful" nations. The middle and upper strata, on the other hand, tended to form the crown of the mushroom; they tended to be somewhat larger in number than the corresponding group in other nations, with a greater propensity to spread out horizontally into new positions of privilege or control over new territories, populations, or capital resources, and correspondingly with at least somewhat greater opportunities to accept in their midst newcomers from the less favored strata of their own nation.

It is perhaps this sociological explosion into a mushroom cloud that has been at the heart of the transitory popularity of empire-building. Nationalism typically has led to attempts at empire or at least at establishing privileges over other peoples. The essence of this empire-building has been perhaps the attempt at ruling without sharing, just as the essence of nationalism has been the attempt at improving the position of one's "own" group without any sharing with "outsiders." To the extent that this process was successful it could only tend ultimately to transform the whole nation into a privileged class, a *Herrenvolk* lording it over servant peoples, as the Nazis dreamed of it, or a small, select population monopolizing vast natural resources or accumulations of technological equipment regardless of the fate of the rest of the world. In reality, this state has probably never been achieved; and where it was even partially approximated, the results in the long run were anything but lasting. Invariably, thus far, the same nation-building process which had permitted one nation to get temporarily on top of its neighbors subsequently raised up other nations to weaken or destroy it.

From this it might seem at first glance that the whole process of the rise and decline of nations has been cyclical, with only the names of the actors changing in an endlessly repeated drama. Closer scrutiny may show that this is not the case, and that some tentative inferences may be drawn from the events and processes surveyed.

THE UNIQUENESS OF THE PRESENT PERIOD

Our survey offers no support for the belief of many nationalists that nations are the natural and universal form of social organization for humanity. But neither does it confirm entirely the opposite view held by many thoughtful and distinguished observers—the view that nations are exclusively the product of the modern period and of Western civilization.[36] Perhaps the impression that remains might be summed up by saying that the West has gone much farther on a road which all the world's great civilizations have traveled to some extent.

At this moment we might well pause to question the ease with which we accept the designation of our present-day civilization as exclusively "Western." By Western civilization we mean a civilization which arose from the mingling of the Graeco-Roman tradition with the Celtic, Teutonic, and Slavic barbarian cultures north of the Mediterranean; but this Western civilization was Semiticized and Orientalized by the twin influences of Judaism and of Christianity, even if we allow for the very appreciable element of Greek tradition in the latter.[37]

Subsequently, this Hellenic-Barbarian-Judaeo-Christian civilization was partially Arabicized during more than five hundred years of culture contact from the seventh to the thirteenth century. During the thirteenth and fourteenth centuries, this Arabicized Western civilization was then Mongolized and Sinicized. The details of the origin and acquisition of almost all of these innovations offer room for controversy, but there should be little controversy about the cumulative picture. Nor should there be much controversy about the massive "Amerindianization" of that Western-Arabic-Mongolian world from the sixteenth century onward, once the Indian culture plants of corn and potatoes permitted an entirely new balance of populations on the land, and once the availability of plentiful sugar, cotton, and tobacco transformed food, clothing, and consumption habits. What we call today Western civilization is in a very real sense a World civilization, not merely in what it brought to other countries, but also very significantly in what it received from them. Perhaps its "Western" peculiarities lie, then, not only in its ability to originate, but also in its ability to innovate, that is, to learn actively from others.

All these traits of creativity and of the ability to learn are present in all great civilizations of the world, and the West here, too, has perhaps gone faster and farther on a road traveled to some extent by all. In a real sense, Western civilization is carrying on some—though certainly not all—of the traditions of all other civilizations, and its crisis in the world today is also their crisis, and not merely in externals.

It is this universal aspect that also characterizes the growth of nations in the present. During the last eighty years, there seems to have been growth in all the important regions of the world. Everywhere there has been growth in population, in gross economic wealth, and in national awareness. In no region has there been a decline to compensate for an advance elsewhere. Many of these advances in widely different areas have been the continuation of long-standing trends, which have been helped and speeded by the new resources and possibilities offered by the diffusion of science and technology during those last eighty years.

[36] Cf. A. J. Toynbee, *op. cit., passim;* Kohn, *op. cit., passim;* Carlton H. Hayes, Nationalism," *Encyclopedia of the Social Sciences.*

[37] For this tradition of the poorest strata of the Hellenic world, see the intriguing case presented by A. J. Toynbee, "Christus Patiens," *op. cit.,* VI, pp. 376–539.

The result is that today all peoples are involved in the growth of national awareness, and that soon there will be no peoples left to play the role of submerged nationalities or underlying populations, or passive bystanders of history, or drawers of water and hewers of wood for their better organized neighbors.

The process has gone further. Within each people, all social strata have been mobilized, socially, economically, and politically, or are in the process of being so mobilized before our eyes. Wherever this social mobilization has progressed, it has undermined the patterns of authority and privilege inherited for an earlier day. The time could be envisioned in 1953, and it is close at hand now, in 1977, when the majority of the world's population will have shifted to non-agricultural occupations. There has never been a period like this in the history of the world.

SOME QUESTIONS FOR RESEARCH

The experiences and prospects of supra-national federations or unions must be evaluated against this background. For evaluating the future prospects of any one of these, be it an existing federation[38] or a project, old or new, our survey may suggest a series of questions:

1. What is the immediate relevance of integration? Is there a clear-cut economic or political *advantage* in the union? For which group?

2. What are the cultural and social prospects for integration? Can there evolve a single people, at least in the sense in which the English, Welsh, and Scots are British? How *compatible* are the cultures and the social and economic institutions of the participating peoples, and how much actual communication and migration among them has occurred thus far? What are the present levels and what are the prospects of communication, of future growth, of social mobility, and of the ease of mutual cooperation and substitution among the bulk of the individuals and groups making up the population?

3. What are the prospects for substantial *new investments* to tie the economy together and for the accumulation of new capital to keep it going?

4. What are the *costs* of integration? How large and important are the *mutually incompatible investments*, i.e. the investments in plants or resources which are likely to be made obsolete or partially worthless by the economic results of the union? How effective are the specific institutions and resources, if any, which would be used to deal with such destructive results?

5. Has this union or federation become associated with a better *way of life* in terms of the potentialities and aspirations of the individual? Will it actually provide higher standards of health, education, and of living?

6. Are there *leaders, leading groups,* and *symbols* to give expression to the actually existing facts and trends referred to in the four preceding points?

7. Are there any great *constructive tasks* for this federation, tasks imaginable

---

[38] On some of these, cf. K. C. Wheare, *Federal Government,* 2nd ed., New York, 1951; Oscar I. Janowsky, *Nationalities and National Minorities,* New York, 1945.

now as well as practicable enough so that the first steps toward their fulfillment can be taken immediately with the resources actually available?

The answers to these seven groups of questions in regard to cases of successful federations in the past might prove of some interest to historians and social scientists. As regards any existing or proposed federations today, answers to those questions might go some distance toward indicating their prospects for success or survival in the future.

Whatever the fate of any particular federation or project at this time, there seems to be little doubt that the numbers of fully mobilized nations, as well as of attempts at federation, will increase. The world-wide awakening of nations as well as the world-wide search for wider federations are characteristic of our unprecedented age. Both are steps in the world's new and groping search not for a shallow "universal state" but for an enduring world community based on the social and technological mobilization of all people.

2 | The Trend of European Nationalism: The Language Aspect

The first version of this chapter was written in 1940–41, and it was my first effort to use verifiable quantitative evidence to decide a question of political analysis. The text has now been somewhat updated and revised for inclusion in the present volume, but all the contemporary case references and quantitative data have been preserved, with only some supplementary information from 1977 added in some places.

What could be shown for Europe in 1941 had by 1977 become evident throughout the world. A large number of popular languages in Asia and Africa, and at least three such languages in Latin America, have emerged in politics and business; in print and education; in judicial, military, and administrative practice; and in the electronic media. Of the 131 more or less independent states listed for 1969 in the *World Handbook of Political and Social Indicators,* Second Edition, only sixty-six had been in existence in 1941. The number of such states in the world thus has approximately doubled since the first version of this chapter was written.*

The documentation published then and now amounts to about one-fourth of the original. For reasons of space, the rest has not been included, but many of the titles are now listed in K. W. Deutsch and R. L. Merritt, *Nationalism and National Development: An Interdisciplinary Bibliography* (Cambridge, Mass.: MIT Press, 1971).

In recent years, public opinion in the democratic countries has become increasingly aware of the dangers inherent in the unlimited competition of a host of rival nationalistic movements and sovereign nation-states. Having recognized it as a danger to be overcome, many liberal thinkers, like the experts of the Royal Institute of International Affairs, or Mr. Max Lerner,[1] assumed about 1940 that the trend toward nationalistic disintegration had already reached its peak. Many

*C. L. Taylor and M. C. Hudson, eds., *World Handbook of Political and Social Indicators,* 2d ed. (New Haven: Yale University Press, 1972), pp. 26–29.

[1] *Nationalism; A Report by a Study Group of Members of the Royal Institute of International Affairs* (London, 1939), p. 336; Max Lerner, "The War as Revolution," *The Nation,* Vol. 151, pp. 68–71 (July 27, 1940).

Updated from *The American Political Science Review* 36, no. 2 (June 1942): 533–541. Reprinted by permission of the Publisher.

consequent suggestions of policy to this day have been based on the assumption that nationalism is declining, or about to decline.

The following inquiry into some of the evidence as to the actual direction of the general trend of European nationalism will be limited in two respects. First, it will be concerned at this stage with the surface trend alone, irrespective of its causes. Second, the evidence examined will be limited primarily to the language aspect of nationalism, that is, to the assimilation or diversification of national languages. It should be borne in mind, however, that the other major elements of nationality, such as political and educational institutions, literature, territory, group loyalties, and nationalistic movements, and frequently even sovereign states and customs areas, are all closely interconnected with the language factor. There is hardly a national language in all Europe for which there could not also be shown the existence of many of the other political and economic factors of nationality. In different nations, the proportions of these factors may vary; there will be border-line cases. But a view of the evidence over a longer period of years is likely to show how closely the language factor is linked with the rest of the picture.

<h1 style="text-align:center">I</h1>

Do Europe's nations tend to coalesce, to become one, and to accept one written language for their intercourse, administration, business, and literature? If so, and if in consequence we have been getting fewer and larger language areas in Europe, then the many political proposals for fewer and larger states would seem to have also the forces of nationalism itself on their side. Evidence of increasing willingness to accept economic competition and political rule from other language groups would point in the same direction. What are the facts?

Throughout European history, we find former common languages splitting up into increasingly different local dialects. But the speakers of these dialects accept economic coordination around the common centers of market, town, and capital city. They accept political subordination under a wider territorial administration, and social subordination under an upper class around a central élite. In the process they accept as their common standard language above their dialects the speech of the capital or of the economically central region, as spoken by the élite. Usually it is accepted at first in written intercourse; later, given sufficient intensity of education and daily communication, it becomes the standard for the daily speech of the nation.

Villages become subordinated to towns and states. Dialects become subordinated to standard languages. But what of the number of economic centers, what of the number of social and political élites, what of the number of standard languages themselves?

In the hundred years between 1800 and 1900, the number of full-fledged national languages in Europe increased from 16 to 30, that is, at a faster rate than in any of the preceding ten centuries.[2] And in the 37 years between 1900 and 1937, Europe's standard languages further multiplied to 53, adding almost as many to their number as in the entire thousand years that went before.[3]

The 15 nations that awakened to national language and literature between 1800 and 1900 comprise today a population of more than 80 millions.[4] By 1940, eleven of them had attained, at one time or another, some form of statehood: Bulgarians, Czechs, Croats, Esthonians, Finns, Latvians, Norwegians, Rumanians, Serbs, Slovaks, and Ukrainians. Two others, the Slovenes and the Flemings, had reached a degree of political autonomy; and the last two of the 15, the Welsh in Great Britain and the Yiddish-speaking Jews in the U.S.S.R., had some limited autonomy in matters of language and education. Among all of these the sense of group loyalty has found expression in nationalistic or patriotic movements. Most of these trends visible in 1940 have continued. By 1977, the Croats and the Slovenes each had come to constitute a constituent republic of

---

[2] In 950 A.D., there were in Europe six full-fledged written languages, i.e., languages with a grammar, literature, and some employment in business and public administration—Latin, Greek, Hebrew, Arabic, Anglo-Saxon, and Church Slavonic (Old Bulgarian). See G. Sarton, *Introduction to the History of Science* (Baltimore, 1927-1931), Vol. I. In 1250 A.D., two languages, Anglo-Saxon and Provençal had become submerged, but there were 17 languages flourishing in Europe, as noted in Sarton's survey: Latin, Greek, Hebrew, Arabic, Church Slavonic, High German, Low German, French, Icelandic, Russian, Spanish, Catalan, Portuguese, Italian, Norwegian, Swedish, and Danish, Sarton, *op. cit.,* Vols. II and III. (". . . a deeper study would introduce other languages; I speak only of those [outstanding] . . . by their exceptional vitality or by the creation of masterpieces," *ibid.,* Vol. II, p. 293). In 1800, five of the languages of 1250 had become submerged or relatively inactive: Hebrew, Arabic, Low German, Catalan, and Norwegian; and a survey published in 1809 showed only 16 languages flourishing in Europe: Greek, Church Slavonic, German, French, Icelandic, Russian, Spanish, Portuguese, Italian, Swedish, Danish, English, Dutch, Polish, Magyar, and Turkish (Osmanli), J. Ch. Adelung—J. S. Vater, *Mithridates* (Berlin, 1809). In 1900, a century later, 15 of the above-mentioned languages were flourishing, Church Slavonic being the only one to have dropped out; and to their number had been added Welsh, Flemish, Norwegian (Riksmaal and Landsmaal), Finnish, Rumanian, Czech, Slovak, Serbo-Croatian (a common literary standard language with two sharply different alphabets, traditions, literatures, and loyalties), Slovene, Bulgarian, Ukrainian, Yiddish, Esthonian, and Latvian. See F. N. Finck, *Die Sprachstämme des Erdkreises* (Leipzig, 1911); A. Meillet, *Les Langues du Monde* (Paris, 1925; W. L. Graff, *Language and Languages* (New York and London, 1932); L. Bloomfield, *Language* (New York, 1933); and works on the individual languages.

[3] In 1937, all of the thirty national languages of 1900 were flourishing, and still more were joining their number with new literatures and education or political institutions or movements: Lithuanian, Irish, Scottish Gaelic, Basque, Breton, Catalan, Rheto-Romance, Lusatian Serb, Albanian, Hebrew (modern), Karelian, Byelo-Russian, Moldavian, Georgian, Ossete, Bashkir, Cheremiss, Chuvash, Mordvin, Samoyede, Syryen (Komi), Tartar, and Votiak. Sources as above. The data for 1900 and 1937 have been checked with the survey of Biblical translations in E. M. North, *The Book of a Thousand Tongues* (New York and London, 1938). Nationalities in the European part of the U.S.S.R. of 1937 are listed in accordance with the language map of Europe by A. Drexel and R. Wimpissinger in their *Atlas Linguisticus* (Innsbruck, 1934). Exclusion of the territory of European Russia from consideration would not materially change the picture of the basic trend.

[As philologists disagree in many cases as to what to count as standard languages and what as dialects, the different surveys have been taken in conjunction and their testimony verified, wherever possible, against evidence from sources within the disputed language group.]

[4] Sources as above, and current statistics.

Yugoslavia; and the Flemings had won full legal recognition of their language rights, and to some extent of their majority status in Belgium.

The 23 smaller nations which awakened between 1900 and 1937 contain today a population of more than 30 millions.[5] Seven of these had reached some form of statehood between 1900 and 1941: Albanians, Irish, Byelo-Russians, Karelians, Moldavians—the three last-named only as "Union Republics" within the federal framework of the U.S.S.R., whose constitution grants them, theoretically, the "right to secede"—and the Georgians and Lithuanians, who each formed a sovereign state before becoming Soviet "Union Republics." Of the 13 remaining nationalities, nine have formed administrative units on a national, linguistic basis with various degrees of political self-government within the European part of the U.S.S.R.: the Bashkirs, Chuvashs, Cheremiss, Mordvins, Ossetes, Samoyeds, Syryens, Tartars, and Votiaks.[6] The process was not dissimilar in the rest of Europe; Lusatian Serbs enjoyed some autonomy in education in their own language in Germany from 1918 to 1937; Gaelic-speaking Scotsmen found increased rights for their language in education as well as a number of administrative concessions to the special problems and to the separate identity of Scotland stressed by the Scottish nationalists; Basques and Catalans obtained full political autonomy under the Spanish Republic and played an important part in the Spanish civil war; Rheto-Romans found their ancient language introduced on a basis of full equality into the administration of Switzerland; Hebrew-speaking Jews found a large measure of economic and political autonomy in Palestine, and from 1948 onward in the new state of Israel. A million Bretons in France saw the revival of their old language with a new nationalistic movement in their midst. By 1977, Basque and Breton claims had become more visible in the politics of Spain and France, respectively; Scotland had more autonomy within Britain, albeit not on a language basis. Albania and Ireland were sovereign states; and all other groups listed for 1940 were still in existence.

Most of these nationalistic movements, new states, and new autonomous districts have grown up from already existing language groups, among people who were already speaking some old vernacular in their families and in their simple, mostly rural, life. These now, on becoming commercialized, industrialized, and literate, are elevating their idiom to the status of a written standard language with its own grammar, literature, and claims for social recognition. If this process should continue, we may expect, with the spread of literacy and industrialization, the rise of nationalistic movement all over the world. In order for one to visualize the possible scope of this process alone, one should recall the estimate that there are more than 2,700 spoken idioms or dialects in the

[5] Sources as above.
[6] See note 3, second paragraph, above. On the Moldavian language and nationality, see *Eleven Union Socialist Soviet Republics* (Moscow, 1938), p. 33 (in Russian); and H. Kloss, "Sprachtabellen," in *Vierteljahresschrift für Politik und Geschichte*, Vol. 1 (7) (Berlin, 1929), pp. 111–112.

world,[7] while not more than half of humanity was as yet literate in 1942.[8] The halfway mark was passed in 1955, and by 1977 more than two-thirds of the world's population could read and write.

II

If this were the entire story of the rise of modern nationalism, we could at least expect that this increase of new nationalistic movements would eventually stop, first in Europe and later in the rest of the world, as the supply of historically inherited language groups became exhausted. Actually, however, the rise of standard national languages is a more complex process, and no simple limitation upon the number of existing dialects can be hoped for.

First of all, a standard language is not merely a standardized single local idiom. It may be regarded rather as a combination of several idioms in that it is usually a language accepted as a common standard by the speakers of several different dialects. It may be a combination of several different elements of speech, such as the Greek Koiné. It may be the language of the capital or central city or central region around which some social, economic, cultural, and often, though not always, political integration has taken place, and where an élite has been assembled, whose composition is to some extent reflected in the language.[9] English, the language of London; Danish, the language of Copenhagen; French, the language of Paris, the Ile de France, and the Champagne; standard Italian, the language of educated Florence—all these show that the national standard language is itself the result of economic, cultural, and political cooperation and affiliation.

These elements of affiliation, in their turn, are subject to change. In the twelfth and thirteenth centuries, the Netherlands were united with Cologne and Lower Germany by a chain of wholly fluid transitions in their written languages. Netherlands writers, such as Jacob van Maerlant and Heinrich von Veldeke, have their place in both Dutch and German literature. In the sixteenth century, the Netherlands broke away from the rest of the German dialect area, and the speech of Brabant was regarded as standard. In the seventeenth century, with the

---

[7]"The actual number of languages recently computed by officers of the French Academy is put at 2,796," *World Almanac,* since 1929. A more recent survey by E. Kieckers lists almost 3,000 living languages. *Die Sprachstämme der Erde* (Heidelberg, 1931), pp. 237–257.

[8]F. C. Laubach, *Toward a Literate World* (New York: Columbia University Press, 1938); quoted in North, *op. cit.,* p. 18, note 3.

[9]While standard languages are evolved in the capital cities, they are not necessarily dominated by the original dialect of the metropolitan region. Rather, they will be based on the speech of the new urban population, and particularly of its most important social group, even if its members have been recruited from all over the country. O. Jespersen, *Mankind, Nation, and Individual from a Linguistic Point of View* (Oslo and Cambridge, Mass., 1925), p. 65.

decline of Flanders and the rise of the northern provinces, the speech of Amsterdam became the standard for what is today modern Dutch. At present, the speakers of the Lower Saxon, Plattdeutsch vernacular of Gelderland, of Frisian in Friesland, and of genuine Lower Frankish, Dutch dialects are all united in using Dutch as the language of school and church and as the medium of their common national allegiance. On the other hand, the continuous area of Germanic dialects, mutually intelligible from village to village without a break, is now split into three standard languages, Flemish,[10] Dutch, and German, with another offshoot in a fourth national language, Afrikaans, across the sea. It was not at first these languages that made history; it was history that made these languages.

The acceptance of a common national language contains an element of choice. Macedonians, speaking an intermediate range of dialects, may equally well accept integration into the Serb or into the Bulgarian nation, or else hold out for a nationhood of their own.[11] Slovaks may break away from their common written language with the Czechs, as they did in 1845; later, they may join them in a state based on the idea of a common Czechoslovak nationality, as they did in 1918; and again later their nationalists may protest against attempts of any of their own Slovak countrymen to reduce the relatively small grammatical differences between the two mutually intelligible languages, as they did in the disputes about the new Slovak grammer in 1932.[12] By 1977, Macedonia had become another of the Republics of Yugoslavia, and the Slovaks, too, had obtained a federal arrangement within Czechoslovakia. In both cases, Communist governments had found it worth while to concede some degree of autonomy to nationalistic aspirations.

There is, then, room for new changes and new combinations among the local idioms and ways of speech integrated into the national languages of any given time. Serb and Croat, Russian and Ukranian, Danish and Norwegian, may be brought closer together or foced farther apart. Provençal, Frisian, Plattdeutsch, and Schwyzerdütsch have all had their literary renaissance in the nineteenth century and form today potential instruments for future new political alignments in case such should come to be desired by strong groups among the populations involved. Thus the elevation of Schwyzerdütsch to a political language of equal rank with standard German was actually suggested in March, 1938, in the Swiss legislature; its informal use among the younger generations increased during World War II at the expense of standard German; and by 1977 its use had

---

[10] "Gradually the language of the Dutch Republic began to be considered in Belgium as that of the enemy and the heretic, and an opposition was created between Dutch and Flemish. . . ." G. Duflou, "The Flemish Language," in *Encyclopedia Britannica* (14th ed., 1937), Vol. IX, p. 371.

[11] ". . . the movement for an autonomous Macedonia . . . tends to wean away from the main national body one-fifth of the total Bulgarian population and set it up as a separate nation." S. Christowe, in *An American Symposium on the Macedonian Problem* (Indianapolis, Ind., 1941), p. 21.

[12] C. A. Macartney, *Hungary and Her Successors* (London, 1937), pp. 88, 127.

become still more prominent among German-speaking Swiss and on the Swiss radio and television. In considering the possibilities of future national differentiation, we should bear in mind, therefore, not only the present number of dialects and of their present groupings under national standard languages, but also their possible new combinations in times of exceptional change and stress.

III

In the second place, we find a new development since the middle of the nineteenth century, and particularly strongly in the twentieth: a tendency to increase deliberately the differences between kindred, and particularly between neighboring, languages. The rise of the Slavic written languages and literatures in the first half of the nineteenth century had been characterized by the ideas, if not of Pan-Slavism, at any rate of "Slavic mutuality," of a broad give-and-take among Slavic languages and literatures. Less than a century later, in 1937, the Czech philologist, M. Weingart, found that the old give-and-take of the romantic period had been replaced by "an evident distaste for the influence of the other Slavic literary language, particularly of the neighboring one. Thus the Ukrainian language is struggling against Polonisms as well as Russisms, Slovene against Serbo-Croatisms, and . . . Slovak against Bohemisms, not infrequently only imaginary ones. There is in this a visible turning away from the ideas of romanticism and the direct opposite of what then was demanded by Jan Kollar."[13]

Under favorable circumstances, the new trend has gone even farther. Considerable population groups begin here and there to mark themselves off more sharply from their neighbors by accepting *new languages* which they themselves never spoke, but which are derived from some language used at one time by some of their actual or reputed ancestors. Scottish and Irish nationalists struggling with their unfamiliar varieties of modern Gaelic;[14] young Zionist Jews diligently learning modern Hebrew; Norwegian patriots changing their historical written language, Dano-Norwegian, for a mixture of Norse peasant dialects, Landsmaal or Folkemaal[15]—all these are examples of a new trend to increase consciously, indeed even to *create*, new linguistic differences by an act of the political will. It can be done; the languages of whole communities, in time of whole nations, can be changed to suit the desire for nationalistic separation. That seems to be the evidence of Palestine-Israel, Norway, and Ireland.

[13] M. Weingart *et al., Slovanské spisovné jazyky v době přitomné* (Prague, 1937), p. 5.
[14] Cf. the section on Scotland in A. J. Aucamp, *Bilingual Education and Nationalism* (Pretoria, 1926); also M. C. Brogan, "Linguistic Nationalism in Eire," in *Review of Politics,* Vol. 3, pp. 225–242 (1941).
[15] "It does not often happen that a language form created by conscious deliberation and planning wins the warm support and widespread acceptance which has fallen to the lot of New Norse, the creation of Ivar Aasen." E. I. Haugen, "The Origin and Early History of the New Norse Movement in Norway," repr. from *Publications of the Modern Language Association,* Vol. 48, No. 2, p. 558.

The development of modern philology and modern education has made it possible to revive, modernize, and utilize any ancient language sufficiently known to history, if it should so suit any group's desire for separate identity. At the same time, new ways of speech are formed through the changing and splitting up of old languages into new accents and idioms under the influence of time and geographic separation. With the possibility of changing alignments and combinations between all of these elements, the national languages of today appear not only as a cause, but also as a result, of national differentiation. So far as the linguistic factor is concerned, the nationalistic disintegration of people may go on with hardly any limit so long as the economic possibilities and the political desires for it remain effective.

IV

For each of the 53 European language groups, we found some form of political organization or movement. Further powerful nationalistic loyalties have developed in Europe which are not bound to a separate language of their own: one long before 1800, the Swiss; a second in the nineteenth century, the Belgian; a third at the beginning of the twentieth century, the Macedonian;[16] and a fourth, a border-line case, the nationalism of those Scottish nationalists whose loyalties are attached to Lowland Scots.[17] Non-linguistic nationalistic organizations claim members from among the speakers of four languages in Switzerland, of two languages in Belgium, from members of the whole kaleidoscopic language map of Macedonia. In all these cases, there are at least two loyalties open to the members of many language groups. The Bulgar-speaking Macedonian may follow the Macedonian IMRO or the Bulgarian government; there have been Flemish separatists and Belgian patriots among the Flemish-speaking Belgians, often in intense conflict during the first World War and ever since; there are regionalistic Bretons and Provençals who are ardent French patriots—and there are those who were accused of separatism;[18] there are patriotic, and there are Pan-German, Swiss in German-speaking Switzerland; and in Austria, Chancellor Engelbert Dollfuss died in 1934 for what he conceived to be his patriotic duty to Austrian independence and the "Austrian spiritual character," while the Austrian storm-trooper who killed him went to the gallows for what he had been taught was his duty to Greater Germany. The enumeration is by no means complete. More hopeful features for a possible solution are to

[16] The Macedonian movement calls for the support of "all Macedonians regardless of nationalities, religion, sex, or political convictions . . . for the establishment of Macedonia as an independent Republic within her geographical and economic boundaries." Cf. Ch. Anastasoff, *The Tragic Peninsula; A History of the Macedonian Movement for Independence since 1878* (St. Louis, 1938), pp. 308–310.
[17] W. A. Craigie *et al.*, *The Scottish Tongue* (London, 1924), pp. 3–46.
[18] P. Pansier, *Histoire de la Langue Provençale à Avignon* (Avignon, 1927), Vol. IV, pp. viii–ix.

be found in that British loyalty which today unites the overwhelming majority of the English, Welsh, and Scots. But elsewhere there is a considerable list of cases where within the same communities of language the loyalties of nationalism are in intense conflict on both sides, demonstrating their disintegrating power.

V

The growth of linguistic diversity in Europe from 16 languages in 1800 to 30 in 1900 and to 53 in 1937 has been paralleled to some extent since 1871 by the growth in the number of modern sovereign states in Europe from 15 to 1871 to 21 in 1914 and to 29 in 1937,[19] as well as by the steady rise in the height of the tariff walls and other economic controls separating their national economies from each other. Already by 1941–42, when this essay was originally written, the second World War had shown little indication of a reversal of the trend. The great European powers had been careful to reckon with the vitality of nationalistic feelings, trying to utilize them wherever practicable. By the spring of 1941, Hitler's armies had created two new states, Slovakia and Croatia, and had tried for a time to foster a movement for a third new state among the Bretons in France.[20] The Soviet government had set up, largely along linguistic lines, two new "Union Republics," the Finnish-Karelian and the Moldavian.[21] Iceland, under British occupation, dropped her last tie of personal union with Denmark in order to emerge in full legal sovereignty. For the Allied nations in particular, the liberation of small nations has become both a major war aim and an important political weapon.

So far as the language factor is concerned, the bulk of the evidence shows for the years from 1800 to 1941 a steady increase in the diversity and strength of nationalistic feeling within Europe. Already in 1942 it could be predicted that, in the long run, the peaceful unification of Europe may have to be brought about against this very current. To deal with it democratically and constructively, our understanding of the functioning of nationalism will have to be further developed and extended.

[19] F. Martin (ed.), *The Statesman's Year-Book, 1871* (London, 1871), pp. v–ix; also *1914*, pp. xix–xxix; and *1937*, pp. ix–xiii.

[20] *New York Times*, July 14, 1940, p. 21: 1–3; July 26, p. 3: 7; July 27, p. 6: 3.

[21] A representative of still another European nationality—the 54th—spoke at the "All Slav Conference" in Moscow on Aug. 10 and 11, 1941. According to the report, he represented 400,000 Slonzaks or Lakhs, a Slav people on the borders of Czech and Polish Silesia. *The Slavic Peoples Against Hitler* (New York, 1941), pp. 20–21. The most prominent spokesman of this group, a poet using the name Ondra Lysohorský, was treated as an ally by the Communists in the 1930s and during World War II. After the emergence of Communist rule in postwar Czechoslovakia, however, Lysohorský's activities were increasingly frowned upon by the authorities, and he eventually emigrated to the German Federal Republic.

3 | Nationalistic Intolerance and Economic Interest

This chapter represents another early effort to apply some methods of social science—this time, economic theory—to problems of national, ethnic, or racial conflict. It deals with some powerful economic rewards which may reinforce habits of discrimination and intolerant behavior against poorer and politically weaker groups—ethnic, national, or racial—whose members can be readily labeled and singled out for such treatment. It tries to show some conditions under which such prejudiced behavior may pay off, more often than not, for its practitioners and some of their associates over a considerable span of time. In its substance, therefore, such behavior cannot be called "irrational" for them, so long as those conditions last; however, it may sooner or later damage the larger society within which it takes place, so that it rightly may be called irrational or counterproductive on that score.

Viewed under this aspect, the problems of intolerance and group conflict are larger and more persistent than the classic laissez-faire school of economists from Adam Smith in the eighteenth century until our own days had assumed. The free play of economic forces in the market place does not necessarily produce harmony and equal opportunity. On the contrary, it may often and for many decades reward and teach discrimination, and with it fear and hatred among groups. Where such conditions hold, active political and governmental intervention, together with changes in social values and popular awareness, remain as remedies.

An attempt to analyze briefly the economic factor in intolerance cannot pretend to deal with the problem of intolerance as a whole. The work of the sociologist, the psychologist, the historian, the religious leader, the educator and

The substance of Section I of this chapter, "Some Considerations of Economic Theory," was written in the summer of 1940 and published under the title "Some Economic Aspects of the Rise of Nationalistic and Racial Pressure Groups" in the *Canadian Journal of Economics and Political Science* 8 No. 1 (February 1942): 109-115. The rest of the chapter was published in substance under the title "The Economic Factor in Intolerance" in Lyman Bryson *et al.*, eds., *Approaches to National Unity Proceedings* (New York: Fifth Conference on Science, Philosophy and Religion in Their Relation to the Democratic Way of Life 1945), pp. 368-386. Reprinted by permission of the Publisher.

many others all remain indispensable for a full understanding of the subject. The best any investigation of the economic factor in intolerance can do is to try to find out how far economic analysis can go and where the other disciplines must of necessity take over.

Even within its limited field, the economic factor in intolerance, national, racial, or religious, has sometimes seemed insignificant to previous observers. Discrimination and intolerance appear economically unsound and frequently meaningless when analyzed with the tools of classical nineteenth-century economics with its assumptions of perfect or near-perfect mobility and competition. It is only with the more realistic assumptions of the modern economics of monopolistic competition, particularly with the assumptions of very imperfect mobility and the presence of monopolistic elements throughout the economic structure, that the economic significance of intolerance and discrimination can be investigated. Without the economic techniques developed by Joan Robinson and Edward H. Chamberlin, this analysis could not have been attempted.

I. SOME CONSIDERATIONS OF
ECONOMIC THEORY

An economist, M. W. Reder, has pointed out how members of a trade union, racial group, or fraternal organization, by establishing a consumers' preference for the goods and services of those firms which comply with their demands, may succeed in increasing the value of their own services to the employer and thus gain a higher wage, while at the same time decreasing the value of the services of those outside the group, whose wages will be lowered.[1] Since the outsiders must either try to join the group or organize other groups, if they wish to protect their earning power, it follows that "economic pressure groups tend to breed one another." This economic reason for joining a social group is "a potent force making for the cohesion of ethnic entities," and it is most effective among sections of the middle class, "salespeople, doctors, small businesspersons, and others whose value productivity depends largely upon their ability to sell (and hence) . . . upon the personal relationship with the buyer . . . . " The result is a tendency towards strained relationships between national and racial groups, and the rise of "a world of competition, not between individuals, but between rival groups, which often leads to extremely undesirable consequences."

Mr. Reder's study shows the effectiveness of the analysis of monopolistic competition when applied to the economic factor in group intolerance and nationalistic disruption; but it touches only one corner of the problem. In its relevant sections it deals mainly with the reward of labor engaged in selling, but it can be shown what happens to the rewards of "anonymous," physically pro-

[1]M. W. Reder, "Inter-Temporal Relations of Demand and Supply within the Firm," *Canadian Journal of Economics and Political Science*, (February 1941): 26–30.

ductive labor, as Mr. Reder refers to them, and to the rewards of capital and entrepreneurship under conditions of group competition and discrimination.

It is well known that single buyers—technically called "monopsonists"—can increase their gains by discrimination, if there are differences in the elasticities of supply of the various sources from which they buy, and if they are able to divide them effectively, so that they may offer different prices in each submarket. Single employers, hiring labor out of a large number of applicants, stand to gain if they can break up the labor market into submarkets for each group of laborers whose conditions of supply differ to a relevant degree from the others. While the same wage may have to be paid within each group, the wages as between groups will vary; the total amount of labor employed will be such that its marginal costs is equal to its demand price; "and the wage of each type will be equal to the supply price of the amount employed."[2]

There follows the apparent paradox that rationally discriminating employers may find it profitable to hire less labor precisely from the cheaper sources, and more labor from the more expensive sources, than they would have done in the absence of discrimination—in those cases, namely, where by reducing their employment of the cheaper laborers they are lowering their wages to a still greater degree. Given the same slope of the supply curves from different sources, cheaper labor is likely to be in less elastic supply. If so, discrimination against it becomes profitable; "the amount bought from the less elastic sources of supply will be reduced below what would have been bought from those sources under simple monopsony, and the price to them will be lowered. The amount bought from the more elastic sources will be increased, and price to them will be raised."[3]

Discrimination becomes practicable once a dividing line is found along which the monopsonistic employer can separate the cheaper or more urgent job-seekers (i.e., the less elastic sources) from the others, and the cost of maintaining effective discrimination does not exceed its benefits to the monopsonist. Conspicuous physical characteristics may fulfill both these conditions, if they happen to distinguish groups with different needs for employment. Mrs. Robinson does not consider in her book any other examples than those of discrimination between men and women, and men and boys.[4] The analysis of monopsonistic discrimination, however, appears to be still more closely applicable to the economics of national or racial intolerance.

"A notable fact about farm labor in California is the practice of employers to pay wage scales on the basis of race, i.e., to establish different wage rates for each racial group, thus fostering racial antagonism and . . . keeping wages at the lowest possible point."[5] In this case up to half a dozen different racial groups

[2] Joan Robinson, *The Economics of Imperfect Competition* (ed. 3, London, 1936), pp. 302–3, and Fig. 80.
[3] *Ibid.*, pp. 224–5. It is assumed that the supply curve from each source is rising (*ibid.*, note 1, with further details).
[4] *Ibid.*, pp. 224–7.
[5] Carey McWilliams, *Factories in the Field* (Boston, 1939), p. 118.

appear to have been imported during the years, each to be excluded again, according to the same writer, when they began to demand wages more nearly on the American White level,[6] i.e. when that particular source of labor was no longer cheaper and in less elastic supply than native White labor.

The paradoxical position of such racial groups, which are tolerated, imported, and employed, while restricted in their employment both as to numbers and to occupations, corresponds to the paradox of discriminating monopsony itself; buying from the cheaper source may have to be restricted more than from the more expensive sources, if the full gain from discrimination is to be realized.

In practice different wage rates to different races or language groups are often ascribed to differences in efficiency, or in cost of instruction and supervision in the group's language. To the extent in which such differences exist there is no discrimination. But discrimination does exist wherever "the efficiency of one group is less than the other in a smaller proportion than their wages."[7] Only in those rare cases in which the conditions of supply from each group of labor are equal would it pay the monopsonist to offer wage rates in exact proportion to relative efficiencies. In all other cases wage differences will be best arranged with regard to the elasticities of supply in terms of efficiency units from each source of labor.

Discrimination may be present and profitable wherever the monopsonist is paying one uniform wage rate to persons of different efficiency. Discrimination against a group with a cheaper, less elastic supply of efficiency units can be practised by restricting the number of persons hired from that group at the uniform wage to a smaller percentage of the total, and reserving a larger percentage of positions to labor from more elastic sources. An open or tacit *numerus clausus* against a group seeking more urgently than others the employment in question may yield to the employer more efficient service from the members of the disfavored group, exceeding any loss of efficiency due to the employment of larger numbers of their favored competitors. A *numerus clausus* against, for example, Jews or Catholics will not, in practice, originate from any such calculation; yet, if members of these groups should offer themselves more cheaply or more urgently for employment, such a *numerus clausus* may not only fail to carry an economic penalty for the moderately discriminating employer, but it may even yield some economic reward.

Just as a small group of sellers will arrive by rational foresight at an aggregate monopoly output sold at a monopoly price (oligopoly output and oligopoly price, if we consider costs),[8] so a small group of far-sighted buyers will arrive at

---

[6] *Ibid.*, especially chap. VII, "Our Oriental Agriculture," pp. 103–33.

[7] Robinson, *Economics of Imperfect Competition*, p.302, note 1.

[8] E. H. Chamberlin, *The Theory of Monopolistic Competition* (Cambridge, Mass., 1933); and A. J. Nichol, "Prof. Chamberlin's Theory of Limited Competition" *(Quarterly Journal of Economics,* vol. XLVIII, February, 1934, pp. 317-37). Mr. Nichol also points out a modification in the case of equal but decreasing costs, where the oligopoly price will be higher than the monopoly figure as each oligopolist is producing his share of the aggregate output further up and to the left on the declining cost curve than a single monopolist

buying only an aggregate monopsony amount at a monopsony price (oligopsony amount and price, if we consider demands). In other words, in a group with similar conditions of cost or demand, the rational long-run interest of each member will approach more or less closely that of the group as a whole. Discrimination, then, should be profitable to a group of discriminating oligopsonists. The same gains from restriction and discrimination, however, which a small group would reap from rational calculation, can also be gained and maintained by a large group, if their emotions and prejudices happen to direct them generally to exclude, restrict, and discriminate in those directions and against those groups where exclusion, restriction, and discrimination will yield in the long run higher total returns. More intense emotions and a higher group morale, so long as they do not seriously overstep the limits given by economic rationality (i.e., the underlying supply-and-demand situation), will further improve the group's long-run chances for higher revenues. In many—though not in all—regions and countries the prevailing discriminatory emotions and prejudices do run against groups with an initial lower standard of life, such as Slavic or Latin nationalities, Blacks, Catholics, Jews (especially on the clerical and professional levels of occupation), who are in more urgent need of employment and can be induced to start work already at a lower rate of pay—that is, precisely against the less elastic sources of labor supply.[9] Where this is the case, long-run aggregate revenues of firms may even be somewhat higher than they would be in the absence of discrimination.

Higher revenues in any field, unless entry is restricted, will lead to the entry of new firms. As competition usually is not pure, there will remain eventually in business a larger number of somewhat smaller firms each producing at profits reduced to normal by the higher costs due to the less efficient scale of production. Such higher revenues, leading to a multiplication of firms, may occur in the trades which directly employ both kinds of labor, from the favored as well as from the disfavored sources. Most frequently it is likely to occur indirectly through a kind of product variation: the disfavored type of labor, cheapened by discrimination, may cheapen costs and increase prevailing revenues by being employed mainly in producing certain kinds of goods and services, complementary to the rest of the economy. In either case there will be more opportunities of investment for capital and entrepreneurship at normal, i.e. minimum returns. The surplus profits from discrimination will be turned, under free entry, into surplus livelihoods: numbers of less efficient firms just covering their higher costs, depending now on the maintenance of discrimination for their further

---

(ibid., pp. 319-25). An oligopoly price higher than the monopoly figure is already implied, however, in Professor Chamberlin's chapter on product differentiation, where also the falling parts of U-shaped cost curves are considered.

[9] The practice of discrimination against any group, for whatever emotional, political, or historical reasons, will already in itself tend to impoverish the disfavored group, and thereby render its supply of labor less elastic. Thus it is possible for the relationship to be reversed time and again, and the economics of discrimination may work with equal efficacy against the favored group or nationality of yesterday—a process several instances of which can be found in the Central Europe of the last two generations.

existence. In practice we may find a number of sheltered or larger firms, drawing from the general practice of discrimination some additional revenue, and next to them a zone of smaller trade and professional people, some of them barely at the margin of covering their costs—a few at the peak of a business boom, many more, perhaps even the bulk of the small firms near the bottom of a slump in particularly badly hit regions or countries.

An important part of the discriminatory interest pattern may be furnished by the favored labor group. As against the situation of simple monopsony, the unorganized members of the favored group stand to gain in terms of wages and employment. If they should not be content with the relatively better terms granted to them by the discriminating monopsonist, they will have to organize for collective action, either by excluding the cheaper sources of labor from the field, or by organizing both their substitutes and themselves in a common organization seeking the best monopolistic bargain on that wider basis.[10] In the many intermediate situations where neither full exclusion nor a strong all-embracing organization appears practicable, even groups of organized labor may become willing to accommodate themselves to a favored status under discrimination.[11] furnishing important aid to the stability of popular opinions favorable to the whole discriminatory system.

All this applies to those sections of the labor field where substitution of disfavored for favored labor is in itself readily practicable and hence mainly left to the employers' decisions. In such cases each worker in either group stands to gain if his or her fellows get high wages and if there are few of them. Wage discrimination may be combined, however, with the variation of occupation to such a degree that the favored group, effectively monopolizing certain occupations, comes to look upon the disfavored workers no longer as upon substitutes, but rather as upon complements—and the larger their number and the lower their wages, the better.[12] A diminution of the economic incentive to solidarity between labor of different nations or races would have to be achieved, in the long run, by diminishing their possibility of substitution. But as soon as the favored labor group would then exact a monopoly price for their irreplaceable services (i.e., if they could not be economically replaced by labor-saving machinery) it would become again to the interest of entrepreneurs and consumers

[10]The larger the difference in costs, or supply conditions, between any two sources of goods or services, the wider apart is the optimum price and output of each from that of the others, and the more difficult will it be to establish or maintain any explicit or tacit oligopolistic agreement between them. A common high wage level might penalize the low-cost source by an unnecessarily high share of unemployment. Free competition between independently organized sources would tend to bring the price nearer towards the oligopoly figure of the lowest-cost group, and hence injure the high-cost or high-standard source. The latter might stand to gain from a revival of discrimination.

[11] A case where the favored group (men) are organized, while the disfavored group (women) are not, is illustrated in Robinson, *Economics of Imperfect Competition*, pp. 304–5, Fig. 81.

[12]Cf. Bertil Ohlin, *Interregional and International Trade* (Cambridge, Mass., 1933), pp. 71–2, 348–9.

to restore substitution. To the extent to which substitution cannot be lastingly
abolished, then, this economic incentive towards some degree of international
solidarity seems ineradicable.

Fragmentary as it is, the foregoing analysis suggests that the economic factor
in intolerance may be more than a mere sum of specific interests. In each situation monopolistic competition and discrimination were found to increase the
aggregate revenues, and often the numbers, of enterprises—increasing the proportions of capital and entrepreneurship as against both labor and output. Under
such conditions of approximately equal cost, the abolition of group prejudices
would lead to the disappearance of numerous firms in the crowded industries
and to a fall in revenues in the sheltered ones. Pure competition would mean
fewer opportunities for capital and entrepreneurship, and as even the rewards of
the employed amounts of both would be brought down more closely to the
minimum, the rewards for the entire factors of entrepreneurship and capital,
both employed and unemployed together, would be reduced still more, with corresponding implications for business confidence and the functioning of the whole
economic mechanism—particularly in periods of latent or actual depression.

Attempts to abolish national or racial conflicts by the clearing away of economic barriers and by enlightenment and education have to proceed in the
teeth of serious obstacles. If it were desired to reduce these obstacles, and
to enlist stronger economic factors on the side of cooperation and equality between nations and races, a substantial widening of opportunities for initiative and productive investment in tangible equipment as well as in skills and
knowledge, would be essential: be it through sustained business prosperity,
through a widening of the world market, or through planning and continued
public investments.

So far as economic motives are concerned, monopoly and monopolistic competition are natural and unavoidable in an exchange economy where economic
agents are assumed to be motivated by a desire to maximize their incomes.
If left to itself, such an economy may be expected to produce ever new impulses towards the rise and clash of discriminatory interest groups along national, racial, or religious lines. The proviso "if left to itself" may serve to
indicate in this field some of the problems and responsibilities of democratic
government.

II. INTOLERANCE AS AN
ECONOMIC PRACTICE

By *intolerance* is meant, for the purposes of this paper, the *recurrent denial of
social and economic opportunities to individuals because of their classification* as
members of a certain group. This group is usually different from that of the
discriminators. By *recurrent* denial is meant a denial more frequent against cer-

tain individuals than would be the probable case under conditions of randomness.

By *opportunities* are meant actual possibilities for desired actions or omissions by an individual. The supply of opportunities to individuals depends on the wealth, technological development, and social and economic organization of the community in which they live. If individuals are to feel that opportunities are being denied to them, the *demand* for opportunities must exceed, either in number or in kind, the amount of opportunities available to an individual or individuals at that particular time. For the study of intolerance, people's demands for opportunities may broadly be classified into two main groups: demands for control over nature and demands for control over people. With the advancement of science and technology, opportunities to control at least some parts of nature can be increased for everybody; opportunities for each individual to command others, on the other hand, must remain scarce by definition.

The struggle for power and all the persecution implied by it has been considered eternal and inevitable by all theorists who believed that the individual's urge to boss others was a fundamental drive of human nature. Men and women would fight each other for power, the argument has run from Machiavelli to this day, even if no economic opportunities for greater security of life and greater individual control over nature depended on the outcome. But this oft-repeated claim could only be verified by an experiment which has never yet been made. So far in history there seems to have been no large-scale struggle for power involving great numbers of people in which their economic fortunes were not also at stake, whether they knew it or not. Only by abolishing scarcity, poverty, and even the chance of insecurity for large masses of people could we come into a position to find out whether they would continue to fight each other with the same persistence and intensity for abstract power alone. In all major historical cases of intolerance, it would appear, the long-run economic interests of the group, though necessarily not of each individual, have been a significant factor.

If we define intolerance as the denial of opportunities, the concept of intolerance will overlap the concept of *discrimination*. Both intolerance and discrimination presuppose competition for scarce opportunities.

Any competitive situation involves some degree of *automatic discrimination*, because the very concept of competition implies competition on some definite terms. The *terms* of each competition determine to a large degree the probabilities of success or failure for differently qualified competitors. Modern economic competition, with its heavy premium on social contacts and linguistic skills in many middle-class occupations, automatically imposes heavy barriers on all those who do not share the language, experience, and culture pattern of the locally dominant group, or in other words, on those who have not succeeded in securing at least local domination for their own language and culture. This factor of automatic discrimination in a seemingly free labor market is increased in significance by the fact, common to most markets, that a small difference in quality or price may result in a large difference in sales and economic success.

The difference in linguistic skill between two salespeople may be small. The difference between securing or not securing the desired position may be considerably greater.

The automatic discrimination, implicit in competition within the terms of a given national, racial, or religious culture pattern, is subject, however, to continuing and unequal change. Political, technological, and economic changes frequently upset previous relationships of dominance; new languages and new centers of activities may take leadership away from their competitors.

Seemingly free competition involves an automatic process of discrimination, clashing not infrequently with an automatic process of social and economic change. It is not surprising, then, if we find deliberate discrimination employed by the currently favored group in order to resist or forestall further changes, or if we find deliberate discrimination employed by a new and rising group in order to initiate or accelerate an improvement of their position in the competitive struggle.

Not all discrimination is intolerance. In any general attempt to widen the total amount of scarce opportunities, the appearance of "priorities" will be unavoidable. If no deliberate priorities are employed, the actual priorities imposed will merely be those due to the automatic discrimination implicit in the given terms of competition. If, for instance, educational opportunities were to be allocated exclusively on the basis of recent scholastic achievement with no other consideration whatever, the result might easily be a severe handicap for students from regions or nationality groups with less developed traditions of scholarship. Easier admission for students, let us say, from the southwest of the United States, may mean correspondingly stiffer conditions for the acceptance of students from the more developed northeastern section of the country. Yet, such discrimination may be in the interest of the educational development of the country as a whole; and therefore, indirectly in the interest of the seemingly disfavored northeastern region. Whether any particular case of discrimination or priorities represents part of a genuine attempt to widen total opportunities in the community, so as to become ultimately available even to the descendants of the most disfavored group, will be a question of fact in each particular instance. The outcome will depend not only on the subjective intention of the discriminator, but also on the actual result achieved, and, as in most judgments about ultimate results, considerable uncertainty and guesswork may be unavoidable.

In spite of this uncertainty, it should be possible in a wide range of cases to arrive at judgments sufficient for practical purposes. In such cases, we may define *genuine intolerance* as a total or partial denial of opportunities to individuals with no significant increase of total opportunities for the community and with no concern for any future widening of opportunities for the disfavored group. Under certain conditions, the results of unlimited "survival of the fittest" competition may approximate genuine intolerance as closely as any openly discriminatory pattern of behavior.

III. INTOLERANCE AS AN
IRRATIONAL HABIT

Prejudices, though frequently irrational, may lead to rational results. No less an observer of politics than Edmund Burke emphasized the value of prejudices as savers of time and energy in arriving at the innumerable judgments of every-day life. Customers' preferences for goods, brands, or firms, whether rational or not, are the coveted object of much economic effort in the sales and advertising fields. If the sellers of any particular good or service are too numerous to be united by a formal monopolistic agreement, they may yet reap the profits of oligopoly, if any prejudice, rational or not, should induce them to display sufficient unity of behavior. Wherever in a market a single monopolist could gain increased profit or security, a host of competing sellers may reap similar, though not equal, profits if they are sufficiently united by agreement or emotion.

A group prejudice which parallels a group interest under monopolistic competition may easily involve individual sacrifices for some members of the group. If its economic results should appear to benefit most of the members of the group for most of the time, general experience is quite likely to perpetuate and fortify the habit. For this purpose it is not necessary that the detailed economic mechanism involved should be understood by the participants. All that is needed is that "the visible blessings of Providence" should be found sufficiently often to follow upon the seemingly irrational practice. Employers, for example, who deny in ordinary times more skilled positions to Blacks or Jews, need not be aware of the possibility that such discrimination may tend to cheapen the supply of Jewish or Black labor as a whole and that, therefore, all employers taken together may benefit from cheaper Black labor in the unskilled and service occupations or from relatively cheaper Jewish bookkeepers in a restricted field of employment. Mr. Carey McWilliams's study of California's "factories in the field" contains a whole chapter of cases of profitable discrimination against agricultural labor drawn from various separate minority groups.

If the economics of group monopoly are to reinforce an existing habit of intolerance, all that seems to be needed is favorable economic results in what some economists call *"the middle long run."* In such cases, their influence may be sufficient to overbalance a short-run toll of individual sacrifices, but also extremely serious long-run damage to the group itself. Thus a large number of ordinarily nonpolitical Germans consented to some individual sacrifices for the sake of Hitlerism and showed themselves much impressed with the transitory material gains in prestige and prosperity during much of the first ten years of Nazi rule. During the same years, a startlingly small number of the German public showed any appreciation of the extreme long-run dangers which Hitlerism would eventually bring to the German people as a whole. The difficulty of large numbers of people to take into account considerations beyond the "middle long run" in judging the wisdom of intolerance could be paralleled from many situations outside Germany. Here again science, education, and religion, each in its way committed to the "long run" point of view, may find a serious task on their hands.

A survey of historical examples of intolerance, whether deliberately fostered or unconsciously acquired, confirms the usual parallelism of emotional idea and economic "middle long run" interest. Economics and ideas, in most of the major cases of intolerance in history, appear not to have clashed but rather to have reinforced each other.

Regarded in this light, intolerance is rarely totally irrational. The most extreme conclusions of Adolf Hitler's "Mein Kampf" follow logically from his basic assumption on a point of fact. In his passages on German population policy, Hitler merely assumes as truth an extreme version of the theory of the Reverend Robert Malthus, that populations must necessarily, under normal conditions, outgrow their food supply and therefore struggle for survival. Once this assumption is accepted, even the depopulation policies of the Nazi government acquire an insane logic of their own.

Intolerance is usually adopted because, on the basis of accepted "facts," it is believed or felt in some form to benefit the group, or at least to cause it no significant damage. Intolerance would become openly irrational only if persisted in after the realization that it will do the group continued and serious damage. Such irrational intolerance, which may approach group suicide, occurs in situations where the present members of the group have become convinced that they can no longer make the social and psychological readjustments necessary for a change of behavior. No new knowledge or insight has meaning for those who believe that they have lost the capacity to change. Wherever individuals or groups seem to have hardened irreversibly in the major behavior patterns of intolerance, long-run consequences have to take their courses and only the hard, ultimate impact of these consequences may open the way for that unpredictable phenomenon which religion and folklore have variously described as "conversion" or "a change of heart."

IV. BASIC CONDITIONS FOR INTOLERANCE

The first condition for the rise of intolerance is a strong *demand for opportunities together with scarcity* of important opportunities in relation to it. It is significant to note that the demand for opportunities tends to increase with the growth of mobility and general education inherent in the rise of modern technological civilization.

The second condition for the growth of intolerance is the distribution of existing opportunities through some form of *competition* among individuals. Individual competition also grows with the modern increase in individual mobility.

The third main condition for the practice of intolerance is the existence of suitable facilities for the *classification* of individuals for discriminatory purposes. Such classification must be *economically or politically meaningful.* That is to say, the group singled out by it must have something: positions, property, or services, which makes discriminations against them economically rewarding. Any group, however, which has been subject to discrimination for some time may develop by this very fact into a source of cheaper labor, and intolerance, which was initially unprofitable, may thus in time acquire an economic premium. It is this last peculiarity, incidentally, which make discrimination reversible. The history of Central Europe and the Balkans shows a number of striking instances where the underdogs of yesterday found occasion to discriminate with profit against former favored groups.

In addition to being economically meaningful, discriminatory classification should be *predictable in its incidence.* Since fair-haired parents may have a dark-haired child, for instance, discrimination on the basis of eye or hair color is usually unsuitable.

Classification, moreover, should be *durable;* that is to say, easy to maintain. Earlier discriminations on the basis of religion, for instance, had the drawback that they could be evaded by a change of religion, a practice which became particularly frequent in the nineteenth century.

Finally, classification should preferably be *conspicuous;* that is to say, easy to establish. The visible characteristic of color, or the audible characteristic of language would seem particularly suited to fill these requirements.

The facilities for classification tend to grow with the increased registration, documentation, and identification of individuals under modern government with all its paraphernalia from birth certificates to fingerprints. The potential economic importance of classification and discrimination grows with the increasing economic importance of regulation and administration in modern life, whether imposed by governments or by quasi-governmental private organizations such as cartels, trusts, trade associations, and others.

V. SOME PATTERNS OF INTOLERANCE IN HISTORY

1. *Intolerance in the Pre-Industrial Age.* Even a very brief survey of history would indicate that the growth of human civilization to date has been accompanied more frequently by shifts in the criteria of discriminatory classification than by any abandonment of the practice itself. Classification by physical descent by *family* or kin gave way to the intolerance of the "in group" against the "out group" on the level of savage tribes. When the demand for scarce hunting grounds and food was supplanted by the demand for scarce opportunities for higher skills and leisure, discrimination became effective along the lines of *sex* in the exploitation of women and along the lines of *status* and *class* in the treatment of

the prisoner, the serf, or the slave. Discrimination against women, however, was limited in practice, since men had to identify themselves at least to some extent with their wives in order to be able to identify themselves with their children. Discrimination against slaves led to the notorious difficulties of the ancient slave economies. In addition, slavery was not wholly predictable in incidence, since it frequently depended on the fortunes of politics or war. It is interesting to note that Plato attempted to reinforce slavery through the barriers of language and and race by proposing that the Greeks should make slavery more stringent but limit enslavement to barbarians.

With the growth of transportation, discrimination against slave and serf was supplemented by the growth of *empires* which discriminated against the populations of whole provinces in favor of the *metropolitan region*. Even where empires crumbled, common patterns of culture, law, and written language could spread in the form of great religious civilizations, such as the Latin, Christian, the Byzantine-Orthodox, or the Moslem-Arabic civilization of the Middle Ages. Each of these was centered around definite regions. Each involved some social subordination for recent converts and some intolerance against unbelievers.

After that peculiar departure in European history, the rise of the self-governing mediaeval town, discrimination became a more thoroughly established practice than before. At first the rise of cities brought freedom to their artisans and to those of the peasantry who could flock behind the protection of their walls. The freedom of the cities, however, and the relative wealth and security enjoyed by the members of the monopolistic guilds were bound eventually to attract far more would-be burgesses than the narrow town economy could support. Discriminatory practices flourished. The entire town discriminated against the rural population and frequently succeeded in suppressing all crafts and commerce in the nearby villages. Town discriminated against town, so bitterly that the hatred between the citizens of two north Italian commercial towns became proverbial. Within the town, entry into the guilds was made increasingly difficult by constantly increasing requirements for longer years of apprenticeship and more expensive masterpieces. Local and regional qualifications were introduced, limiting entry to those trained in the town or region or even to those who married a master's daughter. Whole categories of persons were excluded from entry by the fiction of "dishonest" birth. This discrimination was sometimes extended from the children of vagrants or unmarried mothers not only to descendants of actors and dentists, but also to all children of peasants. Even barriers of descent and language were utilized. Burgesses of some Spanish towns attempted to discriminate against baptized Jews. In the sixteenth century North German guildsmen in Lusatia denied admission to their guilds to persons of Slavic descent, and the dominant German guilds in the city of Budapest made proof of four German grandparents the condition of admission.

In some towns the situation was eventually eased by the growth of long-distance and overseas trade and the replacement of the leadership of the guilds by new forms of economic organization. Elsewhere, however, conditions remained stagnant or even became retrogressive. The reports about the distress of the local artisans, the small volume of business for each individual master, and the complaints about the excessive number of competitors for a meagre livelihood sometimes read like a commentary to a modern textbook on monopolistic competition. It is perhaps not surprising if the frequent preoccupations with the too large number of competitors should have provided an emotional and economic background for the waves of mass intolerance which decimated the ranks of the urban populations toward the end of the Middle Ages and the beginning of the Modern Era. The persecution of those suspected of witchcraft, the driving out of Protestants from the cities of Austria and France, the stringent discrimination against Catholics in Britain and Ireland, and the whole holocaust of the Thirty Years' War showed the force of irrational ideas reinforced by the economics of discrimination.

2. *The commercial and industrial revolutions and the rise of territorial patriotism and national languages.* The practices of oppression and intolerance, whether in the name of status, class, or religion, all seem to have one effect for those most successful in their employment: they left them with greater economic privileges and with greater stocks of accumulated capital. While in some of Europe's disfavored regions feudalism and petty guild monopoly lingered on for centuries of stagnation and partial decay, the conquest of monopolistic markets and the accumulation of capital enabled the more favored regions of the Continent to begin the transition to new forms of economic life.

The first changes were usually those related to markets, capital, and the growth in the unit of economic organization, still on the basis in many cases of the traditional artisan's technology. Sooner or later, however, these changes were speeded up and vastly increased in effect by the introduction of machine technology and the coming of the industrial age.

The new changes mobilized a new class of captains of affairs, the enterprisers in business and industry. The widening of markets with the development of transportation shifted the demand for military security and political control from the city to the territory or region as the most effective unit of power. The growth of wage labor, the shift of some industries to the villages where labor was untrammeled by guild restrictions, the influx of farmers' sons and daughters into military or domestic service in the princely capitals, the beginnings of a territorial bureaucracy, the sending of ministers, schoolteachers, and tax collectors to the rural areas and the building of roads to the outlying country districts—all led to a growing contact of the population of the towns with large numbers of the country people. The result of these processes was the slow mobilization of more competitors for the opportunities of the new age. Another result was the discovery of the common people and their language by educated persons in the towns. One of the first things eighteenth-century writers found about this common people was that it spoke and understood everywhere only its own vernacular language. Within three generations after the construction of roads into Brittany and into the Scottish Highland well before the French Revolution, Breton folklore and Gaelic poetry attracted the attention of the educated. Two generations before the French Revolution, in the period of Gottscheld, German housewives fined each other small amounts of money for each French word used in conversation. Fourteen years before the French Revolution, in 1775, the Italian writer, Alfieri, decided to abandon the French language in his diary and to create an Italian dramatic literature equaling or surpassing that of France. English nationalism had already become a substantial force in the days of Milton and Cromwell; and the classical battle hymn of British nationalism "Rule Britannia" stands from the 1740's.

Despite some genuine cosmopolitan sentiments in the thin upper layer of the educated, the increasing concern with the people of one's own territory did not make for more amicable relations with other regions. The monopolistic and protective techniques of the mediaeval cities were modernized and magnified into the even more ruthless mercantilism of the new kingdoms and principalities. At the same time territorial patriotism began to take the place of the earlier rivalries between town and town or district and district. The age was called enlightened and its wars were called commercial; but its decades witnessed the fiery nationalism of Thomas Cooper's poetry and of Gleim's German "War Songs of a Prussian Grenadier," until it culminated, decades later, in the blazing nationalism of "La Marseillaise."

The eighteenth century brought the discovery of the common people and began their mobilization, as individuals and groups, for the competitive struggle. The nineteenth century continued the work. But while the eighteenth and nineteenth century increased the advantages of certain leading nationalities, they also mobilized competitors. The lure of markets in the growing industrial regions induced landowners to pay more attention to the training of their villagers in more efficient methods of agriculture and even industry. Such training, however, could be given to the villagers only in the language which they spoke, if the process was not to take up centuries. What was true of the landlords' need for better peasants and workers was true of the government's need for better soldiers and officials. Thus we find in the eighteenth century English-speaking landowners founding the Cymrodorian Society for the study of the Welsh language and culture while other noble landowners organized a similar society to study the Gaelic language and to improve conditions in the Scottish Highlands. The Austrian monarchy started the first academic course in the Czech language at the Royal Military Acedemy in German-speaking Wiener Neustadt in order to enable their future officers to understand their Czech conscripts. Prominent among the founders of the Bohemian Industrial Union which was to become noted for its spreading of industrial knowledge and Czech nationalism was the German-Bavarian landowner, Count Oettingen-Wallerstein. Parallel examples for this process could probably be found from most countries of Europe.

3. *The free-trade interlude and the discovery of the competitive importance of Nationalism.* The nationalistic wars which ended the Napoleonic age were followed by a strange interlude of peace and good will. In its economic aspects

the period is associated with the growing practice of free trade and the rise of what is known as classic economic theory. While this interlude of free trade was real enough in many of its aspects, events soon began to reveal its transitory nature. If it can be said that the age of free trade won one of its major victories with the repeal of the English Corn Laws in 1846 and the Anglo-French Cobden Treaty of 1860, the back swing to protection can be said to have begun in the same 1860's with the new United States tariff after the Civil War. During the next decade, the 1870's, the trend became obvious, underlined for all to see with the transition of recently united Germany to high protection in 1879.

Near the end of the century the British economist, Sir Alfred Marshall, pointed out what seemed to him the basic condition which had been underlying the period of free trade, and which in his judgment did not seem likely to return. According to Sir Alfred the basic condition for the working of free trade had been the industrial monopoly of Great Britain. Britain had been so far ahead of most other countries in her industries, and her costs of production in her special fields were so much lower than those of any possible competitors that monopolistic agreement and governmental protection were in most cases unnecessary. Modern monopolistic competition could express the situation in a diagram: If the costs of production of two or more competing sellers are nearly equal their only alternatives are either unprofitable all-round competition or an open or tacit monopolistic agreement; if single sellers, however, have considerably lower costs of production than their competitors, then their own most profitable price may easily be below any common price level acceptable to their high-cost competitors, and the low-cost producer or group of producers may stand to gain most by setting their own lower monopolistic price independently. This lower price may, of course, quite possibly be well above the price which would result from the pure competition of some nineteenth-century textbooks. It is in fact quite likely to be somewhere near the optimum monopoly price for the low-cost group; but it is equally likely to be advertised to the world in the vocabulary of "free competition."

Small differences in cost, to put it briefly, tend to put a premium on monopolistic organizations and agreements; while great differences in cost tend to encourage what will look like free competition. Toward the end of the nineteenth century the great differences in industrial costs between the European Continent and the British "Workshop of the World" began to dwindle and finally to disappear in one field after another. With the growth of competition among several countries of similar industrial development, such as Germany, Britain, France, and the United States, old and new patterns of monopolistic organization, now called "Neo-Mercantilism" were likely to make their reappearance.

In the meantime, however, the interlude of free trade had done more than to equip *laissez-faire* doctrines with some theoretical and practical prestige. It had mobilized broader masses both of leading and of backward nationalities for competition in its markets. It had gone far in mobilizing country people, labor, and the middle classes. It had impressed millions with the thought and the desire to rise into the ranks of the middle class, and perhaps even higher. It had taught millions to think of economic life not in terms of co-operation or service but as a struggle against other people for survival. The nineteenth-century business-person's contempt for the improvident could not but make people somewhat more afraid to be among the losers in the struggle, and the prophets of Social Darwinism hammered home their conclusion, so wholly at variance with centuries of religious thought: that life was essentially a struggle between human being and human being, and that it knew nothing of pity.

In some ways the competitive-liberal nineteenth century appears to have been the incubation period for the intolerance of the twentieth. Its liberal division of labor had been based on great differences in the cost of production between advanced and backward countries, and within each country on similar great differences between metropolis and province, and between industrial and rural areas. Millions had been mobilized for the competitive process. As much perhaps as all the speakers and writers, experience had taught them the very real importance of nationality.

Nationality can perhaps be defined as a set of correlated slow-changing habits of social communication and co-operation in each individual. Such habits usually include language, accent, patterns of family education, patterns of acquired knowledge, habitual preferences, aversions, and ways of responding to experience. Almost all these, it may be noted, are acquired by each individual largely without his deliberate choice by the simple facts of education and training in a given community. In addition to these there may be present specific values and loyalties, depending upon specific indoctrination or the deliberate allegiance of the individual. Nationality is thus perhaps more complicated than a single and somewhat mystic "national character," and it is perhaps more objective and less dependent, at least in the short run, upon personal decisions than a mere "state of mind."

The set of habits which makes up nationality functions as an important factor of production and social co-operation, materially affecting the fortunes of individuals, whether or not they wish it. If persons share a common language and other common habits of co-operation, they are better able to complement each other's work, and they can train themselves more easily to substitute for each other's services. Nationality, in other words, functions like a special skill or, to use an economic term, like a *specific factor of production*. Nationality, under certain circumstances, makes its possessors efficient complements and substitutes in the economic process, while, in other situations, when economic life is dominated by another nationality, it may become partly useless to its owners or may even constitute a handicap. In addition to this effect of nationality on an individual's efficiency, account must be taken of the valuation put upon nationality by other persons. Persons of the same nationality as our own are more likely, other things being equal, to have habits similar to ours, and we feel therefore with some justification that we may predict their probable reactions to future events from our knowledge of our own. What we can predict we can trust; and the stranger whose acquired habits are so different from our own that we cannot predict his reactions becomes in our mind the stranger "who is not to be trusted." All these facts became operative, at least to some extent, in nineteenth-century competition. They operated to some extent regardless of any nationalistic ideology, but where nationalistic ideology was present it was rather likely to be strengthened by the experience.

At the beginning of the nineteenth century German nationalism was the nationalism of Arndt; at its end, it was the nationalism of Bismarck. Early in the nineteenth century Italian volunteers under Giuseppe Garibaldi had helped in the liberation of Uruguay. Near its end, Italian soldiers perished in the attempt to subjugate Ethiopia. If the early nineteenth century had seen Canning follow Castlereagh, the late nineteenth century saw the liberal Gladstone succeeded by Cecil Rhodes and Joseph Chamberlain. The 1870's saw the origin of the term "Jingoism" in England; the preaching of anti-Semitism by the preacher of the German Imperial Court; and the election of the first anti-Semitic Deputy, on the pan-German ticket, to the Reichsrat of Austria. The same decade saw the return of effective discrimination againt Blacks in the South of the United States, and the following decade added the Chinese Exclusion Act. During the following decades there followed discrimination against Japanese in California and British Columbia. The welter of discriminatory and race movements in the twentieth century finally is too well known to need more than passing mention.

4. *A Legacy of Growing Conflict.* The free-trade interlude in the nineteenth century thus ended with three main changes. Costs of production became more competitive between several countries. Individuals' nationality was increasingly appreciated as of tremendous significance for their social and economic fortunes, in schools, employment, and business life, particularly where competing individuals were otherwise not too markedly distinguished from each other by training or ability. Finally, group organization emerged as one of the main weapons of the individual in the competitive struggle.

All these three major processes are in all likelihood irreversible. Industrial monopoly of a single country is unlikely to return; the economic significance of nationality is unlikely to disappear, and competing individuals are unlikely to forget or discard the powerful weapon of group organization.

In the meantime the industrial civilization continues to mobilize ever new millions of people and to demonstrate before their eyes the potential opportunities of the scientific age. But the oft-quoted "rise of the masses" now continues not so much as a rise of competing individuals but as a rise of competing organizations.

The results are the processes which threaten to turn our present time into a new age of organized intolerance. Neo-mercantilistic practices in the 1930's converted much of international trade into economic "battles without bullets." The growth of monopoly has been described in serious studies with such titles as "The Decline of Competition." If British booksellers in the 1850's refused to join a trade association for the purpose of maintaining prices against undercutting, their successors in the 1890's responded overwhelmingly to a similar proposal. Today, prices have become rigid and trade associations predominant in most lines of business, while a similar development has taken place in most of the professions. Almost everywhere in western society the relative cost of selling and distribution have increased until a well-known estimate for the United States put the average share of distribution costs as high as 59 cents out of each customer's dollar. At the same time we have witnessed a growth of various preference and patronage organizations in the different countries. Fraternities, Rotarians, political parties, honorable Elks, Odd Fellows, and Foresters, all are joined by individuals not only in search of instruction or conviviality, but not infrequently also in search of contacts and connections. The various national, racial, or religious organizations—all can be, and frequently are, used for the same purpose. To this may be added the growth of farmers' organizations, competing labor unions, veterans' organizations, and many others. It has been said, half jokingly, of modern democracy that its ideal state would be one in which every business beloned to a cartel and a lobby, and every individual to a pressure group.

The basic pattern of group competition today is still the same monopolistic behavior as that of the mediaeval guild: to restrict the group's output and to increase the group's price. But, as the Czechoslovak economist, Karel Englis, pointed out, restriction cannot possibly be practiced with success by all members of an economy at one and the same time. It is not possible for everybody successfully to hold up everybody else. Either the entire economy falls into deadlock and stagnation or else, more likely, some foreign or domestic group must be defeated and its organization destroyed or made ineffective, so that the conflicting claims of the remaining pressure groups may be settled at its expense.

Since 1870 large parts of the world have seen a significant decrease in the effectiveness of the automatic discrimination operative in any competition between advanced and backward areas. Moreover, there has been a widespread revolt against competition wherever it appeared to lead to adverse results. Nevertheless, during the same period the basic fact of unguided competition has remained unchanged, while the spread of science and technology has increased the demand for wider opportunities for new millions of people. The automatic result of these factors was bound to include increased group pressure and intolerance. Today their legacy includes the growing difficulties of immigration even into extremely thinly populated countries, the spread of various exclusion acts and practices, the persistence and sometimes even the spread of practices of disenfranchisement, the increasingly ingenious classification techniques of modern racialism, and finally the unprecedentedly vast movement of race hatred and intolerance spearheaded before and during World War II by Hitler's Germany and by Imperial Japan.

VI. CONCLUSIONS: A LONG PERIOD OF RECURRENT DANGER

It has been frequently predicted from the most different quarters that a blind continuation of present trends with no attempts at their conscious guidance would in some manner lead the western world to ruin. We could now perhaps add that one of the most specific forms of the growing forces of destruction would be the growth of organized intolerance.

The growth of the basic forces making for intolerance is under present conditions automatic. Any remedial actions must be conscious and deliberate and the actions of individuals will have to be co-ordinated in an organized manner both by voluntary organizations and by civic authorities.

There seems to be little hope that nationalism should automatically become "de-politicized" after the fashion in which religion is sometimes alleged to have become "de-politicized" in the Era of Enlightenment. The growth of intolerance has not been stopped, and seems not likely to be stopped, by a shift in the technique of classification.

Neither a return to the universalism of the Middle Ages nor to the cosmopolitanism of the eighteenth century seems practical at this time. Both these patterns of intellectual culture remained limited to a thin upper layer of society. They were coupled with extreme intolerance along class and status lines. Most important, they were based on the narrow parochialism and the political, and to some extent even cultural, apathy of the vast majority of the population. The desirability of any return to such a state of affairs is open to debate. On practical grounds, however, it should be remenbered that a return to the economics and technology of the past might necessitate the return to the population figures which could be sustained by them; in other words, that it might necessitate a drastic reduction in the present numbers of humanity.

If these solutions seem impracticable, there remains the possibility that *economic and cultural expansion* may be accelerated so as to keep ahead of the process of economic and cultural mobilization. Such expansion would find some real opportunities in the promotion of the orderly industrialization of the world, which has become, at least to some extent, a part of the present foreign policy of the United States. Expansion would find further opportunities, though perhaps of a different kind, in the growing practices of large-scale training and "upgrading" such as were undertaken with success in the course of the United States war effort. A continuation of such widespread training seems implied in the provisions of the "G.I. Bill of Rights" recently adopted by the United States Congress. The further widening of educational opportunities would be in harmony with well-established trends in the United States as well as with similar trends in most of the United Nations.

Any orderly widening of opportunities will in the end place a new emphasis on the question of values. Individuals will have to decide whether they should desire greater opportunities for knowledge and mastery over nature, and for service to their neighbors, or whether they should desire ruthless competition for the eternally limited number of opportunities for arbitrary power over man. It is not an accident that the question of values is receiving new emphasis in the present crisis of our civilization. It is likewise not an accident that the leaders of religion are listened to with new attention at this time, and that people everywhere feel that religion could make a significant contribution to the political and economic decisions of our time. All such decisions, as T. G. Masaryk was fond of pointing out, are at bottom moral and spiritual.

Economic expansion and cultural mobilization will probably mean the rise of a number of new languages and nationalities in Asia and Africa during the time of the next two generations, just as the number of languages with some economic or political significance in Europe increased from 16 in 1800 to 30 in 1900 and to 54 in 1937. This transitory period of the rise of new languages and nationalities contains obvious possibilities of conflict. It can probably be safely bridged if the leading countries of the world succeed in maintaining both at home and abroad a *parallel and simultaneous insistence on both tolerance and development.*

Ultimately, such a policy would open up a perspective of genuine world unification involving the large mass of all people in all countries. The exact chances of such an outcome can obviously not be determined at the present time. A combined policy of tolerance and development may, nevertheless, have to be adopted not so much for the sake of ultimate hopes but in order to enable our civilization to survive in the present and the immediate future. The existence of our civilization seems likely to remain threatened for some time to come by the recurring danger of organized intolerance fed by the blind social forces unleashed by the growth of modern technology. Their successful control during this time of transition may necessitate a long period of co-operation between public and private leadership for their deliberate guidance in the public interest.

4 | Race Discrimination Among and Within Nations

    The ideas sketched in the first three chapters are applied in this essay to the problem of race relations, both within the United States and other countries and in international politics. The result is a series of hypotheses and suggestions for research that seem to me worth further testing and development. Even now, they seem to me more likely to be true than not, and hence they might deserve to be borne in mind by policy makers who may have to decide on actions without having time to wait for more research. In the ancient tug-of-war between the medical clinician who must treat a sick patient here and now and the scientist who asks for more time to test and deepen his knowledge, there is no perfect answer; we should act as quickly as we must, and strive to improve our knowledge as carefully as we can.

This starts with a series of research problems that is based on a definition of race in a context of social communication.[1] *Race* will be defined in terms of the effect of its *visibility* on the social-communication process in which it is a built-in, rapid, inexpensive, and reliable signaling device. It would permit the identification of a group of persons on the basis of some physical characteristic, very quickly, very cheaply, very reliably, and without elaborate procedures for verification. By this device different observers would usually use the same means to classify people as either members or nonmembers of this group.

    If people could be injected with a chemical that would turn them bright green,

---

[1] For general background, see Ruth Benedict, *Race: Science and Politics* (New York: Viking Press, 1959); Anthony de Reuck and Julie Knight, eds., *Symposium on Caste and Race: Comparative Approaches* (Boston: Little Brown, 1967); T. G. Dobzhansky, *Heredity, Race and Society* (New York: New American Library, 1957); E. Franklin Frazier, *Race and Culture Contacts in the Modern World* (Boston: Beacon Press, 1965); M. F. Ashley Montagu, ed., *The Concept of Race* (New York: Free Press, 1964); UNESCO, *The Race Question in Modern Science: Race and Science* (New York: Columbia University Press, 1961, and Research on Racial Relations, Paris, UNESCO, 1966).
The substance of this paper was presented in 1968 at a symposium on Theoretical Approaches to International Racial Factors at the Graduate School of International Studies at the University of Denver and published in G. W. Shepherd, Jr., *et al.*, eds., *Race Among Nations: A Conceptual Approach* (Lexington, Mass.: D. C. Heath, 1970), pp. 123-151. Reprinted by permission of the Publisher.

we would have the equivalent of such a signaling device. The elaborate tattoos of the Maoris would have a similar effect. People wearing these tattoos all over their bodies and faces could immediately and quickly determine whether or not someone else had such a tattoo. Efforts to confuse or imitate these marks would be difficult, expensive, and usually unsuccessful. The first major characteristic of the built-in labeling device is its cheapness and reliability.

The second characteristic of race is its *inescapability:* in most cases, a person so labeled bears that label from birth to death. These are statements of probability. For example, race has the probability that ninety or ninety-five percent of the people with a particular label will be recognizable throughout life. There is a small group of people who, to the geneticists, may belong to this race but who are not immediately recognizable as members of it. I remember a native Czech in Prague with blue eyes, a short nose, full lips, Negroid features, and blond but tightly curled hair. When photographed in black and white, he looked black. Furthermore, he had the athletic build, slim hips, and wide shoulders of many black athletes. I have a picture of this boy in his student days practicing archery which would deceive a racist. This is clearly an example of one of the wonderful genetic cocktails that history has produced all over the world in the course of centuries. In the United States it is estimated that between two and two and a half million people of partial black ancestry have passed or are passing for white. I am talking in these instances of race as a probabilistic definition; for most, however, it is inescapable from birth to death.

The third trait is the *inheritability* of physical characteristics, again with a ninety or ninety-five percent probability.

Race involves, therefore, the probability of conspicuous, easy recognition with a high likelihood of inheritance. Let us assume that one could duplicate such a reliable process of cheap and inheritable labeling artificially, with no correlation to any other genetic attributes of people. If you had such a communication label, what would be its effect in a society? Very clearly, it would depend on the statistical distribution of this particular signaling device.

Suppose that we could divide the population into greens and blues. These signaling devices would have no immediate effect in a society if they were statistically distributed by random numbers so that greens and blues were found with equal frequency, with equal chances of being rich and poor, educated and uneducated, propertied and unpropertied, industrially acculturated (people with obsessive, puritanical compulsions about punctuality, precision, and such) and preindustrially acculturated. But as soon as these physical labels became attached to a probability distribution that made some difference in terms of education, property, training, preindustrial or postindustrial behavior patterns, subculture, or anything else, the racial labeling would function as an accelerator of perceptions, a simplifier of perceptions, and a gross distorter of perceptions.

I think it is quite important to speak about the gross distortion of perceptions. A great deal of social learning occurs through making global judgments based on probability. If you have your fender scraped three times by drivers wearing checkered shirts and smoking cigars, you are very likely to give the fourth driver smoking a cigar a wide berth on the road. You will not stop even to think that a sample of three is not very large or representative. On the other hand, if such an accident happened only once you would probably not draw this kind of conclusion.

It seems that the human mind works as a probability device to a large extent. We learn by probability categories. We tend to use categories that have high and precise correlations, are cheap to compute, and are easy to recognize. Very often one event or experience can be aggregated into a whole series of different statistical groupings. If my fenders were scraped I could aggregate the fender scrapers into compulsive neurotics or near-paranoids. I could classify them as cigar smokers, as people who wear Makinaw shirts, as workers, as hippies, as Sunday drivers, or as amicable drunks. Since, in fact, I do not know whether they are drunk or what their educational level is (they may, for all I know, be poets on their way to a writers' conference), I am very likely to end up with the category that is cheapest to compute. A person who is treated roughly or impolitely by someone who has a very conspicuous skin color probably will associate the unpleasant experience with this easily recognizable skin-color group rather than with some other group. Thus, race biases are the statistical aggregation of our memories and inferences.

I have said that race is based on easily recognizable physical characteristics. How easy is easy? Perhaps whatever ninety or ninety-five percent of the local population can recognize within five seconds is easily recognizable. Race therefore presupposes not only some obvious characteristic in the recognized, but also a trait in the recognizer.

A Polish population in a rural area where most people have round faces, high cheekbones, and short noses is quite likely to impute to a different race a delicate-featured, long-faced, dark-haired youngster. In his novel *The Painted Bird* the Polish author, Jerzy Kosinski, writes of the nightmare of a child like this who is displaced into the Polish countryside during World War II and is assumed to be either a gypsy or a Jewish child.[2] According to the novel he is neither, but the recognition patterns of the local rural population function that way. I am told that Kosinski's personal nightmares have something to do with the unrelieved horror of his book. I am also told that in the Polish countryside during World War II many things occurred that give a cast of reality to some of the events described in his book.

Depending on what a group has been trained to recognize, genetically doubtful features could still be considered racial attributes. If the inheritance of these features occurs with any probability and if the recognition habits of the population are stable, a race will be created in the eyes of the population. The genetic differences between a deep black American and an American the color of old ivory are considerably greater than the differences between the light American

[2] Jerzy Kosinski, *The Painted Bird* (New York: Bantam, 1972).

black and any American of Meditteranean ancestry. The imputation of genetic
relationships depends on the mores, recognition scales, and habits of the local
citizenry rather than on the scientifically determined differences.

A marginal characteristic of race, even in the absence of the physical label, is
the probability of close family or personal associations. On the fringes of almost
every race are people like Walter White, late leader of a "black" organization,
the N.A.A.C.P., who would not give up his friends, family, or childhood associates and who therefore was recognized as belonging to a racial group not by
physical attributes but by association with other persons.[3] To some extent, this
is race by choice.

It follows, for instance, that membership in the Jewish community is treated
as a racial affiliation in areas where the Jewish population is conspicuously different from the rest of the people. Such distinctions may arise even among
people of similar ancestry. For example, a trained Israeli observer may recognize
Yemeni Jews as distinct from European Jews. If the recognition were easy and
instantaneous and if specifically Yemeni traits were inherited with high probability, the differences between Yemenite and European Jews could lead to
racial divisions in Israel. Under these circumstances, such divisions could occur
even though a geneticist might say there were no racial differences between
Yemeni and European Jews.

In other words, I am proposing to define race as a communication syndrome.
This might lead to a series of studies. As a simple social experiment, suppose we
took a school under reasonably controlled conditions where youngsters lived
together and where, as happens in many schools, the population is somewhat
stratified. To make it very simple, let us say that the stratification included a top
elite, a middling group, and a number of youngsters at the short end of the stick.
This could be a scholastic or an athletic classification, or one based on social
scales with the popular versus the unpopular. The elite would involve the football team, the class president, and the students who win the scholarships. We
could divide this group into halves, separating the different strata unequally. One
group would wear blue shirts for the next three months, and the other group
would wear green shirts. The same color scheme would apply to all other apparel
so that they would really remain conspicuously labeled for most hours of every
day.

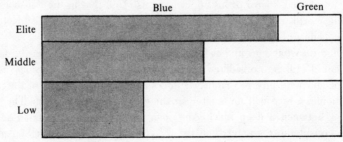

[3] Walter White, *A Man Called White: The Autobiography of Walter White* (Bloomington:
Indiana University Press, 1970).

After three months we would probably witness a kind of *Herrenvolk* behavior in perception on the part of the blues whose membership consists of three quarters of the elite, half of the middle group, and less than one quarter of the bottom group. An underdog psychology and perception would develop among the other group. Psychologists could find out by interviews and observation that each group would perceive the other group as it was labeled. This would be particularly true if they had not known each other before and thus did not know how artificial the distinction was between blues and greens. You would find probably that the self-perception of the groups would be distorted after three to six months. This is a hypothesis to be tested. After a while the people in the different groups would start believing this elaborate swindle themselves.

In this experiment we have deliberately taken away history and ethnicity and, through using random numbers, we have taken away individuality. We have combined a clear-cut stratification situation with a clear-cut device for unequal cross-strata labeling. The important thing is to use unequal cross-strata labeling that is diagonal, but not orthogonal to the stratification line, and to see that it is consistent and transitive. The hypothesis asserts that with a significant probability there would be then a development of something like racism: an in-group, out-group perception pattern.

A second hypothesis follows from this: the political effect of visible race distinctions, of the visual identifiability of groups, will be higher as the stratification of society is greater. This social stratification, plus economic and subcultural distinctions, is the matrix, the source of strength, of race conflict.

These propositions may be amplified by noting that the social and political importance of visible and inheritable physical characteristics will increase in a society roughly in proportion to seven factors. First is the degree of inequality in the stratification of rewards. The second factor is the degree of insecurity. You could have very unequal rewards but assign these unequal rewards in a very predictable and reliable way to certain people and their children. This would be a closed-class system. The class distinction would be very sharp, but everyone would know that he belonged in a particular class and that he would be likely to stay there. In an open-class system the classes remain highly unequal, but people and their children can change their class position through either effort or accident. Those who are up are not quite secure in staying up, and those who are down have some chance of moving up.

I suggest that in an open-class society the effects of race would be more severe than in a closed-class society. In this sense, the American combination of a persistent high inequality of rewards and a considerable degree of openness may be a more powerful engine for manufacturing race conflict than the more closed British or continental European class systems. You should read de Tocqueville again with a more jaundiced eye and without the eagerness of the apologist for the excellence of our national condition. You may find that the de Tocquevillian democracy can become a stick of dynamite when combined with the racial conditions of economic inequality and physically recognizable characteristics diagonally distributed across the different strata. I think it is possible to predict that the racial conflicts are in danger of becoming worse as the vertical social mobility of the disadvantaged groups increases, and as the likelihood of this mobility increases. Later I will discuss some ways this situation could be relieved, but first let us continue the diagnosis.

The third hypothesis indicates that conflicts become more serious in proportion to the density of settlement and the probability of encounters among relative strangers. This is an important point for metropolitan areas.

The fourth component is that conflict will increase in proportion to the volume of communication flow and the volume of transactions. Again, this goes up as modernization occurs.

The increase in conflicts with the equalization of aspirations is the fifth factor. That is, to the extent that the disadvantaged learn to aspire to the same things as the advantaged, race conflicts will get worse. Therefore, the communications media will increase the danger by using the most powerful tool of subversive education ever invented—mass advertising.

The sixth point is the probability that race conflicts will increase with the impersonality of the society. This can be measured by seeing what proportion of an individual's personal contacts are with previously unknown people. In the preindustrial society, most people deal with others whom they have known for a long time and whom they will see again. In the mass industrial society, people in both their working and their social lives will again and again meet individuals they have never seen before and are not likely to see again. You can measure the proportion of the two types of contracts, and from this you can get an index of the impersonality of transactions. Valid indicators could be constructed to measure the importance of personal to impersonal transactions.

Finally, factor seven is competitiveness. This is the degree to which the rewards to people depend not on their ability to perform according to some scale vis-à-vis space or time, but on their ability to perform better than the next person. For instance, you could arrange at a school to give prizes to athletes who can run a hundred yards in thirteen seconds. This would be very different from giving a prize to the fastest runner. In the latter case, the runners' situations become more insecure if they have fleet-footed colleagues. The same goes for students. If you give a certain prize or reward to all students who have passed a particular measurable level of competence you have a less competitive situation than if you stress relative standing in class. Law school students know that if they have bright fellow students they will rank lower in their class than if they are lucky and have weak students sitting next to them.

Since most of our schools are based on competitive ratings, standings in class, grading on curves, and so on, we are grossly increasing the insecurity of precisely those minority-group students whom we recruit into our top colleges. We are destroying with one hand what we are trying to build with the other by putting these students into competitive situations that create insecurity.

The seven factors I have named—stratified rewards, insecurity, density of settlement, high volume of transactions, equalization of aspiration, impersonality, and competitiveness—are characteristic of ordinary modernization and industrialization as it has occurred and is occurring in many countries of the world. With the economic, political, and social evolution in most of the world's developing countries, one can conclude that this situation will get worse, not better. This is particularly true of the thirty-odd countries in the last three columns of Marie Haug's classification, quoted in George Shepherd's essay in the volume *Race among Nations.*[4] A glance at these countries unfolds a world map of future troublespots.

This entire line of study will combine the techniques of communication research with the theory of probabilistic reinforcement learning. This is essentially Pavlovian learning. While Pavlov's dogs can be taught to give a physical reaction to a bell or a buzzer, simply because it happens to be associated with food, a conditioned reflex can be increased by making the association probabilistic rather than completely certain. You could subject populations to Pavlovian conditioning by combining visual signals about race with some other perception of competition, insecurity, threat, fear, social distance, or whatever was salient to them. B. F. Skinner more recently has shown that, if this combination is merely very probable but not certain, and if later the probability declines but does not become insignificant, the conditioning effects are likely to be stronger and more lasting. In this sense, the social communication process becomes a mechanism for manufacturing Pavlovian and Skinnerian conditioning in the population on a large scale. This is essentially social-reinforcement learning.[5]

ECONOMIC THEORIES AND DISCRIMINATION

A second line of research would examine more closely the reward half of this conditioning process. For Pavlovian learning, you need an easily discriminated signal in association with an undoubted reward. The reward only has to be probable, not certain. What research can we do about the rewards associated with race? A number of points come to mind. I will take my examples from the United States, about which we know a little and ought to know more. I would venture to suggest, however, that we would find similar problems already existing in other countries. These would be more extreme in some cases, as in South Africa; in others, they would be milder but growing, as in certain parts of Brazil. The first point would be the economic rewards associated with the economics of

[4] George Shepherd *et al.*, eds., *Race Among Nations* (Lexington, Mass. D. C. Heath, 1970).
[5] See Y. Frolov, *Pavlov and His School* (trans. from the Russian) (New York: C. P. Dutton, 1970); B. F. Skinner, *Contingencies of Reinforcement: A Theoretical Approach* (New York: Appleton, 1969), and oral communication, Cambridge, Mass., December 1973.

noncompeting groups. The economic theory was worked out by E. J. Cairnes in the 1920s and 1930s and is reported in a textbook by Gottfried von Haberler.[6] Von Haberler, however, did not draw the inferences for the race situation which I think come clearly from Cairnes's theory.

Cairnes deals with the following problem. Let us assume that we have two kinds of labor in the labor market and that people performing these two kinds of labor cannot move from one group into the other. When one group, called Labor Group A, gets a higher wage, the workers in Group B cannot move over into Group A to take advantage of the higher wage. In this case, these two "noncompeting" labor groups will exchange their products as two countries would do in international trade. The cheaper products and services of the relatively underpaid Group B may then serve to enhance the living standards of the better paid Group A, without threatening A's wages by their competition so long as the two groups still do not compete for jobs.

Cairnes was using this kind of theory for international trade to show that, given these supplies and conditions, it was quite possible for poorer countries to be exploited by richer countries. Von Haberler and Taussig pointed out that this did not happen very frequently in international trade. More often other countries would come into the market or countries would shift the nature of their exports or start different crops. On the whole, therefore, the Taussig model rather than the Cairnes model would hold. This is where Von Haberler left the argument in 1937.

If you consider this argument more closely, however, you will see that it affects to a nightmarish degree the situation inside a country where racial labeling of different groups of wage earners is concerned. Assume that among the twenty-two million blacks in the United States there are approximately ten million wage earners. The supply of black labor is an almost vertical curve, so that, no matter how badly black workers are paid, their numbers will not decline. Similarly, if many women need to work, or want to work, higher or lower wage levels may not change by much the number of women seeking jobs. A few women may have fewer children, but other black women stay home on welfare and have more babies if their wages are very poor or if their jobs are very unattractive. On the whole, then, being more realistic, the curve would not be completely vertical, but would be very steep. Racial discrimination from the possible wage to what the blacks are really offered will lead to a drastic reduction in their average wage level. The lower level of wages of the labor group that does not compete with the bulk of the labor force becomes an invisible subsidy for the rest of the society.

In a newspaper plant, a white person may be a highly skilled mechanic working at some complicated machine such as a typesetter, and a black person may sweep the floor. If the whole newspaper has a limited wage fund, then the cheaper the wages of the worker who sweeps the floor, the more money there is for the type-

[6] Gottfried von Haberler, *The Theory of International Trade* (trans. from the German) (London: William Hodge, 1950), pp. 190–191, with reference to Cairnes.

setter's union to get higher wages for its members. It is therefore the floor-sweeper who subsidizes the typesetter's wages. If the typesetters' union is skilled in the ways of the world, it may even take two black people into its ranks in order to prove to everyone that it does not practice racial discrimination. It is obvious, however, that the children of meritorious elderly typesetters have priority claims to be received into the union. The result will then be that the ninety-eight percent white group of typesetters will be subsidized by a ninety-eight percent black group of floorsweepers, and the typesetters will, in fact, have a share of what would have been the floorsweepers' wages if there had been full mobility of labor and no discrimination.

What is true of the black subsidy of the newspaper wage fund would be true of the subsidy paid by black janitors to white teachers in the New York school system. The New York taxpayers are only willing to pay a fixed sum of money for the school system. Thus racial discrimination that forces blacks to sweep the school buildings at a cheaper rate than white workers would charge makes it possible for the teachers to get a little more money or better seniority or other fringe benefits. In all these cases, the labor group that is subject to discrimination, if it cannot escape from its status, can be forced to subsidize the favored group. Under these monopoly conditions it is possible for one labor group to have a share in exploiting the other. The classical Marxist notion of virtuous workers and wicked exploiters has to be replaced by a more complex situation in which the role of worker and the role of exploiter may become unhappily intermingled.

I would suggest that this is the kind of study that too few economists have undertaken. We have large numbers of radical sociologists in the world today. We have bearded and unbearded radical political scientists and psychologists, although scant research on race by radical economists. I would like to know where the economics departments of Howard University and Fisk University have been recently. I would suggest that the economic theories of monopoly, monopolistic competition, discriminating monopoly, and the Cairnes model of noncompeting groups all give us intellectual tools to find out why there is a significant amount of potential economic reward in racial discrimination.

Let me make a bridge from reward to behavior. In an article on ethnocentrism, Carolyn Ware points out that many groups follow a behavior pattern that has become ritualized and accepted as a folkway, but not understood analytically, simply because it has come to be associated with the statistical probability of reward.[7] This is a prosperity policy. People may never know what trichina worms are, but in an area where trichinosis is frequent, people who do not eat pork may somehow discover that they are better off than their neighbors who do eat pork. In this way the religious taboo—Muslim, Jewish, or otherwise—against eating pork might become established or at least reinforced.

Such a prosperity policy often has a very positive effect, but unfortunately it

[7]Caroline Ware, "Ethnic Communities," *Encyclopedia of the Social Sciences* (New York: Macmillan, 1931), vol. V, pp. 607–613.

also applies to the folkways of racial exploitation. If it turns out that a group discriminates profitably in racial matters, without having to analyze the complicated economics, the group can simply ritualize its practice. If the discriminatory practice happens to be associated with prosperity, a very stable cultural pattern could develop because the ritual is being restored and strengthened by a reinforcement learning process.

I have discussed the noncompeting groups first. One important way to reduce the average wage of the disadvantaged group is by withholding employment opportunities from them. This can be done in two ways. They can be denied employment on a probability basis. For example, black people of all age groups could be laid off from work by random numbers for a certain percentage of the time. If white unemployment in the United States is about three percent and black unemployment is about six percent, we could simply lay off all black people six percent of the time by random numbers and this would effectively reduce wages, according to Cairnes' theory. We can do something else. We can concentrate this layoff in a particular age group—say, sixteen to twenty-five years old—and keep twenty-five percent of this age group unemployed. At the same time, we could employ older black people much more frequently.

This is what may be occurring in fact. For about fifteen years I have read statements by sociologists and psychologists expressing great alarm about the unemployability of young black people in the age group between sixteen and twenty-five. The people who alarmed the sociologists fifteen years ago because they were unemployable at age twenty—they were dropouts, they could not hold jobs, they did not show up at work, they were drug takers, they were petty criminals, they were all this, that, and the other—seem to evaporate by the time they are thirty-five. I do not read statements about their unemployability now. I would therefore urge some age-cohort research on picking people who were born in 1935 and who therefore belonged to the problem group of young people in 1950. I would ask *Newsweek* the famous question, "Where are they now?" I suspect, as a hypothesis, that consciously or unconsciously (and I am pretty sure unconsciously, in that kind of fit of absent-mindedness in which empires are acquired) we are using the unemployment of the young as one of the most cruel and wasteful processes of forced socialization of black men to the work process. By the time a young black man has been out of work almost all of the time, has been a drifter, a casual worker, moneyless and miserable from his sixteenth to twenty-fifth or thirtieth year, he has a great deal of resistance and hope knocked out of him. He is very likely to pick up that broom and show up on the job from age thirty to age sixty-five. It is in one sense a wonderfully cheap method for taming and subjugating the male labor of the group (for black women it is cheaper—they are more willing to work steadily and they have fewer complaints). With black men this terribly cruel process replaces the old slave gang. It is fantastically wasteful because we are throwing away the intelligence, the initiative, the energy, and the sparkle of millions of people. We are impoverishing not only the black minority but the whole United States by doing it.

I must point out that cruel and wasteful as this is, from a certain short-range point of view it is highly functional. Consider New York City with its people who wash windows, sweep floors, wash dishes, make beds in hotels, and do all the other service functions required by the great corporate headquarters and batteries of white-collar workers along the Avenues. A city planner from the University of California, Richard Meier, estimates that if New York had to be run at white industrial wage levels, the cost of keeping the business and communications headquarters of the nation in the New York area would go up by about twenty percent.[8] You could estimate roughly that twenty percent of the turnover of the white-collar industries of New York is the hidden subsidy paid by a million black and Puerto Rican laborers to the predominantly white white-collar workers in the corporations. The division of this subsidy between the corporations and their white employees depends on the labor market and on the bargaining skill of unions and management. According to this theory, the subsidy is hidden. I would not widely publicize this argument immediately, but I would put it before scholars in order to stimulate thinking about the kind of research that should be done to get the details and data.

Another hidden subsidy comes in the cost of land. According to the economic theories of Joan Robinson, if the buyers of any commodity can be divided into two submarkets that are cheaply and reliably labeled, so that no customer can move from one market into the other,[9] and if a seller has a monopoly or a group of sellers makes gentlemen's agreements not to undercut one another, the sellers can charge an optimum price in each market. Robinson's diagram is shown below. Assume the existence of a Demand Group A, a Demand Group B, and a

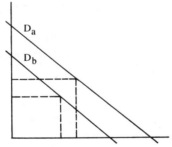

monopoly. You could charge Group B one price and Group A another price and get more money for your total commodity than if you had to charge a uniform price to both groups. By keeping the two groups permanently and reliably separated, you can milk each submarket separately for the maximum it will bear. Robinson developed this paradigm of imperfect competition to show why

[8] Richard Meier, oral communication, Ann Arbor, Mich., c. 1966.
[9] Joan Robinson, *The Economics of Imperfect Competition* (New York: St. Martin, 1969). Cf. also E. H. Chamberlin, *The Theory of Monopolistic Competition: A Reorientation of The Theory of Value,* 8th ed. (Cambridge, Mass.: Harvard University Press, 1962), and William J. Fellner, *Competition among the Few* (Clifton, N.J.: Kelley, repr. of 1949 ed.).

and how it was profitable in a country to pay women less than men for equal work.

The preceding discussion of discrimination against black people applies as well to women, who are also a conspicuously labeled subgroup. Being a woman is not inheritable, however, with the reliability to which being black is inheritable, so women can at least escape discrimination across the generations. Also, women can marry members of the favored group and thus recapture some of the results of the exploitation. The black group does not have integenerational change and does not have much intermarriage. Joan Robinson's paradigm applies with even greater force to the economics of race discrimination than it does to the economics of sex discrimination.

The classic example of this pattern is the real estate market. If you can clearly segregate real estate buyers who are black from real estate buyers who are white, you exploit the blacks *and* the whites. In the Cairnes labor situation the white worker benefits to some extent from the exploitation of the black. In the real estate market the white suffers side by side with the black.

Recently I obtained figures on the size of this exploitation. In the city of Baltimore a journalist analyzed thirty-six real estate sales in a white lower-middle-class neighborhood into which blacks had moved. The white lower-middle-class people sold their buildings in a panic. The buildings each had an average assessed valuation of $9,000, and they were sold to real estate corporations for an average of $6,000. Within a short time these buildings were resold to black purchasers at an average price of $12,000. The whites lost, on the average, one third of their savings in these houses, taking a cut from $9,000 to $6,000. The blacks were then charged twice as much as the real estate developers had paid. The journalist's work was carefully verified. He even looked into the real estate groups and discovered that they were dummy corporations. When he dug behind the dummy he found some plausible but dubious Jewish entrepreneur, usually with a characteristically Jewish name. The Jewish entrepreneur turned out to be a front man, and behind him were the most respectable banks in Baltimore with the most respectable old-stock families on the boards of directors. The work was done in August of 1968. The newspaper in Baltimore printed the article after nearly one year's delay and several rewritings.[10]

This is the kind of economics that should be investigated. Such economic processes might work this way in Johannesburg and they might work this way in Rio de Janeiro. They might work all over much of the world.

So far I have discussed monopoly, monopolistic competition, and Cairnes's noncompeting groups. Let me take another economic theory that is applicable to race relations. This is John Maynard Keynes's multiplier effect. It is known that if you pay a man a wage he will spend it somewhere. If a country exports products, the money it receives will be spent not only by the farmers who raised the coffee or cocoa or cotton, but also by the people who sell goods to the

[10] See Thomas B. Edsall, "How Speculators Profit as Neighborhoods Panic," *Baltimore Sun*, May 4, 1969, p. K–1.

farmers. Ordinarily in international trade, the multiplier effect is about two. For every dollar a country earns in international trade, the economy of that country gets two dollars in real benefits.[11]

A good deal of my argument has been based on the proposition that in a country with racial discrimination, some of the economic relations among race groups take on the characteristics of international trade, just as some of the political relations among these groups assume several of the qualities of international relations, including its dangers. Let us say that fifty-five percent of the school children in New York City are black. If fifty-five percent of the teachers' positions in the New York school system were also held by black people, approximately eight to nine thousand school teachers in New York would be black. If we assume that the average salary of a teacher in the New York school system in the 1960s was about $8,000, the black community would receive $64 million a year just from the income of its teachers. Besides benefiting the teachers and their families, a good deal of this money would be spent in black stores and neighborhoods, stimulating a multiplier effect that might double the amount of the salaries. The economy of the million blacks in New York might eventually end up with more than $100 million. Not all the teachers' income would go to blacks, but if the black community were tightly knit, blacks would probably get about $120 million of the $128 million.

The number of black teachers in the New York school system was then below three percent. The subculture technique of requiring written examinations that minimize the things at which black teachers are good and maximize those at which other teachers are good is likely to keep the percentage about the same.

Blacks usually pay their rent to white landlords and do most of their shopping with white shopkeepers (probably forty percent of Harlem's stores are Jewish-owned), while only one fifth or one third of black business goes to black-owned stores. As a result, the multiplier effects of black earnings are siphoned out of the black community. It is very important to understand the economic-reward probabilities involved in the integration-segregation argument. Offering the black people of the United States complete integration under the present distribution of land ownership, store ownership, intermarriage possibilities, availability of medical and professional services, and all the rest means that most of the multiplier effect from increased black earnings would disappear again.

If on the other hand community control and black power increased, despite the similarities of this situation to segregation, the multiplier amount of money would stay in the black community to a much larger extent. The same argument that led to the victory of protectionism over free trade in many countries during the last fifty years is now applicable to intergroup relations within this country. The possibility arises that blacks could gain more through building their own self-contained multiplier economy than they would lose through missing some of

[11] J. M. Keynes, *The General Theory of Employment, Interest and Money* (New York, Harcourt, Brace, 1936), pp. 115–131. Cf. also P. A. Samuelson, *Collected Papers*, Vol. 2 (Cambridge, Mass.: MIT Press, 1966), pp. 1140–1196.

the jobs that integration would open up to them. In the long run this is not ideal and this is not the last word on the question. Nevertheless, we cannot discuss black interests, white interests, and our common interests realistically and intelligently unless we know the real economics behind it and not the superficial free-trade textbook economics that has been out of date for fifty years.

Thus the segregation discussed above may benefit the minority if it creates higher multiplier effects in the black community. Let me add to this that there are also discriminatory effects on confidence and risk, on the availability of credit, and on the probability of capital formation. All these are superimposed on the multiplier effects. In some senses, rewards for the economic nationalism and protectionism that exist in international trade have implications for the problems of racial minorities inside national markets. We need essentially an adaptation of the theories of international economics to the theories of inter-racial economics within both developing countries and highly developed countries.

We must balance the rate of gains versus the rate of costs from the economic processes I have just outlined. These are all research tasks. In the field of inter-racial economics we need a far more thorough development of economic analysis and economic modeling than we have ever had before. We have to gather and to test in empirical research the data concerning the magnitudes of these gains and costs. Wherever we do not have aggregative data we should take sample surveys. There are techniques for taking well-chosen representative samples which could apply to market research for race discrimination and its consequences as well as to market research for shaving cream. If necessary to discover what the effects are, we will have to send mixed black and white teams of interviewers to everybody in order to be sure that they are getting frank and effective answers on both sides of the dividing line.

The theory suggests that gains from racial discrimination are different for different groups. We ought to do some intensive research on those groups benefiting most from this discrimination. These will be the real estate brokers and the credit interests and, therefore, the banks where real estate and credit operations come together. In the short run, the banks get richer, but over a longer period the banks often saw off the limbs on which they are sitting by making the big metropolitan areas almost uninhabitable and depressing real estate values. Short-range interests and long-range interests may be quite different, but this should be worked out in considerable detail.

ETHNICITY AND CULTURE

Let me now leave economics and turn to an approach based on looking at race in the context of ethnicity and culture. We are really dealing with economics, competition, stratification, ethnicity, and culture, to which race is only added as an accelerating and reinforcing signaling device. Race has been defined as a probability. The biological characteristics of race tend to change over a time span of at least six hundred to a thousand years and at most three thousand to five thousand years. I do not think there is evidence of any race older than that. Ethnicity involves traceable descent, concentration of childhood experiences, family associations, peer-group associations, and probability of intermarriage. Where these have a coefficient or correlation of .8 or more, you would have a closely knit ethnic group. We could make a quantitative definition of ethnicity by finding the actual probabilities and determining how strongly they cluster. Essentially culture is a distribution of similar or interlocking memories relating to facts, images, preferences, and basic orientations, as derived in part from childhood learning. One can show how the probability of ethnicity will lead to a probability of culture. The two go together but are somewhat distinguishable.

This distinction is quite important because the distorting and simplifying device of a dark coloring lumps into one category very different individuals. On one hand is a man like Ralph Bunche whose culture was the success-oriented, precision-oriented, performance-oriented, obsessive, puritanical, northwest European, North American culture of the modern industrial age, complete with its risk of stomach ulcers and with all its strengths and weaknesses. Labeled in the same category is the man who subscribes to the kind of culture that leads to what Eldridge Cleaver says about the beauties of rock 'n roll. Now Ralph Bunche is not easily pictured as dancing rock 'n roll to the satisfaction of Eldridge Cleaver. Nevertheless the racial label fantastically oversimplifies and hides not only individual differences among human beings but also the deep cultural differences.

Every people in the world moving from a preindustrial to an industrial system has a tendency to assign to some people still the preindustrial role of spontaneity, warmth, irascibility, willingness to fight and willingness to take strong stimuli, while others have taken on the pattern of tight-lipped repression, ceaseless work, and willingly accepted frustration in the hope of distant goals. In Germany it is the Bavarians who are cast in this spontaneous role and the North Germans who have taken on the characteristics of the highly industrialized people. Among the Czechoslovakians, the Czechs are placed in the industrial posture and the Slovaks are seen as the people who are better singers, better dancers, and, reputedly, better lovers. You will find this stereotyping between the highly industrialized and the preindustrial culture pattern in country after country. Even white American Southerners have some of this stereotype compared with the Connecticut Yankees. In Israel the oriental Jews get stereotyped as opposed to the Jews from Europe or the so-called Anglo-Saxons in Israel, namely the Jews coming from America and Britain.

Culture is a distribution of interlocking habits of communication and cooperation, including language, and coordination of expectations and role structures which each group wishes to keep distinctive. Ethnicity in terms of family relations and childhood patterns seems to change in two to three generations at the fastest or in fifteen hundred to two thousand years at the slowest. Immigrants usually change language within two generations, but settled populations change languages over a period of five hundred to seven hundred years. Culture, pre-industrial to industrial, changes most rapidly, passing from parents to children within ten to twenty years. Think of the industrial revolution or of the great political and social revolutions. Fundamental and fantastic cultural changes, as distinct from language changes, can occur in about fifty to one hundred years. One must keep distinct the race label, which changes very, very slowly; the ethnicity label (family associations and intermarriage probabilities), which changes faster; and the cultural label, which can also change fast.

Culture implies coordinated patterns of aspirations and motivation, coordinated patterns of capabilities, and coordinated practices and institutions for the acquisition and reinforcement of all these characteristics. Special contiguity and high frequency of interaction are usually associated with culture, but they are not essential to it. Separated by thousands of miles, Jewish communities in Eastern Europe and in Baghdad managed to maintain a surprising amount of cultural community. The whole notion of ethnic solidarity is based on the assumption that West African blacks and American blacks share some cultural traits as well as a visible pigment. Whether or not this is true is a research question. Harold Isaacs notes that American blacks going to West Africa discover that they have become much more American than African and that their main culture has become American at the same time.[12]

Nationality is primarily based upon culture. Ethnicity and race may contribute to it, but they are not essential. During the course of time a single people may emerge across barriers of ethnicity, as within Ireland and England, respectively. If race becomes weakened by intermarriage so that the physical signs are no longer spectacular, a common people arises across race barriers. Germanic Vikings were conspicuous. A tall redhead from Scandinavia stood out among small, dark Irish, and certainly among small, dark Italians. After the migration of nations, Lombards became over a period of time an inseparable mixture of Germanic and Mediterranean populations. We find racially mixed populations in Hawaii, Hungary, Finland (in Hungary and Finland there is an Asian-European mixture), Russia, Sicily (where Arabs mixed with Italians and Greeks), Egypt, India, Mexico (an Indian-European mixture), Brazil, and many others. Alternatively, whole peoples can be built across different languages, as in Switzerland.

Trends toward a disintegration of populations occur along cultural cleavages, often as a result of the pressure of social mobilization and heightened competition for vertical social mobility. These trends are strongest along lines of language. Social mobility makes language more salient as, for example, when more people become white-collar workers and become more dependent on language for their careers. These are also cleavages for the disintegration of peoples and of nations, particularly when either of these partly overlaps with

[12] Harold Isaacs, *The New World of Negro Americans* (New York: Viking Press, 1964). Cf. now also H. Isaacs, *Idols of the Tribe: Group Identity and Political Change* (New York: Harper & Row, 1975).

class. Disintegration rarely occurs along lines of mere ethnicity or of weak or unreliably transmitted racial characteristics. Even here, however, a combination of culture cleavages with class and social stratification can split up or disintegrate a nation. In this sense, Ireland was split away from the developing integration of Britain, and the same phenomenon may occur in Scotland.

We are now living in a period where in some parts of the world disintegration is more frequent than integration. In another part of the globe, six Ibo tribes of Nigeria became one Ibo people over the last forty years, and the survivors of the civil war there may remain Ibos now that they are even more unified by their sufferings. For most of the world, however, we now have a reversal of earlier integrative trends, and this may be happening in the United States at the moment. A conscious and deliberate policy may be required to reverse what seems to be a disintegrative trend in this country.

Let me briefly discuss sociological and psychological effects. We can look at jobs, for example. If the population of schoolchildren in all urban districts changes rapidly while teacher populations remain the same because of tenure, we will get an alien occupation of metropolitan schoolrooms that has never existed before. As a result, we will find a culture conflict superimposed on the racial and economic conflicts which will ruin the effectiveness of the educational system in all central cities. Here is a clash: irresistible changes in the ethnic and racial composition of the schoolchildren in the core cities hit an immovable object, the justified insistence of teachers on job security.

We are running into the shop problem, too. As the minorities develop shop-keepers of their own, they will run into the shopkeepers of the other racial groups. This happens in Harlem right now. It will be expressed in municipal votes and patronage. Newark, New Jersey, has a majority of black residents but a minority of black voters. The voting districts of Baltimore preclude any chance of adequate representation of black voters of Baltimore, even where they are enfranchised. Washington, D.C., has changed the other way, but Washington is not fully self-governing. We will see this problem becoming quite acute in metropolitan politics everywhere.

Something similar will happen within the next thirty years in that model country of racial peace, Brazil, when more and more dark-skinned poor people of the north move into the growing cities of Rio de Janeiro, Sao Paulo, and Brasilia. Conflicts will deepen as the Brazilian educational system slowly improves and dark children begin to compete more effectively for white-collar jobs, government positions, and business opportunities. Brazil is now where the United States was forty or fifty years ago, and it may be moving toward the condition in which we find ourselves.

We face the problem of standards again. We tolerated flagrant corruption in New York under Boss Tweed and in Boston under James Michael Curley. From one point of view, this could be defended because it permitted the immigrant Irish and others to learn how to run a city. After the Curleys came the Kennedys. We have to accept Adam Clayton Powell with equal good grace. We are not enthusiastic about it, but I do not think that we can afford to have different standards of morality for Senator Dodd and for Congressman Powell.

We may have to separate the areas in which revenues are raised from the districts where revenues are spent. To prevent a flight of taxpayers from areas of high welfare needs, each area must be decentralized in order to tailor its spending effectively to the needs of the people it is supposed to serve. We must decentralize the service functions of the government in order to shorten the feedback from the government to the people it is serving, and we must increase and centralize the revenue-raising functions in order to make them more explicit. This means that the old and traditional Anglo-American tradition of making the tax-raising and tax-spending units identical is becoming untenable. Research problems could be developed along these lines.

The same applies to our admission system in education. Admission to the better schools in the country is highly competitive, but after students have been admitted, they still must compete to a much greater degree than either in Britain or on the European continent. Norman Podhoretz describes in his revealing book, *Making It*, the blessed feeling of relief when he discovered that at Cambridge he was not going to be graded for a solid year.[13] He had to talk to a tutor, but his tutor gave him no grades. If this is good enough for Cambridge University, why should it not be good enough for a black student on our college campuses? I would suggest teaching black students by the Cambridge and Oxford system, where the grading comes not day after day and week after week, but after two or three years. Examining is done by outside examiners after a period of time long enough to show the results of the student's education.

The steady and ceaseless feedback of competitive grading may have or have had advantages, but today it is superfluous. I think the students who go to Harvard today know one thing. They know how to compete. If they did not, they would not be there. There is not the slightest point in making them prove over and over again what they have proved already. Incidentally, students in Germany did not pass many exams; instead, they had years in which they just have to grow up. The process of growing up intellectually and emotionally should not be a competitive process.

Our present performance tests, both for teachers and students, are fantastically biased. If students have learned French, this shows that they have high intellectual standards. This is equally true for New York teachers, even though French is rarely spoken in Bedford-Stuyvesant. If they have learned Navajo, this also shows a high standard and they get some academic credit. If they know the slang spoken in the black districts of Baltimore, they get no credit. I submit that it takes as least as much verbal skill to understand black slang as it takes to learn elementary or high school French, but the one is a credit subject and the other is not. Many times I have seen poems written by young black students that show high sensitivity and first-rate verbal skills, but not the kind of verbal skills to

[13] Norman Podhoretz, *Making It* (New York: Random House, 1967).

which the Princeton educational testing service can attach a number.

I surmise that we have a badly warped method of culturally biased testing and, as a student of international and comparative politics, I find that this is not an American peculiarity. All over the world examination systems for government, public service, and business are devised around traditional testing techniques that fit a class of literati. These tests favor certain groups of people and grossly disfavor others. The favored groups naturally defend these tests grimly as a protective tariff around the market for their talents. They use this technique because it looks legitimate and impersonal. Such a practice splits countries and leads to hatreds. The technique of written examinations stressing literary talents in India favored the Hindu clerk and disfavored the Muslims for decades. The result was that these tests produced in the short run a highly literate and cheap Indian civil service, and in the long run a murderous hatred between Muslims and Hindus. This led to the split of India and Pakistan and contributed to the massacres of 1947 that cost one million lives.

You get something similar in Nigeria where the written examinations in the British civil service favored the Ibo tribesmen. I suggest that these examination systems first favored the Ibo and produced or enhanced as a result the Muslim, Hausa, and Fulani hatred of the Ibo. The next step was the massacre of the Ibo, winners of the examination system, which contributed to the Nigerian civil war.

I think that this use of examination and recruiting methods that looked neutral but that were in fact ethnically discriminatory certainly made situations worse. We should do more work on finding out how the full range of human abilities can be effectively used.

On the other side, just as a privileged minority overreacts in defending these tests (such as New York's Jewish schoolteachers) so the underprivileged minority overacts in rejecting all of the competitiveness, compulsiveness, precision, and accuracy. I have heard students, both white and black, tell me that precision, accuracy, and hard work are "white middle-class prejudices." In that case, I say that if my child had an inflamed appendix, I would much rather have it removed by a white middle-class doctor who knows where the appendix is than by a very poetic, spontaneous, hippie individual who remembers it only vaguely and did not do so well in medical school. A cat that lives on catching mice must have a long attention span in front of mouseholes. Whether we call it a white middle-class cat or a black tom cat is irrelevant. There is a degree of performance characteristics which is inherent in catching mice, and there is a degree of performance characteristics inherent in doing surgery or in managing machines.

Today at least half or more of the American people, probably nearly three quarters, could not eat and survive without a machine technology. That is true for blacks and whites equally. Black farmers of West Africa are now learning to use strains of wheat—call them white middle-class strains of wheat—which have been raised with the help of white middle-class chemical fertilizer. Every successful nationalism has a phase where, after the rejection of alien values, there comes a demand from within to internalize the values of performance and efficiency in the name of self-respect. This has happened in Japan; it is happening now in India and China, and I think it is going to happen in the black community. The Black Muslims are a striking example of this process.

It ought to be possible to do this on a broader front than just in association with one particular denomination. In the meantime, must we have the biased examination systems? Perhaps we ought to give a black student from the ghetto area veterans' points and combat points for having grown up in such a situation, just as we give our soldiers special consideration for their service and hardship. I think it takes character and resourcefulness for blacks to get where they are now.

It also may be that we have to change the way we teach the top groups. If we are to train the future leaders of the United States at Harvard, we have to have black students at Harvard, regardless of their test scores, because a student who has not worked with black students, the way they are, not the way they are supposed to be, is not qualified to lead the United States. They would be an essential educational resource, even if they themselves learned nothing. If we had to say that they do not study anything, that instead we are studying them, their presence would still be important. But in actual fact they are studying something; they are learning something. The more we make this less competitive and more spontaneous and creative, the better the educational process will work.

This means that we have to remember the task of education which is, first of all, to develop identity, self-respect, and motivation. If we destroy motivation, everything else is lost. If we keep motivation, everything else can be added. To paraphrase Nkrumah, "Seek ye the kingdom of motivation and all things will be added to the educational process."

Second, we need to teach communication skills and the accessibility of a much wider range of sources. We would need renovation schools. There is a distinction between a renovative school and a school that teaches its children mainly cognitive additions to the culture of performance, achievement, and self-control which already has been presented to them in their homes. When my children go to school, the schools essentially add something or continue what is already happening in the home. Our children have lots of books at home; the schools teach them to read a few more books. This is quite different from a school that has to teach an industrial culture to children coming from a preindustrial home—for example, the homes of recent migrants. To think that these are the same tasks is a self-deception, and to count educational budgets as equal per capita expense of all students is both a deception of the students and self-deception on the part of the community.

We should do analyses of what schools really have to do and should distinguish information schools from renovation schools. Information schools add information to children who already live in families and in cultural settings which are on the whole adequate and appropriate to much of the industrial culture in which we live. On the other hand, schools for children who are deprived, whether white or black, have a renovative task. They have to provide an industrial element of culture that the family never had or even make up for deprivations from which the family has suffered.

I would assume that renovation schools, serving one fifth of our people (perhaps as many as one quarter of the schoolchildren in this country, since the poor have more children), ought to be based on the assumption that they may require the spending of at least twice as much money per student as information schools. Basically, the latter can run quite successfully as they have in the past on class sizes of twenty-five to thirty students, where the teacher maintains discipline, silence, and long attention spans. Renovation schools cannot possibly have classes with more than fifteen students, and they should have classes of between ten and twelve pupils.

This requires federal financing; it cannot be done by the central cities. The renewal of this country is at stake here. If it is undertaken, however, it will turn out that such conflicts as those seen recently with the New York teachers will disappear. If Oceanhill-Brownsville shifted to a twelve-student class size, the district would need every one of the union teachers, and would make the best of every current teacher and of every new teacher it could possible recruit, whether white or black or any other shade. The class size and the manpower budgets might make a decisive difference. This might then involve using the existing buildings because you can hire teachers fast, as Oceanhill-Brownsville demonstrated, but you cannot build schools quickly. School buildings would have to be run in shifts and would have to double their maintenance budgets. They would have to develop a staff paid for by the community to make sure that these schools are as well equipped as any of the good suburban schools. If necessary, one ought to get together the Office of Economic Opportunity, the local civic groups, and the local plumbers' union to see what can be done to introduce some civilization and decency into the old buildings. Perhaps they will have to invade some of the old schools with armies of renovators, but I think this can be done. At the moment we have an environment that telegraphs to the child every day, "No one cares for you." If a teacher says once in a while, "We do care for you," it is almost inaudible over the environmental voice that shouts the opposite.

This has some implications for foreign policy. First, the demonstration effects of the American success or failure in handling its own race relations will be worldwide and will be quite decisive for what is now still politely called the "free world." The same will be true for the demonstration effects of what happens in Britain (whether Enoch Powell will prevail or something better), in France, the Soviet Union, Japan, and China. All of these countries are less racially homogeneous than they look.

There will be crucial alignment choices for all the major countries in the world; for example, whether they will support black Africa in its confrontation with Rhodesia and the Union of South Africa. On the whole, we may find that many of the Western countries are unwilling to put serious pressure on South Africa or Rhodesia, but also are unwilling to make sacrifices in their defense. One should realize that this unwillingness cuts both ways, and analytic studies of foreign policy should be done to determine what these two kinds of unwillingness imply. There are similar problems of alignment between Arabs and Israelis, and it will be very important to prevent a possible racialization of that conflict.

There are risks of an arms race between racial groups since the white minority populations, both within countries and in charge of small countries in nonwhite regions, insist on making up for their lack of numbers by higher concentrations of fire power. This is true of Rhodesia and South Africa as compared to the manpower of black Africa and of Israel as compared to the manpower of the Arabs. We will find continually that arms control and disarmament negotiament negotiations have this hidden dimension, that the smaller numbers of the privileged white groups are to be made up for by the superiority of armaments. Sometimes this is openly averred, but much more often it is in the back of the minds of the negotiators.

In the long run this has an effect on the proliferation of weapons systems. We have to try to de-escalate the regional conflicts, the Rhodesia-Southern Africa discord, the Israeli-Arab confrontation, through multination guarantees, arms reductions, United Nations presence, and in particular resettlement and economic construction plans. If one cannot throw out South Africa, one might possibly get her to pay reparations to black Africa for development purposes. Such a plan might tide the situation over for ten or twenty years and give a new generation of South Africans a chance to become more reasonable. Israel and the United Nations might finance a plan that would give every Arab country two acres for every acre of irrigated Arab land lost in Palestine. I do not know whether this would work, but we have to think of the foreign policy of conflict management in the short run as opposed to conflict resolution in the long run.

The main task of foreign policy is to keep people alive. A potentially suicidal international conflict must be kept within limits just as a patient with a heart condition must be managed. We have risks of nuclear genocide through the proliferation of nuclear weapons. If the South Africans, Rhodesians, Malawians, and Zambians all get nuclear weapons in the next twenty or thirty years and if the Syrians, Egyptians and Israelis get them, we might suddenly find that these countries have been literally blown off the map. There will be very few survivors to argue the merits of each side in the conflict.

In doing something about this very real point, we may get into the politics of international population transfer. Someday the United Nations may transfer white Rhodesians to a country where they will be welcomed, perhaps to New Zealand, and give them farms or other opportunities which will prevent them from becoming déclassé. The problem would be preserving the prestige and economic and social status of ruling ethnic minorities after moving them from their homelands where their old powerful position is untenable. People fear a loss of social status more than they fear death. People prefer murder and suicide to a downward fall in their social mobility and this, I think, is relevant to the problem of compensating the transferred *Herrenvolk*.

Let me finish with some implications of these research problems for world politics. What will happen when, near the end of the century, the world's non-white peoples achieve nuclear parity or, in President Nixon's more appropriate term, "nuclear sufficiency"? Almost certainly by the year 2,000 the nonwhite population of the world will have enough weapons to be able to kill all the whites in the world at least once. We may be able to kill them three times, but that would be useless. This is something that is coming and we ought to know that it is coming. It will come in a world which will have six billion people, in-sufficient food, and which may contain some people who prefer to die with a bang instead of a whimper. These problems are now in the pipeline; they are not pipedreams. We ought to begin preparing for them.

A second problem for basic research in world politics is the national owner-ship of land and capital throughout the world, which is analogous to private property within the nation. This is a problem that Marxists have neglected and hidden from themselves as eagerly as have non-Marxists. There is a concept in Roman law which includes the right of the individual to neglect or to destroy his property. This is the right of exclusion and denial against others, which is largely obsolete in most Western countries and which has been replaced by a steward-ship concept. In Britain it is called the residual property right of the crown. In America we speak of property as being imbued in certain cases with a public interest. We speak of a law of eminent domain that entitles the community to expropriate certain items of property from a property holder if it is in the com-mon interest to do so, but it also obliges the community to compensate the owner.

One could argue that the establishment of the state of Israel in 1947 was an absent-minded act of eminent domain performed by the international com-munity with the concurrent votes of the United States, Britain, the Soviet Union, and most of the United Nations. The United Nations, however, did not compensate the former owners, the Arabs of Palestine. I believe that, if there is a law of eminent domain in international politics, the obligation to compensate property owners should be included in it. This has not been worked out yet.

Among the so-called socialist countries, the Russian people are currently property owners over the emptiness of Siberia vis-à-vis the Chinese and their views on that issue seem to resemble closely the collective, nationalistic property owners of the Western world.

Property in the Roman-law style was not the last word in the national develop-ment of countries. I cannot imagine that national property will be the last word in international relations, but very little thought has been given to these prob-lems—which apply to the possession of capital as well as land.

This leads us to the third point. Within the nation we accept those men as our countrymen by whom we are willing to be outvoted. The question arises concerning the sense in which we consider black Americans as participants in local government. A crucial test of true political integration is the willingness of a group to be outvoted. To what extent and on what issues will we consent to be outvoted in the world community? This is a question that not only we but also the Soviet Union must answer, and most countries, particularly large ones, are not very enthusiastic about relinquishing any voting power.

The willingness to be outvoted is related to the agreement to pay taxes. Indeed it is possible for a community to consent to pay taxes before it consents to be outvoted. Harvard pays taxes voluntarily to the city of Cambridge but does not accept the tax jurisdiction of the Cambridge City Council. We may need to study ways in which we could gradually transform what is now international charity, development programs or bribes for joining alliances, into the concept of an international income tax. We seem to be thinking already of the rate for such a tax, and American diplomacy has set as a yardstick about one percent of the gross national product. We ought to think seriously on the international level of what Oliver Wendell Holmes said, "I like paying taxes, that is the way I buy civilization." When will the Congress of the United States be willing to pay an international income tax as the cheapest way of buying survival at a time when national armaments are clearly becoming incapable of guaranteeing survival?

Finally, there is a fourth field for research in international politics. So far as we know, approximately one child with an IQ over 140, the so-called genius level, is born among every thousand babies. Although our intelligence tests are culture-bound, almost all we know is that this statistic varies within a factor of two. Scottish-Americans have twenty-five percent more highly gifted children than the national average while Jewish-Americans have about twice as many. These figures may reflect a kind of cultural development. On the whole, however, the ratio of one extremely bright child per thousand births is true throughout the world. Two thirds of the world's geniuses are nonwhite. Among the twenty-two millon blacks in America, potentially twenty-two thousand are geniuses as far as geneticists can tell.

We identify less than one quarter of the highly gifted people in most countries. Among whites in the United States we may identify and train as many as one third of the gifted. Remember, one half of the highly gifted are women, and that is an additional problem of discrimination. But among American blacks we probably ignore around nine tenths of the highly gifted. The cure for cancer that could save the lives of elderly Southern senators twenty years from now could easily be found by some young black scientist in the United States or elsewhere.

The nonwhite people of the world discovered iron, the number zero, gunpowder, papermaking, and many other things that we now consider characteristic of Western culture. We ought to include in international relations a cooperative effort to identify talented individuals and to train them early. We should subsidize and finance them so that they can follow their inclinations into medicine and science, medical research, scientific work, finding new sources of food and of art and beauty, and doing more social-science research in order to discover additional ways in which people of different races can live together peacefully and benefit each other.

I think these will be some of the tasks which a race program in international relations could study quite profitably and which in time might lead to legislation at both the level of individual nations and at the international level of the United Nations.

5 | Social Mobilization and Political Development

If a general theory suggests the importance of quantitative relationships, and particularly of their changes, then serious scholarship must examine the evidence of statistical data. The data that form the basis of this article and are presented in the appendix to it are by no means trivial, once we learn how to read them. They summarize important aspects of the conditions of life, the needs and capabilities, the behavior and actions of many millions of people.

Much of this behavior is habitual, and the habits of millions are a terrible force. They cannot be quickly changed or easily broken, except quite rarely, under extraordinary circumstances. Yet those occasions of vast quick change occurred in the great revolutions, violent like the American, French, Mexican, Russian, and Chinese Revolutions—five in nearly two centuries—or predominantly nonviolent, like the Industrial Revolution that started in eighteenth-century England, later spread to North America and Western Europe, eventually to Eastern Europe, Japan, Australia, and in our own time to sections of countries around the globe.

The size, scope, speed, sequence, and partial coincidence of such large-scale changes in mass habits and behavior have much to do with the changing needs of people, with the burdens and demands placed upon governments, and with the willingness of population to obey and support them.

The present chapter attempts to identify and measure some indicators of such changes in the 1950s for nineteen countries, projecting them to two common base years, 1945 and 1955, and then projecting them forward to 1960 and 1970, as set forth in Tables 5-3B and 5-5, respectively, in the appendix to this chapter. These tables, like the entire text, have been left unchanged in order to illustrate how much—or how little—foresight could be attained with the data and methods available in the late 1950s.

What then was the dimly foreseen future has since then happened. For the present edition, two new tables, 5-6 and 5-7, have been added, comparing the projected data of the original analysis with the actual data that are now available. For the projections of literacy, for example, these show that the average error of the projections for all nineteen countries was

This chapter was published in substance in *The American Political Science Review* 55, no. 3 (September 1961): 493–514. Reprinted by permission of the Publisher.

relatively small, of the order of minus one percentage point, but that the variance among the errors for particular countries was much larger, with a range between errors of up to more than plus or minus 12 per cent. The direction of the process of increasing literacy, however, and its general order of magnitude have been confirmed.

If the analysis were to be repeated today, better data and much longer time series would be available for most of the countries of the world, more effective computer methods could be used, and more deep-probing questions could be developed. But I believe that the general image of the set of basic processes of social mobilization established in the original article would stand, even though it might have to be modified for some particular countries and historical periods, and for the tightness or looseness of coupling with political effects in such cases.

Critical discussions on these matters have been contributed by Douglas A. Hibbs, Jr., *Mass Political Violence* (New York, Wiley, 1973), and Jorge Dominguez, *"Social Mobilization, Traditional Political Participation and Government Response in Early 19th Century South America"* (Ph.D. dissertation, Harvard University, 1972).

Social mobilization is a name given to an overall process of change, which happens to substantial parts of the population in countries which are moving from traditional to modern ways of life. It denotes a concept which brackets together a number of more specific processes of change, such as changes of residence, of occupation, of social setting, of face-to-face associates, of institutions, roles, and ways of acting, of experiences and expectations, and finally of personal memories, habits and needs, including the need for new patterns of group affiliation and new images of personal identity. Singly, and even more in their cumulative impact, these changes tend to influence and sometimes to transform political behavior.

The concept of social mobilization is not merely a short way of referring to the collection of changes just listed, including any extensions of this list. It implies that these processes tend to go together in certain historical situations and stages of economic development; that these situations are identifiable and recurrent, in their essentials, from one country to another; and that they are relevant for politics. Each of these points will be taken up in the course of this paper.

Social mobilization, let us repeat, is something that happens to large numbers of people in areas which undergo modernization, *i.e.*, where advanced, non-traditional practices in culture, technology and economic life are introduced and accepted on a considerable scale. It is not identical, therefore, with this process of modernization as a whole,[1] but it deals with one of its major aspects, or

[1] For broader discussions of the modernization process, see Rupert Emerson, *From Empire to Nation* (Cambridge, Harvard University Press, 1960); Harold D. Lasswell, *The World Revolution of Our Time* (Stanford University Press, 1951); and Gabriel A. Almond and James S. Coleman, eds., *The Politics of the Developing Areas* (Princton, Princeton University

better, with a recurrent cluster among its consequences. These consequences, once they occur on a substantial scale, influence in turn the further process of modernization. Thus, what can be treated for a short time span as a consequence of the modernization process, appears over a longer period as one of its continuing aspects and as a significant cause, in the well known pattern of feedback or circular causation.

Viewed over a longer time perspective, such as several decades, the concept of social mobilization suggests that several of the changes subsumed under it will tend to go together in terms of recurrent association, well above anything to be expected from mere chance. Thus, any one of the forms of social mobilization, such as the entry into market relations and a money economy (and hence away from subsistence farming and barter) should be expected to be accompanied or followed by a significant rise in the frequency of impersonal contacts, or in exposure to mass media of communication, or in changes of residence, or in political or quasi-political participation. The implication of the concept is thus to assert an empirical fact—that of significantly frequent association—and this assertion can be empirically tested.

This notion of social mobilization was perceived early in intuitive terms, as a historical recollection or a poetic image. It was based on the historical experiences of the French *levée en masse* in 1793 and of the German "total mobilization" of 1914–18, described dramatically in terms of its social and emotional impact by many German writers, including notably Ernst Jünger. A somewhat related image was that of the long-term and world-wide process of "fundamental democratization," discussed in some of the writings of Karl Mannheim.[2] All these images suggest a breaking away from old commitments to traditional ways of living, and a moving into new situations, where new patterns of behavior are relevant and needed, and where new commitments may have to be made.

Social mobilization can be defined, therefore, as the process in which major clusters of old social, economic and psychological commitments are eroded or broken and people become available for new patterns of socialization and behavior. As Edward Shils has rightly pointed out,[3] the original images of "mobilization" and of Mannheim's "fundamental democratization" imply two distinct stages of the process: (1) the stage of uprooting or breaking away from old settings, habits and commitments; and (2) the induction of the mobilized per-

---

Press, 1960). *Cf.* also Daniel Lerner, *The Passing of Traditional Society* (Glencoe, 1958), and Lerner, "Communication Systems and Social Systems: A Statistical Exploration in History and Policy," *Behavioral Science*, Vol. 2 (October 1957), pp. 266–275; Fred Riggs, "Bureaucracy in Transitional Societies: Politics, Economic Development and Administration," American Political Science Association Annual Meeting, September 1959, multigraphed; Dankwart Rustow, *Politics and Westernization in the Near East* (Center of International Studies, Princeton University, 1956); and Lyle Shannon, "Is Level of Development Related to Capacity for Self-Government?" *The American Journal of Economics and Sociology*, Vol. 17 (July 1958), pp. 367–381, and Shannon, "Socio-Economic Development and Political Status," *Social Problems*, Vol. 7 (Fall 1959), pp. 157–169.

[2] Karl Mannheim, *Man and Society in an Age of Reconstruction* (New York, 1940).

[3] Edward Shils, at the Social Science Research Council Conference on Comparative Politics, Gould House, Dobbs Ferry, June 1959.

sons into some relatively stable new patterns of group membership, organization and commitment. In this fashion, soldiers are mobilized *from* their homes and families and mobilized *into* the army in which they then serve. Similarly, Mannheim suggests an image of large numbers of people moving away *from* a life of local isolation, traditionalism and political apathy, and moving *into* a different life or broader and deeper involvement in the vast complexities of modern life, including potential and actual involvement in mass politics.

It is a task of political theory to make this image more specific; to bring it into a form in which it can be verified by evidence; and to develop the problem to a point where the question "how?" can be supplemented usefully by the question "how much?" In its intuitive form, the concept of social mobilization already carried with it some images of growing numbers and rising curves. In so far as the constituent processes of social mobilization can be measured and described quantitatively in terms of such curves, it may be interesting to learn how fast the curves rise, whether they show any turning points, or whether they cross any thresholds beyond which the processes they depict have different side effects from those that went before. Notable among these side effects are any that bear on the performance of political systems and upon the stability and capabilities of governments.[4]

I. AN ANALYTICAL FORMULATION

Let M stand for the generalized process of social mobilization, and let us think of it as representing the general propensity or availability of persons for recommitment. In this sense, M could be measured by the average probability that any person, say between fifteen and sixty-five years old, would have undergone, or could be expected to undergo during his lifetime, a substantial change from old ways of living to new ones.

In order to define this change more precisely, it is necessary to make three assumptions: (1) there are different forms of social recommitment relevant for politics; (2) these forms tend to be associated with each other; and (3) these forms tend to reinforce each other in their effects. Two further points may be noted for investigation: (4) each of these forms may have a threshold at which some of its effects may change substantially; and (5) some or all of these thresholds, though not identical in quantitative terms, may be significantly related to each other.

For these constituent processes of social mobilization we may then choose the symbols m_1, m_2, m_3, . . . , m_n. Thus we may call m_1 the exposure to aspects of modern life through demonstrations of machinery, buildings, installations, consumer goods, show windows, rumor, governmental, medical or military practices, as well as through mass media of communication. Then m_2 may stand

[4] For a broader discussion of quantitative indicators, regarding such problems, see Karl W. Deutsch, "Toward an Inventory of Basic Trends and Patterns in Comparative and International Politics." *American Political Science Review*, Vol. 54 (March 1960), p. 34.

for a narrower concept, exposure to these mass media alone. And m_3 may stand for change of residence; m_4 for urbanization; m_5 for change from agricultural occupations; m_6 for literacy; m_7 for per capita income; and so on.

Our m_1 could then stand for the percentage of the population that had been exposed in any substantial way to significant aspects of modern life; m_2 for the percentage of those exposed to mass media, *i.e.*, the mass media audience; m_3 for the percentage of the inhabitants who have changed their locality of residence (or their district, province or state); m_4 for the percentage of the total population living in towns; m_5 for the percentage of those in nonagricultural occupations among the total of those gainfully occupied; m_6 for the percentage of literates; m_7 could be measured simply by net national product, or alternatively by gross national product in dollars per capita. At this stage in the compilation of evidence the exact choice of indicators and definitions must be considerably influenced by the availability of statistical data. In many cases it may be most satisfactory to use the data and definitions published by the United Nations, in such volumes as the *United Nations Demographic Year Book*, the *United Nations World Social Survey*, the *United Nations Statistical Year Book*, and a host of more specialized UN publications.[5]

In a modern, highly developed and fully mobilized country m_7 should be above \$600 gross national product per capita; m_1, m_2, and m_6 should all be well above 90 per cent; m_4 and m_5 should be above 50 per cent, even in countries producing large agricultural surpluses beyond their domestic consumption; and even m_3, the change of residence, seems to be higher than 50 per cent in such a country as the United States. In an extremely underdeveloped country, such as Ethiopia, m_7 is well below \$100 and the remaining indicators may be near 5 per cent or even lower. (All dollar figures are in 1960 prices.)

In the course of economic development, as countries are becoming somewhat less like Ethiopia and somewhat more like the United States, all these indicators tend to change in the same direction, even though they do not change at the same rate. They exhibit therefore to some extent a characteristic which Paul Lazarsfeld has termed the "interchangeability of indicators"; if one (or even several) of these indicators should be missing it could be replaced in many cases by the remainining ones, or by other indicators similarly chosen, and the general level and direction of the underlying social process would still remain clear.[6] This characteristic holds, however, only as a first approximation. The lags and

[5]*Cf.* the pamphlets issued by the Statistical Office of the United Nations, Statistical Papers, Series K, No. 1, "Survey of Social Statistics," (Sales No.: 1954. XVII. 8), New York, 1954, and Statistical Papers, Series M, No. 11, Rev. 1, "List of Statistical Series collected by International Organizations," (Sales No.: 1955. XVII. 6), New York, 1955. For somewhat earlier data, see also W. S. Woytinsky and E. S. Woytinsky, *World Commerce and Governments: Trends and Outlook* (New York, The Twentieth Century Fund, 1955), and *World Population and Production: Trends and Outlook* (New York, The Twentieth Century Fund, 1953).

[6]See Hortense Horwitz and Elias Smith, "The Interchangeability of Socio-Economic Indices," in Paul F. Lazarsfeld and Morris Rosenberg, *The Language of Social Research* (Glencoe, 1955), pp. 73–77.

discrepancies between the different indicators can reveal much of interest to the student of politics, and some of these discrepancies will be discussed below.

The first and main thing about social mobilization is, however, that it does assume a single underlying process of which particular indicators represent only particular aspects; that these indicators are correlated and to a limited extent interchangeable; and that this complex of processes of social change is significantly correlated with major changes in politics.

The overall index of social mobilization, M, is a second order index; it measures the correlation between the first order indices $m_1 \ldots m_n$. It should express, furthermore, the probability that the $(n + 1)$th index will be similarly correlated with its predecessors, regardless of how large a number n might be, provided only that the index itself was appropriately chosen. Differently put, to assert that social mobilization is a "real" process, at certain times and in certain countries, is to assert that there exists for these cases a large and potentially unlimited number of possible measurements and indicators, all correlated with each other and testifying by their number and by the strength of their correlation to the reality of the underlying phenomenon.

In practice, of course, the range of available measurements and indicators is likely to be limited, and ordinarily there should be no need to compile for any particular time and country even all those data that could be found. On the contrary, one's usual aim will be economy: to get the greatest amount of useful information from the smallest body of data. The seven indicators of social mobilization listed above as m_1 to m_7 should quite suffice, in most cases, to give a fairly good first picture of the situation. They were chosen in part on grounds of availability and convenience, but also because they are less closely correlated, and hence less completely interchangeable, than some other indices might be.

Each of the seven processes chosen could itself be measured by several different indicators, but in each case these subindicators are apt to be very closely correlated, and almost completely interchangeable. Literacy, for instance, can be measured as a percentage of the population above fifteen or above ten, or above seven years of age; it could be defined as the ability to recognize a few words, or to read consecutively, or to write. Each of these particular definitions would yield a different numerical answer, but so long as the same definition was used for each country, or for each period within the same country, each of these yardsticks would reveal much the same state of affairs. If applied to Morocco between 1920 and 1950, *e.g.*, each of these tests would have shown how the number of literate Moroccans began to outgrow the number of literate French in that country, with obvious implications for its political future.

Similarly, urbanization could be measured in terms of the population of all localities of more than 2,000 or more than 5,000, or more than 20,000 or 50,000 inhabitants; or it could be measured, less satisfactorily, in terms of the population of all those localities that had a charter or a city form of government. Each of these criteria of measurement would have revealed the same process of large-scale urban growth in Finland between 1870 and 1920, for instance, or in India between 1900 and 1940, which had such far-reaching effects on political life in these countries. A recent unpublished study by Frederick E. Tibbetts 3d suggests once again the close interchangeability of different indicators of urban growth in Canada, as they bear upon the problems of assimilation and differentiation among the French-speaking and English-speaking population of that country. Urbanization, Tibbetts finds, has outstripped in recent decades the learning of English among French-Canadians; he finds among urban residents, and generally in nonagricultural occupations, a growing number of persons who speak no other language but French. The political significance of this development, which was largely concentrated in the province of Quebec, is highlighted by his observation that in 1951 Quebec (omitting Montreal), with 21 per cent of the total population of Canada, had only 4 and 7 per cent, respectively, of the veterans of World Wars I and II.[7]

Among the seven major indicators of social mobilization proposed in this paper, the correlations between economic development and literacy are less complete and the discrepancies more revealing. Ethiopia and Burma both have per capita gross national products of about $50, but Ethiopia has less than 5 per cent literates and is politically stable; Burma reports over 45 per cent literates and is not.[8] Of the states of India, Kerala, with one of the highest rates of literacy, elected a Communist government in the late 1950s.

It may thus be useful to seek answers to two kinds of questions: (1) how good is the correlation between the seven main indicators and (2) how interesting are the variant cases? As regards the first question, it has already been pointed out that the numerical values of the seven main indicators will not be identical. However, if we think of each of these indicators as forming a separate scale, on which each country could rank anywhere from, say, the top fifth to the bottom fifth, then we could measure the extent to which the rankings of a country on each of these indicator scales are correlated. From general impressions of the data, I should surmise that these rank order correlations should have coefficients of correlation of about 0.6 to 0.8, accounting on the average for perhaps one-half of the observed variation. As regards the second question, each of the cases showing substantial discrepancies between some of the main indicators will have to be studied separately, but the examples of Burma and Kerala, just mentioned, suggest that such cases may well repay investigation, and that the comparison of indicators may serve political scientists as a crude but perhaps useful research device.

For a somewhat more refined study the notion of two thresholds may be introduced. The first of these is the threshold of significance, S, that is, the

---

[7]Frederick E. Tibbetts 3d, "The Cycles of Canadian Nationalism," Yale University, typescript, 1959, pp. 24, 26–31. For details of the Finnish and Indian cases referred to above, see K. W. Deutsch, *Nationalism and Social Communication* (New York, 1953, 1966), pp. 102–11, 170–82, 197–204.

[8]Note, however, the comment on Burmese literacy in Note 6, Table 5–3A.

numerical value below which no significant departure from the customary workings of a traditional society can be detected and no significant disturbance appears to be created in its unchanged functioning. For each of the particular indicators, m_1 through m_7, we should expect to find a corresponding particular threshold of significance, s_1 through s_7; and our concept of social mobilization should imply that, once several major indicators move to or beyond this threshold of significance, the remaining indicators should also be at or above their respective levels of significance. The probability that this will be in fact the case should indicate once again what degree of reality, if any, may be inherent in the concept of social mobilization as an overall process.

The second threshold would be that of criticality for significant changes in the side effects, actual or apparent, of the process of social mobilization. At what level of each of the indicators we listed above do such changes in social or political side effects appear?

The indicator of literacy may serve as an example. It has often been remarked that even a considerable advance in literacy, say from 10 per cent to 60 per cent of the population above fifteen years of age, does not seem to be correlated with any significant change in the birthrate, if one compares literacy and birthrate levels of a large number of countries in the 1950s. At the level of 80 per cent literacy, however, there appears a conspicuous change: for the same collection of countries, not one with a literacy rate above 80 per cent has a birthrate above 3 per cent a year.[9] As a provisional hypothesis for further testing, one might conjecture that a literacy rate of more than 80 per cent might indicate such an advanced and thoroughgoing stage of social mobilization and modernization as to influence even those intimate patterns of family life that find their expression in the birthrate of a country. Obviously such a hypothesis would require other evidence for confirmation, but even in its quite tentative stage it may illustrate our point. If it were true, then the 80 per cent level would be a threshold of criticality on the particular scale of literacy as an indicator of social mobilization.

Since we called the indicator of literacy m_6, we might write c_6 for the particular threshold of criticality on that scale and put it as equal to 80 per cent. It would then be a matter for further investigation to find out whether other critical changes also occur near the passing of the 80 per cent literacy level. If so, c_6 might turn out to be the main threshold of criticality for this indicator. If important side effects should show critical changes at different literacy levels, we might have to assume several thresholds of criticality, which we might write c_6', c_6'' and so on.

Other indicators might well have their own thresholds of criticality at other percentage points on their particular scales. It might turn out, for instance, that most of the countries with more than 80 per cent literacy were also more than, say, 40 per cent urban, and that the apparent side effects observable above the

[9] Rosemary Klineberg, "Correlation of Literacy Rates with 1956 Birth Rates," Fletcher School of Law and Diplomacy, 1959, unpublished.

80 per cent literacy mark were also observable above the 40 per cent level on the urbanization scale. If such different but correlated thresholds of criticality could be found for all of our seven indicators, then the concept of social mobilization could be expressed as a probability that, if for some country n different indicators should show values equal to or greater than their respective critical levels, then any relevant $(n + 1)$th indicator also would turn out to be at or above its own critical threshold.

Much of what has been said thus far may be summarized in concise notation. If we write P as the conventional symbol for probability, M_s as the symbol for the overall process of social mobilization in regard to the thresholds of significance, and M_c as the symbol for the same process in regard to the thresholds of criticality, then we may write the general concept of social mobilization briefly as follows:

(1) $M_s = P$ (if $m_n \leqslant s_n$, then $m_{n+1} \leqslant s_{n+1}$)
     or briefly,
(1a) $M_s = P (m_n \leqslant s_n)$
     and
(2) $M_c = P$ (if $m_n \leqslant c_n$, then $m_{n+1} \leqslant c_{n+1}$)
     or briefly,
(2a) $M_c = (m_n \leqslant c_n)$
     and perhaps also
(3) $M = P (M_s = M_c)$

None of these shorthand formulas should require further comment here. They merely summarize what has been said at greater length in the preceding pages. Readers who find such formulations uncongenial may skip them, therefore, without loss, so long as they have followed the verbal argument.

II. SOME IMPLICATIONS FOR THE POLITICS OF DEVELOPMENT

In whatever country it occurs, social mobilization brings with it an expansion of the politically relevant strata of the population. These politically relevant strata are a broader group than the elite: they include all those persons who must be taken into account in politics. Dock workers and trade union members in Ghana, Nigeria, or the United States, for instance, are not necessarily members of the elites of these countries, but they are quite likely to count for something in their political life. In the developing countries of Asia, Africa and parts of Latin America, the political process usually does not include the mass of isolated, subsistence-farming, tradition-bound and politically apathetic villagers, but it does include increasingly the growing numbers of city dwellers, market farmers, users of money, wage earners, radio listeners and literates in town and country. The growth in the numbers of these people produces mounting pressures for the transformation of political practices and institutions; and since this future growth can be estimated at least to some extent on the basis of trends and data from the recent past, some of the expectable growth in political pressures—we may call it the potential level of political tensions—can likewise be estimated.

Social mobilization also brings about a change in the quality of politics, by changing the range of human needs that impinge upon the political process. As people are uprooted from the physical and intellectual isolation in their immediate localities, from their old habits and traditions, and often from their old patterns of occupation and places of residence, they experience drastic changes in their needs. They may now come to need provisions for housing and employment, for social security against illness and old age, for medical care against the health hazards of their crowded new dwellings and places of work and the risk of accidents with unfamiliar machinery. They may need succor against the risks of cyclical or seasonal unemployment, against oppressive charges of rent or interest, and against sharp fluctuations in the prices of the main commodities which they must sell or buy. They need instruction for themselves and education for their children. They need, in short, a wide range and large amounts of new government services.

These needs ordinarily cannot be met by traditional types of government, inherited from a precommercial and preindustrial age. Maharajahs, sultans, sheikhs and chieftains all are quite unlikely to cope with these new problems, and traditional rule by land-owning oligarchies or long established religious bodies most often is apt to prove equally disappointing in the face of the new needs. Most of the attempts to change the characteristics of the traditional ruling families—perhaps by supplying them with foreign advisers or by having their children study in some foreign country—are likely to remain superficial in their effects, overshadowed by mounting pressures for more thoroughgoing changes.

In developing countries of today, however, the increasingly ineffective and unpopular traditional authorities cannot be replaced successfully by their historic successors in the Western world, the classic institutions of 18th and 19th century liberalism and laissez-faire. For the uprooted, impoverished and disoriented masses produced by social mobilization, it is surely untrue that that government is best that governs least. They are far more likely to need a direct transition from traditional government to the essentials of a modern welfare state. The developing countries of Asia, Africa and parts of Latin America may have to accomplish, therefore, within a few decades a process of political change which in the history of Western Europe and North America took at least as many generations; and they may have to accomplish this accelerated change almost in the manner of a jump, omitting as impractical some of the historic stages of transition through a period of near laissez-faire that occurred in the West.

The growing need for new and old government services usually implies persistent political pressures for an increased scope of government and a greater relative size of the government sector in the national economy. In the mid-1950s, the total government budget—national, regional and local—tended to amount to roughly 10 per cent of the gross national product in the very poor and poorly mobilized countries with annual per capita gross national products at or below $100. For highly developed and highly mobilized countries, such as those with per capita gross national products at or above $900, the corresponding proportion of the total government sector was about 30 per cent. If one drew only the crudest and most provisional inference from these figures, one might expect something like a 2.5 per cent shift of national income into the government sector for every $100 gain in per capita gross national product in the course of economic development. It might be more plausible, however, to expect a somewhat more rapid expansion of the government sector during the earlier stages of economic development, but the elucidation of this entire problem—with all its obvious political implications—would require and reward a great deal more research. (Dollars are in 1955 prices, unless otherwise indicated.)

The relationship between the total process of social mobilization and the growth of the national income, it should be recalled here, is by no means symmetrical. Sustained income growth is very unlikely without social mobilization, but a good deal of social mobilization may be going on even in the absence of per capita income growth, such as occurs in countries with poor resources or investment policies, and with rapid population growth. In such cases, social mobilization still would generate pressures for an expansion of government services and hence of the government sector, even in a relatively stagnant or conceivably retrograde economy. Stopping or reversing in such cases the expansion of government or the process of social mobilization behind it—even if this could be done—hardly would make matters much better. The more attractive course for such countries might rather be to use the capabilities of their expanding governments so as to bring about improvements in their resources and investment policies, and an eventual resumption of economic growth. To what extent this has been, or could be, brought about in cases of this kind, would make another fascinating topic for study.

The figures just given apply, of course, only to non-Communist countries; the inclusion of Communist states would make the average in each class of government sectors higher. It would be interesting to investigate, however, whether and to what extent the tendency toward the relative expansion of the government sector in the course of social mobilization applies also, *mutatis mutandis*, to the Communist countries.

A greater scope of governmental services and functions requires ordinarily an increase in the capabilities of government. Usually it requires an increase in the numbers and training of governmental personnel, an increase in governmental offices and institutions, and a significant improvement in administrative organization and efficiency. A rapid process of social mobilization thus tends to generate major pressures for political and administrative reform. Such reforms may include notably both a quantitative expansion of the bureaucracy and its qualitative improvement in the direction of a competent civil service—even though these two objectives at times may clash.

Similar to its impact on this specific area of government, social mobilization tends to generate also pressures for a more general transformation of the political elite. It tends to generate pressures for a broadening and partial transformation of elite functions, of elite recruitment, and of elite communications. On all these counts, the old elites of traditional chiefs, village headmen, and local notables are likely to prove ever more inadequate; and political leadership may tend to shift to the new political elite of party or quasi-party organizations, formal or informal, legal or illegal, but always led by the new "marginal men" who have been exposed more or less thoroughly to the impact of modern education and urban life.

Something similar applies to elite communications. The more broadly recruited elites must communicate among themselves, and they must do so more often impersonally and over greater distances. They must resort more often to writing and to paper work. At the same time they must direct a greater part of their communications output at the new political strata; this puts a premium on oratory and journalism, and on skill in the use of all mass media of communication. At the same time rapid social mobilization causes a critical problem in the communications intake of elites. It confronts them with the ever present risk of losing touch with the newly mobilized social strata which until recently still did not count in politics. Prime Minister Nehru's reluctance to take into account the strength and intensity of Mahratti sentiment in the language conflict of Bombay in the 1950s and his general tendency since the mid-1930s to underestimate the strength of communal and linguistic sentiment in India suggest the seriousness of this problem even for major democratic leaders.

The increasing numbers of the mobilized population, and the greater scope and urgency of their needs for political decisions and governmental services, tend to translate themselves, albeit with a time lag, into increased political participation. This may express itself informally through greater numbers of people taking part in crowds and riots, in meetings and demonstrations, in strikes and uprisings, or, less dramatically, as members of a growing audience for political communications, written or by radio, or finally as members of a growing host of organizations. While many of these organizations are ostensibly non-political, such as improvement societies, study circles, singing clubs, gymnastic societies, agricultural and commercial associations, fraternal orders, workmen's benefit societies, and the like, they nevertheless tend to acquire a political tinge, particularly in countries where more open outlets for political activities are not available. But even where there are established political parties and elections, a network of seemingly nonpolitical or marginally political organizations serves an important political function by providing a dependable social setting for the individuals who have been partly or wholly uprooted or alienated from their traditional communities. Such organizations may serve at the same time as marshalling grounds for the entry of these persons into political life.

Where people have the right to vote, the effects of social mobilization are likely to be reflected in the electoral statistics. This process finds its expression both through a tendency towards a higher voting participation of those already enfranchised and through an extension of the franchise itself to additional groups of the population. Often the increase in participation amongst those who already have the right to vote precedes the enfranchisement of new classes of voters, particularly in countries where the broadening of the franchise is occurring gradually. Thus in Norway between 1830 and 1860, voting participation remained near the level of about 10 per cent of the adult male population; in the 1870s and 1880s this participation rose rapidly among the enfranchised voters, followed by extensions of the franchise, until by the year 1900, 40 per cent of the Norwegian men were actually voting. This process was accompanied by a transformation of Norwegian politics, the rise to power of the radical peasant party *Venstre*, and a shift from the earlier acceptance of the existing Swedish-Norwegian Union to rising demands for full Norwegian independence.[10] These political changes had been preceded or accompanied by a rise in several of the usual indicators of social mobilization among the Norwegian people.

Another aspect of the process of social mobilization is the shift of emphasis away from the parochialism and internationalism of many traditional cultures to a preoccupation with the supralocal but far less than worldwide unit of the territorial, and eventually national, state.

A highly enlightening study of American communications before the American Revolution, which has been carried on by Richard Merritt, shows how during the years 1735–1775 in the colonial newspapers the percentage of American or all-colonial symbols rose from about 10 to about 40 per cent, at the cost, in the main, of a decline in the share of symbols referring to places or events in the world outside the colonies and Britain, while Britain's share in American news attention remained relatively unchanged. Within the group of American symbols, the main increase occurred among those which referred to America or to the colonies as a whole, rather than among those referring to particular colonies or sections.[11]

More recent experiences in some of the "developing countries" also suggest a more rapid rise of attention devoted to national topics than of that given to world affairs, on the one hand, and to purely local matters, on the other. This, however, is at present largely an impression. The nature and extent of attention shifts in mass media, as well as in popular attitudes, in the course of social mobilization is a matter for research that should be as promising as it is needed.[12]

[10] See Raymond Lindgren, *Norway-Sweden: Union, Disunion, Reunion* (Princeton, Princeton University Press, 1959); and K. W. Deutsch, *et al., Political Community and the North Atlantic Area* (Princeton University Press, 1957).

[11] Richard Merritt, *Symbols of American Community, 1735–1775* (New Haven, Yale University Press, 1966).

[12] For examples of pioneering contributions of this kind, see the series of Hoover Institute Studies by Harold Lasswell, Ithiel Pool, Daniel Lerner, and others, and particularly Pool, *The Prestige Papers* (Stanford University Press, 1951).

Some data on the flow of domestic and foreign mail point in a similar direction. Of five developing countries for which data are readily available the ratio of domestic to foreign mail rose substantially in four—Egypt, Iran, Nigeria, and Turkey—from 1913 to 1946–51; the fifth, Indonesia, was an exception but was the scene of internal unrest and protracted warfare against the Dutch during much of the latter period. The trend of Egypt, Iran, Nigeria, and Turkey is confirmed in each case by data for the intermediate period 1928-34, which are also intermediate, in each case, between the low domestic-foreign mail ratio for 1913 and the high ratios for 1946–51. Many additional developing countries— including the Gold Coast (now Ghana), the Belgian Congo, Malaya, French Morocco, Kenya-Uganda, Tanganyika, Mozambique, and Malaya—for which data were found only for the 1928-34 to 1946-51 comparison, show upward trends in their ratios of domestic to foreign mail.[13] Here again, a relatively moderate investment in the further collection and study of data might lead to interesting results.

According to some data from another recent study, a further side effect of social mobilization and economic development might possibly be first a substantial expansion, and then a lesser but significant reduction, of the share of the international trade sector in the national economy. Thus, in the course of British development, the proportion of total foreign trade (including trade to British overseas possessions) rose from an average of 20 per cent in 1830-40 to a peak of 60 per cent in 1870-79, remained close to that level until 1913, but declined subsequently and stood at less than 40 per cent in 1959. Similarly, the proportion of foreign trade to national income rose in Germany from about 28 per cent in 1802-1830 to a peak of 45 per cent in 1870-79, declined to 35 per cent in 1900-1909, and by 1957 had recovered, for the much smaller German Federal Republic, to only 42 per cent. In Japan, the early proportion of foreign trade to national income was 15 per cent in 1885-89, rising to peaks of 41 per cent in 1915-19 and 40 per cent in 1925-29; but by 1957 it stood at only 31 per cent. Data for Denmark, Norway, France and Argentina give a similar picture, while the same foreign-trade-to-national-income ratio in the United States fell, with minor fluctuations, from 23 per cent in 1799 to less than 9 per cent in 1958.[14] Here again the evidence is incomplete and partly contradictory, and the tentative interpretation, indicated at the beginning of this paragraph, still stands in need of confirmation and perhaps modification through additional research.

The problem of the ratio of the sector of internationally oriented economic activities relative to total national income—and thus indirectly the problem of the political power potential of internationally exposed or involved interest

[13] See charts 1 and 3 in Chapter 8, pp. 162 and 164, based on data of the Universal Postal Union.

[14] See K. W. Deutsch and Alexander Eckstein, "National Industrialization and the Declining Share of the International Economic Sector, 1890-1955," *World Politics, XIII* (Jan. 1961), pp. 267-299. See also Simon Kuznets, *Six Lectures on Economic Growth* (Glencoe, 1959), esp. the section on "The Problem of Size" and "Trends in Foreign Trade Ratios," pp. 89-107.

groups *vis-a-vis* the rest of the community—leads us to the problem of the size of states and of the scale of effective political communities. As we have seen, the process of social mobilization generates strong pressures towards increasing the capabilities of government, by increasing the volume and range of demands made upon the government and administration, and by widening the scope of politics and the membership of the politically relevant strata. The same process increases the frequency and the critical importance of direct communications between government and governed. It necessarily increases the importance of the language, media, and channels through which the communications are carried on.

Other things assumed equal, the stage of rapid social mobilization may be expected, therefore, to promote the consolidation of states whose peoples already share the same language, culture, and major social institutions; while the same process may tend to strain or destroy the unity of states whose population is already divided into several groups with different languages or cultures or basic ways of life. By the same token, social mobilization may tend to promote the merging of several smaller states, or political units such as cantons, principalities, sultanates or tribal areas, whose populations already share substantially the same language, culture and social system; and it may tend to inhibit, or at least to make more difficult, the merging of states or political units whose populations or ruling personnel differ substantially in regard to any of these matters. Social mobilization may thus assist to some extent in the consolidation of the United Arab Republic, but raise increasing problems for multilingual India—problems which India may have to overcome by a series of creative adjustments.[15] (Politics may outweigh such advantages or handicaps. By 1978, India still was united; Egypt and Syria were not.)

In the last analysis, however, the problem of the scale of states goes beyond the effects of language, culture, or institutions, important as all these are. In the period of rapid social mobilization, the acceptable scale of a political unit will tend to depend eventually upon its performance. If a government fails to meet the increasing burdens put upon it by the process of social mobilization, a growing proportion of the population is likely to become alienated and disaffected from the state, even if the same language, culture and basic social institutions were shared originally throughout the entire state territory by rulers and ruled alike. The secession of the United States and of Ireland from the British Empire, and of the Netherlands and of Switzerland from the German Empire may serve in part as examples. At bottom, the popular acceptance of a government in a period of social mobilization is most of all a matter of its capabilities and the manner in which they are used—that is, essentially a matter of its respon-

---

[15] For more detailed arguments, see Deutsch, *Nationalism and Social Communication, op. cit.,* and Deutsch, *et al., Political Community and the North Atlantic Area* (Princeton, Princeton University Press, 1957, 1968). See also the discussions in Ernst B. Haas, "Regionalism, Functionalism and Universal Organization," *World Politics,* Vol. 8, (January 1956), and "The Challenge of Regionalism," *International Organization,* Vol. 12 (1958), pp. 440-458; and in Stanley Hoffmann, *Contemporary Theory in International Relations* (Englewood Cliffs, N.J., Prentice-Hall, 1960), pp. 223-40.

siveness to the felt needs of its population. If it proves persistently incapable or unresponsive, some or many of its subjects will cease to identify themselves with it psychologically; it will be reduced to ruling by force where it can no longer rule by display, example and persuasion; and if political alternatives to it appear, it will be replaced eventually by other political units, larger or smaller in extent, which at least promise to respond more effectively to the needs and expectations of their peoples.

In practice the results of social mobilization often have tended to increase the size of the state, well beyond the old tribal areas, petty principalities, or similar districts of the traditional era, while increasing the direct contact between government and governed far beyond the levels of the sociologically superficial and often half-shadowy empire of the past.

This growth in the size of modern states, capable of coping with the results of social mobilization, is counteracted and eventually inhibited, however, as their size increases, by their tendency to increasing preoccupation with their own internal affairs. There is considerable evidence for this trend toward a self-limitation in the growth of states through a decline in the attention, resources and responsiveness available for coping with the implicit needs and explicit messages of the next marginal unit of population and territory on the verge of being included in the expanding state.[16]

The remarks in this section may have sufficed to illustrate, though by no means to exhaust, the significance of the process of social mobilization in the economic and political development of countries. The main usefulness of the concept, however, should lie in the possibility of quantitative study which it offers. How much social mobilization, as measured by our seven indicators, has been occurring in some country per year or per decade during some period of its history, or during recent times? And what is the meaning of the differences between the rates at which some of the constituent subprocesses of social mobilization may have been going on? Although specific data will have to be found separately for each country, it should be possible to sketch a general quantitative model to show some of the interrelations and their possible significance.

III. A QUANTITATIVE MODEL OF THE SOCIAL MOBILIZATION PROCESS

For a quantitative description, it is convenient to express our first six indicators not in terms of the total percentage of the population which is literate, or exposed to modern life, etc., but in terms only of that average annual percentage of the total population which has been added to, or subtracted from, the total share of the population in that category. If for some country our indicator

[16] *Cf.* Chapter 7, pp. 144–152.

showed, say, 40 per cent exposed to significant aspects of modern life in 1940, and 60 per cent so exposed in 1950, the average annual percentage shift, dm_1 would be 2 per cent. The seventh indicator, per capita increase, may be broken up into two elements and written as the annual percentage of the total income added, dm_7 and the annual percentage of population growth, p.

Adopting these conventions, we may use in this model, for purposes of illustration, crudely estimated magnitudes from various collections of data. If we add indicators for the increase in voting participation, and in linguistic, cultural or political assimilation, we may write for a case of fairly rapid social mobilization a small table of the sort show in Table 5-1. The case represented by this table is an imaginary one, but the different rates of subprocesses of social mobilization are not necessarily unrealistic, and neither are the consequences suggested by this model, for the stability of the government in any country to which these or similar assumptions would apply.

Before discussing these consequences more explicitly, it should be made clear that the annual rates of change are likely to be realistic, at most, only for countries during the rapid middle stages of the process of social mobilization and economic development—say, for a range of between 10 and 80 per cent literacy and for analogous ranges of other indicators of economic development. In the earliest stages, the annual percentages of the population shifting into a more

TABLE 5-1. A HYPOTHETICAL EXAMPLE OF A COUNTRY UNDERGOING RAPID SOCIAL MOBILIZATION: RATES OF CHANGE

SYMBOL OF INDICATOR		DESCRIPTION	AVERAGE ANNUAL % OF TOTAL POPULATION OR INCOME ADDED TO CATEGORY	
			Range	Median
Group I:	dm_1	shift into any substantial exposure to modernity, incl. rumors, demonstrations of machinery or merchandise, etc.	2.0 to 4.0	3.0
	dm_2	shift into mass media audience (radio, movies, posters, press)	1.5 to 4.0	2.75
	dm_8	increase in voting participation	0.2 to 4.0	2.1
	dm_6	increase in literacy	1.0 to 1.4	1.2
	dm_3	change of locality of residence	1.0 to 1.5	1.25
	p	population growth	(1.9 to 3.3)	(2.6)
Group II:	dm_5	occupational shift out of agriculture	0.4 to 1.0	0.7
	dm_4	change from rural to urban residence	0.1 to 1.2	0.5
	a	linguistic, cultural or political assimilation	-0.5 to 1.0	0.25
	dy	income growth	(2.0 to 8.0)	(5.0)
	dm_7	income growth per capita	—	(2.3)

Note: Figures in parentheses refer to percentage increases against the previous year, and thus are not strictly comparable to percentage shifts among sub-categories of the total population. A shift of 1.2 per cent of all adults into the category of literates, for instance, would refer to the total adult population, including the part just added by population aging; etc.

mobilized state are apt to be much smaller, and in the late stages of the process something like a "ceiling effect" may be expected to appear—once 80 or 90 per cent of the population have become literate, any further annual gains in the percentage of literates in the population are likely to be small.

Within the middle stages of development, however, which are appropriate to the assumptions of the model, a cumulative strain on political stability may be expected. All the rates of change in group I tend to make for increased demands or burdens upon the government, and all of them have median values above 1 per cent per year. The rates of change in group II are related to the capabilities of the government for coping with these burdens, but the median values of all these rates, with only one exception, are well below 1 per cent. If it were not for this exception—the assumed 5 per cent annual increase in national income—one would have to predict from the model an annual shift of perhaps 1 per cent or more of the population into the category of at least partly socially mobilized but largely unassimilated and dissatisfied people.

If one assumes, in accordance with this model, an annual entry of 2.75 per cent of the population into the mass media audience and a shift of only 0.6 per cent into non-agricultural employment, then the expectable increase in the numbers of not adequately reemployed new members of the mass media audience might be as high as 2.15 per cent of the population per year, or more than one-fifth of the population within a decade. This might be the proportion of people newly participating in their imagination in the new opportunities and attractions of modern life, while still being denied most or all of these new opportunities in fact—something which should be a fairly effective prescription for accumulating political trouble. The spread of more effective methods of production and perhaps of improved patterns of land tenure, rural credit, and other betterments within the agricultural sector could do something to counteract this tendency; but short of major and sustained efforts at such agricultural improvements the dangerous gap between the fast-growing mass media audience and the slow-growing circle of more adequately employed and equipped persons is likely to remain and to increase.

If linguistic, cultural or political assimilation—that is, the more or less permanent change of stable habits of language, culture, legitimacy and loyalty—is also a relevant problem in the country concerned, then the lag of the slow assimilation rate, put at only 0.25 per cent per year in our model, behind the far more rapid mobilization rates of 0.5 to 3.0 per cent for the various subprocesses in our model, might be even larger for some of them, and potentially more serious.

Table 5-2 shows some of the implications of our model for a hypothetical country of 10 million population, $100 per capita income, a principal language spoken by 35 per cent of its inhabitants, and a relatively low degree of social mobilization in 1950. Conditions somewhat similar to these can in fact be found in several countries in Africa and Asia. Table 5-2 then shows the expectable state of affairs for our imaginary country in 1960 and 1970, if we assume the rates of change given in our model, as set forth in Table 5-1, and their persis-

TABLE 5-2. A HYPOTHETICAL EXAMPLE OF A COUNTRY UNDERGOING RAPID
SOCIAL MOBILIZATION: ASSUMED LEVELS FOR 1950 AND EXPECTABLE
LEVELS FOR 1960 AND 1970

SYMBOL OF INDICATOR		DESCRIPTION	PER CENT OF TOTAL POPULATION		
			1950	1960	1970
Group I:	m_1	population exposed to modernity	35	65	95
	m_2	mass media audience	20	47.5	75
	m_8	actual voting participation	20	41	62
	m_6	literates	15	27	39
	m_3	persons who changed locality of residence since birth	10	22.5	35
	P	total population (millions)	(10)	(12.9)	(16.7)
Group II:	m_5	population in non-agricultural occupations	18	25	32
	m_4	urban population	15	20	25
	A	linguistically assimilated population	35	37.5	40
	Y	total income (million $)	(1000)	(1629)	(2653)
	m_7	per capita income ($)	(100)	(126)	(159)

Note: Figures in parentheses refer to absolute numbers, not percentages. Because of rounding, calculations are approximate. (Dollars in 1950 prices.)

tence over twenty years. As can be seen from Table 5-2, the cumulative effects of these changes from 1950 to 1960 will appear still moderate, but by 1970 these effects will have become so great that many of the political institutions and practices of 1950 might be no longer applicable to the new conditions.

As Table 5-2 shows, a major transformation of the underlying political and social structure of a country could occur—and could pose a potential threat to the stability of any insufficiently reform-minded government there—even during a period of substantially rising per capita income.

To be sure, many of these political and social difficulties could be assuaged with the help of the benefits potentially available through the 5 per cent increase in total national income, which was assumed for our model. Such a 5 per cent growth rate of total income is not necessarily unrealistic. It is close to the average of 5.3 per cent, found by Paul Studenski in a survey of data from a large number of non-Communist countries.[17] Since the rate of population growth, assumed for the model, was 2.6 per cent—which is well above the world average in recent years—the average per capita income might be expected to rise by slightly more than 2 per cent per year.[18] These additional amounts of available income might well go at least some part of the way to meet the new popular

[17] Cf. Paul Studenski, The Income of Nations (New York, New York University Press, 1958), p. 249; cf. also pp. 244-250.
[18] Cf. United Nations, Department of Social and Economic Affairs, Population Studies No. 28, "The Future Growth of World Population" (New York 1958), and United Nations, Bureau of Social Affairs, Report of the World Social Situation (Sales No.: 1957. IV. 3) (New York, 1957), p. 5. (Estimates in 1978 for growth of population and incomes were lower.)

needs and expectations aroused by the mobilization process, if the income can be devoted to consumption and price levels remain stable. But any increments of income will also be needed for savings (in addition to loans and grants from abroad) to permit a high rate of investment and an adequate rate of expansion of opportunities for education, employment and consumption for the growing numbers of the mobilized populations.

These beneficial consequences could only be expected, however, if we assume that an adequate share of the increase in income would go directly or indirectly to the newly mobilized groups and strata of the population. Unfortunately, no assumption of this kind would be realistic for many of the developing countries of Asia and Africa.

It would be far more realistic to assume that in most of these countries the top 10 per cent of income receivers are getting about 50 per cent of the total national income, if not more. If we assume further, as seems not implausible, that in the absence of specific social reforms the increase in income will be distributed among the various strata of the population roughly in proportion to the present share of each group in the total national income, then we may expect that the richest 10 per cent of the people will get about 50 per cent of the additional income produced by income growth. At the same time, since these richest 10 per cent are not likely to be much more fertile than the rest of the population, they are likely to get only 10 per cent of the population increase; and they will, therefore, on the average not only get richer in absolute terms, but they will also retain the full extent of their relative lead over the rest of the population; and so they will increase in absolute terms the gap in income that separates them from the mass of their countrymen. Under the same assumptions, however, we should expect that the poorest nine-tenths of the population will get only one-tenth of the total income gain, but that they will get up to nine-tenths of the entire population growth; and that on the average these poorest 90 per cent of the people will remain in relative terms as far below the level of the rich one-tenth as ever. The fact that the poorer majority will have become slightly richer in absolute terms may then in the main increase their awareness of the wide gap between their living standards and those of their rulers; and it might at the same time increase their ability to take political action.

Differently put, if for the entire country the *average* per capita income was assumed to rise, we must now add that under the assumptions stated, the "social gap"—the gap between the incomes of the poorest 90 per cent and those of the top 10 per cent—may well be expected to increase. Political stability, however, may well be more affected by changes in the income gap than by changes in the average which in this respect might be little more than a statistical abstraction. Our model would lead us to expect, therefore, on the whole the danger of a significant deterioration of political stability in any development country to which its assumptions might apply. Since these assumptions were chosen with an eye to making them parallel, as far as possible, to the more rapid among the actual rates found in countries of this type, the expectations of rising political tensions in countries undergoing rapid social mobilization may not be unrealistic.

To rely upon automatic developments in economic and political life in those countries of the Free World to which the assumptions of our model apply, would be to court mounting instability, the overthrow of existing governments and their replacement by no less unstable successors, or else their eventual absorption into the Communist bloc. Deliberate political and economic intervention into the social mobilization process, on the other hand, might open up some more hopeful perspectives. Such intervention should not aim at retarding economic and social development, in the manner of the policies of the regime of Prince Metternich in Austria during much of the first half of the 19th century. Those policies of slowing down social mobilization and economic development in the main only diminished the capabilities of the government, paved the way to domestic failures and international defeats and were followed over the course of three generations by the persistent backwardness and ultimate destruction of the state. A more promising policy might have to be, on the contrary, one of active intervention in favor of more rapid and more balanced growth; a somewhat more even distribution of income, related more closely to rewards for productive contributions rather than for status and inheritance; the more productive investment of available resources; and a sustained growth in the political and administrative capabilities of government and of ever wider strata of the population.

The crude model outlined above may have some modest usefulness in surveying and presenting in quantitative terms some of the magnitudes and rates of change that would be relevant for understanding the basic problems of such a more constructive policy in developing countries.[19] Somewhat as the economic models of the late Lord Keynes drew attention to the need of keeping the national rates of spending and investment in a country in balance with the national propensity to save, so it may become possible some day for political scientists to suggest in what areas, in what respects, and to what extent the efforts of government will have to be kept abreast of the burdens generated by the processes of social mobilization. The first steps toward this distant goal might be taken through research which would replace the hypothetical figures of the model by actual data from specific countries, so that the model could be tested, revised, and advanced nearer toward application.

Any cooperation which social scientists and other students of cultural, political, and economic development and change could extend to this effort—by improving the design of the model or by suggesting more precise or refined definitions of some of its categories, or by furnishing specific data—would be very much appreciated.

---

[19] For other highly relevant approaches to these problems, see Almond and Coleman, eds., *The Politics of the Developing Areas,* Princeton, 1960, esp. the discussion by Almond on pp. 58–64. The problem of rates of change and their acceleration is discussed explicitly by Coleman, *ibid.,* pp. 536–558. While this work presented extensive data on levels of development, it did not take the further step of using explicit quantitative rates of change, which would be

APPENDIX

A Glance at Actual Cases: Partial Data
for 19 Countries

(with the assistance of Charles L. Taylor
and Alex Weilenmann)

The following data, presented in Tables 5-3 through 5-5, have been compiled or computed, respectively, in order to illustrate the possibility, in principle, of the kind of analysis proposed in the main body of this paper, and to demonstrate the availability of enough actual data to get such work at least started.

For certain categories—such as voting participation, immigration and internal migration, linguistic and cultural assimilation, and the inequality of income distribution—not enough data were readily available to permit even the simple type of tabulation presented here. Even for the data that we have collected, the gaps in such countries as Ghana, Nigeria and Congo illustrate the need for more research.

Moreover, the data being presented on the basis of the figures that appear in United Nations publications and similar sources make no attempt to estimate the margins of error to which they may be subject, or the differences in significance which a particular indicator of social mobilization may have in the cultural context of certain countries, in contrast with its significance in others. The high literacy rates reported for Burma and Thailand, *e.g.*, include a substantial proportion of literates trained through traditional monastic institutions. These rates show only a weak correlation to other indicators of modernity for those same countries, while the high literacy rates for China by contrast, refer to the effect of a more modern type of school system and are far better correlated to other indicators.

We have tried to take some account of these matters by basing estimates of over-all exposure to modernity not on the highest single indicator but on the average of the two highest indicators for each country, so as to discount to some extent the effects of any single indicator that seems too far out of line with the rest. Despite these precautions, the figures in projection offered here represent at best a crude beginning intended to stimulate far more thorough and critical statistical work, and its critical evaluation by experts on each of the countries and areas concerned.

For discussion of specific data and sources, see the Notes following the tables.

---

needed for the type of dynamic and probabilistic models that seem implicit in the long-range predictions of the authors, as set forth on pp. 58-64, 535-544.

TABLE 5-3A. SELECTED INDICES OF SOCIAL MOBILIZATION FOR NINETEEN COUNTRIES: AGGREGATE LEVELS

COUNTRY	(1) GNP PER CAPITA (1955) US $	(2) GNP (1955) MILLION US $	(3) POPULATION (1953, 1958) 1,000	(4) RADIO AUDIENCE %	(5) NEWS-PAPER READERS %	(6) LITERATES %	(7) WORK FORCE IN NON-AGRIC. OCCUPATIONS %	(8) URBAN POPULATION %
Venezuela	762	4,400	5,440 / 6,320	12.8 ('48) / 48.9 ('57)	— / 30.6 ('56)	43.5 ('41) / 51.0 ('50)	50 ('41) / 59 ('50)	39 ('41) / 50 ('50)
Argentina	374	7,150	18,400 / 20,248	51.2 ('50) / 65.0 ('59)	54.0 ('58)	64.9 ('14) / 86.7 ('47)	75 ('47) / 77 ('55)	53 ('14) / 63 ('47)
Cuba	361	2,180	5,829 / 6,466	42.7 ('49) / 59.3 ('59)	— / 38.7 ('56)	71.8 ('31) / 76.4 ('53)	59 ('43) / 58 ('53)	50 ('43) / 57 ('53)
Colombia	330	4,180	12,111 / 13,522	17.6 ('50) / 24.7 ('56)	— / 17.7 ('58)	55.8 ('38) / 61.5 ('51)	28 ('38) / 46 ('51)	29 ('38) / 36 ('51)
Turkey	276	6,463	22,850 / 25,932	4.8 ('48) / 17.6 ('59)	— / 9.6 ('52)	20.9 ('35) / 34.3 ('50)	18 ('35) / 23 ('55)	24 ('40) / 25 ('50)
Brazil	262	15,315	55,772 / 65,725	19.2 ('50) / 25.5 ('58)	— / 18.9 ('57)	43.3 ('40) / 48.4 ('50)	33 ('40) / 42 ('50)	31 ('40) / 37 ('50)
Phillippines	201	4,400	21,211 / 24,010	1.6 ('49) / 5.2 ('57)	— / 5.7 ('56)	48.8 ('39) / 61.3 ('48)	27 ('39) / 43 ('58)	23 ('39) / 24 ('48)
Mexico	187	5,548	28,056 / 32,348	11.4 ('48) / 34.6 ('58)	— / 14.4 ('52)	48.4 ('40)[a] / 56.8 ('50)[a]	35 ('40) / 42 ('58)	35 ('40) / 43 ('50)
Chile	180	1,220	6,437 / 7,298	36.9 ('49) / 38.4 ('58)	— / 22.2 ('52)	71.8 ('40) / 80.6 ('52)	65 ('40) / 70 ('52)	52 ('40)[b] / 60 ('52)[b]
Guatemala	179	580	3,058 / 3,546	2.8 ('50) / 4.6 ('54)	— / 6.6 ('58)	34.6 ('40)[a] / 29.7 ('50)[a]	29 ('40) / 32 ('50)	27 ('21) / 32 ('50)
Honduras	137	228	1,556 / 1,828	5.9 ('48) / 7.2 ('57)	— / 7.5 ('57)	32.6 ('35)[a] / 35.2 ('50)[a]	17 ('50) / 16 ('56)	29 ('45) / 31 ('50)
Ghana	135	624	4,478 / 4,836	0.8 ('48) / 8.9 ('59)	— / 11.4 ('58)	20-25 ('50)	—	—
Egypt	133	3,065	22,003 / 24,781	4.8 ('49) / 13.2 ('57)	— / 7.5 ('52)	14.8 ('37) / 22.1 ('47)	29 ('37) / 36 ('47)	25 ('37) / 30 ('47)

	1	2	3	4	5	6	7	8
Thailand	100	2,050	19,556 21,474	0.5 ('50) 1.6 ('58)	– 1.2 ('52)	52.0 ('47) 64.0 ('56)	11 ('37) 12 ('54)	– ('47) 10 ('47)
Republic of the Congo (Leopoldville)	98	1,639	12,154 13,559	0.2 ('48) 1.0 ('59)	– 0.9 ('57)	35–40 ('50)	– ('55) 15 ('55)	– ('47) 16 ('47)
India	72	27,400	372,623 397,390	0.3 ('48) 1.6 ('59)	– 2.7 ('58)	9.1 ('31)[c] 15.1 ('41)[c] 19.9 ('51)	29 ('51) 30 ('55)	11 ('31)[c] 13 ('41)[c] 17 ('51)
Nigeria	70	2,250	30,104 33,052	0.2 ('48) 1.0 ('58)	– 2.4 ('58)	11.5 ('52/3)	26 ('31) –	4 ('31) 5 ('52)
Pakistan	56	4,560	80,039 85,635	0.3 ('50) 1.2 ('58)	– 2.7 ('54)	9.1 ('31)[c] 15.1 ('41)[c] 13.5 ('51)[a]	24 ('51) 35 ('54/6)	11 ('31)[c] 13 ('41)[c] 11 ('51)
Burma	52	1,012	19,272 20,255	0.2 ('48) 0.5 ('56)	– 2.4 ('52)	40.2 ('31) 57.3 ('54)	32 ('31) 30 ('55)	10 ('31) –

[a] Unequal age groups (see Notes below, Column 6).

[b] Variation of definition of "urban" (see Notes below, Column 8).

[c] Applies to pre-partition India, i.e., to India and Pakistan together.

Notes to Table 5-3A

Table 5-3A gives the level of economic and social indices at the beginning and end of a period for each of the 19 countries. Gaps in the available data render it at present impossible to find data for equal periods for all of the indices of any one country. To compensate somewhat for this difficulty, projected levels for the same two years (1945 and 1955) have been computed in Table 5-3B by applying the average annual shifts of Table 5-4A to the levels given in this table.

The present state of comparative international statistics is such that the table contains several weaknesses which are discussed below:

Columns 1 and 2. Per capita gross national products in United States dollars for 1955, and gross national products for 1955 were compiled by the Research Center in Economic Development and Cultural Change, University of Chicago, and reported in Foreign Aid Program, 85th Congress, 1957, Senate Document 52, pp. 239 f.

Column 3. Mid-year population estimates for 1953 and 1958 were taken from United Nations, Statistical Office and Department of Economic and Social Affairs, Demographic Yearbook, 1959 (New York, 1959), pp. 109 ff.

Column 4. Column 4 gives the percentage of the population exposed to radio broadcasting. The figures were arrived at on the assumption of 4 listeners for each radio receiver. This factor of 4 seems to be justified by the fact that countries which can with good reason be considered to have reached a level of

(continued)

TABLE 5-3A. (Continued)

saturation in numbers of radio receivers show approximately 4 persons per radio receiver. The outstanding exception is the United States, with 1.2 persons per radio receiver. Canada has 3.6, Western Germany 4.2, the Netherlands 4.3, Norway 3.8, Sweden 3.0, Switzerland 4.1, and the United Kingdom 3.7 persons per receiver set (these figures, for 1952 to 1955, are based on data given in UNESCO, *World Communications: Press, Radio, Film, Television*, Paris, 1956). The factor of 4 is further substantiated by a sample poll of persons above 18 years of age in the German Federal Republic, in which 92% said they listened to radio (see Noelle, Elisabeth, and Erich Peter Neumann, editors, *Jahrbuch der oeffentlichen Meinung, 1947-1955*, 2d rev. ed., Allensbach am Bodensee, *Verlag fuer Demoskopie*, 1956, p. 62), a percentage that corresponds roughly to four times the number of radio receivers per 100.

Sources. The numbers of radio receivers for the years indicated were taken from United Nations, Statistical Office and Department of Economic and Social Affairs, *Statistical Yearbook, 1960* (New York, 1960), pp. 608f. The percentages were calculated on the basis of the population figures given for the corresponding years in United Nations, Statistical Office, *Monthly Bulletin of Statistics*, Vol. XIV, no. 12 (New York, December 1960). For Thailand, 1950, the percentage of radio receivers was taken directly from United Nations, Bureau of Social Affairs, *Report on the World Social Situation* (New York, 1957), p. 90; and the 1958 population figure for Nigeria was taken from the United Nations *Demographic Yearbook, 1959*.

Column 5. This column shows the percentage of the population exposed to daily newspapers. The figures are the result of multiplying the number of daily newspaper copies per 100 persons by a factor of 3. This factor seems justified by the fact that the number of daily newspaper copies in well advanced countries is approximately one third of the total population figure (United States 34.5%, Federal Republic of Germany 31.2%, Norway 39.2%, the Netherlands 25.9%, Switzerland 30.8%; figures based on UNESCO, *World Communications*). Professor Wilbur Schramm also uses the factor of 3 in his "Data on Mass Communications in 90 Countries" (Stanford University, 1957, mimeographed).

Column 5. Only the circulation of daily newspapers has been considered, even though various kinds of periodicals, such as illustrated weeklies and monthlies of general interest, may enjoy greater popularity than newspapers in many countries. Also, popular illustrated magazines may reach isolated and hard-to-reach places more readily than daily newspapers are likely to. Total exposure to the press is thus somewhat understated.

Definitions of "urban" vary widely from country to country, but an attempt has been made to see that the definition remained the same for both dates used in calculations for each country. For Chile, this was not possible. In 1940, "urban" included cities and towns of 1000 or more inhabitants and administrative centers of less than 1000 population. In 1952, the definition was population centers which had definite urban characteristics contributed by certain public and municipal services. It would seem, however, that these two definitions are close enough for our purposes.

A higher 1950 urban population (almost 54%) is given for Venezuela in *UN Report, 1957*, p. 172; if we had used it, it would have made the mobilization rates for Venezuela still somewhat higher.

It was found feasible to give figures for only one year; this column does not therefore appear in the following tables.

Source. The United Nations *Statistical Yearbook, 1960*, pp. 206f, gives the estimated number of daily newspaper copies per 1000 of population. The *Yearbook* defines a daily newspaper "for the purposes of this table as a publication containing general news and appearing at least four times a week." It points out: "In interpreting the data, it should be borne in mind that in different countries the size of a daily newspaper may range from a single sheet to 50 or even more pages."

Column 6. Comparable international statistics on literacy are still difficult to obtain. In their enumerations, countries differ with respect to the age group of the population to be considered and to the definition of literacy or illiteracy. Not only do countries differ among each other, but a country may change definitions from one census to another. Most sources used for this column endeavor to give literacy (or illiteracy) figures based on defining literates as persons able to read and write. The degree of this ability may again vary from country to country (see UNESCO, *Progress of Literacy in Various Countries*, Paris, 1953). An attempt has been made to find or compute data in such a way that the same age limits apply to both years for each country; exceptions are duly indicated. The data in such exceptional cases are still deemed valid for our purposes. In 15 cases in which corresponding calculations have been made, the difference between the percentages of literates in the population of 10 years of age and over and that in the population of 15 years of age and over averages 0.9% and ranges from 0.1% to 2.6%. For the purposes of this analysis, these magnitudes are negligible, particularly regarding average shifts per year.

Column 6. The high literacy rates reported for such countries as Burma and Thailand include to a large, though diminishing, extent men who have received traditional training in Buddhist monasteries and are not necessarily involved in the process of social mobilization.

Several sources used for this column give percentage of "unknowns." To find the percentage of literates, the former was subtracted from 100%. In some cases, this method may count a small percentage of "unknowns" as literate, and thus very slightly overstate the number of literates.

Sources and age groups by countries and years:

(Abbreviations used and summary of sources)

DY 1948—United Nations, Statistical Office and Department of Economic and Social Affairs, *Demographic Yearbook, 1948* (New York, 1948), pp. 204 ff., gives numbers of illiterates and of total population in several age groups, by country (*e.g.*, 10 years and over, and 10 to 15 years);

DY 1955—United Nations, Statistical Office and Department of Economic and Social Affairs, *Demographic Yearbook, 1955* (New York, 1955), pp. 436ff., lists total population, number of literates and percentage of literates in several age groups, by country;

StY 1957—United Nations, Statistical Office and Department of Economic and Social Affairs, *Statistical Yearbook, 1957* (New York, 1957), pp. 599ff., lists percentage of illiterates and total population in several age groups, by country;

UN Report—United Nations, *Report on the World Social Situation*, pp. 79ff, lists percentage of literates;

Progress—UNESCO, *Progress of Literacy in Various Countries*, gives percentage of illiterates;

BFF—UNESCO, *Basic Facts and Figures: International Statistics Relating to Education, Culture and Communications, 1959* (Paris, 1960), pp. 27ff., gives percentage of illiterates.)

Venezuela: 1941: *DY 1948*, age group 15 years and over computed from age groups 10 and over and 10–14; 1950: *DY 1955*, age group 15 years and over computed from age groups 7 and over and 7–14.

Argentina: 1914 and 1947: *Progress*, age group 14 years and over.
Cuba: 1931: *Progress*, age group 10 years and over; 1953: *StY 1957*, age group 10 years and over.
Colombia: 1938: *DY 1948*, age group 10 years and over; 1951: *StY 1957*, age group 10 years and over.
Turkey: 1935: *DY 1948*, age group 10 years and over; 1950: *DY 1955*, age group 10 years and over.
Brazil: 1940: *DY 1948*, age group 10 years and over; 1950: *DY 1955*, age group 10 years and over.
Philippines: 1939 and 1948: *Progress*, age group 10 years and over.
Mexico: 1940: *DY 1948*, age group 10 years and over; 1950: *UN Report*, age group 6 years and over.
Chile: 1940: *DY 1948*, age group 10 years and over; 1952: *StY 1957*, age group 10 years and over.
Guatemala: 1940: *DY 1948*, age group 7 years and over; 1950: *DY 1955*, age group 10 years and over.
Honduras: 1935: *Progress*, age group 15 years and over; 1950: *UN Report*, age group 10 years and over.
Ghana: 1950: *UN Report*, estimate, age group 15 years and over.

(continued)

TABLE 5-3A. (Continued)

Egypt: 1937: *DY 1948*, age group 10 years and over; 1947: *DY 1955*, age group 10 years and over.

Thailand: 1947: *DY 1955*, age group 15 years and over and 10–14; 1956: *BFF*, age group 15 years and over.

Congo: 1950: *UN Report*, estimate, age group 15 years and over.

Pre-partition India: 1931: *Progress*, age group 10 years and over; 1941: Davis, Kingsley, *The Population of India and Pakistan* (Princeton, Princeton University Press, 1951), p. 151, Table 70, quoted in Karl W. Deutsch, *Nationalism and Social Communication*, p. 201, age group 10 years and over, based on a sample and correction factor.

India: 1951: *DY 1955*, age group 10 years and over, based on 10% of census returns.

Nigeria: 1952/53: *UN Report*, age group 15 years and over.

Pakistan: 1951: *UN Report*, all ages, including semi-literates (13.5%). Another figure, 18.9%, excluding aliens and the population of the Frontier Regions, is given in *Pakistan—1959-1960* (Karachi, Pakistan Publications, October 1960), p. 89. Both data are reported to be based on the 1951 census.

Burma: 1931 *Progress*, age group 10 years and over; 1954: *StY 1957*, age group 10 years and over.

Column 7. The percentages of economically active population engaged in non-agricultural occupations (*i.e.*, those other than agriculture, forestry, fishing and hunting) were taken from Food and Agricultural Organization, *Production Yearbook, 1959* (Rome, 1960), pp. 19ff., except those for Guatemala (1950), Honduras (1950), and Pakistan (1951) which were calculated from International Labour Office, *Yearbook of Labour Statistics, 1960* (Geneva, 1960), pp. 14ff.; Cuba (1943) which was calculated from the 1947/8 edition of the same publication, pp. 10f.; and Argentina (1955), India (1955) and Burma (1955) which were taken from United States Senate, *Foreign Aid Program*, op. cit., p. 243.

Column 8. Urban data were reported in United Nations, Statistical Office and Department of Economic and Social Affairs, *Demographic Yearbook, 1952* (New York, 1952), pp. 168ff., and United Nations, *Demographic Yearbook, 1955*, op. cit., pp. 185ff. Those for Nigeria were taken from United Nations, Department of Economic and Social Affairs, *Economic Survey of Africa Since 1950* (New York, 1955), p. 14; and for Cuba (1953) from *UN Report, 1957*, p. 172.

TABLE 5-3B. SELECTED INDICES OF SOCIAL MOBILIZATION FOR NINETEEN
COUNTRIES: AGGREGATE LEVELS: PROJECTED FOR 1945 AND 1955

COUNTRY		(4) RADIO AUDIENCE %	(6) LITER-ATES %	(7) WORK FORCE IN NON-AGRIC. OCCU-PATIONS %	(8) URBAN POPU-LATION %	(9) EXPOSURE TO MODERNITY %
Venezuela	'45	1	47	54	44	63
	'55	41	55	64	56	75
Argentina	'45	44	85	74	62	>95
	'55	59	92	77	65	>95
Cuba	'45	36	75	59	51	83
	'55	52	77	58	58	84
Colombia	'45	12	59	38	33	60
	'55	22	63	52	38	72
Turkey	'45	1	30	21	24	34
	'55	13	39	23	26	40
Brazil	'45	15	46	37	34	52
	'55	23	51	46	40	61
Philippines	'45	0	57	32	24	56
	'55	4	71	41	25	70
Mexico	'45	4	52	37	39	57
	'55	28	61	41	37	64
Chile	'45	36	75	67	56	89
	'55	38	83	71	62	>95
Guatemala	'45	1	32	31	31	40
	'55	5	27	34	33	42
Honduras	'45	6	35	18	29	40
	'55	7	36	16	33	43
Ghana	'45	0	—	—	—	—
	'55	6	—	—	—	21[b] (1950/58)
Egypt	'45	1	20	35	29	40
	'55	11	28	42	34	47
Thailand	'45	0	49	12	—	38
	'55	1	63	12	—	47
Republic of the Congo (Leopoldville)	'45	0	—	—	—	—
	'55	1	—	—	—	33[b] (1947/50)
India	'45	0	18[a]	27	14[a]	28[c]
	'55	1	24[a]	30	16[a]	34[c]
Nigeria	'45	0	—	—	5	—
	'55	1	—	—	5	23[b] (1931/53)
Pakistan	'45	0	18[a]	11	14[a]	20[c]
	'55	1	24[a]	35	16[a]	37[c]
Burma	'45	0	50	31	—	50
	'55	0	58	30	—	55

Data in Columns 4, 6, 7, 8, based on corresponding data in Tables 5-3A and 5-4A.
Data in Column 9 are 125% of means of the two highest figures in each of the other columns.
(See Notes.)   (continued)

TABLE 5–3B. (Continued)

[a]Pre-partition India.

[b]Based on the two highest data for country in Table 5–3A.

[c]No distinction made between pre-partition India and India and Pakistan respectively.

Notes to Table 5–3B

To be in a better position to compare the available data, all indices of social mobilization (Columns 4 and 5–8) have been adjusted to the same two years (1945 and 1955), by applying the annual average shifts of Table 5–4A to the corresponding levels given in Table 5–3A. It is thereby assumed that shifts did not change significantly over the relevant years. While most of the adjustments involve only a few years, the risk of possible slight distortions had to be taken in cases in which a longer period was involved.

As we have only one level for newspaper readers, Column 5 does not appear in this table.

Column 9. The persons exposed to modernity are those who have in one way or another come into contact with aspects of modern life. Since hardly enough surveys in this respect have been made in the countries under consideration, the percentage of the population exposed to modernity must be estimated indirectly. It is initially assumed for the purpose of this table that (1) exposure to modernity includes any one of our indices (Columns 4–8) in addition to other, more informal exposures such as markets, travel, rumor, etc.; (2) the sector of the population in a smaller percentage index is entirely included in the sector of a higher percentage so that the exposed population groups form concentric circles—*e.g.*, all of the newspaper readers would be exposed to radio, and all of the radio listeners would be literate, but that some literates would not listen to radio, etc., (3) the largest sector is that exposed to any form of modernity, and (4) 20% of the population exposed to modernity are unaccounted for in Columns 4 to 8, because the groups indicated there do not overlap completely, and because of less formal ways of exposure. As has been pointed out in the introduction to this Appendix, however, in order to discount to some extent the effects of any single indicator that seems too far out of line with the rest, the procedure followed to estimate the percentage of the population exposed to modernity has been to increase the average of the two highest of the indices for each country and year by 25 per cent. This method reduces the impact of a single indicator with weak correlation to other indicators to such a degree that the percentage of persons exposed to modernity appears to be smaller than that of some other population sector in cases in which the correlation of single index is extremely weak (*cf.* Philippines, Thailand, Pakistan, Burma).

In actual fact, we have good reason to suppose that these assumptions understate in general the total extent of exposure. It is quite likely that some of the population sectors overlap only to a lesser degree. This can particularly be expected in countries with balanced low levels of social mobilization.

Calculated percentages exceeding 95% are assumed to behave differently. They are merely listed as being over 95%.

TABLE 5-4A. SELECTED INDICES OF SOCIAL MOBILIZATION FOR NINETEEN COUNTRIES: SHIFTS AND RATES OF GROWTH

COUNTRY	LEVEL	AVERAGE ANNUAL RATES OF GROWTH			(5) Radio Audience %	AVERAGE ANNUAL SHIFTS			
	(1) Per Capita GNP (1955) US $	(2) Total GDP (1954-58) %	(3) Population (1953-58) %	(4) Per Capita GDP (1954-58) %		(6) Literate Population %	(7) Work Force in Non-agric. Occupations %	(8) Urban Population %	(9)* Population Exposed to Modernity %
Venezuela	762	(8.8)	(3.0)	(7.5)	4.0 (1948-57)	0.8 (1941-50)	1.0 (1941-50)	1.2 (1941-50)	1.2 / 3.2 / 2.2
Argentina	374	(2.4)	(1.9)	(0.5)	1.5 (1950-59)	0.7 (1914-47)	0.3 (1947-55)	0.3 (1914-47)	0.0 / 1.4 / 0.7
Cuba	361	(3)[a] (1957-60)	(1.9)	(1.1)[c] (1957-60)	1.7 (1949-59)	0.2 (1931-53)	-0.1 (1943-53)	0.7 (1943-53)	0.1 / 1.5 / 0.8
Colombia	330	(3.1)	(2.2)	(0.8)	1.2 (1950-56)	0.4 (1938-51)	1.4 (1938-51)	0.6 (1938-51)	1.2 / 1.6 / 1.4
Turkey	276	(8.1)	(2.7)	(5.2)	1.2 (1948-59)	0.9 (1935-50)	0.3 (1935-55)	0.1 (1945-50)	0.6 / 1.3 / 1.0
Brazil	262	(6.4)	(2.4)	(4.0)	0.8 (1950-58)	0.5 (1940-50)	0.8 (1940-50)	0.5 (1940-50)	0.9 / 1.0 / 1.0
Philippines	201	(4.8)	(2.5)	(2.2)	0.5 (1949-57)	1.4 (1939-48)	0.8 (1939-58)	0.1 (1939-48)	1.4 / 1.4 / 1.4
Mexico	187	(4)[a] (1957-60)	(2.9)	(1.1)[c] (1957-60)	2.3 (1948-58)	0.8[e] (1940-50)	0.4 (1940-58)	0.8 (1940-50)	0.7 / 1.9 / 1.3

(continued)

TABLE 5-4A. (Continued)

COUNTRY	LEVEL (1) Per Capita GNP (1955) US $	AVERAGE ANNUAL RATES OF GROWTH (2) Total GDP (1954-58) %	(3) Population (1953-58) %	(4) Per Capita GDP (1954-58) %	(5) Radio Audience %	AVERAGE ANNUAL SHIFTS (6) Literate Population %	(7) Work Force in Non-agric. Occupations %	(8) Urban Population %	(9)* Population Exposed to Modernity %
Chile	180	(2.0)	(2.5)	(−0.6)	0.2 (1949-58)	0.7 (1940-52)	0.4 (1940-52)	0.7[f] (1940-52)	0.6 / 0.9 / 0.8
Guatemala	179	(8.3)	(3.0)	(5.2)	0.4 (1950-54)	−0.5[e] (1940-50)	0.3 (1940-50)	0.2 (1921-50)	0.2 / 0.4 / 0.3
Honduras	137	(6.6) (1954-57)	(3.3)	(3.2) (1954-57)	0.1 (1948-57)	0.2[e] (1935-50)	−0.2 (1950-56)	0.4 (1945-50)	0.3 / 0.4 / 0.4
Ghana	135	(3)[a] (1957-60)	(1.6)	(1.4)[c] (1957-60)	0.7 (1948-59)	—	—	—	— / 0.9 / —
Egypt	133	(2.1) (1954-56)	(2.4)	(−0.3) (1954-56)	1.0 (1949-57)	0.7 (1937-47)	0.7 (1937-47)	0.5 (1937-47)	0.7 / 1.0 / 0.8
Thailand	100	(3.1)[b] (1950-54)	(1.9)	(1.2)[c] (1950-54)	0.1 (1950-58)	1.3 (1947-56)	0.1 (1937-57)	—	0.9 / 0.9 / 0.9
Rep. of the Congo (Leopoldville)	98	(1.7)	(2.2)	(−0.8)	0.1 (1948-59)	—	—	—	— / 0.1 / —
India	72	(3.3)	(1.3)	(1.9)	0.1 (1948-59)	0.6[g] (1931-41)	0.3 (1951-55)	0.2[g] (1931-41)	0.6[h] / 0.6[h] / 0.6

Nigeria	70	(4)[a] (1957-60)	(1.9)	(2.1)[c] (1957-60)	0.1 (1948-58)	—	—	0.0 (1931-52)	— 0.1
Pakistan	56	(1.8)[b] (1950-54)	(1.4)	(0.4)[d] (1950-54)	0.1 (1950-58)	0.6[g] (1931-41)	2.8 (1951-54/6)	0.2[g] (1931-41)	1.7[h] 2.1[h] 1.9
Burma	52	(3.8)	(1.0)	(2.8)	0.0 (1948-56)	0.7 (1931-54)	-0.1 (1931-55)	—	0.5 0.4 0.4

*In each box of Column 9, the first figure is based on the levels in Table 5-3B, Column 9; the second figure is based on the two largest shifts for country (Columns 5-8, this table), and the third figure is the average of the two preceding figures in the box. (See Notes to Table 5-4A, Column 9.)

[a] Growth in GNP.

[b] Growth in national income.

[c] Growth in per capita income.

[e] Based on unequal age groups. (See Notes to Table 5-3A, Column 6.)

[f] Variation in definition of "urban." (See Notes to Table 5-3A, Column 8.)

[g] Applies to pre-partition India, *i.e.*, to India and Pakistan together.

[h] No distinction made between pre-partition India and India and Pakistan respectively.

Notes to Table 5-4A

Column 1. See notes to Table 5-3A, Column 1.

Column 2. Average annual rates of growth in gross domestic product for the years 1954-1958 were reported in United Nations, Statistical Office and Department of Economic and Social Affairs, *Yearbook of National Account Statistics, 1960* (New York, 1961), pp. 265ff. Data for Cuba, Mexico, Ghana and Nigeria are average annual rates of growth in gross national product for 1957-1960, and were taken from P. N. Rosenstein-Rodan, "International Aid for Underdeveloped Countries" (multilithed, Cambridge, Mass., M.I.T., August, 1960), pp. 3ff. Data for Thailand and Pakistan are average annual rates of growth in national income for 1950-1954, and were taken from Paul Studenski, *The Income of Nations: Theory, Measurement and Analysis: Past and Present* (New York, New York University Press, 1958), pp. 229 f. According to the sources, all rates are based on constant prices.

Column 3. The rates of population growth are the geometric means of the differences between the mid-year estimates of populations in 1953 and 1958. They were taken from the United Nations *Demographic Yearbook, 1959*, pp. 109ff.

Column 4. Average annual rates of growth in per capita gross domestic product in constant prices for 1954-1958 were taken from United Nations, *Yearbook of National Account Statistics, 1960*, pp. 265ff. Data for Cuba, Mexico, Ghana, Thailand, Nigeria and Pakistan were calculated on the basis of columns 2 and 3 of this table.

(continued)

TABLE 5.4A. (Continued)

Columns 5–8. While Columns 2, 3 and 4 show average percentage rates of growth per year, Columns 5 to 8, and 9, represent average annual percentage shifts, *i.e.*, that average annual percentage of the population which has been added to, or subtracted from, the total share of the population in that particular category. Thus, these percentages were obtained by dividing the difference between the pair of levels in Table 5–3A by the proper number of years (see explanation of Table 5–1, above). Since the figures in these four columns are entirely based on the data in Columns 4 and 6 to 8 in Table 5–3A, the notes and the sources for Table 5–3A and for its respective columns apply also to Columns 5 to 8 of Table 5–4A.

Since we have the percentage of newspaper readers for only one year (Columns 5, Table 5–3A), shifts into the exposure to newspapers have had to be omitted.

Column 9. Shifts in the population exposed to modernity were calculated in three different ways.

The first figure in each box is based on the levels of modernity given in Column 9 of Table 5–3B, and calculated in the same way as the shifts of Columns 5 to 8. For a discussion of the assumptions made, see Notes to that Table, Column 9.

The second figure in each box is based on the average of the two fastest growing indicators, as expressed by the percentage shifts in Columns 5 to 8. The underlying assumptions in this case are similar to those set forth for Column 9 in Table 5–3B. It is again assumed that the shift into the aggregate of all groups involved in at least one process of social mobilization should grow faster than shifts into any of the particular processes. If two or more sectors of the population did not overlap at all, yet each index was an expression of modernity, the shifts into each of these sectors would have to be added to obtain a basis for the calculation of the shift into modernity, and the fastest shift would constitute a minimum. A conservative estimate of the percentage shift into exposure to modernity, taking into account informal exposures, has been to take the average of the two highest of the percentage shifts in Columns 5 to 8 and increase it by 25%.

The first method used may perhaps best be applied to countries that already have very high levels of minimal exposure to modernity. The second figure may be more representative of the shift to minimal exposure in low-range countries, and of the shift to more intense mobilization in more advanced ones.

The third figure in each box is the average of the first two figures.

TABLE 5–4B. SELECTED INDICES OF SOCIAL MOBILIZATION FOR NINETEEN COUNTRIES: AVERAGES IN SHIFTS AND RATES OF GROWTH

RANGE (ACC'D. TO PER CAPITA GNP) US $	AVERAGE LEVEL	AVERAGE ANNUAL RATES OF GROWTH				AVERAGE ANNUAL SHIFTS			
	(1) Per Capita GNP (1955) US $	(2) Total GDP # %	(3) Total Population %	(4) GDP Per Capita %	(5) Radio Audience %	(6) Literate Population %	(7) Population Engaged in Non-Agricultural Occupations %	(8) Urban Population %	(9)† Population Exposed to Modernity %
400+ (N = 1)	762	(8.8)	(3.0)	(7.5)	4.0	0.8	1.0	1.2	1.2 / 3.2 / 2.2
300–399 (N = 3)	355	(2.8)	(2.0)	(0.8)	1.5	0.4	0.5	0.5	0.4 / 1.5 / 1.0
200–299 (N = 3)	246	(6.4)	(2.5)	(3.8)	0.8	0.9	0.6	0.2	1.0 / 1.2 / 1.1
100–199 (N = 7)	150	(4.1)	(2.5)	(1.6)	0.7	0.5 (N = 6)	0.3 (N = 6)	0.5 (N = 5)	0.6 (N = 6) / 0.9 / 0.8
50–99 (N = 5)	70	(2.9)	(1.6)	(1.3)	0.1	0.6* (N = 2)	1.0 (N = 3)	0.1* (N = 2)	0.9 (N = 3) / 0.7 / 0.8
Total 50–750 (N = 19)	209	(4.2)	(2.2)	(2.0)	0.8	0.6* (N = 15)	0.6 (N = 16)	0.4* (N = 14)	0.7 (N = 16) / 1.1 / 0.9

These averages are entirely based on data of Table 5–4A.

*Data for pre-partition India were used only once in calculating the average.

GDP = gross domestic product.

†In Column 9, in each box, the first figure is the average of shifts based on highest levels, the second figure is the average of shifts based on largest shifts, and the third figure is the average of the first two. (See Table 5–4A and Notes to Table 5–4A, Column 9.)

TABLE 5-5. SELECTED INDICES OF SOCIAL MOBILIZATION FOR NINETEEN COUNTRIES: PROJECTED MINIMUM LEVELS IN 1960, 1970

	(1) RADIO AUDIENCE %		(2) LITERATES %		(3) ECONOMICALLY ACTIVE POPULATION IN NON-AGRICULTURAL OCCUPATIONS %		(4) URBAN POPULATION %		(5) EXPOSURE TO MODERNITY %	
COUNTRY	1960	1970	1960	1970	1960	1970	1960	1970	1960	1970
Venezuela	61	>95	59	67	69	79	62	74	86	95
Argentina	67	82	>95	>95	79	82	67	70	95	95
Cuba	61	78	78	80	57	56	60	65	87	93
Colombia	30	42	65	69	59	73	41	47	79	93
Turkey	19	31	43	52	24	27	26	27	45	55
Brazil	27	35	53	58	50	58	42	47	66	76
Philippines	7	12	78	92	45	53	25	26	77	91
Mexico	39	62	65	73	43	47	51	59	70	83
Chile	39	41	86	93	73	77	66	73	95	95
Guatemala	7	11	25	20	35	38	34	36	44	47
Honduras	8	9	37	39	15	13	35	39	45	49
Ghana	10	17	–	–	–	–	–	–	–	59
Egypt	16	26	31	38	45	52	37	42	51	59
Thailand	2	3	69	82	13	14	–	–	52	61
Rep. of the Congo (Leopoldville)	1	2	–	–	–	–	–	–	–	–
India	2	3	26*	32*	32	35	17*	19*	37	43
Nigeria	1	2	–	–	–	–	5	6	–	–
Pakistan	1	2	26*	32*	49	77	17*	19*	46	65
Burma	1	1	62	69	30	29	–	–	57	61

*On basis of pre-partition India.

The projections, for 1960 and 1970, are based on the levels of Table 5–3 and on the shifts of Table 5–4A. For Column 9, the median shifts (third figure in each box of Column 9, Table 5-4A) have been used in computing the projections of the exposure to modernity.

It is assumed that the average annual shifts will continue to hold. In actual fact, we have good reason to believe that shifts will grow as the countries develop and that these projections represent minima. Since results of the censuses taken around 1960 will soon be available, the reader will be able to check our projections for that year.

Calculated figures close to 100% are assumed to behave differently and are listed as being over 95% (>95).

TABLE 5-6. GROSS DOMESTIC PRODUCT PER CAPITA FOR
NINETEEN COUNTRIES
(FIGURES EXPRESSED IN CURRENT U.S. DOLLARS)

COUNTRY	1955[1]	1960	1970	1973	1974
Venezuela	762	1043	1124		2542
Argentina	374	606	1053		1954
Cuba	361			617	
Colombia	330	253	336		520
Turkey	276	190	365		757
Brazil	262	206	493	768	
Philippines	201	164	192		355
Mexico	187	331	661		1119
Chile	180	273	713		720
Guatemala	179	274	373		543
Honduras	137	182	285		330
Ghana	135	198	257	309	
Egypt	133	129	217	260	
Thailand	100	96	180		323
Zaire	98	92	88		146
India	72	73	100	130	
Nigeria	70	78	145	227	
Pakistan	56	81	176	128	
Burma	52	61	78		101

[1] Figures given for Gross National Product per capita.
Sources. The figures for 1955 are taken from pp. 112–116, Table V–3A. All other figures are taken from United Nations, *Yearbook of National Accounts Statistics 1975,* Volume III, Table 1a.

TABLE 5-7. FORESIGHT AND HINDSIGHT: TESTING PROJECTIONS
AGAINST ACTUAL DATA
(PROJECTIONS IN PARENTHESES)

COUNTRY		(1) RADIO AUDIENCE %	(2) LITERATES %	(3) WORK FORCE IN NON-AGRIC. OCCU- PATIONS %	(4) URBAN POPU- LATION %
Venezuela	1950		52	59	54
	1955	50 (41)	(55)	(64)	(56)
	1960	74 (61)	(59)	(69)	(62)
	1961		63	68	68
	1970	66 (95+)	(67)	78 (79)	76 (74)
	1971		84		
	1973	71	82		
	1975			81	74
Argentina	1947		77	75	63
	1955	59 (59)	(92)	(77)	(65)
	1960	67 (67)	92 (95+)	82 (79)	(67)
	1970	100 (82)	93 (95+)	85 (82)	(70)
	1972		93		
	1973	100			

TABLE 5-7.   (Continued)
(PROJECTIONS IN PARENTHESES)

COUNTRY		(1) RADIO AUDIENCE %	(2) LITERATES %	(3) WORK FORCE IN NON-AGRIC. OCCU-PATIONS %	(4) URBAN POPU-LATION %
Cuba	1950	42			
	1953		78	59	57
	1955	(52)	(77)	(58)	(58)
	1960	64 (61)	(78)	(57)	(87)
	1970	64 (78)	(80)	70 (56)	60 (65)
	1971				61
	1973	81	85		
Colombia	1951		62		38
	1955	25 (22)	(63)	(52)	(38)
	1960	56 (30)	(65)	(59)	(41)
	1964		73	53	
	1970	42 (42)	(69)	(73)	60 (47)
	1973	48	74	74	
	1974				64
Turkey	1950		32		
	1955	17 (13)	(39)	23 (23)	29 (26)
	1960	19 (19)	38 (43)	25 (24)	32 (26)
	1965			28	
	1970	36 (31)	51 (52)	32 (27)	39 (27)
	1973	42	51		
	1974			31	43
Brazil	1950		49	39	36
	1955	24 (23)	(51)	(46)	(40)
	1960	26 (27)	61 (53)	(50)	45 (42)
	1970	24 (35)	66 (58)	56 (58)	56 (47)
	1973	25	66		
	1975				59
Philippines	1948		60		
	1955	4 (4)	(71)	(41)	(25)
	1956			46	35
	1960	9 (7)	72 (78)	40 (45)	(25)
	1970	18 (12)	83 (92)	49 (53)	32 (26)
	1973	18			
	1975			48	
Mexico	1955	35 (28)	(61)	42 (41)	44 (37)
	1960	38 (39)	65 (65)	46 (43)	51 (51)
	1970	100 (62)	74 (73)	61 (47)	59 (59)
	1973	100	76		
	1975			61	63
Chile	1952		80	70	60
	1955	38 (38)	(83)	(71)	(62)
	1960	38 (39)	84 (86)	72 (73)	67 (66)
	1970	57 (41)	88 (93)	79 (77)	76 (73)
	1973	58	90		

TABLE 5-7. (Continued)
(PROJECTIONS IN PARENTHESES)

COUNTRY		(1) RADIO AUDIENCE %	(2) LITERATES %	(3) WORK FORCE IN NON-AGRIC. OCCU- PATIONS %	(4) URBAN POPU- LATION %
Guatemala	1950		29	32	25
	1955	4 (5)	(27)	(34)	(33)
	1960	22 (7)	(25)	(35)	(34)
	1964		38	35	
	1970	(11)	(20)	(38)	34 (36)
	1973	18	38	43	
Honduras	1950		35	17	
	1955	7 (7)	(36)	(16)	(33)
	1960	27 (8)	(37)	(15)	(35)
	1961		45	33	31
	1969				32
	1970	23 (9)	(39)	(13)	(39)
	1973	22	45		
	1974			41	31
Ghana	1955	4 (6)			
	1960	7 (10)		42	23
	1970	24 (17)			
	1971				29
	1972	34			
	1973		25		
	1974				31
Egypt	1947		20	36	
	1955	14 (11)	(28)	(42)	(34)
	1957				36
	1960	23 (16)	21 (31)	43 (45)	38 (37)
	1966			47	
	1970	53 (26)	(38)	(52)	42 (42)
	1973	57	26		
	1975				45
Thailand	1947		52	15	
	1955	1 (1)	(63)	(12)	9
	1960	2 (2)	68 (69)	18 (13)	12
	1970	31 (3)	79 (82)	22 (14)	13
	1973	30		28	
Zaire	1955	0 (1)		14	22
	1960	1 (1)			
	1970	1 (2)			22
	1973	2	12		
	1974				26
India	1951		21	29	17
	1955	1 (1)	(24)	(30)	(16)
	1960	2 (2)	(26)	(32)	(17)
	1961		28	27	18
	1970	8 (3)	(32)	(35)	20 (19)

(continued)

TABLE 5-7. (Continued)
(PROJECTIONS IN PARENTHESES)

COUNTRY		(1) RADIO AUDIENCE %	(2) LITERATES %	(3) WORK FORCE IN NON-AGRIC. OCCUPATIONS %	(4) URBAN POPULATION %
	1971				
	1973	10	34	28	
	1974				21
Nigeria	1952		11		
	1955	1 (1)			(5)
	1960	2 (1)			(5)
	1970	9 (2)			(6)
	1973	20	25		
Pakistan	1951		19	24	10
	1955	0 (1)	(24)	(30)	(16)
	1960	1 (1)	(26)	(49)	(17)
	1961		19	25	13
	1968				27
	1969			31	
	1970	6 (2)	(32)	(77)	(19)
	1972				26
	1973	6	16		
	1974			43	
Burma	1954		58		
	1955	0 (0)	(58)	(30)	
	1960	2 (1)	(62)	(30)	
	1970	6 (1)	(69)	(29)	
	1973		60		
	1975			31	

Sources.
Column 1. UNESCO, *Statistical Yearbook 1963*, Table 39; UNESCO, *Statistical Yearbook 1971*, Table 9-2; United Nations, *Statistical Yearbook 1975*, Table 218. Column 1 gives the percentage of the total population exposed to radio broadcasting. The figures were arrived at on the assumption of four listeners for each radio receiver.

Column 2. UNESCO, *Statistical Yearbook 1964*, pp. 36–44; UNESCO, *Statistical Yearbook 1973*, pp. 67–77; Ruth Sivard, "World Military and Social Expenditures 1976," Table III. Column 2 gives the percentage of literates in the population fifteen years of age and older.

Column 3. International Labour Office, *Yearbook of Labour Statistics 1957*, Table 4; International Labour Office, *Yearbook of Labour Statistics 1963*, Table 4; International Labour Office, *Yearbook of Labour Statistics 1971*, Table 2-A; International Labour Office, *Yearbook of Labour Statistics 1975*, Table 2-A. Column 3 gives the percentage of the economically active population engaged in non-agricultural occupations (i.e., those other than agriculture, forestry, fishing, and hunting.)

TABLE 5-7. (Continued)

Column 4. United Nations, *Demographic Yearbook 1960,* Table 9; United Nations, *Demographic Yearbook 1962,* Table 9; United Nations, *Demographic Yearbook 1975,* Table 6. Column 4 gives the percentage of the population residing in "urban" areas. Definitions of "urban" vary widely from country to country, but an attempt has been made to see that the definition remained the same for the dates used for each country.

Projections are taken from pp. 112-125. The 1955 projections are taken from Table 5-3B, pp. 117-118, while the 1960 and 1970 projections are taken from Table 5-5, p. 124.

I am indebted for these tables to Dr. Andrei Markovits, Assistant Professor at Wesleyan University.

II | *Problems of Integration: National and International*

6 | Problems of Nation-Building and National Development

Written in the early 1960s in the days of President John F. Kennedy, this chapter tried to warn against the illusion that new nations in Asia, Africa, and Latin American could be "built" quickly within each newly independent country by some central government backed by modern weapons and massive foreign aid from one great power or another. One and a half decades later, we have fewer such illusions. We know now that nations develop more from within than from without, and more from the middle than from the top, and generally more from below than from above. We have perhaps also learned that the process of national development is large, complex, and rich in autonomous elements, and that the influence of the political designs is often small and always limited, though it still is very real. "Building a nation," it has turned out, seems to be mainly a "do-it-yourself" job for the people who live there—a job in which outsiders can aid somewhat but can neither direct nor control.

A more detailed discussion of what seems to be our present-day knowledge of the process of national integration is presented in chapter 15.

How and when do nations come into existence, how and when do they pass away, and how and when can people decide the outcome by their actions?

We know that humankind existed long before nations, and we have good reason to hope that humanity will exist long after them. The era of nations and nationalism is a short span in recorded history, but in various parts of the world this age of nations—everywhere succeeding ages of villages, tribes, and empires—has begun at different times.

Scholars who have studied mainly a single geographic or cultural area have been tempted to see the rise of nationalism and of nations in that area either as something alien or as something unique and peculiar to the area. Investigators, however, who have paid careful attention to more than one country or area—and particularly those who have compared the long history of nationalism in Europe

The substance of this chapter appeared, as an introductory essay, in Karl W. Deutsch and William J. Foltz, eds., *Nation-Building* (New York: Atherton Press, 1963), pp. 1–16. Reprinted by permission of the Publisher.

with its shorter histories in Latin America, Asia, and Africa—have soon discovered the intellectual power that is inherent in such comparisons. They have discovered that the making and breaking of nations is a process that is now occurring in most parts of the world and that it is a process which must be studied in its general and uniform aspects, especially if the unique features of each country and epoch are eventually to be understood better than they have been thus far.

The essays in the book (*Nation Building*) are early steps in the comparison and analysis across the continents and centuries. To some degree, each of them combines three concerns: the concerns of the historian, the concern of the social scientist, and the concern of the policy-maker and statesman.

The descriptive and analytical scholars begin with the organized complexity of something that stands visibly before them; the historians deal with processes the outcomes of which are known.[1] Both use their knowledge of general regularities of social processes mainly to understand better the unique configuration of repetitive factors that makes up the particular contemporary institution or past sequence of events with which they are concerned. Historians thus use their knowledge of many general regularities in order to understand a few situations. Social scientists work mainly in the opposite direction: they start from a multitude of particular and seemingly unique facts and then search for general rules that can be derived from them. They study many situations to discover a few regularities. Put into somewhat more modern terms, social scientists often study the distribution of events and the information that can be gained from comparing differing distribution patterns. Policy-makers and statespeople, finally, use both their knowledge of general regularities and their judgment of partially unique situations in order to influence many specific outcomes in the direction of their general values.

Each of these viewpoints tends to favor a somewhat different perception of the problems of nationalism and of the rise and fall of nations. Many historians speak of the "growth of nations"; some historians and many statesmen and policy-oriented political scientists speak of "nation-building"; many social scientists prefer to think and speak of "national development."

Each of these images, however, carries its own cognitive implications which may reach beyond the motives for which the image was originally chosen. "National growth" suggests an organismic image, the growth of a living thing that cannot be dissected without injuring or killing it and, moreover, a growth process that is expected to pass through certain fixed intervals of time and through certain fixed qualitative stages toward a maturity the form of which is known and beyond which there are only decline and death or reproduction which start a new, but essentially identical, cycle.

"Nation-building," by contrast, suggests an architectural or mechanical model.

[1] For an extremely stimulating discussion of certain aspects of the historian's approach, see Leonard Krieger, "The Horizons of History," *American Historical Review*, 53, No. 1 (1957), 62–74; and William L. Langer, "The Next Assignment," *ibid.*, No. 2 (1958), 283–304.

As a house can be built from timber, bricks, and mortar, in different patterns, quickly or slowly, through different sequences of assembly, in partial independence from its setting, and according to the choice, will, and power of its builders, so a nation can be built according to different plans, from various materials, rapidly or gradually, by different sequences of steps, and in partial independence from its environment.

Finally, the concept of "national development" also implies a limited but significant degree of combinatorial freedom. It is reminiscent of the mechanistic and voluntaristic aspects of the "nation-building" concept, but it also includes an awareness of internal and external interdependence in both space and time. This awareness characterizes the organismic image and tends to stress the influence of the past, the environment, and the vast, complex, and slow-changing aspects of the actions and expectations of millions of people. These actions and expectations limit the speed and scope of "nation-building" while offering significant opportunities and choices and strategic decision points for possible intervention and partial control.

How and when do nations break away from larger political units, and how do they triumph over smaller units, such as tribes, castes, or local states, and more or less integrate them into the political body of the nation?

Here there is much unfinished business for research. What exactly is a tribe, and just what is meant by "tribalism"? How uniform a meaning can be attributed to these terms, which are so freely used in political discourse? Anthropologists sometimes call a tribe that social and political unit which is above the kin group and is still small enough to claim common descent although it is large enough to permit intermarriage. This definition is neither rigorous nor uniform, but the variety of groups called "tribes" is still larger, and the political use of the terms "tribe" and "tribalism" is still looser. Nevertheless, even the loose terms refer to real groups and problems, and the accounts of the eventual overcoming of tribalism in medieval and early modern Europe may shed some light on the partly analogous contemporary problems in Africa.

Similar considerations apply to the time and size dimensions of each major tribe. How old is it? How quickly was it formed and from what elements? How long would it be likely to endure under various conditions? Tribes, we know from European history, can change their language and culture; they can absorb other tribes; and large tribes came into existence through federation or mergers of smaller tribes or through their conquest and absorption by a larger one.[2]

[2] For the old Saxon tribe in northwestern Germany between 450 and 750 see, for example, Rudolf Buchner, "Germanentum und Papsttum von Chlodwig bis Pippin," in Fritz Valjavec, ed., *Historia Mundi* (Berne: Francke, 1956) V, *Frühes Mittelalter*, 161–162; and for the changes among the early Slavic tribes, George Vernadsky, "Das frühe Slawentum," *ibid.*, pp. 255–256, 275; for the changes in the barbarian war bands, tribes, or peoples in the territories of the former Roman Empire, see the thoughtful comment by Robert S. Lopez, *Naissance de l'Europe* (Paris; Armand Colin, 1962), pp. 39–40. Also see discussions of early European tribalism by Carl J. Friedrich, Hermann Weilenmann, and Joseph Strayer, and discussions of contemporary African tribalism by Rupert Emerson and William J. Foltz, in K. W. Deutsch and William J. Foltz, eds., *Nation Building* (New York: Atherton Press, 1966).

In contrast to this picture of plasticity and change, many writings on African and Asian politics still seem to treat tribes as fixed and unlikely to change in any significant way during the next decades. Yet in contemporary Asia and Africa, the rates of cultural and ethnic change, although still low, are likely to be faster than they were in early medieval Europe. Press reports from the former Belgian Congo in 1961 mentioned that 26 per cent of natives were free from the (tribal) customary way of life, as against only about 12 per cent a generation earlier. Research is needed to establish more reliable figures, but it seems likely from the experience of ethnic minorities in other parts of the world that the process of partial modernization will draw many of the most gifted and energetic individuals into the cities or the growing sectors of the economy away from their former minority or tribal groups, leaving these traditional groups weaker, more stagnant, and easier to govern.

Research on the speed, scope, and quality of change among the tribes and within them also requires more attention to the relative size and humanpower of these tribes. The distribution curve of tribes and ethnic or linguistic groups, ranked by their numerical strength, usually shows a few relatively strong languages or groups—often about six—which among them comprise more than half the total population of the territory. About ten to fifteen languages or groups are then likely to include over 90 per cent of the population, and the dozens or hundreds of remaining petty tribes or language groups are likely to add up to less than one-tenth of the population. Governments that can obtain the compliance or even the active support of a few of the largest groups—and thus usually of the majority of the population—then have a fair chance to maintain themselves in power over the entire territory of their state.

The dynamic processes of social mobilization and cultural assimilation—or, at least, of political integration even with continuing linguistic and cultural diversity—are thus likely to be more powerful in uniting or destroying an emerging people or a newly-established state than are the mere static facts of the multiplicity of tribes or languages within its territory. To assess these processes, however, richer data and more detailed studies will be needed.

Detailed studies of national integration will also pose a challenge to analysis. Just what do we mean when we say that "tribalism" or any other social and political attachment to a small ethnic, cultural, or linguistic group has been "overcome" in the process of national integration?

Tribes or other smaller ethnic or cultural groups could be politically related to the state and the nation in several ways. They may flatly deny membership in the nation, refuse obedience to the state, and rise in war against other groups of those who are officially supposed to be their fellow citizens. If they are less hostile or less self-confident, they may passively obey the government and comply with its demands as long as they are being supervised more-or-less directly by government officials and soldiers, but they may rise against the state in times of crisis in order to secede. In that event, they will already be a source of taxes and humanpower for some national purposes but they still will require garrisons of national troops whose presence in these districts of the amalgamated national state will express the latent danger of civil war and the continued lack of integration.

If the members of the tribe or minority group have become more reconciled to their inclusion in the state, they may no longer be likely to rise in times of crisis and thus no longer require any garrisons from the rest of the state, but they might still lift no finger to aid the nation in its hour of need. Tribes or minorities in such a situation already may be called not only politically amalgamated under the common government of the national state but also integrated from the viewpoint of military security, since they—like any sovereign but reliably non-hostile state—pose no active military threat against which any significant military resources would have to be committed.

If the political integration of such tribes or minorities has gone beyond this minimum, however, the state may then count on their "good citizenship"—that is, on their unsupervised compliance in most situations and on their active support in case of need—even though they may have preserved their ethnic, cultural, or linguistic distinctness and their reluctance to condone intermarriage or to engage in close social or personal relations across the boundaries of their group. In terms of political loyalty, all the diverse groups may be integrated solidly and dependably into a single nation or united in one amalgamated national state, federal or unitary. In terms of habits of communication, their cultures may have become sufficiently similar to let them communicate and act together as one people, but their ethnic, linguistic, or other group diversity still has been preserved as it has been preserved among the English, Welsh, and Scots that have for centuries made up the British people and the British nation or among the four language groups that have made the Swiss people and the Swiss nation.

Finally, these diverse groups within the same state—and by now within the same people and nation—may become wholly assimilated to the majority of their compatriots in language, culture, probabilities of intermarriage, and close personal relations until they have become indistinguishable as a group.

Open or latent resistance to political amalgamation into a common national state; minimal integration to the point of passive compliance with the orders of such an amalgamated government; deeper political integration to the point of active support for such a common state but with continuing ethnic or cultural group cohesion and diversity; and, finally, the coincidence of political amalgamation and integration with the assimilation of all groups to a common language and culture—these could be the main stages on the way from tribes to nation.[3] Since a nation is not an animal or vegetable organism, its evolution need not go through any fixed sequence of these steps.

[3] For more detailed discussion of these concepts, see Karl W. Deutsch, *Nationalism and Social Communication* (New York: Wiley, 1953); *idem, Political Community at the International Level* (Garden City, New York: Doubleday, 1954); *idem et al., Political Community and the North Atlantic Area* (Princeton: Princeton University Press, 1957); *idem, Backgrounds for Community* (forthcoming).

Linguistic assimilation may long have preceded the amalgamation into a single state, as it did in the unification of Germany and Italy; political integration likewise may develop well before the ultimate decision-making powers of several governments are amalgamated into one, as Richard Merritt's study shows for the American colonies.[4] Yet the most frequent sequence in modern Asia and Africa may well be the one sketched above. How long might it take for tribes or other ethnic groups in a developing country to pass through some such sequence of stages? We do not know, but European history offers at least a few suggestions. In the forcible incorporation of the Saxons into the Frankish empire and their forcible conversion to the Christian religion and culture, the period of open violence lasted thirty-two years, from 772 to 804; and it took more than another century, until 919, for a Saxon prince to don Frankish dress to ascend, as Henry I, the throne of the empire and to symbolize the active integration of his peoples into the common state.[4a]

The speech of Saxons and Franks, though not identical, had been mutually intelligible to a considerable extent. Nevertheless, the assimilation of the two large tribes or peoples in regard to culture and speech did not occur for many centuries. More than five centuries later, several separate translations of the Bible had to be made—one into High German, the standard language gradually being adopted by the descendants of the Franks near Frankfurt and in Southern Germany; another into Low German, the standard language derived from the speech of the Saxons; and a third into Dutch, the standard language derived from the Low Frankish speech of the populations which in 1648 finally seceded from the empire to become the Dutch nation.[5] Smaller linguistic minorities, more interspersed or intermingled with the settlements of other populations, were assimilated in medieval Europe within a time of between one hundred and four hundred years. These were the approximate time spans for the linguistic assimilation of the Langobards in Italy (568-c. 750), of the Scandinavian-speaking Normans in Normandy (955-c. 1050), and later of the French-speaking Normans in England (1066-c. 1400). Modern immigrants, particularly in cities, have tended to assimilate much faster, often within twenty to fifty years, at least in situations where there were strong positive social, economic, and cultural incentives to assimilation as usually was the case in North and South America.

Generally, the political pacification and the establishment of minimal compliance have preceded by far the assimilation of minorities; minorities have often continued to express their particular patterns of social cohesion and political preference within the framework of a common state without neces-

---

[4] R. L. Merritt, "Nation-Building in America," in *Nation Building, op. cit.,* pp. 56–72.
[4a] See Gerd Tellenbach, "Europa im Zeitalter der Karolinger" in Valjavec, *op. cit.,* p. 406; Paul Kirn, "Das Abendland vom Ausgang der Antike bis zum Zerfall des Karolingischen Reiches," in Walter Goetz, ed., *Propyläen-Weltgeschichte, III, Das Mittelalter bis zum Ausgang der Staufer* (Berlin: Propyläen-Verlag, 1932), 106–108, 124; Karl Hampe, "Abendländisches Hochmittelalter," *ibid.,* pp. 301–303.
[5] For references, see the literature cited in Chapter 2, pp. 35–43.

sarily threatening its continued existence. In the case of majority populations, there is often the opposite pattern: a certain amount of social and cultural assimilation—or, at least, compatibility—may have to be established first if a common political regime is to endure.

On these points the European experience may have some relevance. The power of kings and other rulers is not an uncaused cause. Nation-building, Carl Friedrich has suggested, is "a matter of building group cohesion and group loyalty for international representation and domestic planning."[6] How and why are some governments, elites, and policies more successful in attracting support for this undertaking and in evoking loyalties than are their rivals? Who becomes loyal to a group, a tribe, or a nation—when and why? Based on a long study of history as well as much experience in the political and educational practice of nation-building from highly diverse elements in the Swiss democracy, Hermann Weilenmann's thought condenses a great amount of knowledge on this point. What appears as a process of nation-building from the point of view of governments here appears as a matter of nation-choosing by the individual. As Weilenmann sees it, it is an act of personal choice, or rather a sequence of choices, made in terms of the needs inherent in an individual's personality as well as in his or her external situation. Both personality and situation may be changed to some extent and made and remade by the consequences of each choice. This is almost an existential view of nationality, for it goes well beyond the demand for law and order, and it is, perhaps, a realistic view that might be fruitfully applied to the problems of national integration in other parts of the world and that might be advantageously combined with the results of other studies of personality and politics.[7]

The choice of national alignments and national identity is related to the decision to choose a common enemy. This is indeed a decision, even if it has been made unconsciously. Carl Friedrich refers to the Spanish people as having become united in their "struggle against the Arab overlords." Why did they choose to struggle rather than to submit? No such unifying struggles took place at such other boundaries of Islam—or of the Arab language area—as the Sudan, Morocco, Mesopotamia, or India; to see the Arabs as overlords to be resisted was in part a response to a situation of social stratification, but in part it was a decision that changed the destiny of those who took it.

Similar questions are now acute in Asia and Africa. Whom will the populations there choose to consider their common enemy at each particular time and place,

[6] Carl J. Friedrich, "Nation Building?" in *Nation-Building, op. cit.,* pp. 27–32, esp. p. 32.

[7] Hermann Weilenmann, "The Interlocking of Nation and Personality Structure," in *ibid.* pp. 33–55. See, for example, Erik H. Erikson, *Childhood and Society* (New York: Norton, 1950); *idem, Young Man Luther, A Study of Psychoanalysis and History* (New York: Norton, 1958); Lucian W. Pye, *Chinese Guerrilla Communism in Malaya, Its Social and Political Meaning* (Princeton: Princeton University Press, 1956): *idem, Politics, Personality and Nation-Building: Burma's Search for Identity* (New Haven: Yale University Press, 1962); and *idem,* "Personal Identity and Political Ideology," *Behavioral Science,* 6, No. 3 (1961), 205–221; and Daniel Lerner, *The Passing of Traditional Society* (Glencoe, Ill.: Free Press, 1958).

and whom will they choose as their allies? In response to what conditions and existential needs will they make their choices in each case and with what consequences for their own identity? We can say something about the conditions: usually two groups must have something important in common before they are likely to consider a new intruder as a "common enemy" rather than as an ally and to see each other as allies rather than as enemies. But, even if we know the initial conditions well, a crucial element of more or less free choice quite often will remain.

It is with such considerations in mind that we may come to appreciate the thoughtful definition of a nation proposed by Carl Friedrich.[8] Spelled out in greater detail, his definition, if I have understood it correctly, seems to imply at least five major points. A nation, in his view, is any sizable population or group of persons which can be called:

> *independent,* in the sense that it is not ruled from outside;

> *cohesive,* by virtue of its markedly more effective habits of easy and varied social communication and cooperation, compared with their corresponding capabilities and motivations for communication and cooperation with outsiders;

> *politically organized,* in the sense that it provides a constituency for a government which exercises effective rule within it;

> *autonomous,* in that it accords to this government such acclaim, consent, compliance, and support as to make its rule effective;

> *internally legitimate,* in the sense that its habits of compliance with and support of the government, or, at least, toward mutual political cooperation and membership in the nation, are connected with broader beliefs about the universe and about their own nature, personalities, and culture so that their support for the nation, even in times of adversity, is likely and thus ensures its endurance. (This internal legitimacy, anchored in the beliefs of its own population, may be largely independent of the opinions of other populations or of foreign governments.)

This definition does much to bring together a great deal that has been learned and thought about the nature and development of nations. It could be applied to further comparative research on the emerging nations of Asia and Africa, as well as to Friedrich's fascinating question about whether a European nation might be in process of emergence in the 1960's.[9]

If Friedrich has deepened and clarified the concept of an emerging nation, Merritt has demonstrated the usefulness of verifiable quantitative data for the study of such questions.[10] When we have comparable data for other periods and

---

[8] C. J. Friedrich, *op. cit.,* p. 31.

[9] *Ibid.,* p. 32

[10] Richard L. Merritt, "Nation-Building in America: The Colonial Years," in *ibid.,* pp. 61–62.

other parts of the world—such data as are now beginning to be collected by the Yale Political Data Program[11] —and if we have scholars interpreting them with care and perception, we shall know much more about the building of nations.

Robert Scott notes the limits of quantitative data.[12] Weilenmann suggests that men choose groups and nations in answer to their needs and that groups and nations derive their strength from their ability to attract and consolidate such choices.[13] Scott suggests the corollary to this view—the failure of this need-fulfilling, need-combining, and need-consolidating function. Such failure to create sufficient identity and congruity in the relations of nation, government, and individual may be a key element in what Scott sees as the failure of national integration in Latin America. There, as he reports, quantitative indexes of social mobilization would suggest opportunities for far greater progress toward nationhood than seems to have been attained in political practice.[14] He reminds us that economic and social change does not automatically create loyalties and institutions, but, at best, gives people opportunities for their creation and that here, too, the presence or absence of concomitant cultural and moral changes may be crucial.

A study by David A. Wilson illustrates the possibilities of one process—the pattern of revolutionary war that has characterized nationalistic and communist movements in much of eastern Asia—of concomitant cultural, political, and military change.[15] Carried to its extreme by the Communists, the attempt to combine nationalistic appeal and military effort with a policy of far-reaching cultural, social, and economic change has also been used in only somewhat more moderate form by many non-communist regimes. Here again, a comparison with the outcome of revolutionary war in the history of other parts of the world might throw some light on the potentialities and limits of the process. By the late 1970's, the outcome of the wars and civil wars in Vietnam, Laos, and Cambodia had added further weight to Wilson's forecasts.

Studies by Rupert Emerson and William J. Foltz illustrate the problems of applying our very incomplete knowledge of nation-building and national development to sub-Sahara Africa. Emerson writes with insight, wisdom, skepticism, and compassion, recalling the many unsolved problems in evaluating the present and prospective strength of nationalism in Africa. Foltz raises intriguing problems on the contrast between confident African nationalistic expectations and skeptical Western perspectives.

These two studies on Africa point to potentially fruitful lines of research. Emerson raises the whole problem of the persistent or transitory nature of tribal

[11] For a brief description, see Karl W. Deutsch, Harold D. Lasswell, Richard L. Merritt, and Bruce M. Russett, "The Yale Political Data Program," *Yale Papers in Political Science*, No. 4 (February 1963).

[12] Robert E. Scott, "Nation-Building in Latin America," in *Nation-Building, op. cit.*, p. 79.

[13] Weilenmann, in *ibid.*, pp. 38–40.

[14] Scott, in *ibid.*, p. 76.

[15] Wilson, "Nation-Building and Revolutionary War," in *ibid.*, pp. 84–94.

minorities and of the differing but not unrelated rates of political integration and ethnic assimilation—the two rates which may make the difference between a pattern of civil war, as in Algeria, and a pattern of peaceful ethnic bargaining, as in the "balanced ticket" of New York City politics. His study suggests the need for better research on the actual numerical strength of all the various minority tribes and languages, on the number and rates of growth of partially or wholly detribalized populations, and on the prospects of building more powerful and stable political coalitions from some of these variegated elements.

Emerson also notes the imperfectly understood problem of African boundaries. Which ones are "natural," and which ones "unnatural"? Who seems likely to spend how much effort on attempts to change them? To my knowledge, no study of African boundaries had been made by 1963, nor has there been a probing comparison between African boundaries and comparable boundaries in Asia and Latin America—a scholarly enterprise in which the resources of geography, history, political science, and sociology might have to be combined.[16]

Professor Foltz highlights another problem for research: the current scarcity of high-school-educated, "middle-level," elite groups in many parts of Africa and the resulting cleavages between a very small upper layer of university-educated Africans, often with European or American training, and the large mass of their uneducated or poorly educated countrymen. According to Foltz, in the old elite families there is a related cleavage between the small minority of young foreign-trained and technically competent elite members and their older and less well-trained fathers, brothers, or other relatives. He notes the need for broader and deeper studies of African elite recruitment and of the probable changes in the composition of future African elites. African parties are likely to require increasingly the services of local and district functionaries, many of whom will not be rich, foreign trained, or university educated. Labor unions and rural cooperatives are likely to elevate to local and regional leadership a similar elite of urban or rural lower- or lower middle-class origin who have only an elementary or, at most, a high-school education. Any progress in industrialization or economic development will similarly demand expansion in secondary school training. Any gains in literacy will swell the demand for elementary school teachers in towns and villages, and the newly literate young adults may soon furnish a public for mass publication on a relatively low cultural level, resembling the "penny press," tabloids, pulp magazines, and comic strips and catering to similar recently acculturated strata in Europe, America, and, perhaps,

---

[16] Rupert Emerson, "Nation-Building in Africa," in *ibid.*, pp. 95–103. For a beginning in this direction, see George P. Murdock, *Africa: Its Peoples and Their Culture History* (New York: McGraw-Hill, 1959); S. B. Jones, *Boundary-Making: A Handbook for Statesmen, Treaty Editors and Boundary Commissioners* (Washington: Carnegie Endowment for International Peace, 1945); Karl Haushofer, *Grenzen in ihrer geographischen und politischen Bedeutung* (Heidelberg: Vowinckel, 1939); D. Whittlesey, *The Earth and State: A Study of Political Geography* (New York: Holt, 1939).

India.[17] All this may mean the gradual shift in many African states to a new elite with less formal education and more intensely national experience, backed by a similar, widening public for the mass media and for increasingly sustained political participation.

Another set of issues raised by Foltz has wider implications for Africa. He mentions the exploitation of the peasants by the new national states and governments and the frequent lack of appreciation by the latter of any possible economic benefits that might flow from an expansion of their countries' private economic sectors, either native-owned or foreign. Experts from the former colonial administrations, as well as spokesmen for Western business groups or settlers, have often stressed these points. Perhaps just as often, African and Asian nationalists have done the exact contrary, minimizing the economic pressure of the new nationalist governments on the rural population and predominantly casting private business interests in the role of the exploiter. It seems hardly plausible that in this debate all the truth should be on one side, but to ascertain how much truth there is in which claim and under what conditions will require a combination of skilled political and economic research.

In many ways, these studies make a book that is not finished, yet it is a book that is more than the sum of its parts. It suggests the opportunities for insight that come from the comparison of cases and the dialogue of scholars. Neither this book nor this dialogue will be properly finished until much more is known about the complexities of the topic. Yet, even as an expression of the incompleteness of our knowledge, it may suggest by how much our knowledge has grown in recent years and what real promise it holds of increasing in the future.

[17]William J. Foltz, "Building the Newest Nations: Short-Run Strategies and Long-Run Problems," in *Nation-Building, op. cit.*, pp. 117-131. For a discussion of this problem in India, see Selig S. Harrison, *India, the Most Dangerous Decades* (Princeton: Princeton University Press, 1960).

7 | The Propensity to International Transactions

> The broad surmises summarized in this brief chapter seem to have stood up well, but they still deserve more detailed testing. In the nearly two decades since this chapter was written, many more data and volumes of data collections have become available, so that it should have become easier to carry out such tests. Yet much of this work, too, still remains to be done.

In the thinking of some economic theorists, a "propensity" is the average share of efforts or resources allocated to a specific class of activities. Thus, the "propensity to save" is the average percentage of income which people allocate to saving. Such percentages can then be plotted against other variables which are believed to be relevant, in order to find out whether, and how, changes in each variable are correlated with changes in the proportions of resources allocated to the activities in question.

In this manner the average percentages of their incomes which the people of some country save can be plotted against the levels of their incomes, as found in different income groups. Very roughly put, it may then appear that those who are richer save a bigger share of their incomes; someone may infer from this that the "propensity to save" rises with the level of the income; and this inference may be tested by investigating whether, and to what extent, the same people, when and as they get richer, do in fact increase the proportions of their incomes which they save. Similar studies can be carried out for the behavior of members of other social groups, so that one might speak of the "propensity to save" of farmers, or workers, or Protestants, or blacks, or of more narrowly defined subgroups: and other types of behavior can be studied in similar terms, such as the "propensity to invest," the "propensity to hoard," and so forth.[1]

It is impractical to go here beyond this extremely crude sketch of what is

---

[1] For an interesting attempt to extend the concept of propensities even further to aspects of economic and social behavior that cannot be readily measured, see Walt W. Rostow, *The Theory of Economic Growth* (New York, Norton, 1950).

The substance of this chapter appeared in *Political Studies* 8 (June 1960): 147–155. Reprinted by permission of the Publisher.

actually a considerably more complex field of economic theory and measurement. Yet the main points should be clear. A propensity is a quantitative concept; it is a proportion, derived from the measurement of some class of past activities of the members of some defined group, and applied to the tentative prediction of the future frequency of similar activities—and sometimes of related ones—within the same social group, or within similar ones. In its relation to other variables it can be depicted as a curve on a graph, and expected values can be read from it for various conditions. This concept and this technique have long been applied, successfully, in economics. They could be applied to other fields; and it is the purpose of the present chapter to propose their application to the field of international relations.

In its broadest terms, a propensity to engage in international transactions would cover a considerable and ill-defined range of different activities. It might be better, therefore, to break it down into several more specifically defined propensities, referring in each case to a more narrowly definable class of activities, such as trade, postal communications, news reporting and readership, travel, migration, or the allocation of governmental expenditures. These propensities would have to refer in each case to the behavior of the members of some defined group, such as the population of some country.

This approach would call, therefore, for measuring for at least one of these activities the volume of relevant transactions entered into by the members of this population, and for measuring further the proportions of such transactions which cross the boundaries of the country, as against those that remain entirely within it. Considerable statistical data are available in published sources—on national incomes and foreign trade, on the flow of domestic and foreign mail, on residence and migration, on governmental budgets, and on the content of newspapers and other media of mass communication—from which proportions of this kind could be computed.

From such computations propensities could be inferred. It could be supposed tentatively that such proportions should turn out to be fairly stable over longer periods of time; that they should be fairly similar for similar countries; that their variations should appear to be non-random and capable of being accounted for in an orderly manner; and that conspicuous changes or differences in these proportions should suggest interesting questions and potential insights, as to the underlying social and political structure of the countries and communities involved. These suppositions can be tested. In the course of several preliminary studies it has turned out thus far that the proportions discussed here do meet in fact, by and large, the qualifications just listed.

The collection and analysis of such data should be of interest to students of society and politics. The proportions found might be interpreted tentatively in terms of propensities, as defined above, and thus not necessarily in terms of any supposed psychological predispositions or national character traits. Such cultural or psychological assumptions would require additional and independent evidence to count as even strongly indicated. The empirical behavior, measured by the propensities, might be caused simply by external arrangements or constraints, or by broad factors of geography, or industry, or occupation, or religion, or general type of culture, rather than by any peculiarities of inner group structure or individual decision. The study of propensities should start a process of more deep-probing analysis, not terminate it.

With these cautions, however, even tentative findings could serve as more general indicators of the levels and trends of international involvement on the part of groups or nations. In regard to the politics of each country, such findings might tell us something about the relative strength of those political and social interest groups that are directly involved in international transactions, as against those whose primary concerns are domestic. The relative strength of such internationally involved groups, and the share of economic resources involved in direct international transactions, have a direct bearing on the generation and distribution of political power in a country, and on the purposes to which it is applied. In addition to the power process, the processes of communication and decision-making are affected by the proportions of purely domestic messages which compete for the attention of social elites, political decision-makers, and the general population, as against the proportion of messages carrying some direct concern with matters abroad. Both the power process and the attention process are inseparably interlinked in politics; and both are significantly affected by the overall proportions of domestic to international transactions.

It is possible, of course, to deny in principle the significance of such quantitative data, by proposing something like a "vitamin theory" of the social and political importance of international transactions. Even though these were only present in small traces, it could be argued, their presence might still be essential to the functioning of the society or community concerned; and it might be asserted that any changes in the relative amounts of international transactions above this trace level should have next to no effect. Such a "vitamin theory" of politics, however, would require some evidence to sustain it; and it would clash with much that is known about interest-group politics, the importance of economic factors, and the quantitative aspects of mass communication.

If one grants, for the time being, the potential interest of such quantitative data and proportions, what actual ratios have been found and what do they suggest? From such data, would it be possible to construct a more general scale as a background and aid in their interpretation?

A TENTATIVE SCALE OF INTERNATIONAL
AND INTERREGIONAL INTEGRATION

From a survey of the proportions of foreign to domestic mail-flows in a large number of countries, as well as of several other kinds of international and interregional transactions, a tentative scale for the integration of a relatively small community with its larger environment was proposed some years ago.

The most convenient form for giving such a scale would be in terms of per cent international transactions among the total volume of transactions of the relevant class. Such percentages are often given in the published sources, and their interpretation seems intuitively familiar to many social scientists. A somewhat more sensitive yardstick for changes, particularly in cases where international transactions form a small proportion of the total, is offered by the I/O ratio, that is, the proportion of internal transactions to outside ones. For the purposes of the present paper it seems best to give the scale in both kinds of units—percentages as well as I/O ratios. This scale might be most nearly applicable to countries or communities which are comparatively small relative to their total outside environment—say, not above 10 per cent of the latter.

According to this scale, and in regard to the particular type of transactions studied, one might consider countries which show between two and six times as many internal as external transactions—corresponding to a share of 14 to 33 per cent of the total for the latter—as fairly well intermediate between international integration and national autonomy, in so far as this particular type or range of transactions is concerned. Countries with more than ten times as many domestic as foreign transactions—i.e. with less than 9 per cent of the total for the latter—might count as low in international integration and high in national autonomy or self-preoccupation; and they might be rated extremely so, in both regards, if domestic transactions were to outnumber foreign ones by more than fifteen to one, reducing the international share of the total to about 6 per cent, or less. By contrast, international integration might be considered high, if domestic transactions should be equalled or outnumbered by foreign ones. Intermediate values between these "high," "fair," and "low" points on this scale might then receive appropriate "fair to high" and "low to fair" interpretations, as shown in Table 7-1.

TABLE 7-1. A TENTATIVE SCALE OF INTERNATIONAL INTEGRATION
AND NATIONAL AUTONOMY

I/O RATIO: INTERNAL TO OUTSIDE TRANS-ACTIONS	PERCENTAGE OF OUTSIDE TRANSACTIONS AMONG TOTAL	TENTATIVE INTERPRETATION: DEGREE OF	
		Integration to Outside World	Autonomy or Self-preoccupation of Smaller Unit
1 or less	50+	High	Low
1–2	33–50	Fair to high	Low to fair
2–6	14–33	Fair	Fair
6–10	9–14	Low to fair	Fair to high
10–15	6–9	Low	High
15 or higher	6 or less	Extremely low	Extremely high

Source. K. W. Deutsch, "Shifts in the Balance of Communication Flows;" pp. 153–170.

SOME SPECIFIC FINDINGS

If one applies the tentative interpretations, suggested in this table, to the data about postal correspondence for a large number of countries, it appears that the mean share of international mail was less than 14 per cent in 1880, indicating a low to fair level of international integration at that time. This average share of international mail then rose to a fair level of world integration, or at least inter-dependence, with almost 30 per cent in 1913, but declined again to about 25 per cent for the average of the years 1928-34, and further to about 18 per cent for the period 1946-51, while still remaining above the lower limit of the "fair" category.

International integration in regard to mail declined sharply with the area of a country, the size of its population, and the *per capita* number of letters. The last-named of these variables is correlated to some extent with literacy and *per capita* income, and apparently also with some characteristics of the general culture. Low levels of international postal integration, with less than 9 per cent of foreign mail, were found after 1928 for such countries as the United Kingdom, France, Germany, and Italy. Extremely low values, well below 2 per cent, were found for the United States, and the bottom figures of just above 1 per cent was that for the U.S.S.R. for 1936—the last year for which a figure for that country was given by the Universal Postal Union.[2]

The same scale can be applied to the results of a more recent survey of the proportions of foreign trade to national income for a large number of countries in the mid-1950's, and for a smaller number of countries at various earlier dates. The first noteworthy fact here is that levels of international integration are significantly higher in regard to trade than they are in regard to mail. For a group of seventy-one countries in the mid-1950's, the median proportion of foreign trade, as compared to national income, was about 35 per cent. This is almost twice the average percentage of foreign mail found for a similar large group of countries in 1946-51, and it suggests a fair to high level of international trade integration for this group of seventy-one countries as a whole.[3] It should be borne in mind, of course, that the two periods and groups of countries are somewhat different, and that the mean value for one group is not strictly comparable to the median value for the other. The differences between the integration levels for trade and for mail seem too large, however, to be explained away by these discrepancies.

More nearly comparable figures for individual countries confirm the lagging of the share of foreign mail communications behind the levels of the shares of foreign trade. Thus France and Italy, which rated "low" in terms of international postal integration, rate "fair" in terms of international trade, which corresponded

[2] For details, see Chapter 8, pp. 153-170.
[3] From data in K. W. Deutsch and Alexander Eckstein, "National Industrialization and the Declining Share of the International Economic Sector, 1890-1955," *World Politics,* XIII (January 1961): 267-299.

in 1957 to 26 and 32 per cent of their national incomes, respectively. In the same year, the United Kingdom and the German Federal Republic rated "fair to high" in this respect, with foreign trade proportions at about 42 per cent of national income for each country, and thus more than four times as high as their corresponding percentages of foreign mail. Even the United States and the Soviet Union were less self-preoccupied in their trade than they were in the letter-writing of their populations. The share of foreign trade in the United States was a little above 9 per cent of national income in 1957, and a little below 9 per cent in 1958, leaving that country's international integration rating in regard to trade just at the borderline between "low" and "low to fair," but still more than four times as high as the corresponding level of the share of foreign mails. The Soviet Union, finally, with a foreign trade proportion of less than 5 per cent in 1957, remained here, too, in the "extremely low" category of international integration—including, interestingly enough, the level of its trade integration with the countries of the Communist bloc.[4] The large share which these latter countries were getting of what Soviet foreign trade there was should not obscure the remarkably small proportion of all Soviet foreign trade when compared to the Soviet national income. It may be surmised, however, that even this low level of international trade integration in the case of the U.S.S.R. may still lie well above the corresponding level of its international integration in terms of the share of foreign mail, both to the world at large and within the circle of Communist countries.

The level of international trade integration tends to drop sharply with the population size of countries. In the survey of seventy-one countries referred to earlier, the median proportion of foreign trade to national income for countries with populations of about 1 million was about 50 per cent, suggesting an integration rating of "high." For countries with populations near 10 million, the same foreign trade ratio was about 35 per cent, with an integration level "fair to high." For countries near 100 million, however, the theoretical value from the regression curve would have been about 12 per cent; and for countries above 150 million, the share of foreign trade was below 10 per cent, with an apparent international integration level of "low," or "low to fair" at best.[5]

The fact of some decline in international integration with increasing country size should not be surprising, but the speed and extent of the decline are impressive. On the basis of these figures, any state uniting only as much as one-tenth of humankind would have to be expected to fall to a low level of international integration and to devote more than nine-tenths of its economic activities, and perhaps twice this proportion of its postal correspondence, to domestic activities. These figures might deserve the careful thought of proponents of such plans as Western European Federation, Atlantic Union, or Federal World Government, as well as that of students of integrative and disintegrative tendencies within the

[4] *Ibid.*
[5] *Ibid.*, K. W. Deutsch, C. I. Bliss, and Alexander Eckstein, "Population, Sovereignty and Foreign Trade," *Economic Development and Cultural Change*, X (July 1962): 353–366.

Soviet bloc.[6] The trends suggested by the data need not have the inevitability of fate, but they seem to be clearly more than mere statistical artefacts, and they may well count at the very least as serious challenges to any integrative international policies or institutions.

Another type of international and interregional transactions relates to travel and migration. These processes are usually characterized by lower levels of international integration than are trade or mail, and they bring out strikingly the contrast between the high and still rising levels of integration among different regions within the same country, and the low, and sometimes even declining, level of such integration among different countries. Thus, at censuses during the last hundred years, about 30 per cent of the American people were found living outside their state of birth, showing a long-lasting "fair" level of interstate integration in the United States. For Switzerland, the analogous proportion in terms of Swiss citizens born outside their Cantons of residence rose from about 20 per cent in 1860 to about 40 per cent in 1950. In Bavaria the proportion of German residents born elsewhere was below 6 per cent in the 1880's; it is well above 20 per cent now, as it is in the entire Federal Republic, after the dislocations of World War II.[7] These processes may well have tended in all these countries to weaken regional separatism, and to increase the importance of national politics.

At the international level, however, developments in regard to migration have been different. Among most West European countries integration in terms of international migration must rate as "extremely low," with the proportion of foreign-born residents well below 6 per cent. Even in the overseas countries, migration levels during the last several decades have been far below those of the pre-1913 period, and they seem unlikely to recover without deliberate changes in national policies, as well as concerted international action.

International integration is somewhat higher, on the other hand, in terms of news coverage and news attention devoted to subject-matters beyond one's national boundaries. Here, too, however, the proportion of news space devoted on the average to foreign developments may tend to decline with the size and power of countries. According to some preliminary surveys the proportion of foreign news in the average newspaper—as distinct from the elite papers—of such countries as the United States and the Soviet Union may be at or below 14 per cent of total editorial content, suggesting a "low to fair" level of international integration, or at least involvement, while such countries as the United Kingdom, France, or the German Federal Republic are apt to have comparable proportions of foreign news in the "fair" or even "fair to high" ranges of international integration.

The picture of national self-preoccupation is somewhat strengthened if average-reader attention is taken into account; it tends to drop for foreign news. Thus

[6]K. W. Deutsch and Alexander Eckstein, "National Industrialization and the Declining Share of the International Economic Sector, 1890-1955," *op. cit.*
[7]Data from standard statistical publications.

the average share of foreign and international subjects in the news space of American newspapers was a little below 9 per cent, at a time when their share of reader attention was only about 7 per cent—both figures suggesting a "low" level of international integration.[8]

A corrective is introduced, if one notes the much higher levels of attention to foreign news in the elite press of most countries. To cite just one example, about 40 per cent of the editorials in both the London *Times* and the *New York Times* are devoted to international topics, and this proportion has persisted unchanged for about fifty years.[9] It is possible, therefore, that low or declining levels of international integration in the realm of material activities may be offset, to some limited extent, by a higher and conceivably even an increasing, proportion of attention to international matters in terms of news and symbols, particularly at the elite level.

The process of "fundamental democratization" in the twentieth century—to recall a term of Karl Mannheim's here[10]—might then have quite different results at different stages, so far as international integration is concerned. During the first stage, mass politics might develop faster than mass acculturation to elite levels of international attention and interest. During the same period domestic economic development, communication, and migration might all develop faster than their international counterparts, and all these tendencies might be strengthened further through the ending of past colonial relationships. As a result of all these processes the propensities to international transactions might decline, and prolonged periods of increased parochialism and nationalism might occur in many countries just during the critical early decades of the nuclear age.

If these "dangerous decades"[11] could be surmounted without mass destruction, however, a second stage of development eventually might permit mass acculturation to catch up, just as it might permit substantial cumulative social learning and habit-changing on the part of old and new elites. In this event, international attention and concern in the major countries might attain and retain sufficiently high levels of quantitative strength and qualitative competence to permit the world's population to live somewhat more safely with the vast new powers of physical destruction which it has acquired. At a still later stage, structural changes in technology, economics, and social institutions may then reach a point where the material processes of international integration will enable international

---

[8]Cf. data in the excellent collection edited by Wilbur Schramm, *Mass Communications* (Urbana: University of Illinois Press, 1949).

[9]Cf. Ithiel Pool *et al.*, *The Prestige Papers* (Stanford: Stanford University Press, 1951); and *idem, Symbols of Internationalism* (Stanford, Stanford University Press, 1952). The results appear confirmed by more recent unpublished surveys at Yale University and the Fletcher School of Law and Diplomacy; cf. also unpublished survey data from the Center on Communications at Stanford University, collected under the direction of Professor Wilbur Schramm.

[10]Cf. Karl Mannheim, *Man and Society in the Age of Reconstruction* (New York: Harcourt Brace, 1940, 1947).

[11]Cf. Selig S. Harrison, *The Most Dangerous Decades* (Princeton: Princeton University Press, 1960).

and supranational communities, or even a world community, to attain and exceed the present-day integrative levels of the national state.

These last points are, of course, conjectural and cannot be pursued here. The present chapter will have served its purpose if it has managed to illustrate the intrinsic interest, as well as the practical possibility, of using the aid of some measurable indicators in order to trace the rise and decline of some underlying processes of international or interregional integration, and if it should find some response in the research, analysis, and criticism of other students of society and politics.

8 | Shifts in the Balance of International Communication Flows

Since the first publication of this chapter, a fair amount of further research and analysis on communication and transaction flows has been done by several investigators,* including Charles L. Taylor in expanding the forthcoming *World Handbook of Political and Social Indicators*, Third Edition, through the inclusion of international transaction data.

Transaction research remains of crucial importance for the analysis of international relations. Interviews and survey data mainly tell us what people say; transaction data tell us what large numbers of them do. The two kinds of data supplement each other. If their evidence agrees, it deserves more trust; if it does not, it requires further examination. But first of all, both types of evidence—as well as several others—must be obtained and considered, wherever possible.

Studies of communication deal only with one limited aspect of politics. Many kinds of politically significant transactions cannot be reduced to communica-

---

*See B. M. Russett, *Community and Contention* (Cambridge, Mass.: MIT Press, 1963); W. J. Foltz, *From French West Africa to the Mali Federation* (New Haven: Yale University Press, 1964); R. L. Merritt, *Symbols of American Community 1735-1775* (New Haven: Yale University Press, 1966); R. L. Merritt, ed., *Communication in International Politics* (Urbana: University of Illinois Press, 1972); R. L. Merritt and C. M. Clark, "An Example of Data Use: Mail Flows in the European Balance of Power, 1890-1920," in K. W. Deutsch, B. Fritsch, H. Jaguaribe, and A. S. Markovits, eds., *Problems of World Modeling* (Cambridge, Mass.: Ballinger, 1977); K. W. Deutsch, L. J. Edinger, R. C. Macridis and R. L. Merritt, *France, Germany and the Western Alliance* (New York: Scribner's, 1967); H. R. Alker, Jr., and D. J. Puchala, "Trends in Economic Partnership: The North Atlantic Area, 1928–1963," in J. D. Singer, ed., *Quantitative International Politics: Insights and Evidence* (New York: Free Press, 1968), pp. 287-316; Hugh Stephens, *The Political Transformation of Tanganyika, 1920-1967* (New York: Praeger, 1968); Michael C. Hudson, *The Precarious Republic: Political Modernization in Lebanon* (New York: Random House, 1968); G. Schweigler, *National Consciousness in Divided Germany* (Beverly Hills, Calif., and London: Sage, 1975); and P. Katzenstein, *Disjoined Partners: Austria and Germany* (Berkeley: University of California Press, 1976).

The substance of this chapter appeared in *Public Opinion Quarterly* 20 (Spring 1956): 143-160. Reprinted by permission of the Publisher. Most of the material used here was collected under the author's direction at the Center for Research on World Political Institutions at Princeton University. Most of the computations were made then at the Center by Yvette Gurley and Johanna Lederer. The charts were drawn by Professor Manfred Kochen, now at the University of Michigan.

tion: population growth, gross national product, natural and industrial resources, standards of nutrition, geographic location, transport and trade, human resources and firepower. Yet the limited aspect of politics which is constituted by communication processes is a strategic one. It includes the areas of attention, of perception and orientation, of values and evaluation, of goal-seeking and of decision-making.

Since the days of Plato and Machiavelli, classic political theory has aimed at presenting simplified verbal images of politics, of the state, and of the behavior of states toward each other. These classic conceptions contained assumptions about communication, but communication was not treated explicitly as a major aspect of these analytic schemes. More recent treatments of political decision-making, on the other hand, have increasingly focussed on communication and information, and on the related aspects of values and symbols.[1] Part of the same development has been an increasing interest in representing social and political processes by means of abstract models that pay explicit attention to communication problems.[2]

The more ambitious of such models attempt to represent quantitative aspects of the political process. Indeed, there is beginning in political science, as there has been in the field of economics, a gradual shift from the sole reliance on qualitative or literary representation, with its potential richness and sensitivity, to its supplementation by quantitative models with their relatively greater poverty and rigidity, but also their possibilities of greater precision and penetrating power. Where such quantitative models are attempted, however, they raise the question of operational definitions and techniques of measurement for the variables they employ.

WHAT IS MEANT BY MEASUREMENT

What kinds of communications can we measure in international relations, and what can we measure about them? Moreover, what do we mean by measurement in this context, and what kinds of quantities are there that we can try to measure?[3]

[1] Cf. Harold D. Lasswell, "World Politics and Personal Insecurity," in *A Study of Power*, Glencoe, Ill. Free Press, 1950; Richard C. Snyder, H. W. Bruck, and Burton Sapin, *Decision-making in Foreign Policy* (New York: Free Press, 1962).

[2] Cf. Herbert Simon, "Some Strategic Considerations in the Construction of Social Science Models", in Paul F. Lazarsfeld, ed., *Mathematical Thinking in the Social Sciences*, Glencoe, Ill. Free Press, 1954, pp. 388–415; K. W. Deutsch, "On Communication Models in Social Science," *Public Opinion Quarterly*, Vol. 16, No. 3, Fall 1952, pp. 356–380.

[3] For an excellent general discussion of the problem of measurement, see S. S. Stevens, ed., *Handbook of Experimental Psychology*, Cambridge, Addison Wesley, 1949, ch. 1; and the summary in Marie Jahoda, Morton Deutsch and Stuart W. Cook, *Research Methods in Social Relations with Especial Reference to Prejudice*, New York, Dryden Press, 1951, Part I, pp. 92–127.

All measurement depends on repetition. We can measure repetitive events, such as communication flows, that is, streams of messages that resemble each other in some important way, such as in their sources or their topics; or we can try to measure the impact of relatively unique events by noting the changes in the repetitive processes of communication with which their occurrence may have been associated. In either case, it is not the individual message but its statistical context that will most concern us at the outset. At any one time, each message derives its meaning only from the statistical universe of possible alternative messages and silences that could have been transmitted in its stead. Over any longer period of time, again, the significance of each message can be appraised only in terms of the context of the changing flow of other messages between the units relevant for this particular communication process. Statistics of communication flows thus constitute essential background data for almost any effective analysis of international communication.

In looking for measurements to construct and interpret such statistics, it is important not to take too narrow a view of the concept of measurement itself. Measurement in its broadest form consists in assigning in a consistent manner some symbol of quantity to each of a number of events, such as assigning numbers to football players. A slightly less primitive kind of measurement involves the assignment of symbols of rank, such as the words "big" versus "small," or "bigger than," or "faster than," etc. However, even though we know that A is bigger than B, and B bigger than C (and perhaps also that our scale of measurement is transitive, so that C must be smaller than A), we do not know from these statements by how much. Only a more thoroughgoing kind of measurement in terms of some ratio scale can answer the latter kind of question. Many of the measurements most immediately useful, and most readily obtainable, are likely to be in the intermediate category, where exact ratios cannot be relied on, but where some statements in terms of "bigger than," "smaller than," "high in x," "low in x," "faster than," "slower than," "increasing" and "declining" can be made with fair confidence. Has there been growth or decline, or no clear-cut change? Has the ratio between two processes or trends roughly been preserved, or has it become drastically altered? It is with such rough proportions and balances among trends that the rest of our discussion of international communication flows here will be concerned.

Rough quantitative measurements of relative proportions among different communication flows can be made in several dimensions. The most obvious dimension is that of volume, taken either as volume per unit of time, or as a proportion of some total volume of messages, or as a proportion of time or facilities engaged in dealing with them. There are, of course, other dimensions than volume: the speed with which messages are transmitted; the fidelity with which their proportions and details are preserved throughout the process of transmission. There is the effectiveness of communication in terms of the measurable quantities of some response which it may trigger off at the receiving end; and there is the distribution of initiatives among the participating parties in communication.[4] Nevertheless, volume—that is to say, frequency—of communication is the first dimension of international and domestic communication flows that is likely to be measured with any degree of success.

THE INTAKE-OUTPUT RATIO

Perhaps the simplest ratio is that between output and intake of communications of some person or organization, such as a political leader, a party or elite, a government, or a country. How much time is spent in talking and broadcasting, in telling others, and how much is spent in observing, or in listening to what they have to say?

In the case of a relatively simple goal-seeking device, such as an automatic gun director, it has been surmised that the intake-output ratio in terms of bits of information necessary for effective operation, may be somewhere near the general order of one-to-one, so that roughly an equal number of units ("bits") of information per second must be taken in for any level of complexity of effective output information required of the system.[5] It seems clear that this ratio is often widely departed from in politics. In the course of a series of extended interviews of Indonesian political leaders, undertaken as part of the Communications Program of the Center for International Studies at M.I.T., John Rodrigues found that Indonesian political leaders told him repeatedly: "The Indonesian people should do this," but he rarely, if ever, encountered a phrase like: "I hear from my constituents," or "some people think," or "people tell me that."[6] A broad program of interviews among members of the United States Congress on the topic of the reciprocal trade program, showed the opposite pattern. The investigator, Dr. Lewis Dexter, found Congressmen telling him frequently: "I hear," "people tell me," "some people in my district feel," or "other members of Congress seem to think," but that they said much more rarely: "I think we should," or "I think people ought to."[7]

The concept of the intake-output ratio could be used to supplement interview materials and other kinds of evidence in verifying at least in part David Riesman's concepts of "inner-directed" versus "other-directed" personality, and of the changing style of American politics which may be related to the changing pro-

[4] For a more extended discussion of these dimensions, see my *Political Community at the International Level: Problems of Definition and Measurement*, New York, Doubleday-Random House, 1954, pp. 59–62.

[5] Norbert Weiner, oral communication, M.I.T., Spring, 1955.

[6] John Rodrigues, Report in the Seminar on Communication. Center for International Studies, M.I.T., Fall 1955.

[7] Lewis Dexter, report in the same seminar, Fall 1955; and *idem, Congressman and the People They Listen To*, Cambridge, M.I.T., Center of International Studies, October 1955 (C/55–26), multigraphed.

portions among those personality types in our population.[8] It could be applied, in more strictly quantitative terms, to the amounts of human resources and money devoted by certain organizations, such as the State Department or the Associated Press, to the gathering of information from abroad, as against the comparable amounts of money and human resources devoted to sending the "American story" to foreign recipients.

There seem to be no good statistical data readily available, but there are scattered indications that some of these ratios are far from one-to-one, and that rather drastic changes have occurred in some of them in the course of the last decades. Thus according to Russell F. Anderson, the number of U.S. foreign correspondents fell from 2,700 in 1946 to less than 300 in 1951 (excluding those newsmen who were then covering the war in Korea).[9] The causes of the decline, in Anderson's view, were mainly economic: rising costs of paper and printing, together with lack of reader demand for foreign news, led editors to cut down expenses for foreign reporting to an extent often concealed from the readers and advertisers of their papers.

This trend was by no means limited to the United States. A UNESCO survey of seventeen major daily newspapers from as many countries in 1951 arrived at similar conclusions.[10] All foreign newspapers and news agencies together maintained in 1954 only about two hundred regular full-time correspondents in the United States.[11] A significant part of the two-way flow of news in the free market thus seemed to be on the way of being replaced by the heavy output of government-backed information agencies, such as the "Voice of America" and the comparable agencies of other countries.

THE RECEIVING-SENDING RATIO OF
FOREIGN MAIL

Another example of intake-output ratios can be found in the flows of first class mail between countries. Among forty-eight countries for which data were examined, more than three-quarters received regularly more letters from abroad than they sent.

During the decade before the Second World War, the only countries that sent

---

[8] Cf. David Riesman, *The Lonely Crowd*, New Haven: Yale University Press, 1950: and *idem*, *Faces in the Crowd*, New Haven: Yale University Press, 1950.

[9] Russell F. Anderson, "News from Nowhere: Our Disappearing Foreign Correspondents", *The Saturday Review of Literature*, November 17, 1951.

[10] Jacques Kayser, *One Week's News: Comparative Study of 17 Major Dailies for a Seven-Day Period*, Paris, UNESCO, 1953, p. 93. Cf. also Robert Redfield "Does America Need a Hearing Aid?" *Saturday Review of Literature*, September 23, 1953.

[11] The membership of the Foreign Press Association, according to its *1954 Directory of Members*, was 149; this figure was believed to represent about 75% of the regular full-time correspondents in the United States. Data from Center for International Studies, M.I.T.

significantly more letters than they received—for whom, therefore, the ratios of foreign mail received to foreign mail sent (R/S) were well below one—were seven industrial and commercial nations with widely diversified economies and long-established traditions of using mail communications on a large scale. These countries were, in ascending order of the R/S ratios (averaged for 1928 and 1938, or nearest years thereto): France (0.52), Austria (0.62), Germany (0.65), the United Kingdom (0.70), the United States (0.81), Belgium (0.82), and Japan (0.83). Three other countries had R/S ratios very close to one: the Netherlands (0.98), Spain (0.98), and Switzerland (1.01).

At the other end of the rank order scale were about eighteen countries that received substantially more mail than they sent; these countries tended to specialize by and large in the export of primary products from agriculture, forestry and mining, and to import a wide variety of goods and services from countries with more diversified economies. In order of declining R/S ratios, these countries were: Finland (3.18), Mexico (3.12), Argentina (2.93), Brazil (2.78), New Zealand (2.64), Indonesia (2.33), Belgian Congo (2.21), Southern Rhodesia (2.20), Iran (2.19), Iceland (2.10), Gold Coast (1.97), Nigeria (1.89), Union of South Africa (1.87), Bulgaria (1.86), Kenya, Uganda and Tanganyika (1.73), Portugal (1.72), Indochina (1.71), and Turkey (1.63).

The middle range on the R/S scale was taken up by the twenty remaining countries, mostly from Northern and Eastern Europe or from Asia: Poland (1.57), Luxembourg (1.53), Sweden (1.48), Roumania (1.42), Ireland (1.41), Norway (1.40), Egypt (1.31), India (1.26), Iraq (1.25), Yugoslavia (1.25), Hungary (1.21), French Morocco (1.19), Greece (1.18), Czechoslovakia (1.17), Australia (1.15), Lebanon and Syria (1.12), Denmark (1.12), China (1.06), Madagascar (1.04), and the USSR (1.02).

By 1951, the main lines of this picture still persisted, but there had been some interesting changes. Unfortunately, there were no post-war figures available for France, the United States, and Japan, nor for the USSR, Iraq, Roumania, and New Zealand. Among the remaining forty-one countries, nine had R/S ratios below one (figures are for 1951, unless otherwise indicated): Germany 0.66 (1950), the United Kingdom 0.74, Hungary 0.79 (1947), Netherlands 0.80, Yugoslavia, 0.86, Switzerland 0.86, Austria 0.92, Ireland 0.94, and Madagascar 0.98. A tenth, Turkey, had an R/S ratio of exactly 1.00 (1949). At the other end of the scale, there were now only twelve countries with R/S ratios above 1.60, while there had been eighteen such countries in the average of 1928 and 1938; and for many countries the imbalance between mail received and sent was somewhat less. A sharp upturn in mail received in 1951 put Greece at the head of the list with an R/S ratio of 5.07. Greece was followed by Argentina 3.64, Indonesia 3.64 (1949), Kenya, Uganda and Tanganyika 2.59 (1950), Finland 2.11, Iran 2.08 (1949), Gold Coast 1.97, Luxembourg 1.92, Australia 1.91, Nigeria 1.81 (1950), Belgian Congo 1.76, and Bulgaria 1.65 (1947). The middle group with R/S ratios between 1.60 and 1.01 included the remaining nineteen countries: Iceland 1.57 (1950), China 1.50 (1947), Egypt 1.47, Brazil 1.43

(1948), India 1.42, Sweden 1.34, Lebanon and Syria 1.31 (1950), Portugal 1.30, Czechoslovakia 1.30 (1946), Spain 1.28, French Morocco 1.26, Poland 1.24 (1948), Union of South Africa 1.21 (1949), Southern Rhodesia 1.20, Mexico 1.11, Norway 1.06, Indochina 1.04 (1950), Denmark 1.04 (1949), and Belgium 1.04.[12]

What do these figures mean? Since we know as yet so little about international communication flows, all interpretations must be quite provisional. Even so, some tentative inferences seem suggested.

1. The flows of outgoing and incoming foreign mail, and the imbalances between them, are remarkably stable from year to year in most countries, with the obvious exception of times of war or civil war. Changes tend to be greater in underdeveloped countries. Over longer periods of time, however, such as one or two decades, the cumulative changes are often considerable.

2. An appreciable imbalance between the amounts of foreign mail sent and received appears to be the rule. In the average of the 1928 and 1938 figures, such imbalances exceeded ten per cent in forty-two of the forty-eight states examined; and for twenty-eight of these states, the imbalances were larger than thirty per cent. About 1951, thirty-two of the forty-one countries for which we found data had imbalances greater than ten per cent, and twenty-two had imbalances larger than thirty per cent.

3. The number of countries receiving appreciably (i.e., by a difference of more than ten per cent) more mail than they are sending is much larger than the number of countries in the opposite condition.

4. It is conceivable that there might be some correlation between the excess of mail which a country habitually receives from abroad, and its position as an "importer" (rather than as an "exporter") of other kinds of communications. Whether this is true to any significant extent could only be established by further research.

From this brief look at some national intake-output ratios we may move on to consider another relationship between communication flows: the ratio between the flow of messages within a system—such as a country, or an organization—and the flow of messages across its boundaries.

THE RATIO OF INTERNAL TO
EXTERNAL FLOWS

The ratio of intra-boundary processes within any organization to cross-boundary processes originating or terminating in the same organization offers one basic operational measure for the cohesion of any such organization, as well as of the extent of its integration with others outside it.

Local to Non-Local Mail. In this manner, the ratio of local letters—that is,

[12]Sources of data: statistics of the Universal Postal Union, Bern, for the relevant years.

TABLE 8-1. RATIOS OF LOCAL TO NON-LOCAL MAIL IN 20 MAJOR U.S. CITIES

L/N RANK IN 1952	CITY	L/N RATIO IN 1952	1949
1	Atlanta	0.49	0.54
2	New York	0.50	0.54
3	Cincinnati	0.53	0.49
4	Kansas City	0.56	0.68
5	Minneapolis	0.58	0.53
6	Los Angeles	0.59	1.17
7	Brooklyn	0.63	0.71
8	Washington, D.C.	0.66	1.03
9	Chicago	0.73	1.10
10	San Francisco	0.78	0.89
11	Cleveland	0.87	1.16
12	Dallas	0.92	1.27
13	Pittsburgh	0.98	0.51
14	Philadelphia	0.98	1.03
15	Seattle	1.04	0.87
16	Boston	1.08	0.89
17	St. Louis	1.10	1.30
18	Detroit	1.12	1.19
19	Baltimore	1.29	1.18
20	Milwaukee	1.38	1.44

those originating and delivered in the same city (postal district)—to non-local letters (that is, letters originating in the city but delivered outside it) can tell us something about the normal level of integration between some of the large cities of the United States and the rest of the country.

The figures in Table 8-1 show that the ratio between local and non-local first class mail in New York City was 0.50 in 1952, and 0.54 in 1949. New Yorkers thus sent two letters to the rest of the United States for every letter they sent to someone in their own city. For twenty major cities in the United States, these L/N ratios—local versus non-local first class mail—ranged in 1952 from 0.49 for Atlanta to 1.38 for Milwaukee; and in 1949 from 0.49 for Cincinnati to 1.44 for Milwaukee. The median ratio was about 0.96 in 1949 and dropped slightly to about 0.89 in 1952, suggesting for the latter year a ratio of about nine local to ten non-local letters as somewhere near "normal" for a "normal" large city in the United States. The aggregate predominance of non-local mail was somewhat stronger, for the ratio between the aggregate local mail of those twenty cities and their aggregate non-local mail was 0.85 in 1949, and dropped to 0.73 in 1952, i.e., four non-local letters for every three local letters in the twenty cities taken together.

For the United States as a whole, the ratio of local to non-local mail has remained remarkably stable over almost a quarter century. It was 0.46 in 1928 and 0.45 in 1952, with only minor fluctuations in the non-war years between.[13]

[13]From data in the U.S. Post Office *Cost Ascertainment Reports* for 1928-1940, and 1949-52.

**TABLE 8-2. RATIOS OF NON-LOCAL TO FOREIGN MAIL FOR 20 MAJOR
U.S. CITIES, 1952 AND 1949**

GROUP	N/F RANK IN 1952	CITY	N/F RATIO IN 1952	1949
I. N/F Below 15:	1	Washington, D.C.	9.07	8.19
	2	New York	10.04	8.03
	3	Boston	10.38	12.15
	4	Brooklyn	11.81	11.73
	5	Chicago	13.37	11.39
II. N/F 15–25:	6	Detroit	15.08	15.23
	7	Cleveland	17.09	20.80
	8	Seattle	17.51	22.30
	9	Philadelphia	19.32	20.22
	10	Milwaukee	20.03	18.00
	11	San Francisco	21.25	19.97
	12	Los Angeles	23.45	15.02
III. N/F Above 25:	13	Baltimore	29.25	33.08
	14	St. Louis	30.69	21.37
	15	Minneapolis	40.04	38.15
	16	Cincinnati	47.13	42.25
	17	Pittsburgh	55.35	48.52
	18	Kansas City	57.28	44.95
	19	Dallas	95.33	76.86
	20	Atlanta	121.13	148.40

Non-Local to Foreign Mail. For each city, non-local mail sent to the rest of the United States exceeded greatly, of course, the amounts of mail sent to foreign countries, but there were some striking differences. The ratio of non-local to foreign mail—let us call it the N/F ratio—ranged in 1952 from 9.07 for Washington, D.C. to 121.13 for Atlanta, Georgia. More detailed data for twenty major cities in 1949 and 1952 are given in Table 8-2. They offer some interesting statistical sidelights to our usual intuitive judgments of the degree of "world involvement"—as against more local or national preoccupations—of the populations of each of these centers.

The series of N/F ratios for the twenty cities showed a slight increase in the N/F ratio from 1949 to 1952 for most individual cities, as well as slight increases in the average—from 31.8 to 32.2—and in the median—from 20.5 to 20.6—for the entire group. For the United States as a whole, however, and over a longer period of time, the ratio of non-local to foreign mail has increased considerably. Between the years 1928 and 1952, it grew from 35.77 to 46.79.[14]

Domestic versus Foreign Mail. An outstanding example of a ratio of internal to outside message flows is, of course, the ratio of domestic to foreign mail for a country as a whole. For the United States this ratio—let us call it the D/F ratio—

[14] From U.S. Post Office Department *Cost Ascertainment Reports* for the relevant years.

rose for first class mail from 58.09 in 1928 to a peacetime high of 86.39 in 1938, and again after the war from 76.31 in 1949 to 79.42 in 1952.[15]

By 1952, the United States had the highest D/F ratio of all the countries for which contemporary data were available. Earlier, in 1880, the United States with a D/F ratio of 25.6 had ranked third, after Japan and Hungary; and in 1913, when its D/F ratio had declined to an estimated level of about 21.7, it still ranked a close second after Japan.[16] The significance of the high D/F ratio of the United States in recent years, however, can only be appreciated against a background of comparisons with many other countries in the same terms.

Chart 8-1 shows the average D/F ratios for forty-six countries for the years 1946-51, plotted against an index that takes into account the geographic area A, population P, total letters L, and letters-per-capita L/P for each country. It seemed plausible that domestic mail should predominate more strongly over foreign, and hence the D/F ratio should be higher, the greater the geographic area of a country, the larger its population, and the higher its level of economic, social and cultural activity, as expressed, among other things, by a higher number of letters written per head of the population each year. The graph confirmed the surmise: the D/F ratios of the forty-six countries, when plotted on a logarithmic chart against a base AL^2/P, fell into a pattern that permitted the drawing of a regression line with the relatively high coefficient of correlation of 0.78.

Chart 8-1

$D/_F$ vs $\frac{AL^2}{P}$

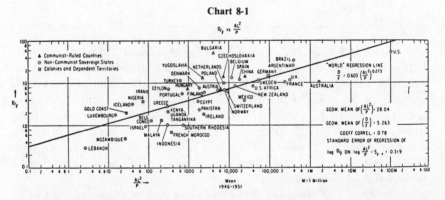

This means two things. First, if we know the geographic area, population, and average number of letters per capita of a country, we can predict—albeit only very roughly—its approximate D/F ratio. In the second place, we can use even the extent to which our prediction will prove wrong for some particular country. For the distance of any country on this chart from the regression line, common

[15] From figures in U.S. Post Office Department *Cost Ascertainment Reports* for the years 1928-40, and 1948-52. D consisted of total first class domestic mail plus domestic air mail. F comprised total foreign surface and air mail minus publishers' second class mail.

[16] From data in Universal Postal Union, *Statistique générale du service postal*, 1875-79, and later years.

to the group of all countries, indicates some particular condition in respect to which this country differs so significantly from the rest that its D/F ratio is much larger, or much smaller, than would ordinarily correspond to its size, population, and level of letter writing. Thus the countries furthest below the regression line of Chart 8-1 are either colonies, such as Mozambique, or recent ex-colonial territories such as Southern Rhodesia or Indonesia; or they are small countries with some special relationship to large numbers of compatriots or co-religionists abroad, such as Lebanon, Israel, and Ireland. On the other hand, countries with D/F ratios far above "normal," as represented by the regression line, often turn out to be Communist dictatorships, such as Bulgaria and Yugo-slavia, or at least fairly large and still partly underdeveloped countries with strongly nationalistic trends in government and policies, as well as in economic and cultural life, such as Turkey, Iran, and Brazil. These correlations are not air-tight, to be sure, but neither do they seem entirely fortuitous.

Chart 8-2

1936-39 $D/_F$ vs $\frac{AL^2}{P}$ FOR COUNTRIES FOR WHICH THE 1946-51 DATA IS NOT AVAILABLE

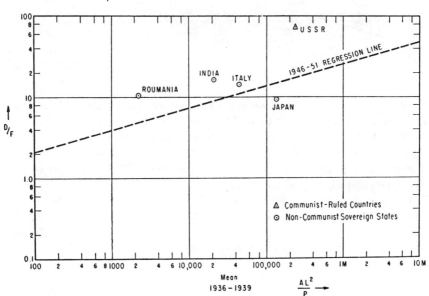

No D/F data for Roumania, India, the USSR, Italy, and Japan were available for the 1946-51 period, but their D/F ratios for 1936-39, as shown on Chart 8-2, would place the first three of these countries well above the regression line of the forty-six countries of 1946-51. The D/F ratio of Italy, by the same token, would appear close to "normal," and that of Japan would appear somewhat below the line. The extreme position of the USSR deserves a special comment. Its 1936 D/F ratio of 96 seems to represent the world's record to date in postal isolationism.

But may it not have been just an accident that the D/F ratios of forty-six countries in 1946–51 appeared to group themselves along a common regression line with such relative regularity? Chart 8–3 shows the corresponding data for forty-seven countries for the period 1928–34. Their average D/F ratios, as shown on the same logarithmic chart, again formed a relatively regular pattern against the same area-population-letter-writing index (AL^2/P), with a coefficient of correlation of 0.80. The greatest downward deviations were again found in the cases of dependent territories, such as Mozambique, French Morocco, Southern Rhodesia, and the Belgian Congo, but Japan in that period appeared well above the line.

Chart 8-3

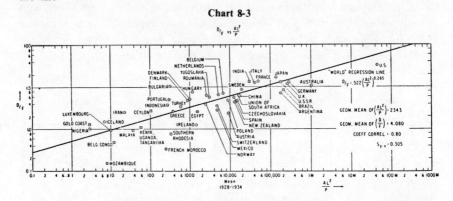

The same charting method was applied to the twenty-nine countries for which we found data for the year 1913. Their D/F ratios for that year are shown on Chart 8–4; their coefficient of correlation is 0.83. Finally, we charted on Chart 8–5 the D/F ratios for 1880 for the twenty-five countries for which we had data. For that period, the correlation was much weaker, with a coefficient of only 0.46, but still perhaps not insignificant.

The regression line itself—the "normal" standard for the D/F ratio of each country in comparison to other countries—has been shifting, albeit only slightly, from each period to the next. What has been the direction of these shifts, and what meaning, if any, can we infer from them?

Chart 8-4

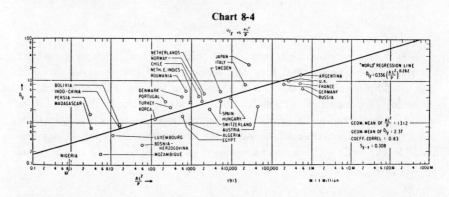

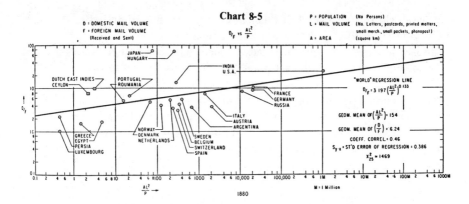

Chart 8-6 shows the four regression lines for the situations 1880, 1913, 1928-34, and 1946-51. Each of these lines represents, more or less approximately, the distribution of the D/F ratios of somewhere between two and four dozen countries. The chart shows that the regression line dropped considerably from 1880 to 1913, but became more steeply tilted. It then shifted again upwards from 1913 to 1928-34, while retaining its new tilt; and it shifted further upward, still keeping its tilt, from 1928-34 to 1946-51. Correspondingly, the "normal" level of the D/F ratio for a country of given size, and given activity in regard to mail communication, seems to have declined from 1880 to 1913, and to have risen again from 1913 to 1951.

At the same time, the average size and activity of these countries themselves

Chart 8-6

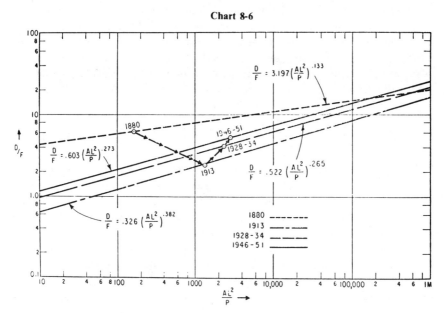

VARIATION OF WORLD REGRESSION LINES WITH TIME

changed, shifting almost all of them to the right from each period to the next. The combined effects of increasing size and activity, and of changing levels of national self-preoccupation in regard to mails have been summarized on Chart 8-6 by indicating on each regression line the geometric mean of the D/F and AL^2/P values for all countries from which this particular regression line was derived. The vectors linking the four geometric means for 1880, 1913, 1928-34 and 1946-51 thus represent an extremely simplified summary of the way the world has been going, in terms of relative time and attention available to foreign mail communications, as compared to domestic ones, during the last seventy years.

SOME PROBLEMS OF INTERPRETATION

Are there other processes of communication, or other kinds of transactions between regions or countries for which I/O rates between the relative frequencies of internal and outside events can be found? If so, how do these I/O rates compare to the ratios of inside to outside mail, such as the L/N ratios of local to non-local mail, or the D/F ratios of domestic mail to foreign? And what inferences, if any, could such comparisons suggest?

Detailed answers to these questions would go far beyond the framework of this chapter. All that can be attempted here are a few brief indications of some I/O ratios found in diverse kinds of communication or transaction flows, and some tentative inferences they might suggest for possible testing.

Travel is a process both of transport and communication, since every traveler carries in his person a considerable range of messages and memories, many of which he eventually communicates to other persons en route or after his arrival. Data for a number of states or regions in the United States concerning the ratio of passengers carried in 1933 by all public carriers within a particular state, as against the number of such passengers carried between the same state and the rest of the United States, are shown in Table 8-3.

It appears that ten of the twelve states for which data were computed had I/O ratios between 1 and 4; only two states on the West Coast—Washington and California—had higher rates, the latter considerably so.

Another way in which experiences are communicated between countries or regions is the movement of students who cross their boundaries in search of higher education. In the United States in 1949-50, the overall I/O ratio for college students—that is, the ratio of the number of students attending college in their home state to the number of students going out of their home state in order to study elsewhere in the United States, plus the number of students from elsewhere in the United States but attending institutions in the same state— ranged from 0.67 for New Jersey and 0.82 for Rhode Island to 5.7 for Texas and 6.1 for California. Table 8-4 presents I/O student ratios for the same twelve

TABLE 8-3. RATIOS OF INTRA-STATE TO INTERSTATE PASSENGER
TRAFFIC FOR 12 STATES IN THE UNITED STATES IN 1933
TRAFFIC RATIOS: STATE/U.S. MINUS STATE

ALL CARRIERS			RAILROADS ONLY		
Rank	State	St/U Ratio	Rank	State	St/U Ratio
1	Illinois	1.23	1	Ohio	0.85
2	Missouri	1.27	2	Missouri	0.93
3	New York	1.66	3	Illinois	1.00
4	Tennessee	1.70	4	New York	1.64
5	Louisiana	1.78	5	Louisiana	1.80
6	Georgia	2.20	6	Washington	1.84
7	Virginia	2.36	7	Tennessee	1.93
8	Ohio	2.48	8	Pennsylvania	2.00
9	Pennsylvania	2.96	9	Virginia	2.31
10	Massachusetts	3.57	10	Georgia	2.95
11	Washington	5.24	11	Massachusetts	3.71
12	California	18.57	12	California	18.97

TABLE 8-4. RATIO OF STUDENTS ATTENDING COLLEGES AND UNIVERSITIES
IN THEIR OWN STATES OF RESIDENCE VS. STUDENTS ATTENDING COLLEGES
AND UNIVERSITIES IN OTHER STATES OF THE U.S. FOR 16 STATES IN 1949/50

RANK	STATE	H/M RATIO
1	New Jersey	0.7
2	Rhode Island	0.8
3	Delaware	0.96
4	Virginia	0.98
5	Massachusetts	1.3
6	Missouri	1.6
7	Tennesse	1.7
8	Illinois	1.93
9	Pennsylvania	1.94
10	Georgia	2.2
11	New York	2.4
12	Ohio	2.8
13	Louisiana	3.0
14	Washington	3.3
15	Texas	5.7
16	California	6.1

(H/M Ratio = Ratio of Home State Students to Migrating Studies, i.e. Ratio of Number of
Students Attending Home State Institutions vs. Number of Home State Students Studying
at Out-of-State Institutions plus Number of Out-of-State Students Attending Institutions
Within State.)

states, for which I/O ratios for passenger traffic were given in Table 8–3. Six states have similar ranks on both tables: California, Washington, Ohio, Georgia, Tennessee and Missouri, but others for obvious reasons show striking differences, such as Massachusetts, Virginia, Louisiana and New York. For an ideal "average state," the I/O ratio of students in 1949/50 should have been 2.0, for about eighty per cent of all American students in that year attended institutions in their home states.

"The proportion of *graduate* students who migrate tends to be larger than that of the college population as a whole. About seventy-one per cent of all graduate students remained within their own states to pursue advanced programs."[17] This would correspond to an I/O graduate student ratio of about 1.2 for the "average state"; the I/O undergraduate student ratio for the "average" state is about 2.1. "The unchanging percentages of students who migrate (as shown in this and the two previous studies [of 1930–31 and 1938–39, respectively]) indicate that stability is being reached with respect to the percentage of students who seek their higher education in out-of-state institutions. While the factor of facility of transportation tends to increase migration, this factor is evidently offset by the expansion of higher educational facilities into local areas."[18]

As regards other kinds of migration, not just that of college students, United States censuses for the last hundred years have shown that somewhere near thirty per cent of Americans have been living in states other than those in which they were born, so that the theoretical "average state" has had an I/O ratio of intra-U.S. migration of about 1.2. This would contrast with corresponding I/O ratios for the sovereign states of Western Europe, which as a rule would be certain to lie well above 10, if we took the trouble to compute them. So would, presumably, the international I/O ratios for students in most countries. For the United States in 1949/50 it was well above 45, since foreign students then comprised 1.1 per cent of the total student population,[19] and the number of American students studying abroad in that year was certainly not larger.

The two orders of magnitude of such I/O ratios—below, say, 6 and above, say, 10—thus illustrate perhaps some aspects of the difference between certain levels of communication among communities or states that are more or less integrated in a common country or federal union, and among those that are not. Thus the I/O rate of migration for Scotland in 1951 seems to have been somewhat below

[17]Robert C. Story, *Residence and Migration of College Students, 1949–50* (Washington D.C.: Federal Security Agency, Office of Education, 1951), p. 13. Italics supplied.
[18]*Ibid.* Cf. also Fred J. Kelly and Ruth E. Eckert, *Residence and Migration of College Students*, Washington, U.S. Government Printing Office, 1945 (Federal Security Agency, U.S. Office of Education, Pamphlet No. 98), p. 5; F. J. Kelly and Betty A. Patterson, *Residence and Migration of College Students*, Washington, U.S. Government Printing Office, 1934 (Department of the Interior, Office of Education, Pamphlet No. 48); George F. Zook, *Residence and Migration of University and College Students*, Washington, U.S. Government Printing Office, 1926 (Department of the Interior, Bureau of Education, Bulletin 1926, No. 11).
[19]Story, *op. cit.*, p. 9.

4.9.[20] Similarly, the I/O rate of Swiss citizens in the theoretical "average canton" in Switzerland was 4.8 in 1860, and it fell to 2.3 by 1930.[21]

Inside-outside ratios of communication or transaction flows can also suggest something about the extent to which some particular human activity, such as science, is "international" or "national," and in what direction, if any, it may be changing. Thus a survey of samples of leading American scientific journals in seven fields showed that on the average they contained in the 1890's about two citations of foreign scientific work for every citation from an American author. By 1954, the proportions had become more than reversed: there were almost three references to work published in the United States for every reference to scientific work in the rest of the world. A survey of the I/O ratio of scientific contributions—that is, of American versus foreign contributions summarized in *Chemical Abstracts*, and of American versus foreign Nobel prize winners—showed a closely parallel increase during the same sixty years. The American I/O ratio of scientific citations in the 1890's was roughly four times the I/O ratio of contributions of that time; and the same habit of seeing national contributions loom four times as large in the area of citations than they did in the area of actual contributions seemed to persist without significant change in 1954. Even in the latter year, however, the average I/O ratio of American versus foreign citations in the American scientific journals surveyed remained below three, indicating perhaps the somewhat diminished but still continuing international traditions of scientific work.[22]

Most of the work on the measurement of international communication flows is yet to be done. Taken together, however, even the few scattered data now available could begin to give us a somewhat better understanding of some aspects of the integration or consolidation of communities, countries, or other kinds of organizations. Generally, if a community, country, or organization is small relative to the larger organization or group of organizations with which it is in communication, then we might tentatively call it "highly integrated" if the I/O

[20] In rounded figures the population of Scotland in 1951 was 5,096,000, of which 406,000 were born outside Scotland; at the same time, according to D. J. Robertson, "there were 560,000 Scots living in England." The ratio of the 4,690,000 Scottish-born residents of Scotland to the sum of non-Scottish-born Scots and of Scottish-born residents of England was about 4.9, and this does not take into account the numbers of born Scotsmen who had migrated to other countries than England. Cf. D. J. Robertson, "Population Growth and Movement," in A. K. Cairncross, *The Scottish Economy: A Statistical Account of Scottish Life by Members of the Staff of Glasgow University*, Cambridge (Eng.), University Press, 1954, pp. 12, 16–17.

[21] In 1860, 86.4 per cent of the Swiss lived in their Cantons of origin, while nine per cent lived in other Cantons, and 4.6 were foreigners; in 1930, only sixty-four per cent of the Swiss lived in their native Cantons, while 27.3 per cent lived in others, and there were 8.7 per cent foreigners. This last group, of course, does not enter into this particular calculation. Cf. the data in George Sauser-Hall, *The Political Institutions of Switzerland*, Zurich and New York, Swiss National Tourist Office Publishing Department, 1946, p. 15.

[22] K. W. Deutsch, George Klein, J. J. Baker, and associates, *Is American Attention to Foreign Research Results Declining?*, Massachusetts Institute of Technology, 1954, multigraphed.

ratio of the smaller unit was below 1.5. We might tentatively consider the extent of integration "fair to high," if the I/O ratio was between 1 and 3; "fair," if it was between 3 and 6: "low to fair," if it was between 6 and 10; "low," if it was between 10 and 15; and "extremely low," if it was above 15. Conversely, reading this extremely tentative scale from the opposite end, we might use it to aid us in forming and checking some judgments of the degree of "autonomy," or "relative self-sufficiency," or "self-preoccupation" which we might be trying to study in some particular organization or social group.

To be sure, this scale will have to be changed, if the relative size of an organization or region increases vis-à-vis its relevant environment. For a very large region, even an I/O ratio between 10 and 15 may be quite compatible with a high degree of integration with its environment. Furthermore, the meaning of any such scale of I/O ratios is likely to differ significantly for different kinds of communications or transactions. All this, however, still leaves us with the surmise that there may be some verifiable and useful scales of social or organizational integration in terms of relative communication flow, and that it may be up to us to find them.

9 | A Generalized Concept of Effective Distance and Political Development

Until now this particular approach to research on the possible aspects of political and social integration does not seem to have been followed up. A related aspect has been continued on a larger scale. It consists of a matrix approach toward measuring the improbably high or low frequency of transactions, such as trade or communication, between two countries or provinces as an indicator of trends toward integration or secession between them; and references to more recent literature are given here.*

Distance is usually conceived of as geographic distance in terms of miles and is used accordingly for mapping, for flight computations, and related purposes. Economists use a more sophisticated concept of "economic distance," which is measured in terms of transport cost,[1] for analysis of location and space. The economic distance between two points is then the cost of transporting a commodity from one to the other. Since effective transport rates differ from commodity to commodity, the resulting computations of economic distance differ for each commodity. Writers such as Chauncy Harris have tried, however, to construct an average transport cost for an aggregate class of commodity flows.[2]

Similarly, more-or-less sophisticated notions of distance apply to communications. The telephone distance between two places is not always the distance as the crow flies, but may involve the shortest distance in the network of available telephone lines. It may have to be weighted not only by a cost factor, such as the rate set by the telephone company, but also for expected delays and frequency overloads.

Sociologists have used a concept of "social distance" emphasizing the interac-

*See K. W. Deutsch, "Toward an Inventory of Basic Trends and Patterns," *The American Political Science Review* 54 (March 1960); 34–57).

[1] See Walter Isard, *Location and Space-Economy* (New York: Wiley, 1956; Cambridge, Mass.: MIT Press, 1960).

[2] See C. D. Harris, "The Market as a Factor in the Localization of Industry in the United States," *Annals of the Association of American Geographers,* 44 (1954).

The substance of this chapter appeared as "A Note on a Generalized Concept of Effective Distance," by Karl W. Deutsch and Walter Isard, *Behavioral Science* 6 (October 1961): 308–311. Reprinted by permission of the Publisher.

tion among members of similar or different social groups or cultures. "For example, the analyst thinking in terms of social distance recognizes that the Puerto Rican who migrates to New York is, from a social distance standpoint, migrating to the closest location of significance to him."[3] Some sociologists have used the concept of intervening opportunities to amalgamate economic and social distance. Other sociologists have attempted to measure the possibility of interactions and of friendly relations between ethnic and racial groups by constructing a "social distance scale," based upon interview materials and responses to questionnaires.[4]

A number of social scientists have tried to trace the effects of distance on the frequency of a given kind of transaction (interchange, interrelations, etc.) between actors. The most frequent relation that has been asserted resembles the well-known mutual energy concept of gravitational (Newtonian) physics. The frequency of transactions, it has often been suggested, ought to be directly proportional to the product of the masses of the two actors and inversely proportional to the distance, d, separating these actors. The simplest formula for predicting transactions between two spatially separated actors or categories is thus

$$G \frac{M_i M_j}{d_{ij}}.$$

Here G is a constant, and M_i and M_j represent the two masses, d_{ij} being the intervening distance. M_i and M_j may refer to the population of two cities, or to the incomes of two cities (or of two groups of actors, or simply two individuals), or to telephone installations of two metropolitan areas, or other relevant political, economic, and social magnitudes.

Slightly more complicated models would raise d_{ij} to a power other than unity, such as two, or even consider the exponent of d_{ij} as a variable. Other models might (1) weight the masses by a simple measure (such as the average number of years of schooling), or by an index constructed from several properly weighted measures; and (2) raise each mass itself to a constant or even variable power.[5]

---

[3] Isard, op. cit., p. 542.

[4] See E. S. Bogardus, "A Social Distance Scale," Sociology and Social Research, 17 (1933): 265–271: Isard, op. cit., pp. 506, 542–544; O. Klineberg, Tensions Affecting International Understanding (New York: Social Science Research Council, 1950), p. 135.

[5] The most rigorous form of the relation indicating interaction, I_{ij}, between i and j is:

$$I_{ij} = G \frac{w_i (P_i)^\alpha \cdot w_j (P_j)^\beta}{d^b{}_{ij}}$$

where w_i and w_j are the weights applied to the respective masses, where α and β are exponents applied to the respective masses, and where b is the exponent (constant or variable) applied to distance. For a discussion of such formulas, see Isard (1960, p. 493–566). The formula cited is on page 510; a survey of the literature is given on pages 566–568.

Finally, they may even employ a different mathematical formulation than the above to encompass the attenuating influence of distance. It seems clear, however, that the different ways of defining and computing distance will have an effect on the attempts to predict the volume of a given kind of transaction for a given pair of actors.

One of the purposes of the present paper is to suggest that it might be worth-while to invert the implied computational procedure, and by so doing overcome the difficulty of accounting separately for the many different economic, social, and political factors bearing upon the concept of distance. For example, suppose we view the flow of economic transactions, T_{ij}, as the prime indicator of inter-action, and initially employ the simplest model, namely,

$$T_{ij} = G \frac{M_i M_j}{d_{ij}}.$$

Hence,

$$d_{ij} = G \frac{M_1 M_2}{T_{ij}}.$$

If transactions depended on some power b of the distance then

$$T_{ij} = G \frac{M_1 M_2}{d^b_{ij}}$$

and

$$d_{ij} = G \frac{M_1 M_2}{T^{\frac{1}{b}}_{ij}}$$

or

$$\log d_{ij} = \log G + \log M_1 + \log M_2$$
$$- \frac{1}{b} \log T_{ij}.$$

Then, if relevant characteristics of populations (actors) and volume of given transaction flows are available, it ought to be possible to use these known data to make a first approximation of the effective distance between the two actors or actor categories. The old procedure takes the estimate of distance as given and treats the transaction flow as the unknown to be found. The method proposed here treats past data about transaction flows and known data for the relevant populations as given, in order to determine what the effective value of distance between the actors may have been for the period in question.[6] It is explicitly taken for granted that the two variables, transaction flows and population characteristics of each of the actors, can be established independently by standard methods.

The resulting value for effective distance between any two actor categories, however imperfect this value may be, does obviate the difficulty of obtaining standardized methods, theoretically satisfying to the different social science disciplines and investigators, which will reflect approximately the relative significance of transport costs, cultural affinity, political bonds, legal channels, credit availability, and the host of other factors relevant for the definition of distance. In essence, our procedure may be viewed as yielding an estimate of "effective distance" as some weighted average of many component elements where it is fully recognized that different weightings of the elements can give the same average result; and it is only this average result which the proposed method of computation would measure. The determination of the basic component elements and their proper weights still would wait upon major theoretical advances in the several social sciences.

Mathematically put, we define the effective distance d_{ij} between actor categories (places) i and j as:

$$d_{ij} = x_{ij} \cdot w_{ij}$$

Here x_{ij} is a vector in n dimensional space. Each component of this vector measures one aspect of distance; e.g., the first one may be said to measure physical distance; the second one, to measure economic (transport cost) distance; the third one, to measure political distance as indicated by quotas and other trade restrictions; the fourth one, social distance as measured by attendance at certain meetings, etc. Also, w_{ij} is a weight vector in n dimensional space, each of its components being a weight to be applied to the corresponding elements of x_{ij}. Thus, the first element of x_{ij} is to be multiplied by the first element of w_{ij}, the second by the second, and finally the nth by the nth. The value d_{ij} is obtained as the sum of the resulting n products. From this computation it is clear that in general many w_{ij} vectors can yield that value of d_{ij} which it is our purpose to estimate roughly from empirical study.

It is to be reiterated that our approach does recognize that the distance between two cities or two countries or two ethnic groups may, of course, be different for each different kind of transaction. It may turn out that the distance between Egypt and Syria in terms of international trade in 1951 was different

---

[6] On the general problem of distance for estimating the political, economic, and social relationships between actors, see Karl W. Deutsch, *Political Community at the International Level* (New York: Doubleday, 1954).

from the distance in terms of the exchange of letters between those two countries, and still another distance figure might result from a computation based on
the frequency of travel or migration.[7]

Inquiries of this kind might lead to a more critical view of the entire distance
concept. The naive notion of distance as expressed solely in miles assumed that
all these different operational definitions of distances would, for practical purposes, coincide. The same assumption was implied in the even older but slightly
less naive idea of measuring distance in terms of hours, or days of travel, which
implied a primitive sort of weight for different kinds of terrain. All these traditional measures suggested that the distances relevant for trade, for travel, for
intermarriage, for communication, or for military affairs all were somehow
related to each other. If two towns were neighbors in terms of one of these
transactions, it was thought that they were very likely to behave as neighbors in
all of them.

Whether modern countries do or do not behave in a similar way is precisely
one of the things that could be found out by applying the method proposed in
this chapter. Our suspicion is that they do not, and this question can be examined more meaningfully once we have measures of effective distance based upon
transaction data. We may find out, in other words, whether the English and
Irish, or Americans and Puerto Ricans, or Americans and Cubans, are as close to
each other in terms of trade as they are in terms of travel, or in terms of communication, or in terms of intermarriage, or in terms of their radio broadcasts
and newspapers.

As so often in social science, some of the most interesting results might appear
in the deviant cases, that is, cases of countries or groups that are very close in
some kinds of transactions but very distant in others. Colonies, for example,
might be much closer to the metropolitan country in economic than in geographic distance, but much farther in social distance as it applies to a significant
range of human relations. An analysis of such deviant cases might tell us something about possible situations worthy of particular attention.[8]

An obvious first working hypothesis to be tested would be that in the course
of the political development of a country the generalized distances within it
would tend on the average to decline. If the decline in generalized distance
would largely apply to rewarding transaction, any such integration could be considered a part of the successful political development of a new or previously

---

[7]This is a consideration quite different from the consideration of different weights
attached to distances in the earlier case discussed above in the text, where weights are
attached to transport costs, availability of credit, etc., all in terms of their effects on the
same transaction category of, say, trade. In the problem discussed now, we are dealing with
the different distances, the weighting of which may or may not have changed, for each different category of transactions.

[8]On the general utility of deviant case analysis, see Paul F. Lazarsfeld and Morris Rosenberg, eds., *The Language of Social Research* (New York: Free Press, 1955).

existing political unit. If a decline in general distance should apply on the average mainly to conflict-promoting transactions, rewarding to one party but often penalizing or frustrating to another, then it may tend to lead to attempts at economic protectionism, increased social or cultural barriers, or politcal secession, and thus in any case to a restoration of a larger and less stressful distance between the parties concerned.

III | *Integration: Some Recent and Contemporary Cases*

10 | Large and Small States in Regional Integration

This chapter was written in 1955 and presented in that year at the World Congress of Political Science in Stockholm, but it has not been published until now in the United States. It is printed here with only minor corrections and additions. The conclusions as to which conditions and policies might tend to help integration, and which ones might hinder it, are those of 1955. They may suggest how much or how little about the problems of Western European integration in the late 1970s could be foreseen from the evidence available in the mid-1950s.

Research on some of the questions touched upon in this chapter has been continued by many scholars. Some of its results have been published in such works as K. W. Deutsch, S. A. Burrell, et al., *Political Community and the North Atlantic Area* (Princeton: Princeton University Press, 1957, 1968); R. Lindgren, *Norway-Sweden: Union, Disunion and Scandinavian Integration* (Princeton: Princeton University Press, 1959); R. A. Kann, *The Habsburg Empire* (New York: Praeger, 1957); B. M. Russett, *Community and Contention: Britain and America in the Twentieth Century* (Cambridge, Mass.: M.I.T. Press, 1963); W. J. Foltz, *From French West Africa to the Mali Federation* (New Haven: Yale University Press, 1965); R. L. Merritt, *Symbols of American Community, 1735-1775* (New Haven: Yale University Press, 1966); K. W. Deutsch, L. J. Edinger, R. C. Macridis, and R. L. Merritt, *France, Germany and the Western Alliance* (New York: Scribner, 1967); G. Schweigler, *National Consciousness in Divided Germany* (Beverly Hills and London: Sage Publications, 1975); and P. Katzenstein, *Disjoined Partners: Austria and Germany since 1815* (Berkeley: University of California Press, 1976).

Some of the results of this research have been taken into account in a more recent summary, presented in Chapter 15, below.

This chapter can only offer some tentative and limited data on a particular sector of the broad problem of large and small states in international relations. The research from which it is derived dealt only with a number of specific

A German version of this chapter was published in Abraham Ashkenasi and Peter Schulze, eds. *Nationenbilding-Nationalstaat-Integration* (Düsseldorf: Bertelsmann, 1973), pp. 72-93. Reprinted by permission of the Publisher.

regions and specific historical experiences, even though these were chosen with
the hope that they might serve as samples for more general aspects of a political
process of integration which might interest political scientists in the fields both
of comparative politics and international organization.

THE BACKGROUND OF THIS RESEARCH:
CASE STUDIES OF REGIONAL
POLITICAL INTEGRATION

The study on which most of this chapter is based was begun in 1951 at the
Center for Research on World Political Institutions at Princeton University.
The purpose of the Center, in the words of its director, Richard Van Wagenen,
is "to promote the study of problems of international organization as they
apply to the eventual elimination of the institution called 'war'."[1] After a
survey of contemporary research, the Center adopted as a major focus for its
own work the problem of the expansion of political community to a larger scale,
so as to include several smaller and potentially hostile communities, such as
states or peoples, within a larger political community in which war would be
eliminated.[2]

It follows that we were interested in the relations only between those states or
peoples which already formed a larger political community in the sense that the
leaders of each state might look upon the others either as allies or rivals, that is,
they could not afford to ignore each others' actions. Each government or political elite had to consider the behavior of the others as highly relevant for the
making of its own decisions. From this viewpoint one could in general define
any political community as the set of individuals or groups—such as states—
which is linked by the mutual relevance of their behavior for political decision-
making.[3]

Within this broad class of political community, however, we were interested in
a still more special division. We looked for the particular kind of political community within which the expectation of warfare had been abolished, together
with all specific preparations for it. We call this a *security community*. Our
study then dealt with some historical examples of the establishment or dissolution of a security community in a particular geographic region, in the hope
that something might be learned from these regional experiences which might be
helpful for the establishment and preservation of wider ones in other regions,

[1] Richard Van Wagenen, "Political Community: Historical Experience and Contemporary
Problems of International Organization—Preliminary Findings," draft prepared for Panel 29
of the Annual Meeting of the American Political Science Association, Boulder, Colorado,
1955, mimeographed, p. 5.

[2] See Richard Van Wagenen, *Research in the International Organization Field: Some Notes
on a Possible Focus* (Princeton; 1952).

[3] See Quincy Wright, *The Study of International Relations* (New York, 1955), pp. 268–
300, 565–567.

and perhaps eventually of a worldwide one. Its findings, we hoped, might bear at a number of points on the role of large and small states in the building of a security community that eventually is to include both.

Whether a security community exists among two or more states (or countries, or peoples) can be tested in several ways. One test might be made in terms of the subjective opinions of the political decision-makers, or the politically relevant social strata, in each country. These could be sampled or surveyed by well-known methods of studying public opinion.[4] Do they generally believe that a firm political consensus exists throughout the wider community? Do they think that peaceful change within this wider group has become assured with reasonable certainty for a long period of time?[5]

Another test would be essentially objective and operational. It would replace the recording of opinions with measurement of tangible commitments, and of resource allocations people make to back them up. What specific preparations are made for the possibility of war against any other group within the wider community? Are a certain number of troops maintained and indoctrinated? Are fortifications and other strategic facilities built and kept up? Are these preparations in the nature of general national defense? Or do they suggest that war against some particular political unit—a state, a people, or a country—is considered a practical possibility? If there is such an allocation of resources for war against a particular opponent, some other kind of political community, but not a security community, may exist between the two political units in question.

The tests by opinions and by allocations should usually coincide in their results, but they may differ in marginal cases. A war between two states may still be considered possible by some of their leaders, even though no specific preparations for it are made by either side. Or routine preparations for defense of a border may continue even though conflict across it may already seem unthinkable. Even in such rare instances, however, the achievement of a security community involves something like the crossing of a threshhold, from a situation where war between the two political units appears possible and is being prepared for, to another situation where it is neither. The crossing of this threshhold, and with it the establishment of a security community, we have called *integration;* it is in this sense that the term is used in this chapter.[6]

---

[4] For some developments in the field of opinion research as applied to international relations, see Quincy Wright, "Criteria for Judging the Relevance of Researches on the Problems of Peace," in Q. Wright, W. F. Cottrell, C. Boasson and I. Gullvåg. *Research for Peace* (Oslo: North-Holland Publishing Co., 1954), pp. 3–94, esp. pp. 15–18. See also W. B. Buchanan and Hadley Cantrill, *How Nations See Each Other* (Urbana: University of Illinois Press, 1953); Otto Klineberg, *Tensions Affecting International Understanding* (New York, 1950); Harold D. Lasswell, *The World Revolution of Our Time: A Framework for Basic Policy Research* (Stanford: Stanford University Press, 1951); Ithiel de Sola Pool, *Symbols of Internationalism* (Stanford: Stanford University Press, 1951), and *idem, The Prestige Papers* (Stanford: Stanford University Press, 1952), International Press Institute, *The Flow of the News* (Zurich, 1953).

[5] Van Wagenen, *Research, op. cit.,* pp. 10–11.

[6] Members of a security community may, of course, continue to expect the possibility of war against outsiders and continue to prepare for it. For a fuller discussion of integration,

We further distinguished two types of security community. One was the *amalgamated* security community, with a single government and a single sovereignty, such as the United Kingdom or the United States of America. The other was the *pluralistic* security community, which includes more than one sovereign government, not merged, such as Norway and Sweden after 1907 or the United States and Canada after 1819.

In order to study the conditions and policies favorable to the establishment of a security community, and to its maintenance against disruption, we concentrated on eight major cases from the Western world, each of which had come to some climax in recent times. Five of those cases led to the establishment of an amalgamated security community, one to a pluralistic security community after a previous failure of amalgamation, and in two cases amalgamation as well as integration broke down more or less indefinitely. Each case was studied by a competent historian especially interested in the area, according to a common plan of inquiry. The cases and historians were: England, Scotland, Ireland, and some attention to Wales, Sidney Burrell; United States, Martin Lichterman; Switzerland, Herman Weilenmann; Italy, Maurice Lee; Germany, Francis Loewenheim; Austria-Hungary, Robert A. Kann; Norway-Sweden, Raymond Lindgren.

To this group of historians were added two political scientists. The author was given the task of providing a comparative analysis of the data obtained and of drafting a volume summarizing the study and its findings. Richard Van Wagenen undertook to draft a final chapter applying the findings to contemporary problems of international organization.[7]

Some tentative findings of the joint study, as they bear upon the role of large and small states in the attainment of a security community, amalgamated or pluralistic, are presented here. It should be remembered that all the communities studied were regional; experiences from them may or may not be relevant to the strengthening of wider international organizations such as the United Nations. However, our cases do reach to some extent into the field of international organization. For as a political community becomes more fully amalgamated, its constituent political units cease to be sovereign states, or even states at all, and political relations among them turn into domestic politics involving merely different provinces, countries, or peoples. As amalgamation is lost, on the contrary, domestic relations between such smaller units may again become international. Our results, therefore, pertain to the whole process of political integration or disintegration, as well as amalgamation or secession. They pertain regardless of

---

security community, and related concepts, see Richard Van Wagenen, *Research, op. cit.,* pp. 10–21; and K. W. Deutsch, *Political Community at the International Level* (New York, 1954), pp. 33–34, 66. See also Quincy Wright, ed., *The World Community* (Chicago, 1948), *passim,* and *idem, Study of International Relations, op. cit.,* pp. 540–543.

[7]A full account of the preliminary results of the project's research undertakings can be found in K. W. Deutsch *et al., Political Community and the North Atlantic Area* (Princeton, 1957, 1968, and New York: Greenwood Press, 1969).

how often the process may cross and recross the boundary between domestic politics and international relations.[8]

LARGE STATES AS CORES OF INTEGRATION

In all the cases studied, the relatively large states or large political units were found to play the decisive role. It was they that furnished the core areas for most of the security communities which developed. The development of their political and economic capabilities was decisive for the integration of each larger community; their responsiveness and adaptability to the needs and values of the various smaller units was decisive for its preservation. Proposals for amalgamation sometimes originated in smaller states and were occasionally backed by their leaders, but it was the commitment of the government of a large state, or a substantial part of its political elite, that in each case set off the effective drive toward partial or general amalgamation of their governmental institutions.

The role of England in the integration of Wales, Scotland, and Northern Ireland is a case in point. So is its role in the establishment of an unsuccessful union with Ireland, which ended in the war of 1918-1921. Other cases are the decisive roles of Piedmont and Prussia in the unification of Italy (1859-1860)·and Germany (1834-1871), respectively; the role of the four largest states, Virginia, Pennsylvania, New York, and Massachusetts, in the establishment of the United States; and the powerful initiative of Sweden in establishing the transitory Norwegian-Swedish Union of 1814 to 1905.

In some of our cases, the core areas were themselves composites, created by the amalgamation or alliance of smaller political units. Thus the core area of the Habsburg monarchy was created by the close association of the several Austrian "hereditary countries," or "Alpine countries," in the fourteenth and fifteenth centuries, which furnished the base for the later acquisition of Bohemia, Hungary, and other territories, and which remained the mainstay of Habsburg power and loyalty to the monarchy until the dissolution of the latter in 1918. The Swiss political community was created around a double core. The alliance of the three original small cantons of Uri, Schwyz, and Unterwalden came to constitute a fairly strong core of power and of economic and political attraction. The other part of the double core was the city state of Bern, which was the largest well-organized political unit in the area, as well as the core of a small alliance in its region.

Together, our data suggest that wider political communities have been built and integrated primarily around the cores of political and economic strength,

---

[8] See the valuable conception by Carl J. Friedrich of "federalism as a process" in his essay "Federal Constitutional Theory and Emergent Proposals," in Arthur W. Macmahon, ed., *Federalism: Mature and Emergent* (New York, 1955), pp. 510-533, esp. p. 519.

and of social or cultural attraction, provided by large states. The feelings of need or dissatisfaction of the inhabitants of smaller countries seem to have been secondary.

THE RELATIVITY OF THE LARGE STATE–SMALL STATE HIERARCHY

The cases we studied tend to confirm the statement of Professor Max Sørenson that "the relativity of the hierarchy of large and small states is essential."[9]

A few examples may suffice. On the eve of the American Revolution, Virginia was by far the largest of the American colonies in manpower and area, including claims to Western lands; Pennsylvania ranked first in industry and economic strength; Massachusetts was first in commerce and shipping; and New York, as subsequent events confirmed, was foremost in strategic location. Even the smallest state, Rhode Island, had considerable shipping. In the unification of Germany, Austria was the largest state of the German Confederation in terms of total area, manpower, and the numerical strength of its standing army. However, Prussia came to outrank Austria in terms of industrial and economic strength, in numbers of German-speaking population, and in administrative and military capabilities. Similarly, in the unification of Italy, the Kingdom of Naples and Sicily outranked Piedmont in terms of size and population, but was well behind it in industry, transport, literacy, and efficiency of administration. Both Naples and Piedmont were easily outranked by Tuscany, particularly Florence, in matters of cultural prestige. Likewise, Norway excelled its larger partner Sweden with regard to shipping and ties to England, as well as in urban development and popular participation in politics.

THE POTENTIAL ROLE OF SMALLER COUNTRIES IN PROMOTING MUTUAL ADJUSTMENTS AND RESPONSIVENESS AMONG LARGER STATES

As suggested above, states or countries form political communities only if their inhabitants are already engaged to a significant degree in mutual relations involving, as a rule, the possibility of frictions and conflicts. Indeed, if the load of such potential frictions and conflict situations grows faster than the capabilities for their peaceful adjustment on the part of the governments concerned, mounting tensions and eventual warfare are likely to result. Conversely,

[9]Max Sørenson, "Large and Small States in International Organization: Introductory Report," Third Congress, International Political Science Association, Stockholm, 1955, mimeographed, p. 3.

if attention to, and realistic perception of, mutual needs and adjustment all grow as fast or faster than the load of potential conflict situations, then a security community—amalgamated or at least pluralistic—seems the more likely outcome. In the race between conflict loads and adjustment capabilities small states, regions, or peoples can play a crucial role.

Smaller or weaker states may act so as to accelerate and sharpen a conflict among larger countries if they have come to consider it inevitable or desirable. A well-known example is the behavior of the governments of Serbia and of Austria-Hungary in 1914, during the critical weeks and months preceding World War I. In the cases we studied we found some instances of similar behavior on the part of minority peoples who possessed effective political organizations but fell short of sovereignty. Thus the small group of Protestants in Northern Ireland—the "Ulstermen"— opposed rather effectively until 1918 any Anglo-Irish compromise likely to be accepted by the two main groups concerned. This traditional policy of intransigence has left its mark on the behavior of the government and politics of Northern Ireland to this day.

Another and still more tragic example is the remarkable role played by the political elite of a large part of the German minority in Bohemia, who sharpened the conflict between Germans and Czechs in the Austro-Hungarian monarchy. They opposed all attempts at compromise advanced by Austrian governments at Vienna, from the days of the cabinets of Hohenwart and Badeni until the last years of the monarchy. This extreme attitude revived in the striking popularity of the Hitler movement among the Sudeten Germans in the 1930s. In the case of Northern Ireland, the Ulster policy of superpartisanship was followed by the secession of the Republic of Ireland, comprising all but six counties of the island, from the British Commonwealth, and, one may add in 1977, by the rise and persistence in the 1960s and 1970s of militant and violent movement among the strong Roman Catholic minority in Northern Ireland. In the case of Bohemia, a similar but still more extreme partisan policy was followed by the Nazi occupation of Bohemia. This brought a fatal deepening of Czech-German antagonism, and the eventual explusion of the great majority of the Sudeten Germans from their homes.[10]

On the other hand, small states or peoples and their leaders can exercise considerable influence toward improving relations between their larger neighbors. They can suggest creative compromise solutions and explore ways of increasing the capabilities of the larger political units for mutual attention, adjustment, and responsiveness. Thus it was Wales and Scotland that furnished the leadership at critical steps toward the eventual English-Scottish union. A ruler of

[10] On the background of the Czech-German case, see Robert A. Kann, *The Multinational Empire: Nationalism and National Reform in the Habsburg Monarchy* (New York, 1950), Vol. I, pp. 55–58, 91–101, 151–152; Vol. II, p. 242; Elizabeth Wiskemann, *Czechs and Germans* (London, 1938), *passim;* Hugh Hantsch, *Die Nationalitätenfrage im alten Österreich: Das Problem der Konstruktiven Reichsgestaltung* (Vienna, 1953), pp. 60, 62; Otto Bauer, *Die Nationalitätenfrage und die Sozialdemokratie,* 2d ed. (Vienna, 1924), pp. 388–391.

Welsh background, Henry Tudor, acquired the English throne with Welsh help. As Henry VII he then arranged the marriage, in 1505, between his daughter Margaret Tudor and James IV of Scotland, which led to the dynastic union of the two countries.[11] A descendant of the marriage, James VI of Scotland, succeeded in 1603 to the English throne as James I. He introduced the style of the "Kingdom of Great Britain" and a union flag. He also secured an English legal decision in 1607 granting the right of English citizenship to all persons born in Scotland after 1603. Together with a corresponding Scots statute of 1608, this secured the eventual mutual exchange of rights of citizenship between the two countries.[12]

In the establishment of the American union, the small states of Maryland, New Jersey, and Connecticut made significant contributions. Maryland refused to ratify the Articles of Confederation unless all states would cede their Western lands to the Confederation. Although the motives of Maryland's policy were self-centered and extremely practical, involving the interests of land speculators, the acceptance of its demand by other states, particularly New York and Virginia, gave the Confederation some of its most important economic and political assets and constituted an important step toward the more complete union that followed in 1789.[13] New Jersey's Assembly likewise at first insisted on various measures to strengthen the proposed federation but after a year ratified the Articles in order not to block its establishment.[14] The cultural, moral, and political contributions of small states and their leaders, such as Tuscany with Ricasoli, or Venetia with Daniele Manin, promoted a unification of Italy rather than a mere expansion of Piedmont. Another case in point might be the initiative taken by the small state Hesse-Darmstadt from 1825 onward—again for highly practical reasons, including financial need—toward a customs union with Prussia. The customs union materialized in 1828, and in view of Hesse-Darmstadt's strategic location it constituted a major breakthrough toward the German Customs Union of 1834.[15]

[11] Historians have noted Henry VII's rejoinder that "the greater would draw the less" in reply to contemporary fears that the marriage might lead to Scotland's annexation of England; see G. S. Pryde, *The Treaty of Union of Scotland and England, 1707* (London, 1950), p. 1, with reference to P. Hume Brown, *History of Scotland* (1909), I: 314; and C. S. Terry, *History of Scotland* (Cambridge, 1920), p. 148. "'If it should fall out so,' said Henry, 'the realm of England will suffer no evil, since it will not be the addition of England to Scotland, but of Scotland to England.'" R. S. Rait, *An Outline of the Relations between England and Scotland, 500–1707* (London, 1901), p. 101.

[12] Pryde, *op. cit.*, p. 4; Rait, *op. cit.*, p. 152; and Theodora Keith, *Commercial Relations between England and Scotland, 1603–1707* (Cambridge England, 1910), p. 15, with reference to J. Hill Burton, *History of Scotland*, V: 411–415.

[13] See Merrill Jensen, *The Articles of Confederation* (Madison: University of Wisconsin Press, 1940), pp. 150–160, 198–224.

[14] *Ibid.*, pp. 187–188.

[15] See W. von Eisenhart Rothe, "Die Entstehung des Preussisch-Hessischen Zollvereins vom 4 Februar 1828: Einleitung," in W. von Eisenhart Rothe and A. Ritthaler, eds., *Vorgeschichte und Bergründung des Deutschen Zollvereins: Akten der Staaten des Deutschen Bundes und der Europäischen Mächte* (Berlin, 1934), II: 3–17, documents, pp. 19–294. See also W. O. Henderson, *The Zollverein* (Cambridge, England, 1938), pp. 50–54; Arnold H. Price,

On the whole it seems from our cases that small states have had few if any effective opportunities to decide situations of *disagreement* between larger states. Schematically viewed, it might appear that when two large states are deadlocked in disagreement, small states ought to be able to swing the balance between them by siding with one large state against the other. The experience from our cases suggests, however, that this analogy of a mechanical balance may be too crude to fit the facts. If the government of a large state cannot or will not respond to the demands of another large state, then the addition of the limited material or moral pressure of several small states usually is not likely to make the dissenting large state more pliant. The behavior of states is to a large extent the outcome of their inner political and social structures for decision-making, and large states in particular tend to respond to outside pressures only very imperfectly and often in unexpected ways. Instead, small states seem to have been most effective when they endeavored to promote compromise and mutual adjustment among larger states within the limits of policies that those large states themselves would find acceptable in terms of their own internal policies, interest groups, and channels of influence and information.

If there is truth in these considerations, then they may well apply also, within limits, to our own time. The small Benelux countries encountered very limited possibilities of adjusting major disagreements between France and Germany in the proposed treaty for a European Defense Community (EDC) in 1953. Their roles in any other major issue related to the efforts toward West European political unification might well be scrutinized in this same perspective. So might the limited opportunities open to small states in the United Nations in situations of deadlock between the large powers. (A comparison of the tactics pursued by the representatives of Australia and Canada at the United Nations Conference at San Francisco in 1945, and of the results obtained, might illustrate some aspects of this problem. Both states were unequivocally committed to the main values and loyalties of the Western world, and both had to rely on moral influence rather than on power to achieve their ends. Yet at various points during the conference the Australian spokesmen appeared more preoccupied with what seemed good and right to them and to their government and home opinion, while the Canadians seemed to take a more lively interest also in what might be acceptable to larger states.)

SOME POPULAR BELIEFS
ABOUT INTEGRATION

The cases we examined throw some doubt upon the validity of certain widely held beliefs about the process of integration of small states into larger communities.

The Evolution of the Zollverein (Ann Arbor: University of Michigan Press, 1949), pp. 199–224.

It has sometimes been claimed that modern economic and social development automatically favors an unequivocal trend toward more internationalism and world community. Neither our cases nor a survey of more limited data from a larger number of countries has yielded any clear-cut evidence to support this view. Many countries in the world today devote a larger part of their resources to their domestic economies, as against foreign trade, than they did in 1911 or 1928.[16] Similarly, as shown in chapter 8, we found a considerable decline in the share of foreign mail among the total volume of letters written in most countries, and that decline was generally larger than would have corresponded merely to the decline in international migration. Other data suggest that discrepancies between average incomes in different countries, and thus perhaps also between national levels of the real wages of labor, may have increased rather than declined.[17] An extended count of the share of references to foreign research in major scientific journals in several leading countries between 1894 and 1954 has left it at least doubtful whether there has been any clear-cut increase in internationalism even in the world of science.[18] The decline in the mobility of persons across national boundaries for purposes of permanent settlement is too well known to require documentation. All these data leave one with the general impression that both large and small states will have to work toward the building of wider political communities without the benefit of any automatic trend toward internationalism.[19]

Another widespread belief has been that the growth of large states was a snowballing process, in the sense that the further expansion of a state was accelerated by its larger size and hence by the extent of its expansion in the past. In this view, as villages joined to make provinces, and provinces to make kingdoms, so states were expected to join into ever larger states.

Some of the evidence we have found, however, points in the opposite direction. It suggests that the growth in the size of states may tend to be accompanied by an increase in the size of their gross domestic product, relative to their foreign trade, and also in their political self-preoccupation. As a state becomes large and its population becomes politically active in large numbers, its government and political elite may become increasingly preoccupied with domestic politics, or with the projection of domestic political pressures, prejudices, and desires into the field of foreign policy. They may find themselves pressured to devote a declining share of genuine attention and responsiveness to the actual messages, needs, and desires of other governments and peoples. To the extent that very

[16]K. W. Deutsch and Alexander Eckstein, "National Industrialization and the Declining Share of the International Economic Sector, 1890–1955," *World Politics,* XIII (January 1961): 267–299.
[17]Calculations made at the Center for Research on World Political Institutions, Princeton University, on the basis of statistics of the Universal Postal Union, 1887–1951.
[18]Surveys made under the direction of the author at Massachusetts Institute of Technology. See p. 169, above.
[19]On the problem of trends, see E. H. Carr, *Nationalism and After* (London, 1945), pp. 1–38.

large states thus may tend to imprison the minds of their rulers in a web of domestic complexities and pressures, the growth of states might turn out to be a self-limiting process. The larger a state in such a situation, the less attention and understanding its political decision-makers may be able to offer to any additional small state, territory, or population tempted to join it. If a new area does join, it still may not get enough attention to consolidate and maintain its loyalty. At the end of a period of integration, then, very large states, empires, or federations may find it impossible to integrate any additional populations or areas, or even to retain the loyalties of some of the smaller groups and political units that joined them in the past.

The possibilities just sketched represent, to be sure, only one side of the process. Governments and elites of large states can learn to increase their capabilities for listening and responding to the more voluminous and diversified communications coming from increased areas and populations. The cases of the United States and the United Kingdom contain many instances of partial successes in this respect. However, in situations where the governments and elites of the largest states may fail—perhaps temporarily—to keep pace with the growing burden of responses and decisions required by the expansion of an amalgamated political community, pluralistic patterns might prove more practicable. It might also be tempting, in the building of larger integrated communities, to look for leadership to the middle-sized countries. They might in some cases be large enough to furnish a potential core of strength, but not so large as to be faced automatically with major pressures toward excessive domestic self-preoccupation.

Another popular notion has been that a major motive for the political integration of states has been the fear of anarchy and warfare among them. Consequently—according to this notion—one of the first and crucial features of an emerging amalgamated security community is strong federal or communitywide law, with courts and police forces or armies to enforce it against recalcitrant member states or populations. Among writers on federalism or international organization, this viewpoint has often implied a stress on legal problems and the problem of coercing member states. In this context we might also recall the suggested importance of maintaining a balance of power among the member states of a larger union or federation, so as to prevent any one state from becoming much stronger than the others.[20] If these notions were correct, the membership of very large states would pose formidable difficulties for federations and other types of political union.

Our findings suggest at least qualifications for all these views. The questions of larger-community police forces and law enforcement, and of the coercion of recalcitrant member states, turned out to be of minor importance in the early stages of most of the amalgamated security communities we studied. The two cases in which problems of policing and coercion played the largest part were England-Ireland and the Habsburg monarchy in its relations to Bohemia and

[20] See the article by Carl J. Friedrich in Macmahon, *op. cit.* (n. 8 *supra*), p. 515.

Hungary. In both cases, integration was precarious for long periods of time and ended in dissolution. There was also some talk in some Swedish political circles about coercing Norway during the crisis that preceded the dissolution of the Swedish-Norwegian union. The Swedish renunciation of any coercive policy was then followed by the development of a pluralistic security community including both countries.[21] In the case of the United States at the time of the establishment of the federal government and the United States War Department in 1789, the federal army numbered less than 600 men, and it was not greatly enlarged thereafter.[22] No federal Navy department was established until 1798. For many decades, Americans continued to rely on their militia—that is, on the forces of the individual states—for defense. The federal government long remained unable and unwilling to coerce any member states, even on some critical occasions. Similarly, no significant role was played by the federal police forces, armies, or courts in the evolution of the Swiss political community from the thirteenth to the early nineteenth century, while its member cantons retained all means of military power.[23]

The problem of the balance of power between member states may have been significant in the cases of the American and Swiss federations, in the sense that no one member state in either of these political communities was far stronger than all others. However, in both cases, groups of member states became clearly predominant over the rest of the federation. The Northeastern states were predominant in the United States between 1865 and 1900. In Switzerland the liberal and industrial cantons were predominant after 1847. In both cases, amalgamation progressed and integration was maintained. In nonfederal types of political amalgamation, considerations of an internal balance of power between major political units seem to have been far less important. Neither England within the United Kingdom, nor Prussia in Germany after 1871, nor Piedmont in Italy for some time after 1860, was balanced by any other member or group of members. Yet each of these larger political communities achieved integration.

Several other conditions have sometimes been considered essential for the establishment of an amalgamated security community. Among them are previous administrative or dynastic union; ethnic or linguistic assimilation; strong economic ties; and foreign military threats. All but the last seem somewhat more likely to occur in association with large states than with small ones. While all of them appear to have been helpful to amalgamation and integration, our cases suggest that none of them were essential, since some amalgamated security communities were established without one or another. No previous administrative union had linked the Italian states for almost 1,500 years. No ethnic or

[21] See Raymond Lindgren, *Norway-Sweden: Union, Disunion and Scandinavian Integration* (Princeton, 1957).

[22] See James Ripley Jacobs, *The Beginning of the U.S. Army* (Princeton, 1947), pp. 43, 236, and *passim*.

[23] See Hermann Weilenmann, *Die Vielsprachige Schweiz: Eine Lösung des Nationalitätsproblems* (Basel and Leipzig, 1925), for a detailed historical survey of the problem.

linguistic assimilation had wiped out the difference between the language groups of Switzerland. No strong economic ties existed between England and Scotland, or Norway and Sweden, or among the Italian states, prior to union in each case. No foreign military threat played any important role in the union between England and Wales or in the adoption of the Swiss Federal Constitution in 1848. Even where foreign threats were present, their effects were transitory. They most often provided an impetus toward temporary military alliances, while more permanent unions derived their support from other factors.[24]

SOME ESSENTIAL REQUIREMENTS FOR THE ESTABLISHMENT OF AMALGAMATED SECURITY COMMUNITIES

A number of other conditions, however, do appear to be essential, so far as our evidence goes, for the success of amalgamated security communities. In all of our cases we found that the main values held by the politically relevant strata in all the participating units were compatible. Sometimes this compatibility included a tacit agreement to prevent other incompatible values from acquiring political significance. Likewise, we found in all our cases of successful amalgamation a distinctive way of life, that is, a set of socially accepted values and of institutional means for their pursuit and attainment. In developing and promoting such compatible values and distinctive ways of life, small states have sometimes been remarkably effective. Thus Bavaria in the late eighteenth and early nineteenth centuries played a significant role in bringing together the Catholic and Protestant elements in its population and in bringing North and Central German linguistic standards into its schools. The small Swiss Forest Cantons were the first to develop the characteristic Swiss way of life—including freehold tenure, local self-government and mutual cooperation, and freedom from feudal oppression—that was to play a major role in the rise and consolidation of the Swiss Confederation.[25]

Several other essential conditions for successful amalgamation seemed to be associated primarily or mainly with the larger states involved in each situation. One such condition was an increase in the political and administrative capabilities of the main political units to be amalgamated. Pennsylvania, Virginia, Massachusetts, and other states adopted important and effective state constitutions prior to the adoption of the Articles of Confederation and the Federal Constitution. Other such conditions included superior economic growth, com-

[24]Other criteria of political community must be invoked to determine when and for whom a "foreign threat" will appear as such. American colonists in 1763 considered France a foreign threat and looked upon Britain as their mother country. Fifteen years later they saw Britain as the foreign threat and welcomed France as an ally.

[25]Hermann Weilenmann, *Pax Helvetica: Oder die Demokratie der kleinen Gruppen* (Zurich, 1951).

pared to the recent past of the territories to be amalgamated or compared to neighboring areas; expectations of joint economic rewards and of strong economic ties as a result of amalgamation; and free mobility of persons prior to, or concurrent with, amalgamation.

Finally, our research turned up two other essential conditions for integration. First, there must be a broadening of the political elite in the course of the amalgamation movement. Second, there must be particular groups or institutions that form unbroken links of communication between several social strata within one unit and between *some* of the politically relevant strata in several of the units.

An example of the broadening of the elite is the emergence of a new type of political leader. George Washington retained the respect of his peers, the landowners of Virginia, but he also know how to gain the votes of poorer farmers and frontiersmen at county elections held well before the American Revolution.[26] Another example might be the shift in leadership in Prussia from nobles like von Manteuffel, who was unwilling to work with the middle classes, to someone like Bismarck, who retained the respect of his fellow aristocrats but knew how to attract and retain middle-class support.

An example of unbroken links of social communication could be seen in the Scottish Presbyterian Church, which in seventeenth-century Scotland had considerable political importance. Its ministers were recruited from the younger sons of the lairds, as well as from the more educated classes in the Scottish cities, but they lived in close contact with their congregations, whose lives they influenced, even in remote villages. At the same time, they followed theological controversies in England. They played a prominent part in the acceptance of English rather than Lowland Scots as the standard language for Scotland, and at several critical junctures they shared strong common interests with English Protestants and, after the 1670s, with the Whigs. Another example would be the German financial and industrial community that came to link major interests in the Rhineland, Berlin, Darmstadt, Leipzig, and other German centers and states during the 1850s and 1860s. As the Scottish example shows, broader elites and unbroken links of social communication may be found in small states as well as in large ones, but it is in the latter that their presence is most often likely to be crucial.

SOME CONDITIONS TENDING TO DISINTEGRATE AMALGAMATED POLITICAL COMMUNITIES

Several conditions were found to be common to all the cases of disintegration of amalgamated political communities we studied. They appear likely to promote disintegration wherever they occur.

---

[26] See Charles S. Sydnor, *Gentlemen Freeholders: Political Practices in Washington's Virginia* (Chapel Hill: University of North Carolina Press, 1952).

Increases in Political Participation and Mass Expectations

Some of these conditions appear equally effective regardless of whether they occur in large or in small political units within the political community. One of these is a substantial broadening of political participation. The needs, wishes, and pressures of newly mobilized social strata or regions have to be accommodated within an old system of political decision-making, which may be ill-suited to respond to them in an adequate way. Increasing political participation among peasants led to the formation of a new peasant party in Norway during the second half of the nineteenth century. There was no corresponding increase in responsiveness on the part of the Swedish governments of the time, and this inequity greatly increased the difficulties of the Norwegian-Swedish Union. Similarly, the Anglo-Irish union became increasingly strained with the rise of Irish mass participation in politics. The destruction of Austria-Hungary was greatly advanced by the rise of mass politics, both among the politically and economically underprivileged peoples—Czechs, Slovaks, Slovenes, Serbs, Croats, and Rumanians—and among the privileged nationalities, the Germans and Magyars. Among all of those groups, mass participation in politics brought more nationalistic parties and leaders. There was more and more stress on ethnic in-group values and interests, along with a growing disregard for the claims and feelings of other groups and regions.

Broadening political participation usually causes an increase in ethnic or linguistic differentiation, as well as a rise in the political awareness of such differentiation as already may exist. There follows a rise in political participation within such groups that are thus differentiated from the predominant nationality or regional-cultural group within the political community. The growing differentiation of the German-speaking Swiss from the Germans during the fifteenth, sixteenth, and seventeenth centuries, and the rapid differentiation of American colonists from Englishmen after the middle of the eighteenth century, may serve as examples of this process. The acute awareness of Belgian-Dutch differences, which helped to end the Belgian-Dutch union of 1815–1830 might be explored from this standpoint, and so might the trend toward the rise of new states based on language differences within the federal system of India.

Political participation can be directly inferred, within limits, from voting statistics; and it is usually closely related, as discussed in chapter 5, to such large-scale trends as participation in urban life and industry, literacy, the use of mass media of communication, and other such criteria of "social mobilization." These in turn often can be gauged from available economic and social statistics, as well as statistics of transport and communication. It is thus possible, in principle, to project the trends of these large-scale series, which are usually rather stable, and to gain from them an impression of the probable future scale of political participation and potential political conflict in particular states, regions, or larger communities.[27]

[27]For a fuller discussion of this point with some statistical examples for Scotland, Finland, Bohemia, and India, see Deutsch, *Nationalism and Social Communication, op. cit.,* pp. 97–138, 169–213.

Taken together, this evidence suggests that the growth of political and economic democracy may not be an unmixed blessing for the persistence of large integrated political communities. The rising tide of mass participation in politics and of mass expectations of social services may imperil the independence of small states, because their limited capabilities to act may fall short of the claims put upon them. The same basic process may imperil large states by overtaking their limited capacities to perceive, and to respond quickly and accurately to, the rising volume of messages, needs, and claims with which their governments and political elites may be confronted.

It is even conceivable that both small states and larger political systems may be thrown into a crisis at one and the same time by the increase of burdens thrown upon their governments. The governments of the small states may be jeopardized by their lack of power to act, and those of large states or federations by their lack of capability to pay adequate attention, to think, and to respond. Such a simultaneous—though transitory—lack of capabilities for either independence or integration may have characterized certain aspects of the situation of the states of Germany and Italy during the first half of the nineteenth century. It may have contributed to the peculiar mood of political frustration often expressed there at that time. A similar dilemma may have contributed to the peculiar difficulties of some of the East European states between World Wars I and II. They seemed unable to enjoy fully their sovereign independence or to achieve a stable integration in some wider union.

Excessive Military Commitments

One of the outstanding disintegrative conditions indicated by our research is the effect of excessive military commitments. Joint armies with light burdens and conspicuous gains in prestige or privileges or short wars with similar characteristics were helpful, though not essential, to the consolidation of a political community. But heavy military burdens with few conspicuous gains over the status quo tended to have the opposite effect. Thus the British attempt to impose a larger defense burden on the American colonies after 1763 contributed to the movement that ended in the American Revolution. The Napoleonic Kingdom of Italy made the idea of Italian unification unpopular for a considerable time afterward through its conscription policies and other military burdens. The strain of war played as essential a part in the destruction of Austria-Hungary in 1918. The same year saw the beginning of the secession of Ireland from the United Kingdom after a period of common war burdens and sacrifices. It appears that the British attempt to introduce conscription in Ireland in April 1918 accelerated the trend toward secession.

On the other hand, in several instances deliberate efforts were made to avoid placing heavy military burdens on weaker or smaller states or regions, or upon populations psychologically and socially unready or unwilling to bear them. These were generally followed by the successful preservation of the wider political community. No burdens in manpower or money were imposed by Britain upon French Canada between 1776 and 1783; and as late as World War II, French Canadians were not drafted for overseas service. In Northern Ireland as in French Canada, Britain relied on volunteers rather than conscripts for overseas service in World War II. In the case of the American union, effective conscription for the Federal army was introduced only in 1917. Throughout the formative years of the union, including the wars of 1776–83 and 1812–15, the military strength of the union remained based on state militias and voluntary enlistments for limited terms, with no effective federal coercion of unwilling states or populations. Even as late as the Civil War of 1861–65, which was fought for the preservation of the union, volunteer enlistments, not conscription, formed the mainstay of the Union forces.

In the light of these experiences, it seems reasonable to expect serious difficulties for any attempt to build a lasting union of states in Western Europe, or around the North Atlantic, primarily around a common army with conscription. It may be particularly vulnerable to difficulties under conditions of heavy military risks and burdens. Relaxations of international tensions may offer the Western countries the opportunity to shift the bases of their community toward more promising foundations of economic growth and social and cultural cooperation.

While excessive military commitments most often result from policies of the larger states in a political community, they may sometimes arise also from the particular policies or involvements of smaller units. In this connection, it would be interesting to study more closely the devices adopted by the Swiss cantons from a very early time onward for limiting strictly the possible commitments of the Confederation that might otherwise arise from the policies of its member units.

Economic Stagnation or Closure of Elites

Another group of disintegrative conditions seems most likely to be found among the larger states within a political community. One such condition appeared to be prolonged economic decline or stagnation, comparing unfavorably with conditions in neighboring areas. Another disintegrative condition was a relative closure of the established political elite, promoting the rise of frustrated counter-elites among ethnic or cultural outgroups or in outlying regions. Related to this were the disintegrative effects resulting from any excessive delay of social, economic, or political reforms that had come to be expected by the population and sometimes had already been adopted in neighboring areas.

Failure to Adjust to Loss of Dominance

Another aspect of the same complex of factors was the disintegrative effect of any major failure on the part of a formerly strong or privileged state, group, or region to adjust psychologically and politically to loss of dominance as a result of changed conditions. The cases of the Northern Irish Protestants and of the Bohemian Germans are relevant in this connection, and so are the attitudes of most of the Austro-German and Magyar political leaders during the last years of the Habsburg monarchy. The attitudes of many British conservatives toward Southern Ireland in 1918–21 and, to a lesser extent, the attitudes of some Swedish conservative leaders toward Norwegian claims between 1895 and 1905 were similarly inflexible.

Instances of successful adjustment to a loss of dominance, on the other hand, tended to contribute to the preservation of a greater measure of political community than otherwise would have been likely. Examples include the British adjustment to American independence and equality after 1819, together with the American adjustment to the continued separate existence of Canada, which permitted the demilitarization of the American-Canadian frontier and the maintenance of a pluralistic security community between the two countries.

Other examples of successful adjustment include the Swedish acceptance of Norwegian independence after 1905 and of Finnish cultural and social equality or near equality after 1918. The first adjustment permitted the establishment of a pluralistic security community between Norway and Sweden, and including Denmark, after 1907. The second may have contributed to bringing Finland ever closer into the Scandinavian community. Still another example might be seen in the successful British adjustment in 1947 to the loss of dominance in India, which permitted the continuing membership of India in the Commonwealth.

Many of these cases involve the acceptance by the leaders of a formerly "large" state or people of the fact that their political unit in some important respects is not quite so "large" any longer. In a time when even the largest countries are becoming small in relation to the destructive force that their physicists have created, these experiences of constructive psychological adjustment on the part of certain governments and political elites to the loss of much of their former coercive power might be worth particularly careful study.

CONCLUDING REMARKS

This chapter has not adequately summarized the results of the research undertaking from which it has been derived; and since the entire project was based on a limited number of cases (although these were selected with some care), it is quite possible that the addition of further cases—or even of one case—might modify some of the findings indicated. At best, this entire investigation should represent a beginning of more thorough and critical studies in the field.

Within these limitations, a few points should be emphasized. Our findings suggest that pluralistic security communities have succeeded repeatedly where amalgamated communities failed. Requiring far less stringent conditions for success, pluralistic political communities thus seem to offer a particularly promising pathway toward the establishment of widening areas of peace and security in our time.

Consistent with this finding, it has also appeared from our cases that both amalagamated and pluralistic communities can be approached functionally and by steps. Partial mergers of particular functions and organs helped rather than hindered further progress toward amalgamation—as they did in the case of the German Zollverein and the Anglo-Scottish union of crowns—so long as a measure of respect for, and responsiveness to, the needs and desires of each of the participating governments was preserved.

This last qualification is important. Political scientists are familiar with the extreme difficulty of maintaining a joint organization or function in cases where there is a basic divergence of political will between the states that are supposed to control it jointly.[28] What appears as "will," however, in the conflict of state or group policies that have become fixed may be treated as a problem of mutual attention, perception, and responsiveness in the case of policies that are still in the process of formation or already in the process of revision.[29]

It is for reasons such as these that our emphasis has centered on the openness of governments and political decision-makers to information coming from outside their own state or group and upon their quick and sensitive responsiveness to its implications. Political discussions have often centered on the notion of power, divorced from its essential context of information, intelligence, and self-control. Where the "power" approach has stressed the muscles of states, so to speak, I have tried to pay more attention to their nerves and to the adequacy of the reflexes and responses that depend on them.[30]

What does this approach suggest in working toward supranational integration? In practical terms, perhaps we should place less confidence in the usefulness of straight majority voting in international organizations and more reliance on the requirement of concurrent majorities and on composite forms of representation. These considerations have been discussed by Professor Sørenson and others in the literature of federalism and international organization.[31] Most such schemes imply, of course, the deliberate granting of greater political influence to some smaller states, territories, or minority groups than would be proportionate to their numerical strength. If this overrepresentation of small states or districts is carried to the point where their particular voting power greatly exceeds their stake in the general broad development of the larger community (its "general welfare"), their votes may become political commodities, and a new "rotten borough" system may result.

[28] See William Diebold, "The Relevance of Federalism to Western European Economic Integration," in Macmahon, ed., *op. cit.,* pp. 433–457, esp. pp. 443–445; also the article by Ingvar Svennilson, *ibid,* p. 468; and Bauer, *op. cit.,* p. 424.

[29] This point is stressed for the case of Switzerland in Weilenmann, *op. cit.,* pp. 273–311.

[30] See K. W. Deutsch, *The Nerves of Government* (New York: 1963, 1966).

[31] Sørenson, "Large and Small States," *op. cit.;* pp. 4–5; Robert R. Bowie, "The Federal Legislature," in Robert R. Bowie and Carl J. Friedrich, eds., *Studies in Federalism* (Boston, 1954), pp. 3–62.

Even at this risk, it may be wise within fairly broad limits to hold to the principle of "overcompensating the weaker partners"—the smaller states—in federal or international organization. Small states should be valued not merely in terms of the quantitative pressures they could exercise but also as potential qualitative resources of new ideas, new information, and new patterns of organization. The basic test of any such policy, however, would be its effect in increasing the capabilities of each of the participating states—both small and large—to respond more effectively to the needs and messages of its own population, as well as to those of the other states that are its partners in the building of some wider political community.

11 | Symbols of Political Community

Many of the data of the 1949–52 period, which had become available by 1954, show the effects of the Great Depression of the 1930s and of World War II, which had tended to depress cumulatively the proportions of private international transactions, such as trade and mail, relative to comparable activities within each nation-state. Thus comparing data from about 1950 with those from 1928, 1913,·or 1890 would lead to an image of increased national self-preoccupation on the level of daily life, while comparing the same 1950 data with corresponding figures from the 1960s and 1970s would lead some later writers to images of growing shares of international transactions. Establishing the long-term trend of actual developments would require, of course, the construction of relevant time series from, say, the 1890s to the mid-1970s, but most of this work still remains to be done or is still in prograss.

In regard to policy, the data available in 1954 and reported here offer some basis for judging some of the accomplishments and limitations of Western politics in the nearly one-quarter century that followed. By 1978 the plans for a European Defense Community had faded, but much of the mutual distrust and dislike between French and German public opinion had been overcome, and trade and travel between the two countries increased. These developments are discussed in Chapter 14. As late as 1977 some remnants of resentment had survived sufficient to become visible in that year in many of the French mass media, despite the positive responses of 62 per cent of French mass opinion to the struggle of the government of the German Federal Republic against the German terrorists, and the expressed readiness for friendship with the Federal Republic by 82 per cent of French respondents, in a survey reported in *Der Spiegel*, 31, No. 48 (November 21, 1977): 143-154. It seems clear that the moral, political, and economic integration of Western Germany into the Western

The substance of this chapter, which has been revised and updated, was written in 1954 and appeared in Lyman Bryson, Louis Finkelstein, Hudson Hoagland, and R. M. MacIver, eds., *Symbols and Society* (New York: Fourteenth Symposium, Conference on Science, Philosophy and Religion in Their Relation to the Democratic Way of Life, Inc., 1955; distributed by Harper & Row, Publishers), pp. 23–54. Copyright 1955 by Harper & Row, Publishers. Reprinted by permission.

community of nations, still recent and highly vulnerable in 1954, has become very much stronger and more dependable by now.

The doubts, expressed in 1954, as to whether the bipolar division of the world into a pro-American and a pro-Soviet camp could be made pervasive and lasting have proved justified by the subsequent emergence of the "Third World" of "nonaligned countries" and the breakup of the Soviet-Chinese coalition, as was already then suggested on pp. 209–10.

The contradictions in United States political opinion and foreign policy, noted in this text of 1954, have remained real but have not proved fatal. More light has been thrown on these matters by the more recent work of other scholars, such as R. Bauer, I. de S. Pool and L. Dexter, *American Business and Public Policy* (New York, 1963, 1972); B. M. Russett, *What Price Vigilance?* (New Haven, 1970); B. M. Russett and B. Hanson, *Interest and Ideology* (San Francisco, 1976); and R. Hilsman, *The Crouching Future* (New York, 1975).

For the development of content analysis and research on political symbols, see Zvi Namenwirth and T. Brewer, "Elite Editorial Comment on the European and Atlantic Communities in Four Countries," in Philip Stone *et al.*, *The General Inquirer* (Cambridge, 1966), pp. 401–427; and for the general development of data-based research on international politics, Susan Jones and J. David Singer, *Beyond Conjecture: Data-Based Research in International Relations* (Chicago, 1972).

Experience has shown that the use of quantitative measurement in the study of international affairs is indispensable but limited. As in medicine, it can offer essential aids to clinical experience and diagnostic judgment but cannot replace them.

Symbols of international politics are often studied for two purposes: to find out what can be learned from their observation, and what can be accomplished by their control. In the first case, we study symbols as possible indicators of political change; in the second, we study them as possible "regulators"—a term of Quincy Wright's—or instruments of manipulation of political developments.[1]

SYMBOLS AS INDICATORS

Viewed as indicators, political symbols and their statistical distribution can tell us something about the flow of messages between political groups and organizations, such as states, countries, regions, peoples, special interest groups, or particular institutions, such as governments, foreign offices, legislatures, newspapers, and other media of mass communication or control. Such flows of messages can tell us something, in turn, about the distribution of attention of the

---

[1]*Cf.* Quincy Wright, "Introduction," Ithiel de Sola Pool, *Symbols of Internationalism*, Stanford University Press, Stanford, 1951, p. 2.

individuals, groups, and organizations concerned. By noting which symbols are frequently associated with each other, we may learn something about the context in which political messages are perceived, remembered, and recalled on later occasions. Thus they help us understand political meaning and political perception at different times and in different communities.

New political symbols may be created, and may become associated with old or new patterns of political behavior. Political information, like all other information, may be remembered or recorded piecemeal by individuals or organizations. It may be dissociated into smaller patterns; and these smaller patterns may later on be recombined to new configurations which had not been received as messages before, and which may never have existed until they were now for the first time put together.

Such new configurations of symbols may themselves be completed patterns, readily available for application to decisions about political behavior. Or they may undergo a process of strategic simplification in which they may be stripped of nonessential features for their new employment, and in which they may thus lose all obvious traces of their combinatorial origin. The simplified cross of the Crusaders, the white cross of Switzerland, the crescent-shaped sword of Islam, the simplified world map that serves as the emblem of the United Nations—all these are symbols of this kind.

Political symbols, like all symbols, are orders to recall something from memory.[2] In this respect, they have several functions: 1) they *denote* or designate some particular group, region, event, behavior pattern, or the like, or they designate a bundle of such memories which are to be recalled together as if they formed part of one concept or unit (such as "Frenchman" or "Western Europe" or "United Nations"); 2) they *connote* a number of other memories which are to be recalled in less vivid detail and associated less rigidly than the memories that fall within the denotation, but which are still effective in modifying the denoted concept and its effects on further associating, thinking, and "decision-making" (such as the connotations, "valorous" or "unstable," respectively, when added to the symbol, "Frenchmen"); 3) they *represent* a particular combination of denotative and connotative meanings for at least three different contexts: a) the universe of memories of the speaker or the source of the symbol; b) the universe of the audience, intended or unintended, by whom the message is received; c) the general cultural and social context which may be common to the source and the audience of the symbol, but which may nevertheless differ to some extent from the private universe of memories of either.

The distribution of the flows of political messages, the speed, precision, and economy of effort with which they are understood and responded to, and the experience of reward and satisfaction by which these processes of communication are accompanied, together form a significant indication of the presence or absence of political community among the groups, countries, or peoples among

[2]For an excellent discussion of "signs" and "symbols," see Susanne K. Langer, *Philosophy in a New Key*, New American Library, New York, 1948.

which they occur. From them we may gain indications of the unity or diversity of the memory pools of the groups and individuals participating in the process; of the mutual compatibility of their major political values; and of the mutual compatibility and responsiveness of the political decision systems and control processes by which they regulate their behavior.[3]

"INDEPENDENCE" AND "SECURITY" AS POLITICAL SYMBOLS

Such powerful political symbols as "independence" and "security" must be defined within the context of these processes of social and political communication. People have been willing to fight and die for their independence and security, that is, for the independence and security of the group of which they formed a part or with whom they had come to identify themselves. But the terms, "independence" and "security," could tell neither them nor us just whose independence is to be defended, from whom, and for what purpose.[4]

Within the context of communication, however, the meaning of these symbols can be perhaps more readily discerned. Independence and security are terms that symbolize the freedom and protection of the self from the nonself, and the nonself can be distinguished from the self in terms of communication and responsiveness. Neurophysiologists have noted that patients who lose sensation in or control over a limb of their own body tend to perceive this limb as alien, as not part of the self.[5] In a somewhat similar manner, we may think perhaps of political independence as *independence from an unresponsive political community or political decision system*. We wish to be independent from any governments, countries, or groups of people who do not respond adequately to our messages and to our needs. We wish to be secure from those who might infringe upon our own political autonomy, that is, from those who might hinder or overburden or

[3] For a more detailed exposition of this approach, as well as for a number of qualifications, see Karl W. Deutsch, *Political Community at the International Level: Problems of Definition and Measurement*, Doubleday & Company, New York, 1954, pp. 46–64. See also Quincy Wright, *A Study of War*, University of Chicago Press, Chicago, 1942, vol. II, pp. 970–986, 1240–1260, 1278, 1286.

[4] Perhaps the most to be said, Quincy Wright has observed, "is that a nationalist has identified himself with a group, larger than the local community and smaller than the world, which he regards as sharing some social and political characteristics with himself and as in some way different from other similar human groups. It also implies that he is prepared to support policies which he regards as in the interest of that group. It is clear, however, that nationalism neither defines those interests nor the group that is supposed to have them." Quincy Wright, "Symbols of Nationalism and Internationalism," *Symbols and Values: An Initial Study*, Conference on Science, Philosophy and Religion, New York, 1954, Chapter XXVI, pp. 390–391.

[5] I am indebted to Warren S. MacCulloch for this point. For a related approach, see also Herbert A. Simon, *Administrative Behavior: A Study of Decision-Making Processes in Administrative Organization*, The Macmillan Company, New York, 1947, pp. 154–171, 198–219.

disrupt the chains and channels of communication and decisionmaking by means of which we control our own behavior and the behavior of the group and the environment that have been linked to us by effective processes of communication and control, with such satisfactory results in terms of our own personal memories, habits, and values, that we have come to include them into the "we-group" and the "we" symbols with whom we identify ourselves. Unions or alliances of countries or peoples which lead to such experiences of successful joint adaptation of behavior and mutual responsiveness, followed by significant joint rewards or satisfaction for the politically important groups among the participants, and by expectations for similar or greater rewards in the future, are likely to leave them with favorable memories and with a desire to see the union or alliance continued or renewed.

Virginians between 1763 and 1790 thus did not desire, by and large, independence from, or security against, Pennsylvanians with whom their frontier people were beginning to share the settlement of the Ohio Valley. Rather in the course of the events leading to the American Revolution, the perception of England as part of the political self of colonists in Virginia faded, and the perception of Pennsylvanians, New Yorkers, and New Englanders as allies, associates, and eventually as part of a new political self which preserved the symbol, "Virginia," but linked it ever more closely with a new symbol—"Americans"—came to take its place. Has there occurred any comparable change in our own time, let us say during the past thirty or fifty years, involving a shift in prominence between the symbols of the various nation-states, on the one hand, and the symbols of internationalism, or of regional political integration, such as in Western Europe, on the other?

RECENT TRENDS IN NATIONAL AND INTERNATIONAL SYMBOLS

In order to seek an answer to this question, it may be well to summarize and compare the results of a number of recent research undertakings, at the risk that the data from some of them may be familiar to some readers. It is in the comparison of the findings of the different surveys that the present summary may possibly be found useful.

Among the conclusions of a survey of symbols of nationalism and internationalism in the "prestige papers" of five major countries between 1890 and 1949, carried out by Ithiel de Sola Pool and others, are the following:

> In interaction this world certainly has become one. The whole world has become responsive to events everywhere, or, more accurately, to events in the same main centers of policy formation . . . . There is . . . a remarkable degree of reciprocity in the attitudes of states toward each other . . . .

> Somehow in this interdependent world the attitudes of the elite in one
> state come to be known and returned by the elite of other states . . .
>
> Attention to international organizations set in after the first World War
> and has increased since . . . (Except for Russia), the trend toward increased
> attention to international organizations seems general.
>
> Other types of international political terminology may be showing some-
> what less vitality . . . . Except for *Izvestia*, the greatest emphasis on those
> symbols which are commonly used for talking about the instrumentalities
> and principles of international relations, seems to have been in the period
> between the world wars . . . . The sharpening of conflicts and the growth
> of a certain cynicism may partly account for the recent decline in these
> terms . . . .
>
> While the world community may be increasingly tightly knit as far as
> interaction is concerned, it is certainly not becoming more unified in at-
> titude. On the contrary, hostility is growing, and lines are becoming more
> sharply polarized between friends and enemies . . . . The total picture is
> that of an increasingly bipolar world.[6]

This suggestion of a bipolar consolidation of the world into two closely knit
camps may require careful qualification. The long term study just cited found
evidence for the persistent failure of any integration between Germany and
France; throughout the half century covered by this survey, these two countries
remained most unfriendly to each other. The percentage of unfavorable judgments between them, out of all judgments of one country by the prestige newspaper of the other, averaged ninety per cent, as compared to slightly above
seventy per cent between Russia and Britain, and Russia and the United States.
For the period as a whole, Pool's figures also suggest that Germany remained far
more unpopular internationally than Russia or any other of the countries
surveyed, *i.e.*, the United States, Britain, and France.[7]

If one computes not merely the "psychic distance" in terms of unfavorable
mutual judgments between any two countries, but computes the psychic distances or frequencies of unfavorable mutual judgments for any possible three-
country coalition among the powers surveyed in Pool's study, one can rank the
ten possible three-country coalitions among these five powers in increasing order
of internal dissension or mutual hostility among the partners. This computation
shows that only one of the ten possible coalitions, that between the United
States, Britain, and France, would unite countries which during the past half-
century average less than fifty per cent unfavorable judgments of one another;
the exact sum of percentages of unfavorable judgments for these three countries
is 115 out of a possible maximum of 300, or a proportion of a little more than
one in three. (The latter figure would mean that the three countries attaining it

[6]Pool, *op. cit.*, pp. 60–63. Reprinted with the permission of the author and of the publishers, Stanford University Press. Copyright 1951 by the Board of Trustees of Leland
Stanford Junior University. Published under a grant from the Carnegie Corporation, New
York.
[7]*Ibid.*, pp. 15–19.

had all judged each other unfavorable all the time.) The other three coalitions not including Russia are the United States-Britain-Germany, with an index of mutual hostility of 202; Britain-France-Germany, with a hostility index of 211; and the United States-France-Germany, with such an index of 216. In these three coalitions the chances of mutually unfavorable judgments among the partners tended to be somewhat better than two to one. Somewhat less handicapped by traditional animosities in their prestige papers appear the combinations of the United States-Britain-Russia with an index of 176; Britain-France-Russia with 177; and the United States-France-Russia, with 184. The first two of these coalitions correspond to actual though temporary alliances in World War II and World War I, respectively. The three-country coalitions which include Germany, on the other hand, appear to have little if any precedent in history; and the three-country combinations which include Germany and Russia are at the bottom of the rank list of mutual psychological acceptability (or at the top of the rank list of mutual dislikes) with indices ranging from 242 to 249.[8]

The quantitative study of symbols by Pool and associates, from which the data for this argument were drawn, is confirmed to a large extent by an independent study by Frank L. Klingberg, based on a survey of opinions of experts in international affairs in 1938–1939. The extreme psychic distance between Germany and France is conspicuous in Klingberg's model, as well as in Quincy Wright's separate estimate in July, 1939. Pool's, Wright's, and Klingberg's studies[9] suggest that the alienation between France and Germany persisted regardless, to some extent, of political changes in Germany, and of the changes in French ability and willingness to fight the Germans. The absence of any major psychological rapprochement between France and Germany in the early years after World War II seems confirmed by the results of the UNESCO surveys of public opinion in a number of European countries, studied by William Buchanan and Hadley Cantril;[10] and it appears further confirmed to some extent by the conspicuous French lack of interest in "social," "personal," or "human interest" news from Germany, as shown by the survey of the flow of international news in 1952–1953, conducted by the International Press Institute.[11]

[8]The full list follows: United States-Britain-France, 115; United States-Britain-Russia, 176; Britain-France-Russia, 177; United States-France-Russia, 184; United States-Britain-Germany, 202; Britain-France-Germany, 211; United States-France-Germany, 216; United States-Russia-Germany, 242; Britain-Russia-Germany, 244; France-Russia-Germany, 249. The indices of mutual hostility within each coalition were computed from data in Pool, *loc. cit.* It may be noted that the only coalition which contains no English-speaking country ranks at the bottom of the entire list, and the chances for mutual recriminations among its members would be five to one.

[9]Frank L. Klingberg, "Studies in the Measurement of the Relations among Sovereign States," *Psychometrika*, vol. VI, 1941, pp. 335–352; "Studies in the Measurement of the Relations among Sovereign States," Thesis, University of Chicago Library, 1939; Quincy Wright, *A Study of War*, University of Chicago Press, Chicago, 1942, vol. II, app. XL, pp. 1466–1471; Pool, *op. cit.*, pp. 15–19, 26–29.

[10]William Buchanan and Hadley Cantril, *How Nations See Each Other: A Study in Public Opinion*, University of Illinois Press, Urbana, 1953, pp. 45–55.

[11]*Cf. The Flow of the News: A Study by the International Press Institute*, International Press Institute, Zurich, 1953, pp. 20–21, 25, 131–134, 140–141, 143, 146–148, 259.

A survey in trends in international trade in Western Europe between 1880 and 1952 suggests that Germany and France may have become more estranged from each other in economic terms during much of that period. In 1880, Germany and France had an average share of 9.4% in each other's imports and exports. This share fell to 9.1% in 1913; to 7.3% in 1928; and to 5.5% in 1937. It had recovered somewhat from this low point by 1952, when it rose to 6.6%, that is, to a level roughly one-third below that of 1880. The same trend is found in the average share of their total foreign mail which each of the two countries sent to the other. This average percentage was 15.2% in 1888. By 1913 it had fallen to 12.3%; by 1928 to 5.3%; and in 1937 it dropped to 3.7%. After the Second World War it recovered slightly to 4.4%, that is, to about one-third of its pre-World War I level between 1888 and 1913. These trends in German-French mail communications contrast strongly with mail communication trends among certain countries among whom community appears to have grown. Thus the average percentage of their total foreign mail which the Scandinavian countries—Sweden, Norway, Denmark, and after 1913, Finland—each sent to the others was 31.1% in 1888. It declined only slightly to 29.3% in 1913 and remained at the same level in 1928, but it rose above the 1888 figure to 31.4% in 1937, and further to 39.1% in 1949. Similarly, the percentage of her total foreign mail which Ireland sent to the United Kingdom rose from 77.5% in 1928 to 78.3% in 1937 and 83.3% in 1949.[12]

If one accords some weight to the well known view of Ernest Renan that a national community is the result of a "plebiscite of everyday life," then data of this kind may deserve serious consideration also in gauging the prospects of supranational political communities. Taken together, the evidence of these surveys may convey to us [in 1954] an indication of the deepseated psychological and material obstacles in the way of Western European Union and of any effective realization of current plans for European Defense Community.

Beyond the confines of Western Europe the trends toward a bipolar world, noted by Pool, have to contend with the recent great increase in the prominence

[12] Sources of trade data: Great Britain, Board of Trade, *Statistical Abstract for the Principal and Other Foreign Countries, 1873-1883*, London, 1885, W. Page, editor, *Commerce and Industry*, Constable, London, 1919; League of Nations, *Memorandum on Balance of Payments and Foreign Trade Balances, 1911-1925*, vol. II, Geneva, 1927; League of Nations, *Memorandum on International Trade and Balances of Payments, 1926-1928*, vol. III, *Trade Statistics of Sixty-Four Countries*, Geneva, 1930; League of Nations, *International Trade Statistics, 1938*, Geneva, 1939; United Nations, *Yearbook of International Trade Statistics, 1952*, New York, 1953. Sources of mail data: Universal Postal Union, Bureau International, *Relevé des tableaux statistiques du service postal international (Réception)*, 1887, Berne, 1889; *(Expédition) 1888*, Berne, 1890; *(Expédition) 1913*, Berne, 1915, *(Expédition) 1928*, Berne, 1930; *Statistique générale du service postal (Réception), 1913*, Berne, 1915; *Statistique générale du service postal, 1928*, Berne, 1930, p. 16, col. 65; *Statistique générale du service postal international, 1937*, Berne, 1939; *Statistique complète des services postaux, 1949*, Berne, 1951; *Statistique des expéditions dans le service postal international, 1949*, Berne, 1951. Computations from both trade and mail data were carried out by Mrs. Johanna Lederer at the Center for Research on World Political Institutions, Princeton University, and by the author.

of the symbols of local nationalism and local or regional political activity in such countries as India, China, Indonesia, the Arab countries, and generally the non-white areas of the world. In many of these regions, political attention seems likely to remain concentrated largely on local and national issues rather than upon the claims and counterclaims of the two distant contending giants, the United States and the Union of Soviet Socialist Republics, and the membership of these "new" countries in the Free World implies precisely their unwillingness to accept too close ideological or political leadership from any agency or power outside their own territory. Indeed, it does not seem clear whether the two contending superpowers of today have greatly increased their traditionally limited abilities to keep large coalitions of countries together, nor is it clear whether the many smaller and middle-sized countries of today are easier or harder to keep in line.

There is some evidence, though not conclusive, pointing to the latter possibility. The progress of modern technology has perhaps done more to facilitate the mutual interaction and impact among governments than it had done to equip these governments to deal with its burdens. We have mechanized the transmission of information, but not the process of listening to it; we can use machines to reproduce symbols in vast numbers, but we get little help from machines in understanding them. By increasing our opportunities for domestic, as well as foreign contacts, we have increased the burdens on our attention; and the political decision systems of modern governments may sometimes be so near to being overloaded with urgent business, foreign and domestic, that they may end up by devoting a smaller rather than a larger share of their attention to foreign countries and to international affairs.

Data on recent shifts in the proportion of domestic to foreign mail suggest the possibility of such a shift of our attention. During the past forty years, the proportion of domestic to foreign mail has been increasing in most of the countries of the world for which we have data; in many countries it is now about twice as high as it was before the First World War. There has been a somewhat similar, though smaller, increase in the proportion of domestic national income (as indicated by gross national product) and foreign trade (as indicated by the sum of imports and exports), with the result that foreign trade over the past twenty-five years, at least, has been forming a decreasing share in the national income of many countries. Thus in the United States in about 1951 the ratio of domestic mail to foreign mail was about seventy to one; the ratio of gross national product (minus exports) to total foreign trade was about ten to one; the ratio of domestic to foreign text material in a respresentative sample of ninety-three newspapers in 1952-1953 was about eleven to one. Earlier experiments have indicated that there is a close connection between the extent of a newspaper reader's previous contacts with persons and places mentioned in a news story and the likelihood of his actually reading it. According to data by Wilbur Schramm, about three out of four potential readers actually read news stories dealing with their community, but not with anyone they knew personally; one in five read stores about a place which he knew well, though outside his community; and only about one in seven read stories about persons and places which he did not know well.[13] If this is so, a growth or decline in the absolute or relative frequency of personal contacts through travel, trade, and mails, across national boundaries might be linked to readership interest in foreign news, and conceivably to interest in international affairs.

At present [summer, 1954], the evidence is by no means conclusive; but the 1952-1953 survey by the International Press Institute has some interesting data on this point. About one-sixth of local news published in American newspapers was actually read; and so was about one-seventh of national news; but only somewhat less than one-eighth of international news published was actually read,[14] so that the ratio of domestic to foreign news actually read would be closer to fourteen to one. Foreign news was more likely to be read when the word, "American" or "U.S." was included in the headline.[15] When asked in the spring of 1953, "Would you like to have your newspaper reduce the amount of local news or national news in order to give you more foreign news?", only eight per cent of the respondents said that they would, and seventy-eight per cent said they would not.[16]

Taken together, data of the kind cited in the last few paragraphs may serve as a group of indices of domestic or national self-preoccupation. There is some evidence that such indices tend to be higher the greater the population, area, wealth, literacy, and perhaps general domestic social and political activity of a country. Compared with other countries in these terms, the self-preoccupation of the United States public would appear, if anything, slightly lower than might seem "normal" for a country of its size, wealth, resources, and domestic level of activity.

This, however, is just the salient point. High and rising levels of national self-preoccupation may be normal for most countries in the world at this particular stage in its development, leaving only limited resources for attention and action to international symbols, messages, and problems.[17] Further data on the increase or decrease of self-reference symbols in political communications (such as an increase or decrease of the symbols, "French" and "France," in the French press) would be of interest in this connection.[18] If such a general increase should turn out to be the case, it might indicate an increase in the difficulty of insuring sufficient mutual attention and responsiveness on the part of the political elites

---

[13] Wilbur Schramm, "The Nature of News," in W. Schramm, editor, *Mass Communications,* University of Illinois Press, Urbana, 1949, pp. 299-300.

[14] *The Flow of the News,* pp. 62-63.

[15] *Ibid.,* pp. 63, 66.

[16] Fourteen per cent expressed no opinion. *Ibid.,* p. 58.

[17] Unpublished studies, Center for Research on World Political Institutions, and K. W. Deutsch, C. I. Bliss, and Alexander Eckstein, "Population, Sovereignty, and Foreign Trade," *Economic Development and Cultural Change,* X (July, 1962), pp. 353-366.

[18] In Pool's count of the distribution of geographic symbols, such "self-references" were specifically excluded. See Pool, *op. cit.,* pp. 37-39.

and politically relevant strata of different states to make any international or supranational political integration practicable.

As regards particular countries, Pool's study found:

> Attention to international organizations . . . (like) attention to foreign states . . . had most markedly increased in the *New York Times*, which, since the end of the controversy over joining the League, had reflected American isolationism by giving relatively little attention to these instrumentalities. While America has been abandoning isolationism, Russia has been adopting it, and in her recent symbol flow devotes very little attention to international organization.[19]

In a related study of the most frequently used political symbols, Pool found for the *New York Times* among other changes a decline of attention to the symbols TARIFFS and FREE TRADE; for the London *Times*, among other trends, an increase in the symbols of PATRIOTISM; and for *Izvestia* he found: "The words that have increased most in attention from the 1920's to the recent period are, in order, FATHERLAND, COLLECTIVISM, and PATRIOTISM.[20]

After World War II, according to Pool's figures, Russian attention to international political symbols remained significantly higher than it had been in the 1930's, but somewhat lower than it had been in the 1920's, and much lower than it had been in the "prestige paper" of Tsarist Russia, *Novoe Vremia*, before the First World War.[21]

These findings of a rising trend of national self-preoccupation in Russia appear confirmed by the sharply rising ratios of domestic to foreign mail in that country, from about seventeen to one in 1928 to almost ninety-six to one—a world record, so far as we could find—in 1937; no further data on mail volumes for Russia appear to have been published by the Universal Postal Union since the latter year, but there is reason to think that the Russian ratio of domestic to foreign mail may have risen even above this record level.[22]

A similar trend in the ratio of Russian gross national product to total foreign trade has long been obvious. From these and similar indications it seems plausible that an ambitious Russian Communist might advance his career most effectively by spending most of his time and attention on Russian internal affairs, and very little on international politics. Political decisionmakers in Russia—and perhaps in time in China—may thus share to a particularly high degree a common problem of government in all highly self-preoccupied countries: the problem that a high interest and competence in international affairs may become inversely related to a policymaker's chances of success in the do-

---

[19] *Ibid.*, p. 61.

[20] Ithiel de Sola Pool, *The "Prestige Papers": A Survey of Their Editorials*, Stanford University Press, Stanford, 1952, pp. 76, 80–81.

[21] Pool, *Symbols of Internationalism*, p. 41, table 8.

[22] Unpublished studies, Center for Research on World Political Institutions, and Chapter 8 above.

mestic contest for popularity and power. If these processes should continue unchecked in Russia or in any other large country, they might eventually produce incompetence in international politics by natural selection, and thus promote the eventual disintegration of any international coalition of which such a country formed a part.

SOME TRENDS IN THE UNITED STATES

The comforting finding of a long run trend in the United States away from isolationism, which was suggested by the count of symbols in the *New York Times,* appears to require some qualification in the light of some of the findings of the Princeton study. The ratio of domestic to foreign mail in the United States rose from about twenty-five to one in 1880 to about twenty-eight to one in 1928, and to almost sixty-five to one in 1951. The ratio of United States domestic national income to total foreign trade rose from less than five to one in 1879 to about seven to one in 1890 and 1913, and to almost twelve to one in 1950 and about eleven to one in 1951.[23] A few other indicators, such as the ratios of immigrants to total population, the study of foreign languages—with enrollments in high school language courses dropping to almost one half between the early 1930's and the late 1940's, despite the increase in high school enrollments generally[24]—the conspicuous decline of the proportion of references to foreign research in American scientific publications between 1890 and 1954,[25] all these likewise seem to qualify the finding of the symbol studies.

To this should perhaps be added the consideration that the *New York Times* is perhaps not quite as representative of the thinking of the political elite of the United States as are the London *Times* or *Izvestia,* or as was *Le Temps,* for their respective countries. American political decisionmaking is less concentrated in New York than French, British, or Russian decisionmaking are concentrated at Paris, London, or Moscow. There is no single close knit political elite in the United States, and the constitutional separation between legislative and executive further tends to keep most members of the Senate and the House of Representatives more interested in domestic political affairs than in international relations. A trend away from isolationism in terms of a change in the distribution of editorial attention of the *New York Times* may thus tell us more of the attitudes of an important segment of American public opinion, and perhaps of a

[23] *Ibid.*
[24] *PMLA: Publications of the Modern Language Association,* vol. 68, no. 5, December, 1953, p. xi. The editors of PMLA reported a drop of fifty-two per cent in enrollment in high school foreign language courses in the period 1934-1949, and an estimated drop of forty-three per cent in foreign language entrance requirements by American colleges in the period 1936-1953. (*Ibid.*) The increased enrollment in foreign language courses at Berlitz Schools, reported in the same issue (p. xiv) would not seem to have been large enough to reverse this trend.
[25] Karl W. Deutsch, George Klein, J. J. Baker, and associates, "Is Science Becoming Less International?", Massachusetts Institute of Technology, June 1954, multigraphed.

major part of the executive branch of the government, than it would tell us about any change in the attitudes of Congress or of the American electorate as a whole.[26]

Perhaps the search for quantitative indicators of any American trend toward or away from isolationism are most likely to confirm something that has been intuitively familiar to many observers: that we are facing in the United States a multiplicity of contradictory trends in public opinion, and that even a major trend toward international involvement still leaves many of the trends toward greater national self-preoccupation unimpaired, just as any temporary upsurge of nationalistic or isolationist sentiment would continue to clash with political and social processes making for greater involvement in international affairs. Under these conditions it is perhaps to be expected that our foreign policy resembles less the consistent expression of a single clearcut trend, and more a collection of persistent contradictions. We favor increased trade with the free world but are reluctant to lower tariffs; we seek security through hydrogen bombs and long range bombing planes but are unwilling to spend corresponding sums on the defense of our own big cities; we ask our diplomats to maintain a worldwide system of alliances but expect them to make few or no major concessions to the views of our allies; we take pride in the position of the United States in the United Nations, but many of our patriots protest against the display of the United Nations flag or the use of UNESCO material in our public schools. Many contradictions of this kind may continue to characterize our politics for some time to come, for they may be the visible expression of larger and deeper contradictory processes in our national development. As we come to understand better these contradictory trends within our own national political community, we may learn how to control them and keep them in safe bounds, so as to avoid international commitments that go beyond our capabilities of political self-control, and so as to learn to play an ever more effective part in building a stable political community among the world's free countries.

SYMBOLS AS INSTRUMENTS OF POLITICAL CHANGE OR CONTROL

If the study of symbols as indicators of international communication can tell us something about the difficulty of this task, the study of symbols as "regula-

---

[26] Pool has been careful to point out this particular character of the *New York Times:* "The *New York Times* was most independent (of all the 'prestige papers'), having favored tariff reductions all through the 1920's and having advocated international cooperation even when the administrations, under pressure, had to give allegiance to isolationism. In these respects it was probably closer to the views of our career diplomats than was official policy . . . ," Pool, *The "Prestige Papers,"* p. 5. For an important treatment of the broader subject of decisionmaking, see also Richard C. Snyder, H. W. Bruck, and Burton Sapin, *Decision-Making as an Approach to the Study of International Politics,* Foreign Policy Analysis Series, no. 3, Foreign Policy Analysis Project, Organizational Behavior Section, Princeton University, Princeton, 1954, especially pp. 54–67.

tors" or instruments of political control may tell us something about what could be accomplished toward its fulfillment with their aid. What can symbols do in furthering or hindering the integration of political communities?

Politics is the making and unmaking of enforceable commands. A political community is a group of persons among whom certain commands are backed by a significant probability of enforcement, as well as by a significant probability of voluntary or habitual compliance even without supervision. Such a political community usually becomes established by a process of social learning, in which enforcement probabilities and compliance habits may mutually reinforce each other. The specific study of politics involves under this aspect the study of the ways in which changes in the enforcement patterns of society—legislative, administrative, military, and the like—may accelerate, retard, or otherwise influence these broader processes of social learning.

It is characteristic of these processes of social learning, however, that they may change the boundaries of the political community within which they first developed. Such changes may involve the size of the political community, the interplay of enforcement probabilities and compliance habits within it, and the range of its functions—that is, the range of tasks that are put before the government of the political community by the changing expectations of its own population, or by the changing requirements of the survival of this political unit in its historical and political environment. What can symbols do to influence these processes of change? What can they do, in particular, to influence the processes by which several smaller political communities merge into a larger one; or by which a larger political community becomes divided into small sovereign units; or by which several sovereign states establish a pluralistic political community—such as the British Commonwealth of Nations, or the only partly formalized community of Scandinavian states—within which their populations may securely expect only peaceful and legitimate changes by processes of mutual communication, accommodation, and responsiveness?

Historical processes of this kind have been studied by a team of historians and political scientists at the Center for Research on World Political Institutions at Princeton University.[27]

The areas and cases covered by this study are: 1) The British Isles, including the unification of England, the Union with Wales, the Union with Scotland, the Union with Ireland, and the dissolution of the latter; 2) the United States, including the secession of the Thirteen Colonies, their Confederation and later Federal Union, the failure of their envisaged union with Canada, the temporary disruption of the United States in the War between the States, and the reunion that followed it; 3) the development of the Swiss Confederation; 4) the unification of Italy; 5) the unification of Germany; 6) the development and eventual disruption of the Austro-Hungarian Empire; 7) the Swedish-Norwegian

[27] Karl W. Deutsch, S. A. Burrell, R. A. Kann, M. du P. Lee, Jr., M. Lichterman, R. Lindgren. F. Loewenheim, and Richard Van Wagenen, *Political Community and the North Atlantic Area*, Princeton, 1957, and Chapter 10 above.

Union and its dissolution. Among them, it is hoped, these cases may include a sufficient variety of political, economic, social, and historical conditions to throw at least some light on the processes of political integration and disintegration in political communities in the general area of Western culture. Since some of this work is still in progress, only very tentative and preliminary results can be indicated here, in so far as they may bear on our problem of the role of symbols in the processes of political union or secession.

The first impression to emerge from a study of these cases was that of the *multiplicity* of unifying symbols in cases of successful union, or even of a successful pluralistic political community. Such political symbols can be divided into six broad categories: 1) abstract symbols, such as words, ideas, slogans, works of literature, or songs; 2) pictorial symbols, such as colors, flags, statues, relics, historic objects, buildings, animals, flowers, and the like; 3) personal symbols, such as heroes, kings, leaders, saints, prophets, or poets; 4) symbolic places, such as capital cities, historic sites, national shrines, centers of pilgrimage, battlefields, tombs of martyrs, or places of scenic beauty or grandeur; 5) symbolic organizations or institutions, such as congresses, church synods, political parties, legislatures, law courts, universities, bureaucratic or military organizations, in so far as any of these acquire symbolic functions in addition to their primary activities; 6) religious symbols—this is a category that cuts across the other five in many instances, but it is perhaps not exhausted by them. The potential usefulness of this tedious enumeration rests perhaps in this: when one lists the cases of successful and unsuccessful political integration, it turns out that in the successful cases one finds effective common symbols not in just one or two, but in five and often all six of these categories. There seems to be no case among those surveyed where a single unifying symbol showed overwhelming power. Rather it seems to have been the multiplicity of integrative symbols, their mutual interrelatedness and mutual reinforcement, that seem to have been most effective in promoting political integration.

The second impression that emerges from a study of these cases is the importance of the relatedness of the effective political symbols to the previously acquired memories of the communities to whom they appeal. Successful symbols, it appears, were only partly new; the "Union Jack" combined the old crosses of Saint George and Saint Andrew, the old symbols of England and Scotland; the red, white, and blue of the flag of the United States repeated the red, white, and blue of the flag of Britain; the ancient sign of the cross reappeared in the new flag of the Swiss Confederation. The same was true of abstract symbols: People in Scotland in 1638 united around the Covenant to defend "the King and the true religion," although within a short time they found themselves defending their "true religion," Presbyterianism, against their king, and eventually were instrumental in Charles I's capture, and indirectly in his beheading at Whitehall. Most of the successful political unions, monarchic as well as republican, were solicitous of the existing symbols, habits, and institutions of the smaller units.

A third impression is one of the limited effectiveness of symbols, and even of groups or systems of symbols, in and by themselves. The integrated symbol systems of the American Revolution, or of the nineteenth century German nationalism, were apparently far more powerful than any one symbol by itself; yet even these symbol systems had to correspond to the past memories and present life situations of the populations whom they were to move. Benjamin Franklin pleaded in vain with the citizens of Montreal to throw in their lot with the Americans; and further to the east most of the "Yankees of Nova Scotia" failed to join their New England cousins in the revolution. The appeal of German nationalism, powerful in Schleswig, proved powerless in German-speaking Switzerland and even, to a large extent and to the embarrassment of German nationalists, in German-speaking and German-ruled Alsace between 1871 and 1918. In all these cases, it appears, the life experiences and expectations of the populations concerned did much to decide the relative power or impotence of the political symbols addressed to them.

Taken together, these impressions suggest a paradox in regard to symbols of interdenominational or international unity. The more all inclusive such symbols are intended to be, the fewer may be the specific memories and habits of specific people to whom they can appeal. Moreover, most of the successful symbols offer to those who accept them a better opinion of themselves. They may do this indirectly, by first casting them down as "Little Englanders" or "miserable sinners," as the case may be, but they offer them the eventual prospect of salvation into the ranks of the saved souls or good patriots, with consequent superiority over those who have remained in darkness. Political unions, too, benefit from this appeal of prestige, implicit as well as overt, and it is striking to note how sometimes the greatest reluctance to enter upon a wholehearted union is shown by the group which is the most popular or prestigious among its prospective members. In this manner it was the English Parliament that was most reluctant to accept Anglo-Scottish Union between 1603 and 1707, and the present day reluctance of many French leaders to accept Western European Union, or the reluctance of some midwestern leaders of opinion in the United States to consider closer American integration into an Atlantic community, may well be strengthened—in addition to many other factors—by only partly conscious considerations of prestige.

This leads us to the consideration of the familiar pessimistic claim that political unity essentially requires an excluded out-group that can be despised or feared, and thus used to keep the members of the newly built larger in-group together. Our data do not support this claim. Successful unions have been brought about in which considerations of excluded out-groups played little or no significant role. Such a union was the successful union between England and Wales; the successful acceptance of the Reformation and equality before the law for the Welsh appear to have been the dominant consideration, and the notion of excluding the Papacy from Wales appears to have had little importance for the Welsh of that time. Inclusiveness rather than exclusiveness appears stressed in many of the symbols of the American Revolution. "Life, Liberty, and the pursuit of Happiness" are not exclusivistic symbols, nor is the "decent respect for the opinions of mankind" that is explicitly avowed at the beginning of the Declaration of Independence. It is the symbols, "men," "human," and "mankind" that loom prominently in that document, and so does the reference to the Creator by Whom all men have been endowed with inalienable rights. The theme is echoed in the line of the song, *"My country, 'tis of thee"*: " . . . let all that breathe partake . . . ," and it is echoed again in the humility of Abraham Lincoln's statements on equality in the Lincoln-Douglas debates, in his Second Inaugural Address, and in his image of America at Gettysburg as "a new nation, conceived in liberty and dedicated to the proposition that all men are created equal." That these inclusive symbols have been conspicuously successful, perhaps few will care to deny. Any new fashion to strike the symbols, "men," "people," and "human," from the future utterances of American leaders, and to put exclusively references to "America" and "Americans" in their place, would itself represent a major departure from the American tradition.

In the Old World, too, the political appeal of the Swiss Confederation during its formative centuries appears to have been inclusive rather than the opposite. New cities and peasant communities continued to join the Confederacy, Basel and Appenzell only at the beginning of the sixteenth century, Geneva even later. Like America, Switzerland appealed to a principle and to a way of life, and the openended symbols which expressed it were highly successful.

If we think today of the few symbols of the emerging world community, we find again that the inclusive symbols appear to have more life in them. The International Red Cross, the United Nations, UNESCO, the United Nations Children's Emergency Fund, the World Health Organization, all these aim in principle and spirit to include eventually all people rather than a select clientele of approved nations. The human symbols of a possible world community—people as different as Albert Schweitzer, Frank Laubach, Albert Einstein, and Mahatma Gandhi—all have exemplified inclusiveness rather than exclusion in their lives.

In any case, however, the community of all humanity may be far away, and the building of regional communities among at least some of the world's free countries may be the next step to be faced. Here, too, perhaps, we may find again, as could be found in a study of past cases of political integration, that the fate of a political community seems to depend less on the unattractiveness of the states and peoples who have remained outside it, and more on the positive attractions that people may find within it. Such a community may have to absorb many of the symbols of traditions of its constituent units by a process of partial incorporation. It may have to invent many new symbols, of many kinds, with the aim of bringing about their mutual reinforcement. In so doing, it would not be enough to merge or combine merely the symbols of community. Before common symbols can move peoples, they must have common or complementary memories and experiences to which these symbols can appeal; and the common symbols of any new international community may require a broadening stream of international communication, mutual attentiveness, and actual cooperation among the participating countries.

It is not enough to arrange for the international exchange of benefits: British inventions such as penicillin, radar, and jet engines for the United States, or American methods of mass production for Britain; it is essential that these benefits should be perceived as coming from the other country. The organization of symbols involves the organization of perception and of memory. Each gain toward integration in terms of perceiving and remembering experiences and symbols conducive to a greater sense of community, will make easier the reception of additional unifying symbols, and enhance their effect; each successfully established symbol of this kind, in turn, would make easier additional steps in communication and action toward more community. The actual existence of joint benefits and joint rewards for the participants would be essential for the success of such a development, and perhaps even more important if we are to go by the evidence of the cases studied, would be the continuing perception of these benefits and the common expectation of joint benefits to come.

Once a community has grown among several formerly separate political units through this process of rewarded social learning, it may grow beyond any short range expectation of reward, and it may prove able to withstand great shocks and strains. People are willing to suffer and die for that which they have learned to love; but they must first have learned to love it. A people, Saint Augustine wrote many years ago, is a community of rational beings united in the object of their love. These words might still suggest a fairly realistic approach to the problem of building a community among nations.

12 | Problems of Central European Integration: A View in 1954

The first draft of this chapter was written in 1953, and it is reproduced here with only minor changes. One change against the outlook of 1953 is the considerable economic and industrial development that has occurred between 1953 and 1978 throughout the region.

Another change is the much greater confidence East Europeans in 1978 could have in the democratic character of the German Federal Republic and in its policy of détente toward its Eastern neighbors, as well as in the democratic and peaceful nature of the second Austrian Republic, which had emerged in 1955.

A third point to be noted is the incomplete character of the pluralistic security community among the countries of the region. Troops still are deployed not only along the frontiers between Communist and non-Communist regimes but also along the frontiers of nation-states explicitly professing different versions of Marxist-Leninist doctrine, such as the borders between Albania and Yugoslavia, and between Yugoslavia and its neighbors who are members of the Warsaw Pact, such as Bulgaria, Hungary, and Rumania—somewhat as there are still larger troop deployments farther East on both sides of the frontier between the two Communist giants, the Soviet Union and China. Even within the Warsaw Pact area, several powers—the USSR, Poland, Hungary, and the German Democratic Republic—kept troops close to the borders of their fellow member Czechoslovakia, and in 1968 invaded that country, overthrew its internationally recognized government, and replaced it by another closer to their liking. A security community in that part of the world, as defined in this chapter, still seems far away.

Even so, the interest in Central or East European federation has somewhat faded, both among people living in those countries and among the dissidents who have left them. A new generation has grown up throughout the area. Many of its members might wish for more economic progress; more freedom of speech, travel, the arts; and perhaps even for more freedom of association and organization. But few of them, if any, believe in the powers of the free market for big industry, or believe that bigger

The substance of this chapter appeared in a volume of essays entitled *Challenge in Eastern Europe*, C. E. Black, ed. (New Brunswick, N.J.: Rutgers University Press, 1954), pp. 219–244. Reprinted by permission of the Publisher.

markets would bring them a better life. Beyond this, the critical minds among East Europeans do not know very well what to hope for. Restoring the past does not seem practicable, even if more than a few people should want it; and a plausible blueprint for a better future still remains to be discovered.

But the federalism that seems less urgent in Europe now than it did a quarter century ago has become of greater interest in other regions of the world. In parts of Africa, Asia, and Latin America the old discontents of Eastern Europe with both unresponsive large states and impotent small ones may find their parallels, and so may the old Central European gaps between consumer aspirations and production capabilities and economic, social, and cultural performance. If these experiences of Eastern Europe should at least have helped the peoples of some of the new nations in the "Third World" to cope better with their problems, their study will have been worthwhile.

I

The distribution of sovereign states in Central and in Eastern Europe went through some striking changes during the one hundred years between 1850 and 1950. In 1850 there were six sovereign states between the Baltic Sea and the Aegean: the empires of Austria, Prussia, Russia, and Turkey, the kingdom of Greece, and the small principality of Montenegro. Little more than two generations later, in 1913, there were ten states in the area, for by then Serbia, Bulgaria, Rumania, and Albania had all become sovereign states. Another ten years later, the number of states had increased to sixteen. Serbia and Montenegro had merged into Yugoslavia, but Hungary, Czechoslovakia, Poland, Latvia, Estonia, Lithuania, and Finland had all been added as sovereign states. After the convulsions of the Second World War, thirteen sovereign states remained in what was now called Eastern Europe. They were the same states which had existed there during the 1920's and 1930's, with the exception of the three small Baltic states of Latvia, Estonia and Lithuania, which had become incorporated under the Soviet dictatorship in the style of the federal republics of the Soviet Union.

By 1949, Soviet-style dictatorships had been established in seven of these thirteen sovereign states. In these "Iron Curtain" states, dictatorship was and is exercised through a native minority who could not have won power without the support of the Soviet Union and the Soviet armies, and who—with the conspicuous exception of Yugoslavia—could not retain this power if Soviet support were withdrawn. The indirect rule thus exercised by the Soviet dictatorship, with the help of native personnel, over six of the Eastern European states—Poland, Czechoslovakia, Hungary, Rumania, Bulgaria, and Albania—might remind the observer at first glance of the indirect rule exercised in past centuries by the empires of Turkey and Russia over some of the principalities then existing in the region. Upon this superficial view, it might seem that despite all the violent changes in political sovereignty and national allegiance during the last one hundred years, the fundamental dependence of the peoples of this region upon foreign powers had remained essentially unchanged.

This impression would be quite deceptive. In 1850, the government of Eastern Europe by only six powers had endured for more than two hundred years, with Sweden and Poland rather than Greece and Montenegro playing the roles of the fifth and sixth power at the side of Prussia, Russia, Austria, and Turkey. With the single exception of Poland, which by the end of the eighteenth century had become the victim of her neighbors, the administrative services of these powers were generally based upon foreign personnel drawn from peoples outside the region. Austria and Prussia depended upon the military and administrative services of Germans, Russia upon those of Great Russians, and Turkey in the last analysis had to rely upon the support of the Ottoman Turks. Natives of the different regions supplemented the personnel of these administrative services but did not dominate it. The rule of these foreign or semiforeign empires over the peoples of Eastern Europe was based upon this region's overwhelmingly peasant character, its political apathy and military weakness.

By the middle of the twentiety century, most of these conditions had been transformed. All the peoples of Eastern Europe had literate majorities. They had native professional and middle classes. All of them had at least some more or less modern industries and transportation systems. All of them had two or three generations of broad national and political development, a flourishing of national languages and literatures, and a vigorous growth in native political participation. They had memories of national independence and skills of political organization and action. They could no longer be ruled by alien rulers, and even the Russian dictatorship had to deal with them by indirect methods. Regardless of the surface events of politics, these basic social changes have become deepened and consolidated. The peoples of Eastern Europe today can be governed stably only by native political administrations, by native civil services and school systems, and by the appeal—however distorted—to native symbols and traditions, or they cannot be governed at all.

All these changes seem to be irreversible. It would be as difficult to restore illiteracy, apathy, and fundamental ignorance to the peoples of Eastern Europe as it would be to restore the economic and social institutions of 1850. If history teaches us anything, it is at the very least that the distribution of political and military power is subject to rapid change and that every submerged people that has preserved its identity and its capacity to think and act may well expect to find again some opportunity to determine its own destiny in freedom.

II

Yet all was not well with the growth of sovereign states in Eastern Europe. Perhaps the most characteristic feature of the political institutions of the area

was the widespread discontent with them. If people had resented the oppressive-
ness of the old large empires, many now chafed under the smallness and divisive-
ness of the national states that had come to succeed them. Eastern European
states, large or small, seemed to have a way of frustrating the hopes and ambi-
tions of significant numbers of their citizens. Where people had complained
about the lack of national freedom in the past, many now complained about the
"balkanization" of the region. It is this underlying restlessness, this *malaise* of
Eastern European politics, that gave a peculiar appeal to the demand for Eastern
European federation. If we are to understand the prospects and the problems of
a federal union in this region, we must first turn our attention to the fundamental needs and discontents that gave rise to the proposal.

Eastern Europe was a relatively backward area in terms of economic development. Even some of its most highly developed regions, such as the countries of
Austria, Hungary, and the Russian-held parts of Poland, had lagged in economic
development during the two crucial generations between 1815 and 1875, during
which time most Western countries went through decades of tremendous economic growth.[1] In 1850 Vienna was larger than Berlin and Austria did not
appear to lag conspicuously behind Prussia; but by 1866 the lag had become
conspicuous and was confirmed on the battlefields of the Austro-Prussian War.
There seems to have been a significant acceleration of economic growth between
1880 and 1914; and it has been estimated that between 1900 and 1910 the percentage rate of growth in the national income of Austria was even somewhat
faster than it was during the same decade in Western Europe. The percentage
growth of the low income of Austria-Hungary was unable, nevertheless, to keep
up with the very much higher levels of national income and industrial productivity which meanwhile had been attained in the West.

Such economic growth as did occur was quite unevenly distributed. The
economic position of the Germans and a few other groups was a great deal better
than that of the rest of the peoples concerned, and the attempts of non-German
groups to equal German economic standards often brought them into economic
competition and political friction with Germans. After the economic depression
of 1873, German nationalists raised the cry for the preservation of German

---

[1] Cf. Paul Muller, "Osterreich seit 1848," in Hans Mayer, ed., *Hundert Jahre Osterreichischer Wirtschaftsentwicklung,* 1848-1948, (Vienna: Springer Verlag, 1949), pp. 1-20, esp.
p. 8; and in the same volume, for the old monopolistic traditions of business at Vienna from
1221 to 1848, and "conditions bordering on lethargy" during the decades preceding 1848,
see Otto Gruss, "Ein Jahrhundert Osterreichischer Binnenhandel (1848-1948)," pp. 310-
358, esp. pp. 311-317; for figures on the slow introduction of steam engines, the lag in the
growth of towns, the slow relative growth of the population occupied in industry, the lack
of capital, the national fragmentation of markets, etc., see Karl Heinz Werner, "Osterreichs
Industrie und Aussenhandelspolitik 1848 bis 1948," *ibid.,* pp. 359, 470, esp. pp. 624-678,
esp. p. 659. See also J. Slokar, *Geschichte der osterreichischen Industrie* (Vienna: Tempsky,
1949), pp. 16-19, 46-54, 177-179; Richard Schüller, "Die Entstehung des osterreichisch-
ungarischen Wirtschaftsgebietes," in G. Gratz and R. Schüller, *Der wirtschaftliche Zusammenbruch Osterreich-Ungarns* (Vienna and New Haven: Holder-Pichler-Tempsky and Yale
University Press, 1930), pp. 1-35, esp. pp. 23-24; Oscar Jaszi, *The Dissolution of the Habsburg Monarchy* (Chicago: University of Chicago Press, 1929), pp. 185-212.

supremacy, and the very attempts to mitigate or overcome economic inequality thus led to intensified economic competition and political conflict.

Economic development was poorly distributed between town and country, as well as between nationalities. In most Western countries, country people had come to share many of the educational and cultural standards of the city populations. In Eastern Europe, by contrast, even the German-Austrian peasants were described before the First World War by the Viennese architect, Adolph Loos, as people wearing different clothes, speaking a different language, and having a vastly more primitive way of life than the populations of the cities.

The uneven distribution of economic opportunity was reinforced in its effect by the extreme splintering of national, linguistic, and religious affiliations. A good map of the nationalities, languages, and religions of Eastern Europe would have shown not the large patches of relatively homogeneous populations which are found in so much of Western Europe but rather a polka-dot pattern of intermixed minorities.

The relative national uniformity of the West is perhaps, at least in part, the product of a history rich in the processes of successful social learning and acculturation, which merged and melted the different ethnic groups that were left in the Western countries by accidents of migration, wars, and settlement. In Eastern Europe, such accidents of conquest or settlement may well have been even more numerous, but there is also some reason to think that the processes of assimilation were much slower and less effective.

Greater uniformity of language and culture means greater interchangeability of social roles. This is not merely a contributing cause to the growth in social mobility and in the interchange of social roles but is also to some extent their product. Where societies are rigorously stratified, where religions fail to impress upon people an awareness of their essential unity, where the obstacles to a change in occupation or in social role are great, and the rewards for mobility are uncertain and small—in these societies individuals may best succeed in gaining security by clinging tenaciously to their familiar groups, languages, customs, and traditions, and by rejecting any assimilation to other groups, except the most privileged, as a threat to their existence. The more privileged groups, under these conditions, can only be expected to resent and resist the assimilation or intrusion of strangers, unless these strangers come from regions of clearly greater wealth and greater prestige and seem to bring to the new group assets clearly greater than those they would demand. The lack of unity and assimilation in language and culture in Eastern Europe thus appears as one more aspect of the relative lack in fundamental economic innovation and social learning in that geographic area, if we take the extent of such learning and innovation in the Western countries as our standard.

On this view, the Western way of life—thus far the way of life of a minority of the peoples of the world—has been built upon a certain fundamental willingness to learn, and a basic acceptance of both some mobility, at least in society, and of some innovations in accustomed practices and habits. Against the background of this Western culture, large-scale markets and economic competition, as well as the impact of the modern centralized state, had a chance of functioning as accelerators of technological and social change: they tended to lure or push people away from social roles or economic occupations which were poorly rewarded and into new roles or occupations where the gains were greater. Western economic and political institutions succeeded the better in this function of accelerating social change where they impinged upon individuals who had the economic and social resources for moving, and at least a minimum of cultural and psychological willingness to do so. Where these economic and cultural preconditions did not exist, however, or where they existed only in part, the effect of the impact of Western institutions was bound to be quite different, and these differences became dramatically visible in the area of Eastern Europe.

<h1 style="text-align:center">III</h1>

Eastern Europe, seen from this aspect, was a semi-Western area. It was fully exposed to Western practices and institutions both in the field of higher education, particularly university education, and in the fields of military drill and warfare, and particularly in the use of conscripted armies, although it could operate in this field only as long as no extensive industrial facilities for the use of massed artillery were needed. Large parts of the area were exposed to Western methods of tax collecting, accounting, and fiscal policy, as well as public administration. They were exposed to the activities of modern bankers, and to a considerable extent to the practices of modern commerce, newspapers, and advertising. They were also exposed in large part to compulsory elementary public education.

As a result of these exposures in the nineteenth century, the peoples of Eastern Europe learned to accept completely the prevailing Western standards of theoretical science, as well as of intellectual and artistic life. They accepted to a considerable extent Western ideals of living standards, standards of consumption, wage levels, working conditions, and social welfare. Finally, many of them came to expect Western standards of farm prosperity, rural welfare, and peasant independence and cooperation. In sum, a large part of the populations of Eastern Europe accepted Western living standards as their goal, or at least as a pattern of their claims and expectations.

This rapid diffusion of Western-style claims and expectations was not matched by any comparable diffusion of Western-style work habits, savings and investment patterns, levels of productivity, or propensities to technological innovation. Land reforms in Eastern Europe were not only slow in coming, but they did little to increase productivity. The consolidation of separate strips of land, long accomplished in Scandinavia and Western Europe, was still not completed in Eastern Europe by the time of the Second World War. The tools and implements of artisans and peasants changed their traditional shape much more slowly in

Eastern Europe than they did in Germany or England and pathetically more slowly than they did in the United States. Throughout most of the regions organized labor feared that increases in productivity would only lead to losses of employment. Employers and business people aspired to use the profits of their businesses for the purpose of retiring from business themselves, rather than for expanding their productive equipment.

While productivity grew slowly, public health measures were effective and birth rates remained high. Throughout most of the region, the population pressed upon the limited supply of land and on the limited productivity of existing agricultural methods. At the same time, the lagging growth of towns and industries did not absorb completely the increases in population. The results were underemployment in the towns and industrial districts, hidden unemployment in the rural areas, and a general cheapness of human labor. While labor was thus abundant, and was often wastefully used, the skills of most workers remained low, and there was little incentive to improve them. Since capital goods and capital were scarce, there were fewer opportunities for engineers and applied scientists. And since universities, public administration, and banking had become modernized, there were ample employment opportunities for civil servants, clerks, lawyers, teachers, and research scientists.

The result was a startling precocity of Eastern European intellectual life. First-rate university training was fairly widely available throughout the region. Food, land, and domestic services were relatively cheap. Civil servants, intellectuals, and members of the professions had high prestige socially, and they found no severe economic difficulty in maintaining their families and sending their children to universities. While the top-level jobs in commerce, civil service, and universities under the Austro-Hungarian monarchy were perhaps somewhat more easily accessible to persons recruited from the German or Jewish minorities, there were some opportunities for careers for people of outstanding talent from all national backgrounds. Czech scientists reminisce today about the remarkable generation of Czech and Slovak intellectuals and scientists who made their careers during the last thirty years before the First World War in the Austro-Hungarian monarchy. At the same time, there was relatively little competition for the services of persons of high talent on the part of industry, applied science, or practical politics, since all of these activities remained relatively underdeveloped.

The coincidence of intellectual precocity with widespread social and economic backwardness led to widespread experiences of frustration. Intellectuals, not unlike the ancient philosopher Plato, dreamed of equalling one day the power and prestige of the aristocracy, for which they lacked the land holdings and family connections; and they dreamed of equalling the comforts and securities of the bourgeoisie—the upper middle class—without either owning a bourgeois amount of property or devoting a bourgeois proportion of their time and attention to money-making or to business matters. They resented the influence of the church and the clergy in the rural areas, without being either willing or able to devote a major part of their own time and attention to the needs of the country population. Almost all classes of society had come to desire Western standards of income, comfort, security, and power, without possessing as yet either the means or the skill necessary to produce them. And all these discontented groups and individuals, pushed forward by the fundamental incongruities in their social evolution, turned to politics and to the state as a remedy for their frustrations.

IV

Under these conditions, no type of government and no size of political unit could for long live up to the rising level of popular expectations and the increasingly pressing demands of society. Already, before the year 1914, large states as well as small, national states as well as international, became increasingly strained by social tensions.

In a supra- or multinational state, such as the Austro-Hungarian monarchy, an obvious reaction of the population to prolonged social and political disappointment was an increasing demand for national freedom. The sovereign nation-state would give the Czechs a fuller opportunity for careers for their young people and a more worthy share in determining their own destiny. A nation-state centered on Hungary would give Hungarian industries the protection they wanted and would free Hungarians from the delays and frustrations of the imperial relationship to Austria. The national state uniting Slovenes and Croatians with Serbia would help these peoples at long last to make real headway in escaping from their backwardness. During these same years, the peoples in the small national states of the region dreamed of escaping from the compromises and frustrations of their own small-scale political existence by national expansion into some greater and victorious power in their own area. Serbians and Montenegrins came to hope that their lives would somehow improve once Bosnia, Herzegovina, Slovenia, and Croatia had been joined to their own territories in a new Yugoslavia. Bulgarians, Greeks, and Serbians all came to believe that somehow their own lives would improve significantly if all or most of the territory of Macedonia were added to their respective countries.

Throughout large parts of Eastern Europe, the burdens and demands put upon the existing governments thus exceeded the capabilities of those governments and of the states they represented. The Eastern European states, large and small, were thus becoming overcommitted politically, economically, militarily, and socially. Among their peoples this situation encouraged the belief that things would become better once the size of political units in their region was changed. Citizens of small national states such as Serbia hoped for improvement from expansion. Minority citizens of large states, such as some of the Hungarians or Czechs in Austria-Hungary, began to wonder whether their position could not be improved by secession. All of them thought that they could improve their posi-

tion by finding that exact size of political unit in which their own language and
their own national culture could be made to predominate and in which their
own nationality or ethnic group could be turned into the leading class or social
and political elite.

Nationalism in Eastern Europe was thus a reaction to the rapid diffusion of
Western claims and to the expectations of security and opportunity throughout
a group of societies that were only slowly, if at all, acquiring the productive skill
and equipment to satisfy them. National secession, national expansion, and the
national state appeared to almost all nationalities in the region as plausible short
cuts to the prosperity, power, and prestige they all desired.

In the course of events, the experiment was actually made. The Austro-
Hungarian monarchy was destroyed and a number of successor states arose from
its remains. There is no doubt on the whole that the emergence of these national
states represented a significant step forward toward higher levels of popular
participation in public affairs, toward political democracy, toward popular education, and even, in some respects, toward greater economic opportunities. But
at the same time it seems clear that the change in the size of political units did
little or nothing to come to grips with the fundamental causes of the poverty and
backwardness of the region, or with the fundamental sources of its peculiar
psychological and political frustrations and resentments. National and regional
markets and consumer preferences remained as small and as unfavorable to mass
production in the new states as they had in the old. Capital remained as scarce
and productive investment as uneven and erratic as before. Tools, technologies,
and work habits changed slowly if at all. Poverty persisted. Purchasing power
remained low and prices high. Production remained scattered over many small
and inefficient factories. Innovations were accepted reluctantly or not at all.
Unemployment became worse than it had ever been.

Thus social tensions persisted or grew worse. Sometimes they appeared as
growing tensions between left and right, with the political middle-of-the-road
parties increasingly threatened by fascists or by communists. Sometimes they
appeared as tensions between different nationality groups, such as between
Serbians and Croatians or between Czechs and Germans. Often the same angry
and frustrated individuals could be found backing communism in one year,
extreme nationalism in another, and some more or less supranational fascism in
a third. Whole districts voted for right-wing radical candidates in one election
and for left-wing radicals in another. Nationalism in Eastern Europe was thus the
symptom of a more fundamental maladjustment, even though nationalistic
policies, once adopted, often served to make this maladjustment worse. Nationalistic governments, as well as most other governments in this region, were
becoming increasingly unpopular and during the 1930's showed increasing reluctance to face their own voters. By 1939, before the first German or Russian
soldier stepped on their soil, every country of Eastern Europe, with the exceptions of Finland and Czechoslovakia, had succumbed to some form of dictatorship. Nationalism had thus failed to cure the fundamental maladjustments of

Eastern European political and economic life. From some points of view its failure was hardly less shattering than the failure of the supranational empires that had preceded it.

It was nationalism which first undermined and in part destroyed the traditions of property and the respect for property in Eastern Europe. This attack against property began as early as the era of Prince Bismarck in Germany. The so-called Polish legislation sponsored by the German government and by the German nationalists during and after the Bismarck era showed scant respect for the property rights of the Polish minority in Germany. It was designed to prevent them from acquiring what was considered German land and to deprive them of such German land as they had managed to acquire in the past. In addition to driving the Poles from German soil, this policy was also designed to eliminate Polish minorities in Eastern Germany by assimilation or expulsion, and the German word *ausrotten*—or exterminate—leaves little doubt as to the ruthlessness of the determination behind this policy. After the First World War, when certain parts of Silesia were incorporated in Poland, former German properties in industrial corporations and other valuables had a way of coming into Polish hands. When from 1939 to 1944 German armies in turn occupied a large part, and later all, of Poland, large amounts of Polish property were again transferred to Germans.

In one shape or another, with or without benefit of legal form, this game of transferring property from the temporarily weaker to the temporarily stronger nationalities was played in large areas of Eastern Europe. When in the course of the First World War the Austro-Hungarian government collected large amounts of taxes and additional amounts of ostensibly voluntary war loans for the war efforts of Germany and Austria from the unwilling Czech, Slovakian, and Polish populations, the Austrian empire was in effect transferring important parts of the national wealth of these regions into German hands to be spent for German political and military purposes.[2] After the First World War, formerly Austrian or German mines, banks, and industrial enterprises in Czechoslovakia had a way of becoming Czechoslovakian. After 1939, when the Nazis occupied this country, Czechoslovakian-owned enterprises soon found their way into German hands, and the Dresdner Bank emerged as a major owner of formerly Czechoslovakian property. After Germany had lost the war in 1945, the new government of Czechoslovakia with the support of all political parties—anti-Communists as well as Communists—proceeded to expel all Sudeten Germans and to confiscate their property. Sudeten German anti-Nazis who had been loyal to the Czechoslovakian republic were nominally exempt from these provisions, but the burden of proving their loyalty was put upon their shoulders, and by 1947 the nationalistic atmosphere in the new Czechoslovakia was such that many German anti-Nazis

---

[2] Cf. G. Gratz and R. Schüller, *op. cit.*, pp. 171–188; Wilhelm Winkler, *Die Einkommens-verschiebungen in Osterreich während des Weltkrieges* (Vienna and New Haven: Holder-Pichler-Tempsky and Yale University Press, 1930), pp. 74–78, 219–221; Alois Rašin, *Financial Policy of Czechoslovakia during the First Year of Its History* (Oxford: Clarendon Press, 1923), pp. 7–25.

with proven democratic records preferred to emigrate voluntarily to Germany, leaving behind the properties and savings of a lifetime. At the beginning of the year 1948, shortly before the Communists seized power in Czechoslovakia, there were perhaps 2,000,000 individuals who, in one way or another, had acquired some parts of former German property either in the Sudetenland or elsewhere in the country. These people may have found it rather difficult to resist the power and the confiscatory threats of Communism, so long as they themselves were using other people's furniture and were living in other people's houses.

Throughout the region, property rights thus became the plaything of nationalistic politics between Poles and Germans, Czechs and Austrians, Hungarians, Slovakians, and Rumanians, Serbians and Croatians. Few, if any, of the persons who participated in these confiscations considered themselves criminals. Rather they persuaded themselves that they were patriots. They had perhaps suffered themselves during the preceding periods of war or foreign occupation, and this may have seemed to them the only opportunity for getting some sort of reparation. No rationalization, however, could change the ultimate result: during the last thirty years in Eastern Europe, the ownership of property, the right to travel, and the right to work in desirable occupations, have been dependent not upon peoples' diligence, honesty, or thrift, but upon the accident of their affiliations with the group temporarily in power. Peoples' property and freedom thus came to depend upon the official estimation of their "political reliability" or loyalty, which was defined for them by a rapidly changing sequence of politicians and political regimes. Many of the people who practiced these policies of confiscation and repression considered themselves anti-Communists, or professed themselves as such. Yet in their disregard for property rights and civil liberties they did much to pave the way for Communist systems of government.

V

Perhaps it has been memories of the stagnation under the old empires and the conflict and repressions of the following eras of nationalism that have turned many to visions of a safer, broader, and more generous life under an Eastern European federation.

In the minds of those who accepted this vision, a federation of Eastern European states would offer its peoples military security against invasion by outsiders. It would insure economic prosperity, provide a more stable distribution of economic welfare, safeguard property, provide broader opportunities for all, reward work, thrift, and enterprise, and by all these means serve to insure broad and rapid economic growth. In regard to politics, it would safeguard civil liberties. It would guarantee nondiscriminatory treatment to all peoples and minorities and free mobility to individuals throughout the region. It would assure to both individuals and peoples throughout Eastern Europe respect for their diverse habits and traditions, so that none of them would be forced to change their respective customs, work habits, and social institutions more rapidly or more radically than they might freely choose. To ease the complex and subtle problems of culture, emotions, and psychology, it was hoped that the federation would insure widespread opportunities for education. It was hoped that it would give to the inhabitants of the region both social and international prestige. It was hoped that it would bring them to a status of equality with the reference groups which they had chosen as yardsticks for comparison, or that in some way an Eastern European federation would make its citizens the equals not only of the French and German peoples but perhaps in time even of the English and American peoples, who have now become the reference groups for standards of achievement throughout the world. Finally it was hoped that such a federation would give rise to inspiring common enterprises that would unite the peoples of Eastern Europe in a new sense of their own identity, as in past centuries the monarchies of Western Europe, according to the philosopher José Ortega y Gasset, have united their own peoples into a sense of dignity and nationhood.

In striking contrast to the splendor of these visions was their relative poverty in specific detail. None of the larger projects for federation in this region were ever negotiated by governments or even by responsible political leaders from the different areas. There was a negotiated project for a Polish-Czechoslovakian federation, worked out by Czechoslovakian and Polish leaders-in-exile during the Second World War, but this project which included only two states in the region was not followed up by the established governments or by the major political organizations after the war.[3] Projects for a Balkan union usually failed to include even the Danubian states and practically never reached out toward Poland and the Baltic. Projects for a Baltic union usually remained limited to Poland and the small Baltic states, leaving the latter faced with the prospect of becoming a minority in what would become in practice a greater Poland.

Perhaps most of the substance behind the projects for federation did not consist so much in plans for the future as in memories of the past, and in particular of the Austro-Hungarian monarchy. A reconstituted and enlarged Austria-Hungary, reaching the North through the accession of Poland and the Baltic states to the shores of the Baltic Sea and including in the South all the Balkan states down to the border perhaps of Turkey, would sum up the many projects for uniting Eastern Europe which have been discussed so often from the 1920s to the 1950s. It is the general project of a federation of the Danubian countries,

[3] Cf. United States Department of State, Division of Library and Reference Service, *Danubian Federation: An Annotated Bibliography (Bibliography No. 66)*, Washington, D.C., October 28, 1952 (multigraphed); Feliks Gross, *Crossroads of Two Continents: A Democratic Federation of East-Central Europe* (New York: Columbia University Press, 1945), pp. 28–34, and for the text of the Polish-Czechoslovakian Declaration, signed in London on January 25, 1942, by representatives of the two governments-in-exile, pp. 102–104; Antoni Plutynski, *We Are 115 Millions* (London: Eyre and Spottiswoode, 1944), pp. 33–36, 114–122; etc.

enlarged by the addition of Poland to the north, and conceivably by that of Albania and Greece in the south, which needs closer examination.

It is true that such a federation would carry a certain amount of international prestige by virtue of the sheer numbers of its inhabitants, and of the considerable sums of productive capacities, natural resources, and miles of railroad track scattered throughout the area. Any more fundamental and lasting prestige, however, might well depend upon the effective military capabilities and the actual levels of economic prosperity and growth, and of educational progress and political democracy which the federation could maintain.

The obvious military task for such a federation would be to form a counterweight to Germany or Russia, or to both of them together. Many of these military tasks, however, seem well beyond the capabilities of the region. Such a federation would have no clear-cut advantage in human resources over either Germany or Russia and would be definitely inferior to the heavy industries and economic war potentials of these two countries, as well as to their productive facilities and transport systems. The military security of such a federation would depend primarily upon the military strength of Western Europe, and perhaps even more upon that of the United States. Given sufficient strength and determination in the Atlantic community, an Eastern European federation could be made secure, but its own military contribution would hardly be necessary, and certainly not decisive. In the absence of sufficient strength among the Western Powers, on the other hand, no amount of military effort on the part of these peoples could make them secure. Any situation in which the military strength of the Western and Eastern Powers were in such delicate balance that an Eastern European federation could make a decisive difference in their military prospects would be extremely rare; and if it should occur, it would be a situation of extreme insecurity rather than security, and would be unlikely to last for long.

A commitment to an active military policy might thus be beyond the military as well as the economic capabilities of the area, as commitments in the First World War proved to be fatally beyond the capabilities of the Austro-Hungarian monarchy. In this case, the result of overcommitment was the dissolution of the larger political unit and its replacement by a number of smaller ones, accompanied for decades by the widespread unpopularity of the very idea of union.

As regards economic prospects, projects of Eastern European union are frequently based on a naïve version of the nineteenth-century economic theory. According to that theory, economic growth would automatically result from free competition; no severe depression or protracted unemployment could result under truly free competition, and all actual depressions would be merely the result of political interference in economic life on the part of misguided governments. Under such a *laissez faire* economy, the rates of saving and capital formation would automatically be high, capital would be invested in the most productive uses, and a continuous stream of creative innovations and technological improvements would be introduced as a matter of course.

These visions have little to do with the realities of the economic development of underdeveloped areas, as economists now know them. The propensity to save, the rate of capital formation, the tendencies to invest money in productive machinery rather than in land or liquid funds and to apply science and to accept technical innovations—all these are largely matters of society and culture and, to a significant extent, matters of public policy.[4]

None of all these problems—terms of trade, capital formation, savings rates, investment patterns, and innovation rates—are necessarily insoluble, but their solution is essential to economic growth, and none of them will be solved automatically by the effects of federation. Free trade has resulted not only in the relative wealth of England, but also in the relative poverty of Portugal, and Ireland. If English rather than Portuguese or Irish living standards are eventually attained in Eastern Europe, this also will be due to a considerable amount of careful study of the problems and conditions of economic growth in this region.

As long as major economic difficulties and frustrations persist in Eastern Europe, political democracy in that region is likely to remain in a precarious position. With the persistence of rural tensions resulting from village poverty and overpopulation, with strikes and unemployment among labor, with bitter competition for white-collar jobs, with the ever-present tendency of the wealthy to flee with their accumulations of capital (a tendency likely to become worse under government-imposed currency regulations and controls), economic stagnation or disruption will probably be a constant threat, and always with it will be the twin temptations of nationalism and dictatorship. The fatal gap between the rapid growth of popular needs and expectations and the slow growth of economic and social opportunities might continue to plague and eventually might even shatter an Eastern European federation, much as it plagued and eventually shattered both supranational empires and national states in the past.

If the plans for an Eastern European federation do not offer in themselves any answer to the general problems of economic growth and political stability, neither do they offer any answer to a number of the most burning specific problems of the area.

Just what would be the role of the Austrian and German peoples in an Eastern European federation? In the 1950s, a large number of Germans were demanding rather vehemently the return to Germany of the formerly German territories which at present form the western provinces of Poland and which contain a large part of the industrial capacity of the Polish republic. There are almost 3,000,000

[4]Cf. W. W. Rostow, *The Process of Economic Growth* (New York: Norton, 1952), pp. 12–106; J. M. Clark, "Common and Disparate Elements in National Growth and Decline," in National Bureau of Economic Research, *Problems in the Study of Economic Growth* (New York, N.B.E.R.), July 1949 (multigraphed), pp. 33–37; Joseph Schumpeter, "Theoretical Problems of Economic Growth," *The Journal of Economic History,* Supplement VII, 1947, pp. 1–9; Albert Kervyn. "Approaches to the Problem of Economic Development," *World Politics* (July 1953), pp. 569–578; B. F. Hoselitz, ed., *The Progress of Underdeveloped Countries* (Chicago: University of Chicago Press, 1952); United Nations, *Measures for the Economic Development of Underdeveloped Countries* (New York, 1951).

Sudeten German evacuees scattered through Germany and Austria, and many of
these persons then still cherished hopes of returning some day to the Sudetenland and to their former properties, and perhaps even of gaining additional
properties and power by way of compensation or booty at the next turn of the
wheel of political fortune.

Only slowly did German claims for restoration or new expansion recede into
the background as the first generation of German evacuees grew old and the
children of this generation found new roots and new prospects within the
present boundaries of Germany. (By 1978 it seemed to have dwindled.)

Distinct from the issue of the East Germans is the problem of German Austria.
The German city of Vienna lies east of both Zagreb and Prague. If Boehmia has
been compared by German writers to a Slavic wedge thrust into Germany, then
Austria could be compared to a German wedge pushed into Eastern Europe.
Would the Austrians be included in an Eastern European federation and, if so,
what would their position be? If they were not included in an Eastern federation, would they be permitted to resume their efforts for union with Germany,
as was attempted by both the German and the Austrian Social Democrats after
1918 and again by the Bruening-Curtius government in 1930, and as was finally
accomplished by the violent action of the Nazis in 1938? If Austria were to join
neither Germany nor an Eastern European federation, where would it go, and
how would its people make a living?

The German and Austrian problems are only two of the major nationality
problems of the Eastern European area. What would be done about the Magyars
and Rumanians in Transylvania? Would the former Ukrainian territories of
Poland and Czechoslovakia remain outside the Eastern European federation?

Perhaps more important, where would the center of the federation be? There
seems to be no first-rate rail link east of Vienna between the north and south
of Eastern Europe. Are there one or more potential metropolitan regions for the
East European area, and could they be linked by an integrated transportation
system? If not, could an Eastern European federation function without them?

VI

None of these question could be answered easily or quickly in the early 1950s,
nor could they be so answered in the 1970s. Necessary to their solution are
many more facts than are now available. Among the first steps that can be
undertaken toward strengthening the prospects for an eventual free and democratic East European federation is the undertaking of some of the fundamental
research which has been given insufficient attention in the past.

Such research would enable us to evaluate more correctly the extent to which
political amalgamation of Eastern Europe is practicable and how likely it is that
integration without amalgamation could maintain peace and security. Political
amalgamation would mean the merging of political institutions and would

emphasize particularly the abolition of sovereign national governments in Eastern Europe and the transfer of their powers to a single common government. Integration without amalgamation might mean the retention of national sovereignty, modified by a sense of community among all participating political units that would lead to the conviction that a war among them would be anachronistic and impossible.

Integration without amalgamation can be found between Norway and Sweden, and perhaps among all the Scandinavian countries. It can also be found between the United States and Canada, and perhaps between the United States and Mexico. In all these cases, the nations involved have demilitarized the borders separating them from each other. They stand ready to defend their national soil against foreign invaders, but they do not expect to be invaded or to go to war with their neighbor. The United States and Canada have even entered in substance into a relationship of alliance under which they stand ready to aid each other against outside enemies. The demilitarized borders between Norway and Sweden and between the United States and Canada are visible expression of the development of the habits, practices, and institutions of mutual trust and quick responsiveness possible between neighboring nations.

Common governments, too, require such mutual habits and understanding and responsiveness, if they are to mean more than the forcible subjection of the peoples living under them. It seems significant that the Swedes and Norwegians were on the verge of open hostilities at the beginning of the twentieth century when they were still living under a common crown and that relations between these two peoples have improved continually since Norway, like Sweden, attained its sovereign freedom. It may well be that the greater the degree of common government, the greater must be the amount of effective mutual understanding and responsiveness. And it may also be true that, at a given level of mutual understanding and voluntary self-adjustment, a nonamalgamated community would be practicable where a common government would founder in mutual conflict.

Dependable habits of mutual understanding and responsiveness are indicators—though not the only indicators—of the capabilities of the political institutions which maintain a political community. Some of the many other indicators of such capabilities are the material resources at the disposal of the community and the speed with which these can be recommitted to meet new pressures or new challenges. The number of duties a government must discharge and the amount of expectations and pressures a security community has to meet represent a load upon the institutions or community; there is a balance between the political load of decision-making, responsiveness, and capacity to act on the one hand, and the actual capabilities of a government or a political community on the other hand.

It is this balance between integration loads and integration capabilities which may decide the fortunes of a political community, whether it be a unitary state or a regional federation. A better understanding of the probable loads and strains and of the probable resources and capabilities of the political communities in Eastern Europe will do much to indicate what degree of political amalgamation will prove practicable in this area, and what kind of political, economic, or military overcommitments may have to be avoided.

During the presidential campaign in the United States in 1952 both General Eisenhower and Governor Stevenson agreed that the liberation of the peoples of Eastern Europe would eventually come, not through destructive war, but through the steady pressure and the increasingly attractive example of the strong and successful development of the Western democracies. In the age of atomic energy, the chains of tyranny cannot be burst by atom bombs if men are to liberate anything more than cemeteries. Rather, the chains will have to be corroded gradually by the ever-present and relentless example of Western freedom.

This may be a slow process but it may in the end be a surer one. It will require from the Western world more and better research and a greater understanding of the needs and conditions of the Eastern European peoples. Such research may show that historical developments are not always slow and that centuries are not always necessary for the evolution of conditions necessary to a great and democratic federation. There is much to be accomplished before a free Eastern European federation can emerge from the assembly line of history. But it is possible that preparations can be made quickly as well as slowly, once people know what they must do, and once they have gained faith that tyranny and war can be banished forever from Eastern Europe.

13 | Toward Western European Integration: An Interim Assessment in 1962

The main changes in this chapter, which first appeared in the early 1960s, are additions, not deletions. In Table 13-1, data for 1965 and 1975 have been added in order to let the reader judge to what extent, if any, the trends reported in the original essay have continued. The recent data suggest that there has been economic growth within the European Community (EC), but more or less the same has been true of industrial countries outside it. Periods of stagnation and recession or depression, such as in the 1970s, have slowed down growth within the EC and the United States no less than in the industrial countries outside these large markets. Since the original essay was written, two small industrial countries, Sweden and Switzerland, have overtaken the United States in per capita income.

The passages from 1962 appraising politics and institutions have been left unchanged. Here the need for some revised judgments by 1978 should be manifest. Slowly but observably, European integration has progressed. The European Common Market is now spoken of as the European Community. It now has nine members since Britain, Denmark, and Ireland joined the original six—France, West Germany, Italy, the Netherlands, Belgium, and Luxemburg—in 1973; and the governments of Greece, Spain, and Portugal are now striving for membership.

As to particular policies, the European agricultural policy of protection and subsidization has on the whole proved successful. Thus far, higher food prices in Britain and subsidies paid in effect by West Germany to French farmers have proved acceptable, and agriculture is now widely looked upon as a link that strengthens European unity.

As to domestic politics, France in 1978 seems less divided against itself than it did in 1962; there is less violence, and political cleavage now runs along different lines. The roots of democracy have become stronger in the Federal Republic of Germany and perhaps in Italy as well. Though tensions with the Soviet bloc have slightly relaxed, the positive appeal of European unity does not seem to have become weaker.

The "quiet process" of West European social and cultural integration,

Copyright by the Trustees of Columbia University in the City of New York. Permission to reprint from the *Journal of International Affairs*, vol. 16, no. 1 (1962): 89–101, is gratefully acknowledged to the Editors of the *Journal*. This article is reprinted here with only minor changes.

observed in 1962, has been at work not for "another five or ten years" but for fifteen. Europe now has nine members and may grow to twelve. There seem to be no current prospects for a European Defense Community or a broader European Energy Authority that would deal with oil and nuclear power as well as coal; and the prospects for an early European Monetary Union seem dim. But there are plans to elect the European Parliament in 1978 by popular vote, though as yet without any significant powers. Proponents of the plan, and perhaps some of the governments that have accepted it thus far, hope that such a popularly elected Parliament will enjoy greater prestige, and that greater powers may follow.

Generally speaking, it thus seemed in mid-1978 that the process of European integration would continue on a time scale of decades rather than of years; that the main arenas and instruments of political action for the next decade and perhaps for the rest of this century would remain the nation-states; and that the growing community of Western Europe would continue to be pluralistic rather than amalgamated in character.

More than fifteen years ago, in September 1946, Sir Winston Churchill proposed to cure the ills of war-shattered Europe by

a remedy which, if it were generally and spontaneously adopted, would, as if by a miracle, transform the whole scene, and would, in a few years, make all Europe, or the greater part of it, as free and as happy as Switzerland is today.[1]

To Sir Winston, the prescription was quite clear:

What is this sovereign remedy? It is to recreate the European family, or as much of it as we can, and provide it with a structure under which it can dwell in peace, in safety and in freedom. We must build a kind of United States of Europe . . .[2]

Nor was there any doubt about the main instrument by which this "sovereign remedy" was to be put into effect: "The process is simple. All that is needed is the resolve of hundreds of millions of men and women . . ."[3]

The steps by which Sir Winston's conception became one of the major policies of the Western alliance need not be retraced here. What concerns us is a tentative assessment of the results which the policies of Western European unification have had thus far during their first fifteen years of gradually increasing operation,

[1] Sir Winston Churchill, "Speech at Zurich, Switzerland, September 1946," reprinted in Andrew and Frances Boyd, *Western Union: A Study of the Trend Toward European Unity* (Washington, 1949).
[2] *Ibid.*
[3] *Ibid.*

and of the main steps and problems on the path toward further European unification that remain to be confronted now.

INTEGRATION AND THE CHANGING
CONCEPT OF A REMEDY

In 1946, Europeans were looking for remedies against a number of dangers that seemed to rise up against them. First of all, for the average person in those years, there was the partial economic collapse of much of Europe, the devastation and poverty left by the war, the still vivid memories of the pre-war depression, the loss of overseas markets and long established channels of trade, and the fear that the war-shattered economies of the West European states might never recover, but at best linger on in an irreversible decline. Only the integration into a European Union, it seemed to many, could restore confidence and rebuild West European economies and living standards.

Linked to the specter of unending poverty in the absence of European integration was the fear of irremediable backwardness. American industry and technology had advanced by giant strides, even Russia's economy had been forced ahead (at least in heavy industry) by Stalin's ruthless control of the vast Eurasian land mass under his rule. But how were the much smaller European national states ever to find the resources and the confidence to renew their technologies, to rekindle their inventiveness, and to re-enter the competition with those continent-sized rivals? Only a European Union could offer sufficiently vast markets, it appeared, to permit the application of the new technologies of mass production, to attract and hold scientific talent, and to encourage the stream of innovations that would be required.

Another danger seen by Europeans in 1946 was that of mounting political and military insecurity, stemming particularly from what seemed to many an imminent Soviet military threat from without, coupled with the danger of Communist popularity and subversion from within—a possibility underscored by the presence of avowed members of the Communist Party in the cabinets in France and Italy. Only European integration, so it seemed, could match and conquer the appeals of communism, particularly to young people. And only a European federation could provide the military strength and unity of purpose to preserve the institutions and traditions of Western Europe against the possibility of Soviet military conquest.

In addition to the vividly perceived danger from the East, Europeans were acutely aware of the danger of recurrent wars among the nations of Western Europe—the kind of nationalistic conflicts that had devastated much of the continent in World Wars I and II. The prospect of an unending repetition of such clashes, particularly between France and Germany, seemed intolerable. Already twice, Europe had torn herself to pieces, and only some form of a United States of Europe seemed capable of preventing a revival of the perennial nationalist hatreds and an eventual third intra-European war that might destroy whatever was still left.

Finally, a remedy seemed desperately needed for the declining position of Europe in the world, particularly something to shore up the continent against the threatening loss of her vast colonial possessions which had been so thoroughly shaken up by the cumulative effects of modern education, trade and industrialization, by the events of World War II and its aftermath, and by the twin impacts of Soviet and American anti-colonial ideologies and American economic competition. Only a strong, united Europe seemed likely to summon up the economic strength, the military power, and the political and cultural prestige to overawe the colonial nationalists and to make them accept their place in an essentially European-directed and European-dominated scheme of things. It was perhaps not an accident that some of the outstanding "Europeans" among the political leaders in the early years after 1946, such as Georges Bidault of France and Paul Henri Spaak of Belgium, were also the men who continued to demonstrate a lively concern for the colonial possessions and interests of their respective countries.

If these were some of the main dangers or ills perceived by West Europeans in 1946, then none of them were remedied by European federation, nor by any other form of a common general government. Rather, the very considerable improvements between 1946 and 1961 in the position of the main West European countries in regard to many of their troubles was accomplished primarily by the action of national governments, aided significantly in some important matters by strictly limited functional organizations at the intergovernmental— rather than the supra-national—level. The elevation of these organizations to true supra-national powers, the broadening of their limited functional competences to the areas of actual decisive power over such vital matters as foreign affairs, defense, or finance, and the rise of broad and strong mass support for, and popular loyalties to, any such genuinely supra-national form of government—all these at the beginning of 1962 were still in the future.

The economic and technological recovery of Europe was accomplished mainly by its national governments, with the very substantial and at times crucial assistance of the United States under a series of items of American legislation, most notably the Marshall Plan. The military security of Europe, such as it was during those fifteen years, was maintained almost entirely by the military and nuclear strength of the United States and the firmness of the American national commitment to its use against any possible all-out attack on Western Europe. Compared to this American commitment, the military contributions of Britain— and even more those of the six European Coal and Steel Community (ECSC) countries—were distinctly secondary in importance, not only in regard to nuclear devices and means for their delivery, but generally in terms of heavy equipment and of firepower.

The loss of European colonies proved inescapable and, by present indications, irreversible. Once India, Burma, Ceylon, Indochina, Egypt, Syria, Lebanon,

Tunisia, Morocco, Ghana, Nigeria, most of French Africa, and a host of others had left the European colonial empires, or shown clear signs of leaving soon, the intensity of the emotional reaction of the pro-colonial sectors of West European opinion in the crises of Suez, Cyprus, the Congo and Goa reminds one of the loud slamming of so many stable doors after the horses have departed.

Neither national governments nor any supra-national European institutions proved capable of providing any remedy against the inexorable effects of the "winds of change" that had begun to blow in Asia and Africa. Nevertheless, the years of the final loss of the great bulk of European colonial possessions were not only the years of recovery of the West European national economies, but were also the years of the recovery of much of the international prestige of such European nations as France, Western Germany and Italy—showing perhaps how much more such international prestige had come to depend on domestic economic health, technological advancement, and perhaps cultural creativity, rather than on colonial possessions.

Even the risk of recurrent intra-European wars was not banished, it seems, by any powerful European institution at the supra-national level. There is no European government or court with any power of compulsion, and substantial parts of the armed forces of most European countries have remained outside any direct North Atlantic Treaty Organization (NATO) command.

Perhaps the most important safeguard against a recurrence of war among West European countries, however, may have arisen well below the level of any type of government, but rather at the level of informal opinion among the political elites, and even more among the broader but still politically relevant strata of the population of the various countries. Somehow, war among West European countries has come to be considered senseless, fratricidal and self-destructive, and thus basically illegitimate. In the nineteenth century, such a shift to a perception of mutual warfare as illegitimate preceded by one or two generations the political unification, respectively, of the Italian principalities and the German states.

This last point might be the one that is relatively least subject to possible crises in the near future. Military security is unattainable in the age of the thermonuclear arms race. The best that states can do by armaments and alliances is to try to match the level of armed insecurity of their potential opponents. A power willing to fight an all-out thermonuclear war could depopulate a federated Europe as easily as a Europe of sovereign nations. Whether the outcome would be a policy of preemption or of caution might depend far more on the specific policies pursued by all participating powers and on the high or low levels of threat and provocation they might imply, than it would on the size and number of countries involved.

Similarly, the future levels of prosperity and economic growth might depend not so much on the size of a common customs area that might emerge, but on international economic conditions, on the one hand, and on the specific eco-

nomic policies pursued within each customs area, on the other. The old argu
ment that larger markets make for faster economic growth is oversimplified. A
study by Professor Hollis Chenery suggests that there are strong economic rewards, particularly in regard to industry, in expanding a nation from 2 million to
50 million people, but there is no very good evidence of any sizable economic
premium on expanding the market further above 50 millions at West European
income levels.[4] A study of national market size, in terms of 1955 gross national
product and average rates of growth for the years 1955-1958, may illustrate the
point.

The figures in Table 13-1 and the comparison of such pairs of countries as
Britain and Germany, Italy and Japan, Ireland and Austria, or Portugal and
Greece, all strongly suggest that in 1955-58 there was no close relation between
market size and rates of economic growth; nor, it seems from a cursory inspection of the countries concerned, is there a close relation between such growth
and area, total population, resource endowment or per capita income of these
countries.[5]

An alternative ranking by growth rates likewise would not put the European
Coal and Steel Community (ECSC) countries clearly at the head of the non-
Communist countries. The relatively high growth rates of Western Germany are
still below those of Japan, Turkey and Greece, and scarcely higher than those of
little Austria, even though none of these four states is an ECSC member. In any
case, the high growth of West Germany in 1955-58 might well be credited rather
to the effects of United States economic aid and cooperation than to membership in the European Economic Community (or Common Market), since the
latter became operative only at the beginning of 1958 and no major tariff reductions occurred in that year. Moreover, if at least the ECSC could be credited
for German growth in 1955-58, it might also have to be blamed, by much
the same right, for Belgium's near stagnation in the same period. Generally, if
the large size of the United States' domestic market was praised as a cause of the
past high growth rates and current high living standards of the country, then
its relative stagnation in the late 1950's could not but weaken at least slightly
the case for economic integration. In all these cases, the decisive factors seemed

[4] I.e., at per capita income levels above $600; at the $300 level, a market expansion up to
100 million population might still be highly rewarding. Cf. Hollis B. Chenery, "Patterns of
Economic Growth," *The American Economic Review*, Sept. 1960, pp. 624-54, and esp.
645-46. (In dollars current at that time.)

[5] In computer calculations carried out in November 1977 by Mrs. Brigitta Widmaier in the
International Institute for Comparative Social Research at the Science Center Berlin, there is
no significant correlation between market size, as indicated by gross domestic product in
1958 and the real growth of that product in any of the periods 1955-58, 1960-70 and
1970-74. For the last two of these periods, the weak correlations are negative and are
becoming slightly more so for the more recent ones. Strong positive correlations are found,
however, between growth rates from one period to another, suggesting that other national
characteristics of the various countries tend to have a stronger effect on growth rates than
does market size alone.

TABLE 13-1. NATIONAL MARKET SIZE AND RATES OF ECONOMIC GROWTH,
1955–1975
A. TOTAL GNP GROWTH

	SIZE OF MARKET GNP, 1958	AVERAGE ANNUAL RATE OF GROWTH OF REAL GDP,		
	Total Bill. $	1955–58 %	1960–70 %	1970–75 %
A Non-Communist Countries				
1. Above $100 billion GNP:				
United States	387	2.6	4.3	2.5
2. From 10 to 99 billion:				
United Kingdom	51	1.7	2.8	2.7
France*	45	4.4	5.7	3.9
German Federal Republic*	38	6.6	4.6	2.2
India	27.4	3.3	3.6	1.4
Canada	26.0	4.5	5.9	4.7
Japan	21.3	9.3	10.5	6.8
Italy*	21.2	5.4	5.4	3.8
3. From 5 to 9.9 billion:				
Belgium*	9.6	2.1	4.7	4.0
Sweden	8.4	2.8	4.4	2.6
Netherlands*	7.6	4.0	5.5	3.4
Spain	7.3	6.0	7.2	7.0
Turkey	6.5	8.1	6.0	7.1
Switzerland	6.1	4.3	4.1	1.3
4. From 1 to 4.9 billion:				
Denmark	4.1	2.4	4.7	2.2
Austria	3.7	6.3	4.5	4.3
Norway	3.3	2.5	4.9	4.5
Greece	2.0	6.7	7.5	4.9
Portugal	1.8	3.0	6.4	7.9
Ireland	1.5	-0.7	4.2	5.3
B. Communist Countries				
USSR	150	10.6	7.2	6.0
China (Mainland)	35	14.5	nd	nd
Yugoslavia**	nd	8.8	6.6	6.4
Poland**	nd	8.3	6.2	10.0
Romania**	nd	8.0	8.6	11.4
Czechoslovakia**	nd	7.6	4.2	5.4
Albania**	nd	7.2	8.4	9.2
Bulgaria**	nd	6.5	8.2	7.6
Hungary**	nd	6.4	5.4	6.4

*Members of European Coal and Steel Community (1952–   ), and of Common Market Treaty (1958–   ).
**No 1955 GNP data in source; countries listed in order of growth rate reported by United Nations.
Data for Communist countries refer to net material product.
Source of data: United Nations Statistical Yearbook, 1976; GNP 1955—Research Center in Economic Development and Cultural Change, University of Chicago, "The Role of Foreign Aid in the Development of Other Countries," App. I, in United States 85th Congress, 1st Session, Senate Doc. 52, *Foreign Aid Programs: Compilation of Studies and Surveys* (Washington, D.C., Government Printing Office, 1957), p. 239.

TABLE 13-1. Continued
B. GNP PER CAPITA

	SIZE OF MARKET GNP, 1958		AVERAGE ANNUAL RATE OF GROWTH PER CAPITA		
	Total Bill. $	Per Capita %	1955-58 %	1960-70 %	1970-75 %
A. Non-Communist Countries					
1. Above $100 billion GNP:					
United States	387	2,343	0.8	3.0	1.6
2. From 10 to 99 billion:					
United Kingdom	51	998	1.2	2.3	2.5
France*	45	1,046	3.4	4.6	3.1
German Federal Republic*	38	762	5.4	3.5	1.8
India	27.4	72	1.9	1.3	-0.7
Canada	26.0	1,667	1.7	4.1	3.2
Japan	21.3	240	8.1	9.4	5.4
Italy*	21.2	442	4.8	4.6	3.0
3. From 5 to 9.9 billion:					
Belgium*	9.6	1,015	1.4	4.1	3.7
Sweden	8.4	1,165	2.1	3.7	2.3
Netherlands*	7.6	708	2.6	4.1	2.5
Spain	7.3	254	5.2	6.1	5.9
Turkey	6.5	276	5.2	3.5	4.6
Switzerland	6.1	1,229	3.0	2.6	0.5
4. From 1 to 4.9 billion:					
Denmark	4.1	913	1.8	4.0	1.6
Austria	3.7	532	6.1	4.0	3.9
Norway	3.3	969	1.5	4.1	3.8
Greece	2.0	239	5.8	6.8	4.3
Portugal	1.8	201	2.2	5.5	7.7
Ireland	1.5	509	–	3.8	4.8
B. Communist Countries					
USSR	150	682	8.7	5.9	5.0
China (Mainland)	35	56	10.9	nd	nd
Yugoslavia**	nd	nd	7.5	5.5	5.4
Poland**	nd	nd	7.4	5.1	9.0
Romania**	nd	nd	6.4	7.6	10.4
Czechoslovakia**	nd	nd	6.5	3.6	4.8
Albania**	nd	nd	4.0	5.6	6.2
Bulgaria**	nd	nd	5.5	7.4	7.0
Hungary**	nd	nd	5.9	5.1	6.0

GDP Growth Rates, 1955-58—*United Nations Yearbook of National Account Statistics, 1960* (New York, 1961), Part D, Table 2, pp. 265-69. GDP Growth Rates for Spain are not given in the source just cited. They have been estimated (for the average of the years 1957 and 1958 only) from the estimated increase in Spanish output in the United Nations *Economic Survey of Europe 1958*, (Geneva, 1959) Ch. II, p. 21, and the rate of population increase for Spain in the United Nations *Demographic Yearbook, 1960* (New York, 1961), p. 114. I am indebted to Professor Charles L. Taylor and the International Institute of Comparative Social Research for aid in adding more recent data to this table.

to be not those of market size but rather those of cultural and historical background, of current political and economic conditions, and of the nature and effectiveness of the national political and economic policies.

Despite these unresolved questions in our imperfect understanding of the economic effects of the integration of markets, it seems that some further advances toward a more integrated European political community will doubtlessly be attempted in the 1960's. Their objectives may seem clear: greater prosperity and economic growth; further progress in technology and the application of science; more security from military threats, both from within and from without; greater popular resistance to Communist and Soviet propaganda; and greater respect and prestige for Europeans in the world at large, including not only Asia and Africa but also notably the United States. What seems less clear is the pathway—or pathways—by which these objectives are to be approached. Are these goals to be sought in the main by policies of supra-national political amalgamation or by less formal policies of pluralism?

SUPRA-NATIONAL ORGANIZATIONS IN THE 1960's: UNIVERSAL AND SPECIFIC OR PARTICULAR AND DIFFUSE?

Among the many suggestive formulations of the sociological theorist Talcott Parsons, three generalizations seem relevant for our discussion at this point. In the gradual transition from traditional to fully modern culture and technology, Parsons suggests, social systems tend to rely less on locally or ethnically *particular* organizations and patterns of action, and more on *universal* ones which are applicable over a wide range of groups and places. The same shift to modernity, however, implies a shift from institutions and ways of acting that are functionally *diffuse*—i.e., that serve jointly a great many different functions through one and the same organization—to those that are functionally *specific*, i.e., where any single organization serves only a single specific function or at most a small group of closely related functions. Still another aspect of the transition to full modernity, according to Parsons, is the shift from the allocation of roles, expectations and awards by *ascription*—that is, according to what a person, group, or institution *is* or is believed to be—to an even greater reliance on making such allocations by *achievement*—that is, in accordance with what an individual, group, or organization has actually done in terms of actually meeting some more or less specified criteria of performance.

The traditional community, which the German sociologist Ferdinand Tönnies called *Gemeinschaft*—such as a family or a tribe, or a modern nation and a nation-state—was particular in membership, diffuse in function, and ascriptive in allocation. It performed a wide and ill-defined range of services for the particular set of persons that happened to belong to it and to whom were ascribed, by virtue of the simple fact of their belonging, the intrinsic qualities which entitled them to expect the services, roles and rewards which the community might have to bestow. The opposite of this warm, secure and emotional shelter of the *Gemeinschaft*, in Tönnies' and Parsons' thought, is the modern, highly rational special purpose organization, the *Gesellschaft*—such as a joint stock company, a textile tariff lobby or an international mathematics congress—which is open, in principle, to the universality of all potential members so long as they happen to share this one specific interest and perhaps meet some universal test of achievement, regardless of their other differences. Ideally, such a *Gesellschaft* then allocates its resources, rewards, roles and expectations on the purely rational grounds of what seems most likely to promote its specific purpose and of what seem to be appropriate criteria of actual performance and achievement, rather than by any ascription of any potency or virtue to anyone or anything on other grounds.

In practice, to be sure, these two ideal types are rarely if ever found in this pure form. Even traditional communities pay some attention to achievement, and even rational organizations sometimes tend to make use of ascriptive criteria in allocating facilities or roles. Nevertheless, there is a real distinction between organizations close to the traditional or the modern of these two poles, and it is this distinction that offers some food for speculation about some possible alternative pathways towards further European integration.[6]

Up to the beginning of 1962, most or all of the effective and successful supranational organizations in Western Europe have been functionally specific, such as ECSC, NATO, the Customs Cooperation Council, the European Civil Aviation Conference, and many others. Where new functions had to be dealt with, new specific organizations were founded in preference to broadening the competence of any one of the old ones. Functionally diffuse organizations, such as the Council of Europe, acquired no substantial powers to act; they remained limited, in effect, to the specific function of discussion and advice. As might be expected from the same line of reasoning, the attempts to broaden NATO beyond its specific military function have met with great and continued difficulties. All attempts to give NATO also some "broader" economic, political, or cultural context—and thus to turn it more nearly into a functionally diffuse general purpose organization—thus far have remained unsuccessful. The failure in 1954 of the attempt to add the military functions of the projected European Defense Community and the political tasks of the proposed European Political Community to the limited coal and steel jurisdiction of ECSC—and thus to merge all three into a functionally more diffuse European Community—points in the same direction.

---

[6]For the general distinctions just sketched out, see Ferdinand Tönnies, *Community and Society: Gemeinschaft and Gesellschaft* (East Lansing: Michigan State University Press, 1957), and T. Parsons and E. Shils, eds., *Toward a General Theory of Action* (Cambridge: Harvard University Press, 1951), pp. 77–88.

The persistent difficulties with functional diffuseness in supra-national organizations are matched, albeit to a lesser degree, by difficulties with particularity. The particularly European Organization for European Economic Cooperation (OEEC) has been replaced by the Organization for Economic Cooperation and Development (OECD) which includes the United States and Canada, two extra-European industrial powers which meet its specific functional requirements and are clearly relevant to its specific purpose of economic cooperation and development. By the same principle, however, the inclusion into OECD of such other extra-European industrial powers as Japan, Australia, and perhaps India, seems likely to appear sooner or later on its agenda. Already in 1948, the specific military concerns of NATO had required the extension of that organization beyond the particular orbit of "North Atlantic" geography indicated in its name, and had led to the inclusion of such conspicuously non-North Atlantic countries as Turkey and Greece. A similar fate may yet befall the European Coal and Steel Community if the functional requirements of the coal and steel trade should come to require it; and the Common Market is already beset with problems involving the inclusion or exclusion of Britain, the Commonwealth countries, and the African member states of the old French Community. If functional specificity here counsels expansion of the Common Market, the prospect of growing functional diffuseness may inhibit it. A specific common market for most industrial commodities can perhaps be readily negotiated; a similar market for industrial labor is somewhat more difficult; and the extension of the Common Market to agricultural products—which was to be agreed on by January 1, 1962—proved still more laborious.

There is another hidden but no less serious reef in the way of further progress of the Common Market. So long as national tariffs and other political controls over trade between its member states remain high enough to be effective, the Common Market remains limited to the specific function of facilitating freer interchange of a limited number of commodities without interfering substantially with the national political control of each national economy. Once, however, the sector of freely exchanged goods becomes large in comparison to the domestic sector, the national controls over domestic levels of prices, employment, credit and taxation all may become precarious, or even increasingly inoperative. If there were no business cycle, nor any other economic instabilities or inequalities, this would matter little, or even might be good—as it still might seem good to the remaining believers in the economics of *laissez faire* and the theories of Adam Smith. The matter looks very different, however, if one accepts the continuing need for some national or supra-national agencies of government to perform the functions of economic control, stabilization, development, and the active promotion of greater economic equity, educational opportunity and social welfare. In recent decades the bulk of these services has been claimed by citizens of each state on the ascriptive basis of their nationality, and the bulk of the corresponding functions has been performed by the diffuse and particular community of the nation-state through a host of specific bureaucratic agencies.

In the Europe of early 1962, there is as yet no effective political community, no governmental machinery of either legislation or administration capable of performing these functions at the supra-national level. How soon and how effectively, if at all, such institutions will be created in the 1960's, no one can say. In the meantime, however, the official timetable of the Common Market agreement will drive Western Europe toward an increasingly critical dependence on an international policy consensus and political machinery, neither of which yet exists.

The problem here is deeper than a matter of machinery. The Common Market, much like the European Coal and Steel Community, seems firmly accepted by the most directly interested political elites of the participating countries. The support of these interests has sometimes been purchased by the judicious toleration of the old cartel practices that have long been traditional in Western Europe. No less important, the Common Market and the other European organizations like it have all been tolerated by the elites whose interests they touched only marginally or not at all; and they were further bolstered by the widespread apathy, rather than by any active and determined loyalty, of the broad masses of the voters. Being functionally specific, such European organizations stirred up relatively little opposition. Once they begin to become functionally diffuse, however, as they must become when they move toward amalgamated or federal institutions of multi-purpose government at some West European level, they may come to be perceived as a diffuse threat by many previously unconcerned elite groups and by a large part of mass opinion. The scope and intensity of Southern resistance in the late 1950's in the United States against anything more than token racial integration in the public schools may illustrate the possibilities of the process.

Much of the integration of Europe has been planned by its proponents in reliance on some "spill-over" process through which each item of functional amalgamation would generate relatively quickly an acute need for some other step, so as to give the whole process an accelerating series of impacts.[7] In the 1950's, "spill-over" perhaps was less effective than suggested by this theory. Most of the new integrative organizations were set up by deliberate choice of policy, rather than under the impact of any quickly mounting needs or pressures. If such pressures for more powerful European general purpose institutions should develop in the 1960's, the time needed to bring any such stronger European amalgamated or federated agencies into being might depend most of all not only upon the degree of elite agreement but also of broad popular perception and consensus achieved by that time.

Dependable European integration would imply many things. It would imply the achievement of a steady and high level of mutual transactions between the West European countries, eventually even close to the levels prevailing between

[7] For the best formulation of the concept of "spill-over," see Ernst B. Haas, *The Unity of Europe* (Stanford: Stanford University Press, 1959), pp. 291–98.

TABLE 13-2. GERMANY—FRANCE, 1880–1959

| YEAR | AVERAGE PERCENTAGE OF MUTUAL SHARES IN EACH OTHER'S FOREIGN | |
	Trade	Mail
1880	9.4	—
1888	—	15.2
1913	9.1	12.3
1928	7.3	5.3
1937	5.5	3.7
1952	6.6	4.4
1958	9.4	8.9
1959	11.1	—

Sources. 1958–59 Trade, United Nations, *Directions of International Trade,* 9:9, 1960.
1958 Mail, Universal Postal Union, *Statistique des expeditions dans le service postal international,* 1958.
Earlier years, trade and mail. See pp. 206–207.

the states of the United States or at least substantially above the intra-European levels of the eve of the First World War. The figures in Table 13-2, showing the levels of German-French trade and mail interchanges in various years between 1880 and 1959, suggest how close the percentage shares of the mutual trans-actions between these two countries in 1958–59 still remained to those of 1913. To be sure, this implies a real gain in relative mutual preference, since both France and Germany in the late 1950's comprised much smaller shares of the relevant world totals than they had half a century ago. But it also shows how much more would have to be done to reach mutual transaction levels more nearly characteristic of those prevailing between the member states, cantons or provinces of federated or otherwise amalgamated countries.

ANOTHER DECADE OF
EUROPEAN PLURALISM?

In addition to a high level of mutual transactions, the minimal integration required for internal peace requires a settled unwillingness to resort to warfare for the decision of mutual disputes and an absence of any substantial prepara-tions for the specific possibility of such mutual hostilities. Such minimal integra-tion is attainable not only within a single country, such as the United States, but also among several sovereign countries: for example, neighbors such as Canada and the United States or the Scandinavian states together might form a plural-istic security community. Beyond this, a willingness to devote substantial resources to long-range positive common undertakings—going well beyond mere military alliances—may carry a community of countries to the point of accepting an amalgamated political community under some form of federal or otherwise amalgamated government; and if such a community is effectively free of fears of civil war, we may call it an amalgamated security community.[8]

Given a high level of mutual transactions, minimal integration can be reached and even more far-reaching federation or amalgamation attained, with the aid of three broad classes of favorable conditions familiar to historians. The first of these is the operation of formative events; the second, that of special unifying institutions; the third is that of the almost imperceptible but cumulative change in the political climate, in the "spirit of the times," in short, in the things that a new generation is coming to take for granted.[9] Even well before minimal integration is reached, the "take-off" of the political movement towards integration or union—the transition from the advocacy of unity by a few prophets or intellectuals to its support by some substantial and more or less constantly operating political group—can be hastened by one or more of these three processes.[10]

In the case of Western Europe, our interim survey may suggest that the speed and power of the effects of the formative events of 1945-1950, as well as of the effects of the European institutions put into operation thus far, though impressive, may still have been somewhat overrated; and that the next five or ten years may still belong to a pluralistic approach where sovereign governments in close and effective consultation are coordinating their policies and practices, creating and operating an array of common, specific and functional agencies, and eventually coordinating not only the variegated political demands of their populations but, at a more fundamental level, the habits, expectations, perceptions and self-identifications from which such political demands arise.

This quiet change in the political climate and in the very spirit of Europe may well be under way by now. It is clearly nowhere near completion in early 1962, at a time when even such a major component of Europe as France remains bitterly divided against herself, as well as often stubbornly divided from her allies, when the popular roots of democracy and constitutionalism in Germany and Italy are still none too strong, and when in Belgium and the Netherlands (as

[8] For the conceptual distinction between political "integration" and "amalgamation," see the accurate and perceptive discussion in Richard Rosecrance, "Categories, Concepts, and Reasoning in the Study of International Relations," *Behavioral Science*, 6:3, July 1961, pp. 222-31, esp. pp. 227-28. Cf. also K. W. Deutsch, *Political Community at the International Level* (New York: Doubleday-Random, 1954), pp. 30 ff., and Deutsch *et al.*, *Political Community and the North Atlantic Area* (Princeton: Princeton University Press, 1957; Westport, Conn.: Greenwood, 1976), pp. 5-7. For a discussion of some of these factors, as they apply to another case, see also Bruce M. Russett, *Community and Contention: Britain and America in the Twentieth Century* (Cambridge, Mass.: MIT Press, 1963).

[9] For a discussion of the assessment of these three classes of conditions by several historians in the case of the integration and subsequent federation of the American colonies, as well as for a survey of some evidence from the contemporary colonial press, see Richard Merritt, *Symbols of American Community, 1735-1775* (New Haven: Yale University Press, 1966).

[10] Cf. Haas, *The Uniting of Europe*, p. 29, and Deutsch *et al.*, *Political Community and the North Atlantic Area*, pp. 83-85.

well as in France) the old resentments over the loss of colonial empires are still vivid, bitter and divisive.[11]

Nevertheless, the quiet process is at work. The climate is changing, and another five or ten years may show how much more ready Europe will have become to surmount what today still looks like formidable obstacles to her creative and lasting unification.

[11] For convenient references on these points, see e.g. the relevant country sections in Roy C. Macridis, ed., *Foreign Policy in World Politics,* second edition (New York: Prentice-Hall, 1962). On recent French politics, cf. also Roy C. Macridis and Bernard E. Brown, *The De Gaulle Republic: Quest for Unity* (Homewood: Dorsey, 1960).

14 | Arms Control and Western European Integration: Some Prospects in 1966

This chapter was written in 1965 and reports the results of a fairly large-scale effort of team research to be applied to United States policy, which had to be carried out under the pressure of time.

The research summarized was planned in 1963; most of the interviews were carried out in 1964, and so was the main part of the analysis. The sponsor of the work, the United States Arms Control and Disarmament Agency (ACDA) was informed orally in December 1964 of the main findings, and in a written report in April 1965. The results filled ten multigraphed volumes and were published in part in two books and several articles.

A condition for undertaking this work by the scholars involved in it was their right to publish their findings freely, but the ACDA retained the right to decide whether to keep confidential its connection with the work or whether to admit publicly to having financed it. In the event, they chose the latter course.

Owing to a then still unrecognized difficulty in a computer program for the calculation of indicators of integration in matrices of international transactions, the increase of such integration in the Europe of the early 1960s was somewhat understated. As a result, we reported a temporary "halting" of European integration in regard to actual transactions, where we should have reported a temporary slowing down. In any case, we thought that the advances of the 1950s might possibly be resumed after 1975, and it seems that they have been. Corrected indicator figures were published in 1973,* but the differences were not large enough to change any of the other major political conclusions in this chapter or in the entire study.

Parts of this chapter were written in the present tense—that is, the present tense of 1966. This language has been left unchanged. Now, nearly twelve years later, readers may judge to what extent a realistic analysis and perspective were produced with the aid of the data available at that time.

*K. W. Deutsch and R. W. Chadwick, "International Trade and Economic Integration: Further Developments in Trade Matrix Analysis," *Comparative Political Studies*, No. 6, (April 1973): 84–109.
From *The American Political Science Review* 60, no. 2 (June 1966): 354–365. Reprinted by permission of the Publisher.

Three questions asked of the research group in 1963–65 were: Will there be a common European government and army by 1975? Do the West German people demand nuclear weapons for their country? Or will a European Multilateral Force with nuclear weapons be needed to head off such a future German national demand? Our answer was "no" to all three of these questions, and so has been the answer of the dozen years that have followed.

Another question was whether French reluctance to accept United States leadership in matters of foreign policy would disappear when President Charles de Gaulle left office. We said it would not, and it didn't. We also reported, however, that it seemed likely that France then would drop its opposition to Britain's entry into Europe, and it did. We made these forecasts not from a crystal ball but from empirical evidence, such as extensive elite interviews; and we knew that most often countries do not quickly change their elites, that elites most often do not quickly change their minds, and that their views are often likely to prevail in the long run over those of the political leaders of the day—even the great ones.

Elite members, we found, are often well-informed. Nearly three-fourths of West German elite respondents in 1964 foresaw a Social Democratic government as possible before 1974 and 40 per cent saw it as likely. History proved them right. Very high majorities of French and German elite respondents foresaw improved relations with "the countries of Eastern Europe" and within the next ten years, détente and *Ostpolitik* arrived.

The chapter ends with the suggestion that the United States might have to choose between major commitments "on the continent of Asia" and "opportunities for leadership to European unity and worldwide arms control." The suggestion seemed relevant in the spring of 1965 when the Vietnam War was escalating; it remained relevant after the war ended in 1975; and it may remain relevant under the different conditions of the years to come.

At the heart of our research was a single basic question: What arms control and disarmament measures might be acceptable to Europeans in 1966, in 1971, and in 1976? And differently put: What would be Europe's attitude in those years either to arms competition or to arms control, and what particular policies would be most popular or least popular in Europe in this respect?

This basic question implied four more detailed questions. The first, what is Europe now, in 1966, and where is it going for the 1971 to 1976 period? Is it going to be a Europe of nation-states with only marginal common functional arrangements on matters not central in importance to the concerns of its citizens? Or will it be to some extent substantially integrated, with some major policy decisions made by common institutions? Or will it be a common body politic, speaking with a single voice and developing common institutions for a wide range of decisions?

Second, do Europeans in general approve or disapprove of arms control? Do they welcome the relaxation of tensions between America and Russia and between the East and West, or do they fear such relaxation?

Third, what specific arms control measures are likely to be most acceptable to Europeans, and which arms control measures are likely to be least acceptable?

And fourth, what are the strength, location, and time aspects of political support for specific policies, such as the policies of France and its President de Gaulle vis-à-vis the NATO Alliance and the United States? What is the European attitude to the nuclear striking force of France, the *force de frappe*, and the proposals that other European countries should also have national nuclear striking forces? What is the attitude of Europeans, both in Germany and elsewhere, to the idea of nuclear weapons for Germany, either directly, for instance through purchase by the German Government for the German military establishment, or through the abrogation of the Paris Agreements of 1954 and therefore eventually through the German manufacture of nuclear weapons? And what is the attitude of Europeans to a multi-lateral nuclear force, either limited to European countries alone or including the United States?

To attempt to answer such questions requires a combination of evidence and judgment. The diagnosis of a physician, the verdict of a judge, and the judgment of a political scientist or analyst all are made in the light of many considerations, not all of which can be made fully explicit. A doctor who has seen many sick people, a judge who has listened to many plausible but not always trustworthy witnesses, a political scientist who has gained some experience in his professional work as to how deceptive evidence can be—each of these is likely to do better in his appraisal of reality than one who only looks at mere statistics and interview reports.

Nevertheless, though it must be interpreted with judgment, evidence speaks with its own voice and deserves to be taken seriously in its own right.

I. FIVE STREAMS OF EVIDENCE

We tried to develop five lines of mutually independent evidence. The first was evidence from elite interviews of 147 French and 173 West German leaders.

We also surveyed relevant mass opinion polls, going back for about fifteen years. In many cases the same question had been asked every year of samples of voters ranging from between one thousand and two thousand respondents. On many questions it was possible to compare how mass opinion had changed over time, and how it agreed with or differed from elite views in the early 1960s.

Another source of evidence was a survey of arms control and disarmament proposals which were specifically focused on Europe. This permitted us to trace the growth and decline of interest in this particular approach to arms control, in contrast either to the rejection of all arms control, or else—more realistically—to the shift of interest to more nearly worldwide approaches to arms control and disarmament, as in the 1963 limited nuclear test ban treaty.

We also carried on two content analysis projects. In one, a large number of newspapers and periodicals in four countries (France, West Germany, Great Britain and the United States) were examined for editorial responses to ten major arms control events by coders using their own judgment and "hand-coding" techniques. The other project studied in greater depth the editorials on European integration in four leading newspapers in France, West Germany, Great Britain and the United States by computer or machine content analysis.

Finally, we collected and analyzed a large number of aggregative data about actual behavior. What is happening, not to editorials about trade, but to actual trade? What is happening, not to speeches about universities, but to the numbers of young Germans and young French people actually crossing the border to study in the other country? What is happening to travel? What is happening to migration? What is happening to the exchange of mail? These data were available from the statistics published by the countries concerned or by various international organizations, and they did tell us whether these transactions had increased or declined, relative to other transactions or to the same transactions in other years or with other countries.

Using all these five streams of evidence, we then tried to make our judgments. A few of the points that came out of the combined use of the five types of evidence can be briefly summarized.

II. THE HALTING OF EUROPEAN
INTEGRATION SINCE THE MID-1950's

The first point to emerge was this: European integration has slowed since the mid-1950's, and has stopped or reached a plateau since 1957–58. An analysis of trade data, going back as far as 1890, suggests that in the 1957–58 period Europe reached the highest level of structural integration it has ever had. Most of this high level was reached by 1954, but there were slow advances to 1957–58. Europe now is much more highly integrated than it was between the wars or before World War I, but from about 1957–58 on there have been no further gains. The absolute increases after 1958 in trade, travel, postal correspondence and the exchange of students are accountable for from the effects of prosperity and the general increase in the level of these activities. There have been no increases in integration in regard to all these transactions beyond what one would expect from mere random probability and the increase in prosperity in the countries concerned.

The spectacular development of formal European treaties and institutions since the mid-1950's has not been matched by any corresponding deeper integration of actual behavior.

As far as they go, the transaction data do not suggest that any substantial increase in European integration should be expected by 1970 or 1975, even among the Six, if there should be a mere continuation of the practices and methods of the 1950's and the early 1960's. The expectable pattern for the next ten years, as suggested by a study of the trends in European transactions from 1928 to 1963, is toward a Europe of national states, linked by marked but moderate preferences for mutual transactions, with little growth—and possibly some decline—in the intensity of those preferences as expressed in actual behavior of the populations and business communities of the European countries.

The foregoing observations apply with particular strength to France. France alone of the EEC countries has retreated in part from foreign trade. It has now a much lower proportion of foreign trade to gross national product—28 per cent in 1963—than it had in 1928, when the same proportion stood at 46 percent. France thus has retained a greater amount of national self-preoccupation, and it has accepted in its actions somewhat less of the limited European integration than have Germany, Italy and the Benelux countries.

A different line of analysis of economic data suggests, on the basis of provisional computations, that Western Europe now has traversed about one half of the way toward structural economic integration and that perhaps another 40 years might be needed, at rates of progress from 1913 to 1955, to complete the process.[1] In any case, the pace of actual progress seems much slower than the pace of such legal and theoretical timetables as those in the formal treaties of integration. Difficulties in implementing these timetables in 1966 and thereafter may be in part inherent in this underlying situation.

III. THE DECLINE OF INTEREST IN GENERAL DESIGNS FOR EUROPEAN UNIFICATION

1. *The Evidence of the Elite Press.* The impression of a halt in the growth of integrative sentiment in Europe is confirmed by the evidence of content analysis of "prestige" newspapers. For the years 1953 and 1963, *Le Monde*, the *Frankfurter Allgemeine Zeitung*, *The Times of London*, and the *New York Times*, were selected as the most representative elite newspapers of France, West Germany, Great Britain and the United States, respectively. In these papers, all editorials dealing with European or Atlantic integration or European politics in general were identified, and a sample of 200 editorials was chosen by appropriate procedures. This sample was then subjected to intensive content analysis by computer. The main changes found in the relevant editorials of each elite paper from 1953 to 1963 were as follows:

Interest in Atlantic Alliance, with military emphasis, and seen against the background of a bipolar world, has declined markedly in all three European papers. This decline is moderate but clear in the London *Times*. It is greater in the *Frankfurter Allgemeine Zeitung*; and it is greatest in *Le Monde*. All three Euro-

---

[1]This 40 year period is suggested by unpublished provisional results of research by Robert Schaefer, Yale University, 1965–1966.

pean papers have moved toward greater concern for primarily European integration, seen in economic terms, and against the background of an increasingly
multi-polar world. Only the *New York Times* has not shared in this trend. Its
editorials alone intensified their Atlantic and military emphasis and their view of
the world as a continuing bipolar power system.

There has been a general decline in the attention of all four papers to any
general political or legal designs for a unified Europe, and a corresponding shift
to greater concern with concrete difficulties of European integration or cooperation in regard to such matters as agriculture. In 1963, only the *New York Times*
continued to maintain a reduced but still marked preponderance of interest in
idealized political or legal designs for a unified Europe.

The concern with domestic French and German controversies, as opposed to
any attention given to the requirements and costs of supranational alliances,
remained unchanged in all four papers over the ten-year period. According to
some theories of political integration, such concern with domestic controversies
should have been expected to decline, and the interest in the needs of supra-
national alliances to increase, if there had been major progress toward supra-
national integration during that decade. No evidence of such a shift was found.

In all four papers, concern increased from 1953 to 1963 in regard to United
States pressure for the extension of the powers of supranational organizations,
particularly within an Atlantic framework. By 1963, supranational integration
had become more closely identified with United States initiatives and pressures.
On this issue the *New York Times* alone among the four papers shifted from an
attitude of moderate but marked concern for American initiatives and pressures
for European unification in 1953 to a so much stronger emphasis in 1963 that
in regard to this issue, in the latter year, it seemed to be living in a different
world from that of the European papers.

The chief form of United States activism, as discussed in these editorials,
referred to American efforts to merge military and economic supranational
instrumentalities in Europe or in the Atlantic area. Such a linkage between economic and military policies, however, appeared in 1963 as a theme chiefly
created by American speakers and writers, with no substantial support in any of
the European papers we studied.

References to arms control and disarmament were so rare in the editorials on
European politics and integration, as studied in all four papers, that no statistical
analysis could be undertaken in regard to these topics. These problems were not
seen, it appears, in the context of European unity and general European politics.

2. *The Evidence of Mass Opinion.* A considerable number of French and German public opinion polls from the years 1952–1962 were analyzed for the purpose of making comparisons between the two countries as well as comparisons
of political attitudes among different groups, and comparisons with a smaller
number of comparable polls from Italy and Britain. Methods used included the
charting of time trends with the help of graphs, and factor analysis with the aid
of computers. From these analyses several tentative findings emerged:

There was persistently greater elite and mass attention to national concerns rather than European. Large samples of Germans were asked year after year by German interviewers: "What is the most important task before our country?" In the spring of 1965, 51 per cent said "national reunification," while only 3 per cent said "European union." National interests outpolled European interests fifteen-to-one for the top spot of attention—and had done much the same for more than a decade.

Throughout the period 1954—1962, the difference between French and German mass opinion tended to be larger than those between opinion in either of these countries and that in Italy or Britain, or between British and Italian attitudes.

Friendly feelings in French mass opinion about Germany and in German mass opinion about France increased substantially to roughly one-half of the Germans and the French polled in 1963-64. Feelings of mutual trust increased much less, to about one fifth of the respondents in each country. Answers in the mid-1950's to specific questions "Which country would you trust as an ally in case of war?" showed markedly greater trust of France and Germany in Britain, and still greater trust in the United States than they showed between those two continental countries.

Questions in the mid-1950's about the Western alliance in peacetime, and about the same alliance in case of war, revealed very marked decreases in its support by French or German mass opinion for the latter and more serious eventuality, but stability or even a slight increase in the British popular commitment.

Nevertheless, factor analysis of many French and German opinion poll results between 1954 and 1962 indicated a marked increase in the similarity of underlying images between the two countries, as expressed by the amount of observed opinion variation that could be accounted for by factors common to opinion in both countries. In particular, there was a marked increase between 1954 and 1962 in the importance of an image of a United Europe in both French and German opinion. Most of this increase occurred between 1957 and 1962. During the same years, there occurred a marked decline in the perception of any military threat and of the danger of nuclear war. Increased relevance of European unity thus appeared quite compatible with a decreased sense of military danger.

The increased similarity of French and German perceptions in 1962, as compared to 1957 and 1954, was not matched, however, by any net increase in the similarity of French and German political values. Although the French and Germans had come to agree to an increased extent on what they saw in the world around them, they continued to disagree on what they liked.

The strongest difference between French and German mass opinion in the analysis of these surveys was found in the area of international politics. Germans had a clearly favorable image of the Western alliance and a clearly unfavorable one of the Soviet Union, while the French attitude towards symbols of Western unity was negative in 1962, and their anti-Russian posture was conditional and reserved. French popular opinion became increasingly pessimistic about NATO from 1957 to 1961, and in the confrontations of 1962 it continued to blame the United States for world insecurity, while being divided in blaming the Russians for recklessness. German mass opinion, however, saw United States policy as directed toward world security, and saw the Russians as acting recklessly. Generally, German mass opinion was markedly pro-American, while the French majority was so only with reservations, and a sizeable minority gave outright anti-American responses.

Only in regard to accepting European unity, at least in general terms, the French and Germans agreed to a greater extent in 1962 than they had done in earlier years. Even here, however, on the specific questions of European political unity and federation, French mass opinion remained significantly less "European" than its German counterpart.

The overall impression from the analysis of the trend of French and German mass opinion data from 1954 to 1962 is that of opinion halting or hesitating at a threshold. There is a consensus that European unity is a good thing, and that some steps should be taken to maintain and strengthen what European unity there is, and to go somewhat further in that direction. There seems to be no clear image in mass opinion as to what these steps should be, or how far they should go, nor is there any sense of urgency about them.

There is thus now in European mass opinion a latent clash between the continuing acceptance of the reality of the nation state, and the newly accepted image of some vague sort of European unity. The ensemble of these present public moods may facilitate general expression of good will, combined with policies of temporizing, caution, national consolidation, and only gradual and sectoral advance toward somewhat greater European integration.

3. *The Evidence of Elite Interviews, 1964.* Since the results of the elite interviews conducted in the summer of 1964 with 147 French and 173 West German respondents are discussed at considerable length elsewhere, only a few major points will be summarized here.[2]

Persistent Nationalism with Major Cleavages: The Divided Elites of France. French elite responses show the continuing strength of self-assertive nationalism. Nearly seven-eighths of the respondents see current French policies as increasingly nationalistic, and nearly three-quarters see the world as an increasingly multipolar power system, replacing the earlier bipolar United States-Soviet predominance. Three-fifths definitely approve this new trend, and a majority asserts a "manifest destiny" for France.

There is overwhelming French elite consensus on not trusting Germany beyond a very limited extent. This was expressed in many ways throughout most

[2] Percentages given in this summary are based on all respondents, including those who said "don't know," as well as those who did not comment on the particular question, *if* this category amounted to no more than 5 per cent of the total. If a larger proportion did not touch on a particular question, the percentages given refer only to the "articulate" respondents, that is, to those who did make a comment, even if they only professed themselves to be undecided or uninformed. In this latter case, the actual number of articulate respondents on the question is indicated.

of the interviews. Only 7 per cent of 136 articulate French leaders are willing to trust the German Federal Republic "a great deal." Of the 109 French leaders who express their views on German reunification, only 7 per cent favor it unconditionally, and of the 77 French leaders who comment on its security aspects, 58 percent consider it a threat to French security.

On many issues, outright nationalist views command only strong minority support. A plurality of nearly one-half flatly deny that Europe will be unified within the next ten years; and 41 per cent choose national predominance as their preferred form of European integration, as against 43 per cent who want supranational influences to predominate. Only 30 per cent endorse an independent national foreign policy for France, while 70 per cent prefer a policy of alliances.

Efforts toward some further limitations on national sovereignty are favored, at least conditionally, by 83 per cent of French leaders, and definitely so by 45 per cent, with only 14 per cent even conditionally opposed. French elite consensus seems more favorable to at least some limited further steps toward supranational collaboration than have been the recent policies of President de Gaulle. During the next few years, such limited steps might well be undertaken with elite support by himself or his successors.

The basic pattern of national self-assertion and of French elite preferences and expectations, however, seems likely to persist. Current (i.e., relatively stressful) French policies toward the United States and NATO are most often mentioned (29 per cent) as likely to continue after President de Gaulle.

French domestic cleavages, too, seem certain to persist. Less than one-fifth of our respondents turn out to be clearcut Gaullists. While a majority expect that the Fourth Republic will not be restored, and that some institutions of the Fifth Republic will survive de Gaulle, there is no agreement on just which features will survive. The hopes for a more pragmatic and consensual "new politics" in France have not materialized.

An analysis of elite age groups indicates no major changes over the next ten years. Typically, age accounts for less than 5 per cent of the variance in the answers found. Within these limits, the "middle elites"—those in their fifties and hence the generation of the 1930's and World War II—tend to differ from both their elders and juniors, who in turn often resemble each other. This middle elite group is somewhat more nationalistic and more closely identified with the de Gaulle regime.

The junior elite—those under 50—are more internationalist, more in favor of alliances, and still more opposed to an independent foreign policy for France. A moderate shift toward a somewhat more internationalist foreign policy might be supported by this generation, once its members win full power in the 1970's, but the essential features of French politics are likely to remain.

French elite members themselves do not expect to change their minds. An above-average degree of closure of thinking is reported for 70 per cent of the respondents, and only 1 per cent feel that the policies proposed by them for defending the French national interest might become impractical in the future.

A brief follow-up survey was taken among the same group of respondents in December, 1964, after Khrushchev's fall, President Johnson's re-election, and the Chinese nuclear explosion. It elicited about 60 per cent usable responses and confirmed the stability of French attitudes expressed in mid-1964.

Strengthened National Consensus and Greater Readiness for Supranational Steps: The Integrated Elites of the German Federal Republic. Elite consensus on definite satisfaction with the present West German regime and basic policies includes nearly three-quarters of West German respondents. Adding those indicating moderate satisfaction brings total elite support for the basic GFR regime to 93 per cent. This support extends solidly across all groupings of age, class, occupation, major party, and past political record.

In contrast to their more detached or alienated French counterparts, large majorities of West German elite members see themselves as influential in the policies of their own country, and appear more likely to identify with them. As recorded by interviewers, 73 per cent of German elite respondents indicate that they think they have more than average influence in domestic affairs, and 66 per cent do so in regard to foreign policy, in contrast to only 33 per cent and 18 per cent, respectively, among the French.

The foreign policy of the German Federal Republic is definitely supported by 55 per cent of the West German leaders, in contrast to France, whose current foreign policy is clearly supported by only 33 per cent of French elite respondents. West German support for "all features" of current foreign policy, and particularly for the alliance with the United States, is expected to continue beyond Chancellor Erhard's term of office.

West German leaders are in overwhelming agreement on their country's need for allies: 93 per cent see alliances and international instrumentalities as the best means for defending the national interest of their country. Only 7 per cent name national instrumentalities, and only 6 per cent favor an independent national policy. Enduring common interests with the United States are stressed by 72 per cent; and 71 per cent favor policies aiming at further reductions in national sovereignty.

In contrast to France, two-thirds of the West German leaders continue to see the world as a biopolar power system, dominated by the United States and the Soviet Union, and they believe that it will remain so. Among the French leaders, on the contrary, nearly three-quarters see an increasingly multipolar world around them. Faith in a continuing bipolar world is somewhat weaker among West German politicians (58 per cent), and it is shared only by a minority of German civil servants (44 per cent).

There is less agreement among German leaders as to just how far these internationalist policies will go, or ought to go. A strong plurality—46 per cent—expect European integration to be achieved within the next ten years, while 35 per cent consider this unlikely. A predominantly supranational form of European union—if it should come to pass—is chosen by a bare majority of the responses, but 45 per cent prefer "confederation" or arrangements implying the clearcut predominance of nation-states. In France, only 19 per cent expect European union within 10 years, while 49 per cent explicitly do not; and 56 per cent of responses prefer confederation or national predominance.

Not unconnected, perhaps, with the increased strength of the West German army, German elite support for the 1954 project of a European Defense Community of conventional forces changed by 1964 to definite opposition by a plurality, 44 per cent, against only 35 per cent in clear support. In France, a much smaller trend seems to have gone in the opposite direction; 23 per cent of the French leaders now definitely favor EDC, and only 18 per cent clearly oppose it.

Contrasting French and West German Views of Future Changes. French response patterns generally indicate that the Fifth Republic is not perceived as deeply rooted, and that many pre-de Gaulle institutions and forces—such as the old political parties—may be expected to reassert themselves after President de Gaulle's departure from political activity. French leaders thus expect short-run changes after de Gaulle, restoring a considerable measure of long-run continuity in society and politics.

German leaders, on the contrary, expect the trends of change, initiated by the Bonn Republic, to continue beyond Chancellor Erhard's tenure of office, and in their large majority they expect no return or revival of any of the pre-Bonn political forces or practices from the Nazi or the Weimar period. As many as 86 per cent of articulate respondents consider Nazism dead; 73 per cent see the possibility of a Social Democratic government within the next 10 years, and 40 per cent consider it likely, but in any case a majority feels sure that it would make very little difference to domestic or foreign policies, except at most in regard to personnel recruitment.

French and German elite expectations differ strongly in regard to German reunification, as well as to European union. Of the 173 German leaders in our sample, only 9 do not comment on this point, while over one-third of the French do not. Among articulate German respondents, 20 per cent definitely expect reunification to take place within the next 25 years, but only 2 per cent among the articulate French do so. Another 38 per cent of the Germans have at least conditional hopes for reunification within the next quarter century, but only 11 per cent of the French agree with them; and 83 per cent of the French elite commenting consider German reunification as at least unlikely within that period.[3]

As to European unification, a plurality of 46 per cent among the 158 articulate German elite members see it as likely to succeed within the next ten years, or at least to make substantial progress, but only 19 per cent among the 141 articulate French leaders share this view. By contrast, no success of, nor any substantial progress toward, European union within the next 10 years is expected by 35 per cent of the articulate German leaders but by as many as 49 per cent among the French.

[3] For French preferences in regard to German reunification, see p. 257 above.

Atlantic Alliance and European Aspirations: French and German Linkages and Clashes. French and German leaders agree—90 per cent in Germany and 72 per cent in France—that the ultimate military security of their countries depends "completely" or "in large measure" upon the deterrent force of the United States. Most German respondents use the stronger, and most French the more cautious, wording. Large majorities of elite respondents—79 per cent in Germany and 65 per cent in France—feel sure that the United States is unlikely to abandon its commitments to the defense of Western Europe. Even larger majorities in both countries refer to long-run common interests, linking their nations with the United States.

There is also agreement among 65 per cent of the German and 62 per cent of the French elite respondents that NATO can be relied upon completely or to a considerable extent. The stronger alternative is more popular in Germany, and the weaker one in France. Minorities of 18 per cent of the German and 30 per cent of the French leaders, however, prefer to rely on NATO only "to a limited extent" or not at all.

Large majorities—68 per cent in Germany and 63 per cent in France—agree that Britain ought to be included in an integrated Europe. A majority of 52 per cent in France stress long-term common interests with Britain, but only 28 per cent do so in Germany.

The same elite proportion of 28 per cent in Germany stress common long-term interests with France, and 37 per cent in France feel they share common long-run interests with Germany. In addition, common interests with the other five EEC members, including Germany and France, respectively, are emphasized by 88 per cent of the French and 35 per cent of the German elite members.

The result is somewhat paradoxical but in line with other evidence. Majorities of French and German leaders see their countries as linked by long-run political and military interests more strongly to the United States—and in the second place to Britain—than they are linked to one another. Any weakening of French ties to the United States thus might weaken the German-French relationship. In distinction from the views of President de Gaulle, the majority of French elite respondents prefer to keep strong these links to the United States, if this could be done on terms nearer to political equality.

French aspirations to a greater measure of equality divide many French and German views on NATO. Among articulate French leaders, 78 per cent favor NATO reforms in this direction, and only 2 per cent say no reforms are needed. Among their German counterparts, only 47 per cent desire such reforms, and 38 per cent consider all NATO reforms unnecessary.

When asked to choose between policies of strengthening mainly European institutions, such as EEC, and strengthening NATO, 40 per cent of the 124 articulate French respondents prefer EEC, against only 4 per cent who favor NATO. The 141 articulate Germans are split more evenly, with 15 per cent picking EEC and 11 per cent choosing NATO, but a 72 per cent majority refuses to choose and insists on supporting both—a middle way favored also by a French plurality of 49 per cent. Major attempts, by President de Gaulle or any successor, to put in a forced choice "Europeanism" against "Atlanticism" are thus likely to run into strong elite opposition in both countries.

Despite this reluctance of French and, even more, of German leaders to choose between Atlantic and European alignments, it seems from many subtle indications that the latter had come to command by 1964 much the larger share of elite imagination and emotional involvement. The vision of a rich, multidimensioned and growing Atlantic Community has faded.

Differentiated French and West German Views of Cold War Problems and International Relaxation. French and German elite members strongly agree in seeing in Communist states and activities the greatest threat to the security of their countries, and in opposing the withdrawals of troops or nuclear weapons from Central Europe. The neutralization of Central Europe is definitely opposed by 69 per cent of the 166 German elite members who express their views, but only by a plurality of 38 per cent of the 71 French elite who did so.

Despite the perception of a Communist threat, European integration is seen as primarily nonmilitary in purpose. Strengthening the West against Communism is seen as the purpose of European integration by only 19 per cent of the French and 10 per cent of the German respondents, while 45 per cent of the French and 67 per cent of the Germans emphasize economic and cultural purposes.

There is a near-record consensus among both French and German leaders that in the next few years relations between their nations and "the countries of Eastern Europe" will become more cordial. No fewer than 99 per cent among the 118 articulate French respondents say so, and so do 83 per cent of the 162 articulate German leaders.

There is much less support, however, for the familiar proposals to relax international tensions by formally recognizing either the division or the current boundaries of Germany. Of the former measure, only 25 per cent of 153 articulate Germans and 18 per cent of 55 articulate French leaders think that it might ease international tensions. Recognition of the Oder-Neisse boundary with Poland is seen as probably helpful in easing such tensions by a majority of 52 per cent of the 155 articulate Germans, but by only a plurality of 42 per cent among the 52 French leaders who commented on this matter.

Altogether, French and German leaders produce parallel majorities on six out of ten questions relating to the Cold War complex, but in most cases they differ even there in regard to saliency and perhaps in underlying expectations. A majority of German respondents favor a partial continuation of the "hard line" policies of Cold War days, in the hope that these will ultimately lead to success or to desirable changes in the bipolar struggle; the French leaders seem to back the same policies with much greater detachment, in the expectation that they might best preserve the German status quo in a multipolar world.

It is against this background of manifest and latent differences in French and German views that current and prospective French and German responses to arms control and disarmament proposals have to be appraised.

IV. ATTITUDES TOWARD ARMS CONTROL

1. *The Attitudes of the European Press.* The machine content analysis of 1953 and 1963 editorials, reported in a preceding section, was limited to four elite papers and to editorials dealing with European or Atlantic integration. To supplement it, another content analysis operation was carried out on a large number of newspapers and periodicals from the same four countries, but focusing this time upon editorial responses to specific proposals or events relevant to disarmament or arms control. For this purpose, a list was compiled of ten such major proposals or events, with the first five items spanning the years from the Baruch Plan of 1946 to the Rapacki Plan of 1957, and the second five items, the years from Khrushchev's speech in 1959 to the nuclear test-ban in 1963. For editorial comments on these ten events, 97 newspapers and periodicals were searched, 35 American, 29 British, 16 French and 17 German. A total of 655 issues were consulted for the relevant periods, and 370 editorials were found and analyzed.

Within the selected periods, following major disarmament-related proposals or events, the general issue of disarmament and arms control was perceived as fairly salient. Over the entire period 1946-1963, editorial responses were found in an average of 58 per cent of the journal issues examined for the four countries. The general attitude toward efforts at disarmament or arms control was overwhelmingly friendly, with 63 per cent of all mentions favorable.

Over time, interest in arms control and disarmament rose substantially in all four countries, from an average of 43 per cent during 1946-57 to 70 per cent for the years 1959-63.

Specific arms control proposals were treated most often as serious and sincere, despite a minority current of comments labeling many of them as unrealistic or as propaganda. The emotional attitudes towards specific proposals, however, were fairly evenly divided; they were almost as likely to be negative as positive or neutral.

Among the four countries, most attention to arms control problems was paid by the press of the German Federal Republic (77 per cent) and of France (61 per cent), followed by that of the United Kingdom (48 per cent) and the United States (45 per cent). To the extent that these differences reflect reader interest rather than the accidents of our very crude sample selection, they may indicate the existence of a significant reservoir of public interest in disarmament and arms control in Germany and France.

As targets of attention, Russia, the United States, and France were the countries whose names and comments received most attention over the period as a whole, accounting for about two-thirds of all national comments reported. They were followed by Britain, Red China (and other Asian Communist countries), and West Germany.

Emotional attitudes toward nations varied. Toward the United States they were about 30 per cent friendly and 60 per cent neutral. Toward the Soviet Union they were most often negative (56 per cent), or else neutral (34 per cent).

Toward Great Britain they were almost as often friendly (41 per cent) as neutral (44 per cent). Toward France and Germany they were predominantly neutral.

There was a frequent tendency in the press of the United States, France, and Great Britain, repsectively, to pay most attention to the proposals of its own government, and less attention to the proposals or moves of other countries. Although there were some exceptions to this—the German press paid a great deal of worried attention to many moves by other countries—the evidence confirms the familiar picture of the national press of each country conducting often a kind of national monologue rather than genuine cross-national communication within the Western alliance.

2. *The Decline of Specific Proposals for Arms Control in Europe, 1960–1964.* A survey was done of 64 proposals made between 1947 and 1964 from the United States, the Soviet Union, Britain, France, West Germany, and Poland, for arms control or disarmament in Europe. Included were both official proposals and major public suggestions made by political leaders, parties, or respected writers. Its findings are subject to the limitations that only proposals specifically focused on Europe were considered, that repetitions or minor variations of old proposals were excluded, and that some proposals may have been overlooked, but it seems likely that all salient Europe-centered proposals were included. The survey shows:

(1) French interest in arms control has been much lower than that of any other major country. During the 18 years covered, there were only four French proposals, two of which were made in 1959 by political leaders out of office, Pierre Mendès-France and Jules Moch. No official French proposals were found after 1956, and no significant French proposals from any source after 1959.

(2) In rank order of frequency, proposals came most often from the Soviet Union (18), and the United States (14), followed by Britain (11), the German Federal Republic (10), Poland (7), and France (4).

(3) Over three-fifths of the proposals for Europe made by government officials of some kind, and nearly nine-tenths of the proposals from opposition leaders or private persons, came in the five-year period from 1955 to 1959. During this peak period, official Western and East bloc proposals were equally frequent. From 1960 onward, official proposals from the United States for European arms control diminished; Britain and Western Germany made no such proposals at all, and by the criteria of relevance used for this report they contributed only one unofficial proposal apiece, and France contributed nothing at all. However, the East bloc countries (i.e., the U.S.S.R. and Poland) continued in 1961–64 to make proposals for Europe at nearly the same rate as in 1955–59, with a somewhat larger share of proposals coming from Poland.

This undiminished East bloc activity might have the possible effect of preempting some of the role of champions of European disarmament for the East bloc countries, but also of associating to some extent in the minds of West European elite members the entire topic of arms control with East bloc propaganda, so as to reinforce the partial withdrawal of West European elite interest

from this topic. If Europe-centered United States proposals should again become
salient and frequent, Western European elite interests might again increase.

The shift, however, in United States interest to more nearly worldwide approaches to arms control and disarmament, such as the 1963 nuclear test-ban
treaty, accords well with the preferences of the French and German elite members, most of whom favor further world-wide arms control arrangements of this
kind but many of whom express misgivings about narrowly regional arms control
arrangements for Central Europe alone, which they fear might leave the area
unprotected in a world of military pressures.

3. *The Common Fear of Nuclear Proliferation and the General Support for
Disarmament and Arms Control.* There are clear indications of anti-Communism,
and of "tough-mindedness" in regard to disarmament, among majorities of both
French and German elite respondents. Inspection arrangements are demanded or
desired as part of any East-West arms control agreement by 78 per cent of the
articulate German elite members, but only by 38 per cent of the corresponding
group in France.

Within this context however, support for arms control and disarmament produces a striking number of strong and parallel majorities among French and German elites. Efforts to stop the proliferation of nuclear weapons "to countries
that do not now possess them" are supported by articulate majorities of 78 per
cent in France and 90 per cent in Germany. Discussions of disarmament are
favored by 69 per cent of the articulate French respondents and 76 per cent of
their German counterparts; 20 per cent among the French supporters of disarmament discussions say, however, that the idea is utopian but worth discussing
anyway. Some plan for arms control is endorsed by 66 per cent of French and
61 per cent of German responses, and only 17 and 30 per cent, respectively, do
not favor any plans. The 1963 American-British-Soviet nuclear test-ban treaty—
which France has not joined—is endorsed by a French plurality of only 46 per
cent, but by a strong German majority of 84 per cent.

Further arms control and disarmament agreements are definitely backed by 52
per cent of the 134 French and by 84 per cent of the 165 German respondents
who comment on the matter. Even if their own countries should not be consulted about future arms control agreements, 55 per cent of the 129 articulate
French respondents and 65 per cent of the corresponding 152 Germans still are
willing to support them. (German mass opinion in mid-1954 took the same view
by a majority of 77 per cent of all those envisaging this possibility, or by a
plurality of 44 per cent).

4. *The Lack of Popular Support for National Nuclear Deterrents and MLF
Proposals.* The idea of a national nuclear deterrent is unpopular among the elites
in France, where it is official government policy, and still more unpopular
among the elites of Germany, where it sometimes has been described—by outside
observers—as a possible latent aspiration. In fact, it seems to be not even that. A
national nuclear deterrent is rejected as unnecessary for national prestige or national independence, and as not credible to the nation's enemies, by majorities

ranging between 54 and 63 per cent by France, and 64 and 94 per cent in Germany.

France's current national *force de frappe* is not expected to survive President de Gaulle. Only 22 per cent of all French respondents expect it to be kept and strengthened, while 49 per cent expect it to be turned into a European institution, and another 6 per cent expect it to be abandoned.

Although clear majorities reject the main arguments in favor of a national nuclear deterrent, French respondents are exactly divided between 46 per cent who feel that such a deterrent still is worth its cost, and the same proportion who feel that it is not.

There is no such division in West Germany, where the thrifty rejection of a national nuclear deterrent as not worth its cost is backed by a landslide majority of 95 per cent of the 163 German respondents commenting on this point. This German majority is so large as to swamp all differences among age or interest groups.

These German elite data tend to disconfirm the notion of a supposedly strong German desire for national nuclear weapons—a desire which would have to be bought off or headed off by offering the German Federal Republic some share in a supranational nuclear weapons system. So far as our evidence goes there is no such German desire for national nuclear weapons at this time.

A multilateral nuclear force under NATO is clearly favored only by 18 per cent, and clearly opposed by 27 per cent of the 100 French respondents who comment on this proposal. In Germany, where practically all respondents comment, the same proposal divides the elites exactly, with 34 per cent clearly in favor and 34 per cent definitely opposed. This last division contrasts sharply with the usual propensity for strong elite consensus in the Bonn Republic.

A European multilateral nuclear force, independent of NATO, would be somewhat more popular among elites in France, where a plurality of 40 per cent of 134 respondents clearly favors it, with only 12 per cent clearly opposed, but it would be much less popular in Germany, where no more than 6 per cent of 168 respondents back the project, while a solid 80 per cent express their opposition.

If a multilateral nuclear force within NATO should come into existence, only 16 per cent of the 102 French respondents to this question would definitely wish their country to participate, but another 43 per cent might agree to such a course under certain conditions. Among the 160 German respondents to the same question these proportions are reversed: 58 per cent clearly favor participation in such a NATO development, with another 13 per cent supporting it conditionally; and only 17 per cent definitely oppose it.

The proportions of the various responses to these and related questions confirm an impression from our interviews: there is no substantial German pressure for an MLF, but rather a willingness to go along with such a scheme, if Germany's ally, the United States, should insist on it.

The pattern of responses to this entire complex of questions suggests that neither French nor German elites are pressing strongly at this time for nuclear weapons, either national or collective. Rather, the issues of the national deterrent and the MLF tend to evoke opposition or division. This contrasts with the high majorities in both countries in favor of arms control.

The evidence of the elite survey, as far as it goes, accords well with the data from mass opinion polls and the other types of evidence examined in this study. All of this evidence is limited and incomplete, and must be appraised with judgment. At the same time it should be borne in mind that none of the evidence we have found, in terms of differences among age groups or of trends over time, points to the likelihood of any drastic changes in the next few years due to any autonomously developing changes in the French or West German political system.

V. CONCLUSIONS

The lines of evidence pursued in our inquiry tend to converge. Although there are minor differences, the weight of evidence points to several major conclusions.

1. *The Strength of Nationalism.* The movement toward structural European unification since 1957 has been largely halted or very much slowed down. The next decade of European politics is likely to be dominated by the politics of nation-states, and not by any supranational European institutions.

Within France, and within Germany, the various elite groups generally are closer in their attitudes to each other, and to the mass opinion of their own country, than they are to the opinion of their counterparts in the other country. Nationality continues to be a far stronger determinant—or indicator—of political attitudes than do class, age, occupation, religion, party affiliation, and even, for most respondents, ideology.

A provisional factor analysis of our elite survey data confirms this finding. Its results suggest that nationality seems to be between two and ten times as powerful as any one cross-national factor, such as religion, occupation, socialist party affiliation, etc., in accounting for the distribution of elite responses.

To restore now to the movement toward European unification the vigor and the momentum of the years 1947–1955 would require much larger efforts on the part of Europeans and of the United States than seem to be contemplated now in any quarter of authority. In terms of politics, it would require a visible increase in the share of American attention fixed on Europe rather than on Asia.

2. *The Desire for Alliances and Near-Equality.* Alliances, particularly with the United States, and limited steps toward additional supranational arrangements and institutions are popular among elites and acceptable to mass opinion. National isolationism is being rejected, but increasing national equality—or perhaps a greater share in power and privilege—is being demanded, particularly by the elites of France.

3. *The Desire for Wider Arms Control and Disarmament.* There is striking consensus in France and Germany on the desirability of arms control and disarma-

ment on a more than local or regional scale, and including further direct agreements between the United States and the Soviet Union. There is particularly strong consensus on the desirability of halting the spread of nuclear weapons to nations which do not now possess them.

4. *The Lack of Any Strong German Demand for Nuclear Weapons.* There is strong opposition in Germany to the acquisition of national nuclear weapons, and there is no strong positive desire for any German share in a nuclear weapons system through some multilateral arrangement, such as the MLF project; and there is overwhelming and deep-rooted French hostility to any idea of a German national nuclear weapon, or to a substantial German share in a multilateral nuclear weapons system.

5. *The Possible European Support for a Nuclear Non-Proliferation Treaty.* Under these conditions of European politics, the most nearly acceptable approach to arms control and disarmament might be an international agreement limiting the possession of nuclear weapons to those five powers now posssessing them: the United States, Britain, France, the Soviet Union, and Communist China.

These five are the governments in control of the five countries whose special importance is recognized in the United Nations Charter by giving them the status of Permanent Members of the United Nations Security Council. The legal status of Communist China is currently blocked in this respect, but her acquisition of a nuclear device has been tacitly tolerated by all other nuclear powers; and an explicit or tacit nuclear *modus vivendi* with Communist China does not seem unacceptable to European leaders.

Even without an agreement with China, an anti-proliferation agreement and extended nuclear test-ban among the "Big Four"—United States, the United Kingdom, France, and the Soviet Union—might prove feasible, and might pave the way to further steps to arms control. Such an approach might meet some of the French desire for a full and genuine share in international leadership; and our data suggest that such an accommodation of French desires on the part of the United States and Britain would be acceptable to the majority of the West German leaders.

6. *Prospects.* The picture emerging from this study is complex but not without hope. At moments of crisis the main ties of Western unity will be to Washington rather than among the European countries. For the next decade at least, national political issues will predominate over supranational ones in both France and Western Germany. Viable alliances during this period will have to be concluded on specific matters, among sovereign powers, and on a footing of equality, particularly in regard to France. Greater unity of action, as well as deeper emotional ties in Western Europe, are growing very slowly. In terms of European unification, we may expect after 1975 a possible resumption of the advances of the 1950s, but not much earlier. Until then we can expect to hold the present plateau and improve it slightly.

Western Europeans on the whole, if French and German leaders are representative of their opinions, now favor worldwide measures of arms control. They favor particularly the relaxation of tensions between the great powers, extensions of the ban on nuclear testing, and measures against the proliferation of nuclear weapons to any countries not now possessing them. They favor all of these policies, however, only provided that they can keep the American alliance and the American nuclear shield. Within this very wide range of policies acceptable to Europeans, the United States at this time has a remarkably wide range of discretion and perhaps an unparalleled opportunity for leadership.

Opportunities can be used or lost, together with the work of years of preparation. Once lost, they may be gone, or recoverable only at a great sacrifice. The value of the present American opportunities for leadership to European unity and worldwide arms control must be weighed carefully in the balance against the attractions of any policy of predominant or unlimited United States commitments on the continent of Asia.

15 | National Integration: A Summary of Some Concepts and Research Approaches

The effort to summarize here the results of a fair number of years of research inevitably will encounter several kinds of difficulties. Those quite unfamiliar with its subject may find it too condensed, while those who know the topic well may find much that is familiar to them—and may perhaps overlook some notions that have not been widely applied to this problem before, such as B. F. Skinner's idea of probabilistic reinforcement sequences, Leon Festinger's notion of cognitive dissonance, and the operational definitions suggested for the various aspects of some concepts, such as "class," "stratum," and "assimilation."

In this chapter I shall try to summarize the main conclusions, ideas and research strategies that I have encountered so far in my studies of nationalism, national integration and disintegration, and social and political development.[1] These studies have been carried out since 1939 and they are still continuing. The ideas that are discussed here are arranged not in the chronological sequence in which they were arrived at but, in an effort to provide a systematic sequence, under six headings. The list of headings is long, but the theses will be brief.

The first heading is *ontology*, that is, the inner structure and process of the phenomenon of political integration. What does it look like from the inside? The second is *existence*, that is, the interaction of the system with the supra-systems, the political and physical environment in which national political systems are embedded. The third heading is *essence*, which comes after ontology, or being, and existence. What is that subset of characteristics that we can treat as

[1] See Emerson (1960), Lerner (1963), Deutsch (1966, 1969), Rustow (1967), Snyder (1968), Shafer (1974), Eisenstadt and Rokkan (1973), and also Deutsch and Merritt (1971) and Rokkan et al. (1973).

An earlier version of this chapter was presented at a Round Table of the International Political Science Association at Jerusalem on September 9, 1974. A revised version was prepared at Harvard in 1975 and published in *The Jerusalem Journal of International Relations* 2, no. 4 (Summer 1977): 1-29. Reprinted by permission of the Publisher. The text of the present chapter is based on this latter version, with a few minor changes and additions.

decisive for classification, for deciding whether a given case or phenomenon should be included in or excluded from the concept of integration?

The fourth point is the notion of *genesis*. How does national integration come into existence, and, of course, how does disintegration come about? And genesis implies the possibilities of critical extrapolation and prognosis. The fifth heading is *evaluation*. What is the positive or negative value that national integration seems to have for the people living under it? Also, what is the value it might have for other populations outside the integrated areas and for groups, as well as for the scholar observing it, whether positive or negative, in terms of his or her own value system? Finally, the sixth heading is *opportunities for intervention*. That is, we wish to know not only where the historical process is drifting or moving but also what, if anything, can be done about it and what, in terms of our own values, should be done about it, i.e., what is desirable. Answers to the questions under these six headings should go far towards providing us with a coherent theory of political and social integration.

I. ONTOLOGY: THE INNER STRUCTURE
OF NATIONAL INTEGRATION

If we were to make a list of major characteristics of relations among sub-systems such as, let us say, political units on their way towards integration, and if we would like to know whether or not they are getting closer to it, we would begin with the study of the extent of *structural correspondence*. By *structure* we mean those aspects of a system that change slowly and only at considerable cost but which, when they do change, have large consequences for other parts of the system. These slow-changing aspects of a system must, at least in part, correspond structurally to one another.

This correspondence begins with the structural characteristic of accessibility. The significance of a geographic structure, however, may itself depend very much on the historical state of technology. Given the level of Irish seamanship in the fifth or sixth century A.D., Ireland was effectively separated from England. Given Norman or Viking seamanship, Ireland became much more closely linked. The sea, after having been a barrier, became a highway. The same is true with bridge building and pass traffic in the integration of Switzerland. With the introduction of the camel in North Africa, the desert became a connecting link, instead of acting mainly as a separating element. What matters in such cases is partial structural correspondence; the correspondence need not be complete.

Not all structures need to be visible or tangible. Value patterns in politics and culture can perform as structures, and single values as structural elements, if they can be changed only slowly and at considerable cost and if they make a substantive difference to political behavior and outcomes. The *compatibility of major politically relevant values* and value patterns may then be a crucial condition for political integration. Where such major values are incompatible, common institutions and frequent contacts are likely to produce not integration but bitter and protracted conflict. A testing of the compatibility of major values by survey methods, content analysis and/or historical description or literary methods may, therefore, be of crucial importance for the realism of our analysis.

A second test of integration is a *high level of transactions.* This can be measured in terms of flow measures, rises or declines in the volume of transactions in the boundary zones, and in terms of the distribution of attention.

The first aspect—the structural correspondence of the components in terms of territories and transportation grids—is measured largely by description and in part by the work of human geographers, geographers of settlement, geographers of transportation and the like.[2] The second aspect—the rate of transaction flows—can be determined from aggregate data. The work by Russett and his associates, the volume by Charles Taylor and Michael Hudson and the more specialized collection by J. David Singer and Melvin Small provide us with many of these aggregate data.[3] In addition, we have survey research, but until now no serious effort has been made to collect survey data on a level and in a manner comparable to, and corresponding to, the major aggregate data collections that are now available.[4] The third set of possible measurements are content analysis data, which show the distribution of mutual attention. Literature on these matters is increasing.[5]

2. EXISTENCE: INNER STRUCTURE VS. RELATIONS TO THE OUTSIDE WORLD

Another aspect of integration comes directly from the transaction flow studies, namely, the study of *boundaries*—boundaries not as historical accidents but as the observable thinning out of settlement patterns and the observable falling off of transaction streams. A great deal of literature that claims that the boundaries among African, Latin American or Asian states are accidental and arbitrary, having been determined merely by the whim of colonial administrators, has been erected on a solid basis of ignorance. That is, most people who make these claims have not looked at settlement density maps, and they have not asked themselves why it was that the British seized what is now Sierra Leone, why the French seized the area that is now the Ivory Coast or other African settlement clusters and why the question of the boundary between them often was not a

[2] See, e.g., Kasperson and Minghi (1969).
[3] Russett et al. (1964), Taylor and Hudson (1972), Singer and Small (1972). Cf. also Mickiewicz (1973), Zapf and Flora (1973) and Flora (1973).
[4] An important beginning has been made by Charles E. Osgood and his associates in their *Semantic World Atlas* (forthcoming).
[5] Merritt (1966), Katzenstein (1976). Cf. also Schweigler (1975), Kann (1957), Harrison (1960), Foltz (1965), Stephens (1968), Melson and Wolfe (1971), Mamdani (1975), Weilenmann (1951) and Deutsch (1975).

very serious matter. The answer is, of course, that very often between one settlement area and another there were, and still are, areas of very thin settlement; and colonial administrators, who needed many peole to tax and to exploit as customers and sources of labor, were usually interested in the densely settled areas and not in the thinly settled ones.

To test this proposition, one might aggregate various boundaries into two sets, set A including boundaries that run through thinly settled areas, characterized by relatively low communication and transaction flows, and set B including cases where a boundary cuts through a very densely settled and previously highly interdependent area. Then one might study the distribution of these two sets and the correlations of each of them with political conditions and effects.

Of course, once such a boundary is drawn, it can drastically cut the communication flow. In the case of Yugoslavia, the boundary between the Latin Catholic areas of what previously was a less differentiated group of South Slav peoples has certainly enhanced the difference between those who became the Croatian people and the Serbian populations which stayed in the Greek Orthodox religion.[6]

The next characteristic of integration is the *structural correspondence of communication codes and cultures*, which may or may not be high. This is only partly a matter of transactions, of whether people actually write to each other. It is partly also a matter of structural correspondence. One of the technical social science mistakes of Joseph Stalin was to deny the existence of the Jewish people, because, he argued, there are Jews in Yemen, in Poland and in Argentina, and these dispersed groups had neither a common territory nor very high flows of transaction with each other in 1913, when he was writing his study (Stalin 1935). Stalin thus underestimated the importance of cultural correspondence. Later, in a situation making cooperation among these different Jewish groups salient, the Jews again began to behave like a people. Stalin's theory that they could not do so because they had no transactions and no contiguous territory was based simply on an underestimation of this structural aspect of integration. The members of the Jewish people, even in their period of national dormancy, were proto-integrated; and within this proto-integrated group, integration could be made actual relatively easily and quickly.

Another structural aspect is the *compatibility of value orientations*, meaning that the desires of each of the different elements—whether they are popular elements, regional elements or political units—are compatible with the salient value orientations of the other groups. Given the compatibility of value orientations, one would still have to ask whether there is positive covariance of values, so that what rewards one group also rewards the others. If that is not the case, if the covariance of values is zero, there will be little integration. And if the covariance is negative, we have a conflict system, such as between wolf and sheep, or slave owners and slaves, or slave owners and the abolitionists. Anything that

[6] Cf. the discussions in Pašić (1973), Kohn (1944), and Lederer and Sugar (1969).

strengthened slavery in the south of the United States angered the abolitionists in the north. Anything that strengthened the system of free labor in the north was an embarrassment to the slave power in the south.

Experiments by social psychologists suggest that if there is positive covariance of values and a perceived causal relationship, so that not only does what benefits one group benefit the other and not only are they seemingly accidentally associated with each other but also group A cannot get an increase in value unless it cooperates with subsystem B, then we do indeed get an increase in integrative perceptions and a feeling of growing together (Sherif et al. 1965).

3. ESSENCE: PROPERTIES RELATING TO THE INTEGRATED SYSTEM AS A WHOLE

At the heart of integration is psychological identification with, or introjection of, the integrated system as a whole and its symbols. This too can be tested by surveys, content analysis and depth interviews and by projective tests.

Related to this identification is *behavioral loyalty* to the larger community, which is tested by observing behavior in situations of great strain. A typical indication is whether the governors of provinces or regions begin to conceal their assets from the central government. This started in Austro-Hungary in World War I, after 1917, when the governors of the different parts of the empire began to conceal their food supplies from each other and from the central government. Something similar happened also in the southern Confederacy in the last days of the American Civil War, when the different states began to conceal weapons and food from the Confederate command.[7]

Another test of behavioral loyalty is whether after a defeat, or in a situation of great strain, there is serious agitation for secession, to some extent regardless of whether or not it is successful. If there is no real integration, then secession will be pursued even after victory, just as Ireland seceded from Britain after their victorious joint war of 1914-18. On the other hand, in Germany, where integration was consolidated, even with the defeats of 1918 and 1945 there were no major spontaneous movements for secession. Similarly, the unsatisfactory situation in Italy after the two world wars did not lead to any serious efforts by Sicily or other areas to secede.

Yet another indicator of mass loyalty is the ratio of prisoners to casualties. In an army with low common motivation, one casualty or one person killed may be followed or accompanied, on the average, by three of four people deserting or surrendering. In an area or a community that is highly consolidated, or where the army is highly motivated, the ratio of killed to deserters or to prisoners could be one to one, or even higher. In Vietnam, for instance, it took on the average six killed Viet Cong to get one Viet Cong prisoner.[8] In the Yom Kippur

[7]See Gratz and Schüller (1928, 1930), and Morison and Commager (1942, pp. 699-712).
[8]U.S. Defense Department data, *The New York Times*, Section I, p. 7, April 4, 1969.

War of 1973, in the Sinai Peninsula, as I was told by the Israeli military, the ratio of Egyptian prisoners to killed was one to one. The ratio of both Israelis and Syrians was six killed to one prisoner.[9] In part, there is a technological element involved. It is very difficult to surrender in the middle of a tank battle, and the type of campaign has a major effect on the defection and surrender rates. Nevertheless, we do know from the statistics of Austro-Hungary in World War I that these rates did show a high correlation with nationality. Germans and Hungarians showed a casualties-to-prisoners ratio of one to one. Slavs, who disliked the Hapsburg monarchy, surrendered in prisoners-to-casualties ratios of three or four to one (Moravec 1936).

Finally, in addition to the psychological identification, which could be deeply hidden or latent, there are also the explicit *awareness* of national symbols and the explicit *will* to exclude, suppress or filter out messages that run counter to them, that is, any messages that are secessionist, independentist or particularist in tendency, as against the messages favoring the image of an integrated political community.

4. GENESIS: HOW DOES INTEGRATION COME ABOUT?

When we inquire into *genesis*, we come to the center of gravity of our discussion. How does integration come into existence? And how can we observe and study the process by which it is produced? Here we shall have to deal with four basic aspects of political integration that generate very many different possibilities of interdependence: country, people, ethnic family system and the state.

Before discussing these aspects, I would urge my colleagues to resist the impulse towards excessive professional specialization. We find that, under the varied pressures of professional selection and promotion, our colleagues are under perpetual pressure to say, "Don't look so much at these 'non-political' variables. Why aren't there more 'political' variables?" And, while they carefully recount thirty-one thousand "events data," where people rioted or somebody got shot, because that is politics, they have misgivings about asking how many letters people write to each other, because that supposedly is not politics. Similarly, extent of social mobility and the differences in it among ethnic groups were supposed to belong to another department. And that notion, I think, has greatly retarded our understanding of the process.

Market and Country

I suggested that there are four basic aspects of integration. The first is the integration of a *market* that we call a *country*. Here the salient difference is that

[9] Oral communication, Israeli army officers, Sinai Peninsula, March 1974.

the world system, or the super-system beyond national integration, tends to be—and here I must invest a term—a *paucifunctional* market. Pauci means a few, and there are indeed very few commodities and services for which we do have an elaborate world market. Copper, tin and wheat are typical examples of commodities that have given rise to specialized world markets; and when we add up all these, we may reach fifty or a hundred categories in which there are world markets.

A country is a *multi-functional* market. The commodities and services that are distributed mainly within a country are of another order of magnitude; they number not in the dozens or hundreds but in the thousands. That is, compared to the world market, a country represents an increase in multi-functional market relations by a factor of ten or more. I am offering here only estimates and impressions. But it seems to me that there is indeed a difference in the order of magnitude between the frequency and diversity of functions that are interchanged within a country and the frequency and diversity of goods and functions exchanged in the world market.

In addition, a country of course encompasses also many relations that do not appear in the world market. Within countries that are integrated, for instance, the prices of factors of production are essentially similar. Such a test has been proposed by Gunnar Myrdal (1956) and Charles Kindleberger (1973). Interest rates within an integrated country are roughly the same, as are wages for similar kinds of labor. When there is a wage difference of more than twenty percent in an economically integrated country, labor begins to move (cf. Maclaurin 1943). Internationally, such mobility often does not exist; and the differences in real wages tend to be higher by an order of magnitude among countries than within them—a point that Galtung (1971) seems to stress.

The same is true of many other factor prices. If within a country the factor prices begin to differ from one region to another or from one group to another as much as they differ internationally, that would be a clear indication that in regard to those wages and services the country is not yet integrated (Myrdal 1956, pp. 63-65; 1957).

To give another example, the difference between the richest and the poorest state in the United States circa 1970 was about two to one (Connecticut vs. Mississippi). Thirty-five years earlier, in the 1930s, it was about three to one. In Germany the difference between the richest and the poorest state (probably Hamburg vs. Rhineland-Palatinate) is on the order of roughly one and a half to one. According to provisional figures collected by Jorge Dominguez, in Mexico the difference between the poorest and the richest province or state is about eleven to one, and in Venezuela it was seventeen to one.[10] Perhaps in developing countries we may often find two-digit differences among regional per capita incomes. Just as we have two-digit and one-digit rates of inflation, so we have

[10] U.S. Department of Commerce, Bureau of the Census (1960, 1965); German Federal Republic (1960 *et seq.*); Dominguez (1968, p. 72; the figures for Mexico are for 1960).

also two-digit and one-digit differences in income disparities. Internationally, the difference between the average per capita income of the richest and the poorest nations, such as the United States, Switzerland or Sweden, as compared to Ethiopia or Nepal, is sixty or seventy to one (Russett et al. 1964, pp. 149–54; Taylor and Hudson 1972, pp. 314–21). In sum, the range of income differences is by an order of magnitude bigger among nations than within most of them.

If a country already is economically integrated to some extent and people attach political values to it and begin to identify with other people in the country, we are likely to find there also the beginning of a notion of *patriotism*. This consists of a preference for and sense of solidarity with people who share the *patria*, regardless of the language they speak. Thus, for instance, in the fourteenth century the term *patriota* was used for both the German- and the French-speakers in the Valais in today's Switzerland (Deutsch and Weilenmann 1967). The sources are Latin, but the people who were living there spoke French and German. Similarly, one finds in the nineteenth century a period of Bohemian patriotism; and in the eighteenth century there was a patriotic period among Protestants and Catholics at the time of Grattan in Ireland.[11] One discovers relatively often such a patriotic stage where what counted was the country and not yet the people.

Equalities and Inequalities of Distribution

The consideration of interregional income differences suggests a question about common markets, such as the European Economic Community. Generally, a market functions also as an engine that transfers wealth; we find that markets often transfer wealth from the very poor to the rich. However, this is not always the case. In a market where mobile factors of production, such as capital and management, are relatively abundant, we can observe a *spread effect*, whereby the mobile factors of production move from the most highly developed enclaves or regions, where capital and management do not command high returns because they are in large supply, and flow out to the hinterland. This phenomenon is noted in the classic treatises on international trade and on laissez-faire liberalism. It was the reality that impressed Adam Smith.

But the empirical facts tell us that in the majority of cases in today's world, and for the majority of contemporary humanity, this relation does not exist. For if capital and labor are relatively scarce, we get not what Gunnar Myrdal called the spread effect but, on the contrary, what he called the *backwash effect*. That is, if capital and management are scarce, they command a high rate of return even in the most developed areas. Therefore, these areas will tend to attract what little capital and managerial talent there is, draining them away from the provinces and into the most highly developed regions (Myrdal 1957, pp. 27–29). It is an empirical fact of the greatest importance that this situa-

[11] On the concept of patriotism, see also Kohn (1944) and Potter (1957).

tion of scarcity of capital and of advanced managerial and technological skills is still the norm among something like four-fifths of the world's peoples; and, as a result, markets still tend, more often than not, to move wealth from the poor to the rich.

By contrast, modern states, if they are democratic and if they are responsive to majority desires and votes, tend to function as highly imperfect engines for moving at least a small part of the wealth from the rich to the poor. This is typical of the welfare state, and to that extent states are instruments of a very limited income redistribution. This is seen explicitly in the German Federal Republic, where the principle of "equalization of burdens" was written into the legislation.[12]

In this sense, there is a sharp difference between an empire and a welfare state. An empire operates like a world market; it takes from the poor and gives to the rich. A welfare state takes a little from the rich and thereby reduces inequality. It retains the equality-promoting effects of the market, insofar as they exist, and reinforces them.

Peoples: Culture and Communication Habits

Let us turn to the element of *people* in the integration process. I define a people as a group of persons who have a community of complementary habits of communication and hence a high probability of mutual understanding on a wide variety of topics. This occurs often, but not always, through a community of languages and, perhaps more indispensably, through a community of culture.[13] As is known, English-speakers in Ireland and England, and Catholic and Protestant English-speakers in Belfast, do not understand each other very well. In a less violent context, German-speakers in Switzerland and in southern Germany, even though they both speak Allemanic dialects, have markedly different cultures.

This concept of a people is similar to, but not identical with, the notion of an *ethnie* or an ethnic system (see Glazer and Moynihan 1975). This involves a combination of complementary communication habits and a family system. It is perfectly possible for different groups of people to understand each other, to have common communication habits, but only a very low probability of inter-marriage and therefore a low frequency of either actual or expected family ties. In a people integrated into an ethnie, on the other hand, one ought to find a higher observable frequency of actual intermarriage, which could be determined from statistics on sample surveys of behavior, and a higher expectation of family ties, which could be tested by surveys of opinion and attitudes.

Moreover, in most countries, peoples are in fact also ethnies, and the family system is connected with the system of the transfer of personal property and with the career system; moreover, in private enterprise countries, it is connected

[12] German Federal Republic, *Basic Law*, Art. 72:3; Deutsch (1972).
[13] For a more extensive discussion, see Deutsch (1966, pp. 86–106).

also with the transfer of productive property, insofar as the latter is not tied up in corporations. Thus membership in such a people involves also, through the family system, a connection with the career system and with the property system, as well as with the system of credit and of general confidence and trust. We may call the latter the system of credit and quasi-credit, such as appointing people to jobs of trust and confidence; and here again a people is an engine for spreading the benefits around. In this sense a people, like a state, is an engine that very often works in a direction opposite to that of the market. It tends to even out somewhat or to spread around expectations of a value gain, particularly in terms of careers and status and in terms of property.

The State: Enforcement and Compliance

Finally, there is the *state* with its enforcement machinery, together with the machinery for educating people and confirming people in habits of compliance. It seems reasonable to assume that, where ninety or ninety-five percent of the population comply by habit almost entirely with the commands of the state, enforcement is practical, and the probability of enforcement will in turn strengthen the compliance habits. This operates in the manner of a feedback system, but, just as the chicken is bigger than the egg, the compliance habits are considerably stronger than the enforcement probabilities.

The real drama of politics—and one that often is hidden and silent—lies in the change of popular compliance habits. Our textbooks, written by historians who were trained by lawyers, stress mainly the changes in laws and in institutions. The political reality, as we know in the age of Gallup and others, often moves in the opposite direction. The legislation and institutions of Prohibition in the 1920s and more recently of the marijuana laws in the United States moved in one direction, while the compliance habits of the population went another way. And we know the outcome of these noble experiments. There is an interdependence between compliance and enforcement, but one should know where the asymmetry is in the coupling; and the coupling is asymmetrical in favor of the compliance habits. That does not mean that the flow in the opposite direction is zero; but the effect of laws on habit though by no means negligible often is somewhat weaker.

An Imperfect Assembly Line

Experience shows that integration can occur in very different sequences. The process might begin with the integration of a country, call it C, and might then lead to the integration of some populations, P, and finally to the emergence of a state, S. A sequence such as C-P-S is quite possible. Alternatively, the sequence might begin with the integration of a people. To some extent, the Arab tribes, even before the rise of Islam, were integrated in their language, L, and through the literature that began to emerge among them; later they were further integrated by the Islamic religion, R; and the consolidations of Arab countries and nationalities came much later and were much more imperfect. Nevertheless, as a political reality, there is such a thing as Arab nationalism, and it began on the human side, in a sequence that we might write as L-R-(C)-(S)-P.

In other cases, integration may have begun with some sort of political unification. The sequence of Welsh-English integration into a British people could be written briefly as S-R-C-P. There was a similar sequence in the integration of England and Scotland. But in England's relation to Ireland, consolidation of the state was not followed by consolidation on the popular level. Thus we might write English-Irish integration as $S\text{-}\bar{C}\text{-}\bar{R}\text{-}\bar{P}\text{-}\bar{S}$, the barred symbols denoting negative outcomes. In sum, we find quite different sequences among our cases.

It follows that a simple effort to measure correlations, either simple correlations or multiple regressions, in the manner of Wolfgang Zapf and Peter Flora (1973), offers valuable contributions in many ways but misses an essential point of the way nations are put together The genesis of national integration is not a simple correlation process of synchronized growth. Rather, it is a process that resembles an assembly line that is very poorly organized. In a well-organized assembly line, the flow of all components occurs at about the same speed and they arrive at about the same time at critical assembly points. Nevertheless, even in an ideal assembly line, it is irrelevant whether one begins with a chassis and later puts in the engine, which was assembled elsewhere, and still later adds the wheels, or whether one puts on the wheels first and the engine later. The main thing is that at the end one has a whole car. This is very different from the organismic model, according to which there must be a tadpole before there can be a frog and there must be a kitten before there can be a cat.

Nations are not organisms, and national integration is not an organismic process. It is, first of all, a kind of assembly line process. But secondly it is a non-synchronized assembly line process with long waiting lines, as in a badly organized factory. There might be a great many wheels already assembled at one place, while the chassis are coming through much more slowly, and therefore a lot of wheels are piling up. At another factory there might not be enough wheels ready, and there may be many car bodies awaiting wheels. Nevertheless, even on such assembly lines, from time to time a car will emerge and roll off on its own power.

If this primitive analogy is at all relevant to the process of national integration, then the best mathematical model for analyzing a process of this type is not multiple regression, simple correlation or causal path analysis. What we need are models of stochastic processes with waiting lines. Thus far, this has been purely theory. We now have some mathematical process models of this kind, and present-day political scientists specializing in the study of national integration would be well advised to associate themselves with mathematicians who can handle such models or to encourage some of their students to do so. It took us enough years to learn something about nationalism; we do not have to learn stochastic process mathematics. But we do need to learn enough about it so that we can cooperate with other colleagues; there is no point in always being fifty years out of date in our mathematical models, which has generally been the case thus far.[14] This seems to me to be the one major point that is missing in the two important volumes edited by Stein Rokkan and Samuel Eisenstadt;[15] that is, they give excellent institutional descriptions of what was happening, but the mathematical side of the discussion either is absent altogether or is, to some extent, still tied to relatively obsolete mathematical methods.

To sum up what has been said about the genesis of national integration, it is achieved eventually by bringing all four of these aspects—country, people, ethnic family system and the state—to a sufficiently high level of development. Since these four aspects develop unevenly in most countries, it follows that there will almost always be more than is needed in one of these dimensions and that the sequences and the leading sectors are likely to differ greatly among countries, though they nevertheless lead to the same final result. This final result is a set of interlocking habitual attitudes of mind, habitual patterns of behavior, and habitually accepted and functioning channels of communication and organization.

Integration as a Learning Process

How is this result—this genesis—acquired? Here another theoretical point must be considered. We may think of national integration as owing its genesis to a process of social learning, and this learning can occur only where something is taught, either by a human teacher or, as is more frequently the case, by a sequence of experiences. The work of the American psychologist B. F. Skinner suggests that such a sequence of experiences is most effective if it is not completely deterministic, with reinforcement occurring all the time, but only probabilistic, such that the probability of reinforcement declines during the period of the learning process.[16] I submit that human society can be looked upon as a gigantic human teaching machine working in a somewhat similar probabilistic manner. (We need to remember that, if reinforcements are not just declining but sometimes rising and sometimes declining, the rising sections of the sequence do not hurt. If people get more of a reward for a certain type of behavior, so much the better. But the slowly declining sections will increase their tenacity, so long as the decline is not too frequent or abrupt.)

We can think of society as offering probabilistic and, part of the time, declining reinforcement schedules; and this will produce much more tenacious habits of behavior than if the sequence of rewarding experiences were completely

---

[14] For discussions of mathematical models, see Alker et al. (1973), and Deutsch and Wildenmann (1976). For a broader discussion of methods, see Merritt (1969).

[15] Eisenstadt and Rokkan (1973), especially Eisenstadt, "Varieties of Political Development: The Theoretical Challenge" (vol. 1, pp. 41-72), and Rokkan, "Cities, States and Nations: A Dimensional Model for the Study of Contrasts in Development" (vol. 1, pp. 73-97).

[16] Skinner 1969; and oral communication, Cambridge, Massachusetts, December 1973.

certain. It turns out, therefore, that what happens in society is probabilistic, not deterministic. This does not weaken our basic findings about learning and teaching, but it calls for re-orientation of some of the primitive models we have been using.

Consonant and Dissonant Experiences:
Classes and Strata

A second point can be derived from the work of the American social psychologist Leon Festinger and his associates. Society teaches different aspects of behavior in different learning experiences. These different aspects of behavior can be *consonant* or *dissonant*. If they are consonant, and hence reinforce each other, the behavior is likely to be established much more strongly. If they are dissonant, however, people come under cross-pressures. They become frustrated or disoriented; they withdraw; and they become anxious or angry (Festinger 1957).

If in a particular society a group of people are so located that most of their experiences are probabilistically reinforcing and consonant, we may speak of them as belonging to a social *class*. I suggest that the classical theories of Burke, Barnave, Victor DuPont, Marx, et al., about the political behavior of classes, can be brought together with the Skinnerian notion of the efficacy of probabilistically declining reinforcement schedules and with Festinger's notion of the contrasting effects of cognitive consonance and dissonance. If there is inter-generational stability in the social, economic and occupational position of a family, so that a man who is the son of a wage worker is the father of a prospective wage worker, inter-generational experiences are consonant; childhood experiences are consonant with other life experiences, and thus certain patterns of behavior are taught more strongly. But, if a society is highly mobile, so that a person's father was an immigrant artisan, he or she is a worker and his or her child is a Ph.D.—as did happen, for example, in the New York garment district and in other places—many experiences will be dissonant and many behavior patterns will be inconsistent, weak or vacillating. It follows that society manufactures both classes and strata.

Some empirical evidence on these matters could be obtained from surveys of social mobility. One can ask about the father's job and the offspring's job (bearing in mind the habitual over-reporting of the eminence of the paternal status in such surveys) and organize the results in a social mobility matrix.

In most classic nineteenth-century societies, the majority of people were stable in their classes; they belonged to the same class as their father. Therefore, these societies were, to a large degree, class societies, as Karl Marx and others saw them and reported them. In a more mobile society, such as those of the United States and West Germany in the mid-twentieth century, probably more than half of the population is in the off-diagonal cells of such a social mobility matrix. Therefore, on the whole, well-defined classes and consistent class experiences and class behavior are becoming rarer in such societies.

People who belong to a class and who have consonant experiences are likely to act in politics more frequently and more energetically, as well as more consistently. Therefore, classes will be more politically effective, at least up to a point, while mere social strata will experience more cross-pressures from different experiences and their members will tend to waver. Many Marxists are angered by the lower middle class and the intellectuals, because they so often vacillate in their political and social behavior. But these strata have good reasons to do so, because their experiences do not push them in one direction. For people who call themselves materialists, it seems strange to be indignant about this vacillation of a class or a stratum that behaves exactly as its situation teaches it to behave; and they should note that the proportion of these strata is increasing in highly industrialized countries.

If a society teaches inconsistent behavior with regard to class positions, it may nevertheless teach consistent behavior with regard to nationality. This should be true particularly for people who are experiencing vertical social mobility, which is in part related to nationalism. For nationalism is partly an ideology of vertical social mobility; and we find that, as modern industrial society increases social mobility, it teaches class behavior with declining intensity and ethnic and national behavior with increasing intensity. This seems to me to be one explanation of the increase in ethnic and nationalistic behavior observable in the process of modernization.

Social Mobilization and Cultural Assimilation

Broadly speaking, the process of national integration into some larger or smaller national political community takes place within the framework of two larger processes: the process of *social mobilization*, which makes people available for new experiences, relationships and ways of feeling and acting, and the process of *modernization*, which consists of their actually developing that complex of new attitudes, behavior patterns and institutions that we call modern.

But national integration itself involves several component processes. The first of these is the *relevance* process, which makes people realize that language and ethnicity are important, and that politics is important. Some evidence regarding this process is known from the research on social mobilization. The second component is the *consonance* process, whereby people learn to respond to more consonant impulses and experiences. The third component is a *highlighting* process, whereby certain messages are filtered out or dropped out of the field or focus of attention. By underplaying or disregarding anything that does not fit, one can artificially increase the consonance of one's knowledge. This process could have worked in certain periods in favor of the theory of class, by dropping out the nationalism-promoting experiences; but now it more often works in favor of nationalism. The fourth component is the *activity* process, in which people are actually acting, moving ahead and making things happen.

I have studied the relevance process, mainly through transaction flows and social mobilization data, as have Russett, Merritt, Zapf, Flora and many others.[17] The highlighting process, which occurs through consciousness and will, has been the subject of much work by Hans Kohn (1944) and Carlton Hayes (1960). The activity process, which occurs largely through participation in parties, organizations and the like, seems to me to lie at the heart of much of the work of Stein Rokkan (1967, 1970a, 1970b, 1975), who has made a very important contribution to the study of our subject.

Finally, there is the *introjection* process—the change of personal habits. The latest and, in my opinion, a fundamental work on this aspect of our problem is Alex Inkeles' and David Smith's book, *Becoming Modern* (1974), which shows the effects of factory work and of participation in cooperatives on the whole personality and on attitudes towards modernity. Here again, I believe that if one were to follow up the evidence from their six-country study, one would find an increase in orientation towards the national state (cf. Lerner 1963).

So much for the mobilization process and its aspects. I once noted the general finding that mobilization seems to occur, on the average, at a rate of shift of one-half of one percent of the population per year into the mobilized sector, plus or minus another one-half of one percent or so. It rarely stands still. The *assimilation* process, in which people learn new languages, cultures, habits and loyalties, proceeds much more slowly. Ordinarily, the assimilation process runs at a rate of shift of approximately one-tenth of one percent of the population into the assimilated sector, plus or minus one-quarter of one percent. The process can therefore easily run negatively, reversing the trend, as it did in Quebec, where the number of monolingual French-speakers has increased in the last two decades. In other words, there is a fundamental cleavage between the mobilization and the assimilation processes. If the non-assimilated group forms a large part of the population, it follows that it cannot be assimilated, that national predominance relations will be challenged and may even be reversed.[18]

Self-Steering Capacity

The last two points can be dealt with briefly. If we observe an integrated national political system, we can also look at it from the viewpoint of its capacity for self-steering, feedbacks, goal-forming and goal-changing capacities, and

[17] E.g., Deutsch (1961), Russett et al. (1964), Merritt (1969), Taylor and Hudson (1972), Zapf and Flora (1973), Flora (1973) and the works listed in n. 5.

[18] In his doctoral thesis, Paul Werbos (1974) shows that the rates of these two processes can be projected over a fifty-year period into the past and into the future, with an error margin ranging ordinarily between five and ten percent with regard to the past. Werbos demonstrates that we now have fairly powerful statistical methods for modeling these two processes. For earlier and more primitive calculations, see Chapter 16 below.

capacities for self-transformation, with the preservation of its identity. This leads us to the notion that the size of states should still follow the old principle stated by Aristotle in the fifth book of his *Politics*, to the effect that one should not make either a state or a ship too big to obey the rudder. Aristotle's point still seems valid (cf. Deutsch 1976). World organizations, to be sure, have a much larger domain, but each of them can deal with only very few functions. At present, only the national state can deal with many.

There is yet another point. As the powers we set into motion by a political decision are increasing in terms of people, energy, capital and other resources, we must not look only at their first-order consequences. For their remote and indirect consequences are becoming too big to be neglected. We are being taught this right now by the ecologists. However, as the second- and third-order consequences of political decisions become salient and important, they will transcend the boundaries of particular disciplines and particular types of expertise. Therefore, we are entering an era that witnesses a built-in contradiction in the field of functional international institutions, when each of them is competent only in its particular specialty, such as FAO for food, WHO for health, and the World Bank for money. What is the effect of a change in petroleum prices on the food situation in India or on the health of children in Bangladesh? At the present, there is no international organization of sufficiently broad interdisciplinary competence to deal with such issues. Furthermore, we have no institution capable of forming a common political will, no machinery to enforce decisions and no social fabric to sustain compliance with them.

It follows that, to some extent, functional international organizations may well decline rather than expand, and we will have to seek new methods, not for having nation-states replaced by world organizations but, rather, for having them cooperate more effectively with these organizations which is a very different thing indeed.

5. EVALUATION: WHAT DOES INTEGRATION MEAN IN TERMS OF HUMAN VALUES?

Images of larger integrated political units—Europe, Atlantic union, world government—are often laden with positive values. "Separatism" or "parochialism" seems unimpressive by comparison. But we must note the great emotional charge that "independence" has for Americans, as it has for many other peoples. We do not celebrate "integration day" or the ratification day of the American Constitution; we celebrate Independence Day on the fourth of July. "Independence" is a positive word; while "secession" is a positive word in the south but not in the north of the United States. In many countries, we find such value-laden words as "liberation," "freedom" and "independence." To a large extent, we find a similar value charge in favor of a shift, sometimes to a larger, sometimes to a smaller political unit. What seems to make the difference is the association, in experience or expectation, of the proposed larger or smaller political unit with other values and valued services.

Here we have a task as scientists, to investigate the operational value consistencies. And we may find that, while we may want big decisions to be taken by world organizations, this may be operationally inconsistent with some of our values in regard to their secondary effects in other fields. We may then have to study historical and idiosyncratic choices. Social scientists can try to map out the subset of viable solutions which are not destroyed by fatal operational inconsistencies. Within that subset, however, the choices are likely to be historical, emotional and idiosyncratic. Within the limits of operational necessity, both humanity and each particular people retain an area of discretion or decision latitude, which may be large. Once a choice within that area has been taken, however, it is quite possible that it will become a given in itself.

6. OPPORTUNITIES FOR INTERVENTION

Given that we can talk about what is operationally possible as a viable pattern, about what is historically and idiosyncratically acceptable to a given population at a given time, what intervention could we consider and carry out? What cost-benefit analysis, in terms of these values, could we carry through?

Thus far, political science has done relatively little to develop this line of inquiry; and it cannot be developed very far until the earlier steps in the direction of understanding the national integration process have been carried out to an adequate degree. Knowing more about the structure or ontology, the essence, the existence, the genesis and the value aspects of the integration process seems to be an indispensable requirement to discovering and gauging opportunities for political intervention in a sufficiently realistic manner. I believe we can now study nationalism and national integration or secession and independence movements on a new level of theoretical sophistication because the various preceding approaches are now acting to refine and reinforce each other.

What has been presented here is a relatively short sketch of a large complex of problems. Inevitably, it must raise many questions, some of which are recurrent. Clarifying some of these points—I have selected six—may help to advance the discussion.

1. Mobilization, Modernization and Integration

The first question relates to the nature of mobilization, modernization and integration and a possible later state to which these might lead. *Mobilization* deals with making people available for new patterns of behavior and, to some extent, putting them in situations where they have new needs and new learning experiences. It involves three things: learning situations, needs and availability. *Modernization*, as I understand the term, means that people actually commit themselves in a large part of their thoughts, feelings, and actions to a new, modern pattern of behavior. It is exactly in this sense that Alex Inkeles and David Smith deal with cases of transition from mobilization to modernization, in their book *Becoming Modern.*

Integration, likewise, is to some extent a commitment to integrative habits and patterns of behavior. A later state in this process would probably be something like *consolidation,* that is, continuity of the behavior patterns to which one is committed, even under stress. Thus, even under considerable stress, after World War I and II, neither the Rhineland nor any other major region wanted to secede from Germany. Alfred Doeblin in 1924 described how, after a long war and the destruction of the great cities in Germany, people would revert to pre-industrial barbarism (Doeblin 1924). In actual fact, Hamburg and Dresden were built up again as industrial cities after World War II.

2. Dimensions of Assimilation

The second point deals with *assimilation.* To some extent, political compatibility can be reached with a relatively limited degree of assimilation. After the Scottish uprising of 1745, the British government did not assimilate the Scottish Highlanders, but it found a niche for them in the British scheme of things. At first, to be sure, the British forbade the wearing of the kilt in Scotland and tried to assimilate the Scots forcibly. But by the 1780s they introduced special Highland Regiments, with all the Scottish symbols, bagpipes, kilts, and all, and the Highlanders served Britain loyally in the Napoleonic Wars.

Assimilation should be divided into four aspects. The first is assimilation of *needs.* Does the new group develop the same needs as the others? This often comes very quickly; for example, movement into town means a need for clean water and public health services. A *need* is a want which, if not satisfied, is followed by a relatively high probability of observable damage, whereas a *desire* is something that most people can do without and not be noticeably damaged (although being permanently frustrated in *all* their desires would probably damage many people somewhat). There is thus an empirically verifiable difference between needs and desires.

Second is the assimilation of *aspirations.* Do people want the same things? For a time, the Malayans were not interested in economic and business success to the same degree that the Chinese in Malaya were. Thus they constituted a group with largely pre-industrial aspirations, co-existing with the Chinese group with its commercial and industrial—and hence modern—aspirations; and the latter group was likely to get most of the prizes available in that society. But when the Malayans began to aspire to the same things, there was considerable conflict.

The third aspect is the assimilation of *capabilities.* Are people equally well educated, equally capable in less formalized skills? Finally, there is the assimilation of *attainments.* One of the major causes of disintegration is a situation where a group has already become assimilated in needs, aspirations and capabilities but is nevertheless denied a significant share of the attainments.

An important part of the assimilation of capabilities is, in many cases, the assimilation of *language.* If the spoken languages of different ethnic groups are not very similar, this assimilation takes, on the average, from two hundred to four hundred years. The latter figure is perhaps the median. Sometimes it takes as long as seven hundred years, while two hundred years seems to be the least for populations remaining in their settlements. Rapid assimilation of loyalties would have to be accompanied by major habit-changing and habit-breaking social innovations.

Let us consider two examples. The conquest of Wales by England was completed in the thirteenth century, but the assimilation was to an important extent consolidated after 1536 through the shift to the Reformation, which gave the Welsh clergy the right now to marry legally and to live with their wives publicly and respectably. At the same time, the Welsh gentry enriched themselves through the secularization of the Church's estates. Thus these Welsh groups acquired a major common interest with the English Protestants. Another case was Alsace. The German city of Strassburg was conquered by France only in 1684, but with the French Revolution the Alsatians won human rights and were freed from serfdom. The gained freedom of movement, free selection of residence and occupation, and so in their sympathies the Alsatians became French, as German nationalists later noted with much chagrin. Nevertheless, Alsace produced five times as many refugees from the French Revolution than any other region in France (cf. Ford 1958; Greer 1924).

Whether political integration efforts will succeed or fail and how fast the process will progress are likely to depend in part on the extent to which some *proto-integration* has already been established. For instance, Franks and Saxons in tenth-century Germany had similar languages and many similar culture patterns; therefore, when Charlemagne and his successors were trying to turn the Saxons into Germans by blood and fire, their task was less difficult than it would otherwise have been. Another major factor is deliberate and imaginative government policy that is responsive to popular needs and social realities. King Henry I of Germany, who was a Frank, had himself crowned in Saxon dress and ordered his Frankish court nobles to marry Saxon wives. (Of course, some of these methods are not fully acceptable today.)

Ideally, all four variables—the time variable, the proto-integrative culture, the major habit-breaking changes, and the deliberate government policy—should be consonant with each other. In actual fact, they may come at different times, which brings us back to the observation that, when several conditions are necessary to produce an end result, history often acts like a very inefficient assembly line. If one of the ingredients never arrives, then integation may not be achieved, and political unity may fail or may merely survive for a time by apathy or force.

3. Is Integration a Goal?

We should perhaps reformulate this question and ask what *the optimal size of the political unit* is. The answer may depend mainly on two conditions: the changing nature and scope of the tasks of government, and the power and resources needed to carry them out.

The scope of government consists of the array of functions that we want the government to fulfill. If we want mainly to prevent radioactive fallout, our political institutions should be global, because fallout does not stop at national boundaries. But, if we want mainly to develop a highly elaborate cultural pattern or to protect a unique cultural pattern, such as that of the State of Israel, the political unit had better remain small, because it will be very hard to bring people who do not share this unique cultural pattern, and, in this instance, a biblical heritage, to collaborate for the purpose of achieving that particular goal. Thus, the bigger the State of Israel becomes, the less Israeli it will be. Optimal state size therefore depends very much on what the state's goals are.

Another point, however, is that the bigger a state is—while still remaining stable—the greater are the means of power and the resources that it can employ. If it is too small, it might be too impotent to act. But, the bigger it becomes, the harder it will be to steer. As the size of a state increases, we get a declining curve of impotence, but a rising curve of ungovernability, which together forms a U-shaped trough, so that somewhere in the middle we may get a political unit big enough to be able to act and yet small enough to be governable. The problem is partly one of values—i.e., what we need and want—and partly one of technical design—i.e., how best to get it.

4. Pluralism vs. Structuralism

Within a political community of a given size, what theory and practice of domestic politics seem most likely to strengthen integration and to preserve it during periods of rapidly changing circumstances? Within the limits of this chapter, only brief indications can be given. A basic issue here is that of the approach of *consociation*, or behavioral pluralism, as against the approach of *structuralism* (Piaget 1970).

The familiar political theory of *pluralism* assumes by implication that the differences in power and aspirations among different interest groups will be moderate and that the tempo of change will be slow and the extent of the changes will be limited.[19] Under these conditions, pluralism might well work. However, if some groups are very powerful and others are weak, if some groups are interested in outcomes and needs very different from those sought by others, and if the tempo of required change—the tempo of change exacted by the supra-system, the environment or the needs of major component subsystems—is rapid

[19] The best statement of the pluralist viewpoint is in Dahl (1961; see also 1970, 1971). See also Polsby (1963).

and the only feasible changes come in large, relatively indivisible packages, then pluralism is likely to be unworkable or to become a cloak for an oligarchy of a few favored groups; and the pluralist promise will lead to disappointment.

Structuralism, however, could still work, because the key idea of structuralism is that a structure not only is an ensemble of relatively stable elements that have a certain set of relations to each other at the time that we observe them, but the structure also includes the entire *transformation group* of potentially viable relations among the elements. That is to say, each structure includes not one pattern but several possible patterns among the same basic elements that are connected by a common set of transformation rules. This means also—as we observe in chemistry and other fields—that there can be several states or patterns of relationships that are stable. And it means that a political system can move relatively quickly from a Bourbon monarchy which remained stable for a long time, to a French republic eventually, or even for a time to a Napoleonic monarchy, which had very remarkable capabilities, but that it cannot move quickly to a Japanese shogunate or to a classical Greek city-state. That is, there is a limited set of possible changes of state for each structure within its basic identity, and the differences between these equally viable structural arrangements may be large. This makes structuralism an approach that permits us to deal with large differences, rapid speeds of change, extensive changes and some significant preservation of a larger identity.

In these respects, structuralism seems superior to the pluralist approach. Pluralism may be thought of as a special case of structuralism. The pluralist society may be treated as a structure that is adapted to small increments of change, small differences in waiting capacity and bargaining power among the different groups, and high degrees of similarity, capability and motivation.

5. Learning Capacity and Overloads

Considerations of capability lead us also to the overload problem. The physical power to act does not automatically imply the cybernetic powers to perceive and process information, to think, to know what to do and to control one's own clumsy efforts to do it. Communication and decision overloads can occur in democracies, but the raw power of a dictatorship does not make it any more intelligent. Often a very powerful dictatorship does not have to make itself more intelligent, at least for a time; but even such a dictatorship may not necessarily be able to improve its decision system and its communication system to such an extent that what is an overload for a democracy would not constitute an overload for a dictator.

The learning process and the learning capacity of a country can, in the short run, probably be very high during a revolution. But nobody can make a revolution permanent. No "permanent revolution" has ever been an observed state of affairs; and, over the long run, some democracies have demonstrated high learning capacities. The first obstacle to the continued learning capacity of a political system is the dictatorship itself, as Salazar's Portugal, the colonels' Greece and other countries have demonstrated. Usually dictators end up committing some colossal act of stupidity, launching an enterprise for which they do not have the military capability and equipment, such as Napoleon's march to Moscow, the Greek colonels' Cyprus adventure, Japan's attack on Pearl Harbor, Hitler's march into Russia and Mussolini's plunge into World War II. In each of these cases, we observe vast misappraisals and failures to adapt to—or even to perceive—the realities in a larger environment. It seems fair to say that, in their ability to deal with informational overload, the dictatorial systems are, in the long run, usually even worse off than the democracies. Though a dictator may come to power by responding to a short-term crisis better than his democratic opponents, he then has a license to commit increasing acts of stupidity in the future.

There are many aspects to the learning capacity of social and political systems, and there are empirical indicators for at least some of them. We may compare the number of important innovations produced in the Soviet Union in the twenty-one years between 1917 and 1938 with the number in the thirty-year period 1937-67 or the thirty-nine-year period from 1937 to 1976. Innovation certainly has not died out in the Soviet Union; however, its tempo seems to have noticeably slowed down.

6. Total Efforts, Single Goals and the Costs of Time

The whole theory—that one can use methods of total war for economic purposes, as in a "war on poverty" or in building capital projects—may be applicable in the short run; and the world can live more easily with a country that mobilizes all its forces to build dams or power stations than with a country that mobilizes for a rampage of attempted wars of conquest. But, after a number of years, perhaps ten or twenty, the methods of any total mobilization become self-damaging, and their overt and hidden costs become very large indeed. Even a democracy that mobilizes for total war pays a price to some extent, in terms of narrowing some of its channels of communication and destroying certain of its moral standards. Perhaps the Watergate affair in the United States was a small sample of the hidden costs we have paid for twenty-five years of widespread willingness to let the ends sanctify the means.

This is an open question and one of the major problems of political theory. How can we mobilize all the forces of a society to deal with a high-priority task, and how do we escape or recover from the damages that this distortion of the real needs of a society—which are always multiple—will produce if we give this one need, or group of needs, a long-lasting priority status? This is a question in which timing and time are of the utmost importance. Democratic societies and their peoples can survive and actually benefit by giving high priority to one or a few tasks for a five- or ten-year period, but they may fare poorly if they go through half a century of total methods of government; and we do not know very well what the time problems are for periods in between.

Maintaining political integration, and particularly the integration of loyalties, may depend, in the long run, on some combination of two system capacities: to respond adequately—and hence sometimes quickly, massively and single-mindedly—to short-term emergencies; and to remain sensitive and open-minded towards a much wider spectrum of the needs and desires of diverse individuals and groups, and towards a much wider range of challenges from the human and nature environment. For if an "urgent" crisis has lasted more than ten years, it is almost certain to have changed its character and its setting. The single-minded response with which it was met earlier will almost surely have become inadequate, and only new patterns of attention and of creativity will permit the political system to meet the changed crisis in an integrated and effective manner.

REFERENCES

Alker, Hayward R., Jr.; Deutsch, Karl W.; and Stoetzel, Antoine, eds. 1973. *Mathematical approaches to politics*. Amsterdam and New York: Elsevier.

Dahl, Robert A. 1961. *Who governs? Democracy and power in an American city*. New Haven: Yale University Press.

——. 1970. *Modern political analysis*, rev. ed. Englewood Cliffs, New Jersey: Prentice-Hall.

——. 1971. *Polyarchy*. New Haven: Yale University Press.

Deutsch, Karl W. 1961. Social mobilization and political development. Ch. 5, pp. 90–129.

——. 1966. *Nationalism and social communication*, 2nd ed Cambridge, Massachusetts: MIT Press.

——. 1967. Nation and world. Ch. 16, pp. 297–314.

——. 1969. *Nationalism and its alternatives*. New York: Knopf.

——. 1972. The German Federal Republic. In *Modern political systems: Europe*, 3rd ed., ed. R. C. Macridis and R. Ward, pp. 309–474. Englewood Cliffs, New Jersey: Prentice-Hall.

——. 1975. *Die Schweiz als paradigmatischer Fall der nationalen Integration*. Bern: Paul Haupt Verlag.

——. 1976. On the learning capacity of large social and political systems. In *Information for action*, ed. Manfred Kochen. New York: Academic Press.

——, and Merritt, Richard L. 1971. *Nationalism and national development: an interdisciplinary bibliography*. Cambridge, Massachusetts: MIT Press.

Deutsch, Karl W., and Weilenmann, H. 1967. The Valais: a case study in the development of a bilingual people. *Orbis* 10 (4): 1269-97.

Deutsch, Karl W. and Wildenmann, Rudolf, eds. 1976. *Mathematical political analysis*. Munich: Olzog.

Doeblin, Alfred. 1924. *Berge, Meere und Giganten, Roman*. Berlin: S. Fischer.

Dominguez, Jorge. 1968. The birth of a nation: an inquiry into Mexico's nationalism and politics in the 20th century. Unpublished seminar paper, Harvard University, June.

Eisenstadt, Samuel N., and Rokkan, Stein, eds. 1973. *Building states and nations,* 2 vols. Beverly Hills, California, and London: Sage.

Emerson, Rupert. 1960. *From empire to nation.* Cambridge, Massachusetts: Harvard University Press.

Festinger, Leon. 1957. *Cognitive dissonance.* Evanston, Illinois: Row, Peterson.

Flora, Peter. 1973. Historical processes of social mobilization: urbanization and literacy, 1850-1965. In *Building states and nations,* ed. Samuel N. Eisenstadt and Stein Rokkan, vol. 1, pp. 213-58. Beverly Hills, California, and London: Sage.

Foltz, William E. 1965. *From French West Africa to the Mali Federation.* New Haven: Yale University Press.

Ford, Franklin, 1958. *Strasbourg in transition, 1648-1789.* Cambridge, Massachusetts: Harvard University Press (and Norton 1966).

Galtung, Johan. 1971. A structural theory of imperialism. *Journal of Peace Research,* no. 2: 81-118.

German Federal Republic. *Basic Law.*

——. 1960 et. seq. *Statistisches Jahrbuch der Bundesrepublik Deutschland.* Statistisches Bundesamt.

Glazer, Nathan, and Moynihan, Patrick, eds. 1975. *Ethnicity: theory and experience.* Cambridge, Massachusetts: Harvard University Press.

Gratz, Gustav, and Schüller, Richard. 1928. *The economic policy of Austria-Hungary during the war in its external relations,* English version by W. Alison Phillips. New Haven: Yale University Press. *Economic and social history of the World War* series (translated and abridged), for the Carnegie Endowment for International Peace: Division of Economics and History.

——. 1930. *Der wirtschaftliche Zusammenbruch Osterreich-Ungarns; die Tragödie der Erschöpfung.* Vienna: Hölder-Pichler-Tempsky. *Wirtschafts und Sozialgeschichte des Weltkrieges* series, for the Carnegie Endowment for International Peace.

Greer, Donald. 1924. *The incidence of the Terror during the French Revolution: a statistical interpretation.* Cambridge, Massachusetts: Harvard University Press.

Harrison, Selig. 1960. *India: the most dangerous decades.* Princeton: Princeton University Press.

Hayes, Carlton. 1960. *Nationalism, a religion.* New York: Macmillan.

Inkeles, Alex, and Smith, David. 1974. *Becoming modern; industrial change in six developing countries.* Cambridge, Massachusetts: Harvard University Press.

Kann, Robert A. 1957. *The Habsburg Empire: a study in integration and disintegration.* New York: Praeger (and Octagon 1973).

Kasperson, Roger E., and Minghi, Julian V., eds. 1969. *The structure of political geography.* Chicago: Aldine.

Katzenstein, Peter. 1976. *Disjoined partners: Austria and Germany since 1815.* Berkeley: University of California Press.

Kindleberger Charles. 1973. *International Economics*. Homewood, Ill: Irwin.

Kohn, Hans. 1944, 1961. *The idea of nationalism: a study in its origins and background*. New York: Macmillan.

Lederer, Ivo J., and Sugar, Peter F. 1969. *Nationalism in Eastern Europe*. Seattle: University of Washington Press.

Lerner, Daniel. 1963. *The passing of traditional society*. Glencoe, Illinois, and New York: The Free Press.

Maclaurin, W. Rupert. 1943. *The movement of factory workers: a study of a New England industrial community, 1937-1939 and 1942*. New York: Wiley.

Mamdani, Mahmood. 1975. Politics and class formation in Uganda. Ph.D. dissertation, Harvard University.

Melson, Robert, and Wolfe, H., eds. 1971. *Nigeria: modernization and the politics of communalism*. East Lansing: Michigan State University Press.

Merritt, Richard L. 1966. *Symbols of American community, 1735-1775*. New Haven: Yale University Press.

——. 1969. *Systematic approaches to comparative politics*. Chicago: Rand McNally.

Mickiewicz, Ellen, ed. 1973. *Handbook of Soviet social science data*. New York: The Free Press-Macmillan.

Moravec, Emanuel. 1936. *The strategic importance of Czechoslovakia for Western Europe*. Prague: Orbis.

Morison, Samuel Eliot, and Commager, Henry S. 1942. *The growth of the American republic*, vol. 1. Oxford: Oxford University Press.

Myrdal, Gunnar. 1956. *An international economy*. New York: Harper.

——. 1957. *Rich lands and poor*. New York: Harper & Row.

Osgood, Charles E., et al. *Semantic world atlas*. (Forthcoming)

Pašić, Najdan. 1973. Varieties of nation-building in the Balkans and among the southern Slavs. In *Building states and nations*, ed. Samuel N. Eisenstadt and Stein Rokkan, vol. 2, pp. 117-41. Beverly Hills, California, and London: Sage.

Piaget, Jean. 1970. *Structuralism*. New York: Basic Books.

Polsby, Nelson. 1963. *Community power and political theory*. New Haven: Yale University Press.

Potter, David. 1957. *People of plenty*. Chicago: University of Chicago Press.

Rokkan, Stein. 1967. Geography, religion and social class. In *Party systems and voter alignments*, ed. S. M. Lipset and S. Rokkan. New York: The Free Press.

——. 1970a. *Citizens, elections, parties*. Oslo: Universitetsförlaget, and New York: McKay.

——. 1970b. The growth and structuring of mass politics. *Scandinavian Political Studies* 5: 65-83.

——. 1975. Dimensions of state formation and nation building: a possible paradigm on variations within Europe. In *The formation of national states in Western Europe*, ed. C. Tilly, pp. 562-600. Princeton: Princeton University Press.

——, et al. 1973. Building states and nations: a selective bibliography of the research literature by theme and country. In *Building states and nations*, ed. Samuel N. Eisenstadt and Stein Rokkan, vol. 1, pp. 277–397. Beverly Hills, California, and London: Sage.

Russett, Bruce M.; Alker, Hayward R., Jr.; Deutsch, Karl W.; and Lasswell, Harold D. 1964. *World handbook of political and social indicators*. New Haven: Yale University Press.

Rustow, Dankwart A. 1967. *A world of nations: problems of political modernization*. Washington, D.C.: Brookings.

Schweigler, Gebhard. 1975. *National consciousness in divided Germany*. Beverly Hills, California: Sage.

Shafer, Boyd C. 1974. *Faces of nationalism: new realities and old myths*. New York: Harcourt Brace Jovanovich.

Sherif, Muzafer, et al. 1965. Intergroup conflict and cooperation: the robbers' cave experiment. In *Human behavior and international politics*, ed. J. David Singer, pp. 427–32. Chicago: Rand McNally.

Singer, J. David, and Small, Melvin. 1972. *The wages of war*. New York: John Wiley and Sons.

Skinner, B. F. 1969. *Contingencies of reinforcement: a theoretical approach*. New York: Appleton.

Snyder, Louis. 1968. *The new nationalism*. Ithaca, New York: Cornell University Press.

Stalin, Josef. 1935. *Marxism and the national and colonial questions*. New York: International Publishers.

Stephens, Hugh. 1968. *The political transformation of Tanganyika, 1920–1967*. New York: Praeger.

Taylor, Charles L., and Hudson, Michael C. 1972. *World handbook of political and social indicators*, 2nd ed. New Haven: Yale University Press.

U.S. Department of Commerce, Bureau of the Census. 1960, 1965. *Historical statistics of the United States, colonial times to 1957* and *Continuation to 1962 and revisions*. Washington, D.C.: U.S. Government Printing Office.

Weilenmann, Hermann. 1951. *Pax Helvetica oder die Demokratie der kleinen Gruppen*. Erlenback-Zurich: Rentsch.

Werbos, Paul. 1974. Beyond regression: new tools for prediction and analysis in the behavioral sciences. Ph.D. dissertation, Harvard University.

Zapf, Wolfgang, and Flora, Peter. 1973. Differences in paths of development: an analysis for ten countries. In *Building states and nations*, ed. Samuel N. Eisenstadt and Stein Rokkan, vol. 2, pp. 161–211. Beverly Hills, California, and London: Sage.

IV | *Perspectives*

IV Preparing

16 | Nation and World

The calculations of 1966 reported in this chapter suggested a period of about seventy-two years for taking the world's population to the level of per capita wealth at which the marginal utility of human life would become greater than the marginal utility of some increments in tangible wealth that might still be the objects of intranational or international disputes. It also was then suggested that a continuation of an annual rate of worldwide economic growth of 5 percent of the total gross national product—and hence a yearly growth of about 3 percent per capita—would be adequate to reach this possible "peace level" of world income by about 2038–2040. These growth rates seemed not unreasonable in 1966 and 1967, for the mean and median rates of growth of total GNP in eighty-five countries for the 1950–65 period had been 4.9 and 4.8, respectively. The mean per capita growth rate during the same period, also for eighty-five countries, had been 2.9 percent, and the median rate had been 2.7 percent.*

The experiences of the period that followed—1967 through 1977—require some revision of these estimates. As a result of the recession of the 1970s, economic growth has been somewhat slower, particularly in the non-Communist countries, which comprise somewhat more than two-thirds of the world's population. If the long-term growth rates worldwide should only be 4 percent overall and 2 percent per capita, instead of the 3 percent and 5 percent, respectively, as envisaged in 1966, the "peace level" of world income, then envisaged for about 2040, could only be reached about 2070–2075, more than a generation later.

If we assume that the risk of major wars and civil wars will persist during this dangerous period of transition, and if we also assume that this on the average will be proportional to the time that the world's population will be exposed to it, then prolonging it from about seventy-two years to about

*Charles Taylor and Michael Hudson, *World Handbook of Political and Social Indicators*, 2nd ed. (New Haven: Yale University Press, 1972), pp. 306, 314.

From Ithiel de Sola Pool, ed., *Contemporary Political Science: Toward Empirical Theory*, pp. 204–227. Copyright © 1967 by McGraw-Hill, Inc. Used with permission of McGraw-Hill Book Company. A version of this chapter was presented at a plenary session on "War and Peace," at the annual meeting of the American Political Science Association in New York City on September 9, 1966, and a revised version was published by McGraw-Hill. It is reprinted here with only minimal editorial changes.

105 will increase the risks of mass destruction for humankind by about 50 percent.

These considerations of attainable average income for the world still do not include questions of its distribution—if the present inequalities of incomes among nations and among social classes and strata cannot be reduced during the same period to a more nearly tolerable level, the threats to world peace and survival are likely to increase; and they may persist well beyond another century—if humanity survives that long.

In the short run, there seems to be little support for reducing even extreme international inequalities of income but the long-run changes in the world's climate of opinion, as suggested by such recent studies as those by Inglehart and Charles Osgood et al.,* may offer more grounds for hope.

A larger question has been raised in the 1970s by the Club of Rome. How much future economic growth will be permitted by the available supplies of energy and raw materials, and by the carrying capacity of the natural environment on our planet? This question and some of its implications for the prospects of world politics are discussed in Chapters 17 and 18 below.

Which is the most important political community in the life of the world's population? Which one is most important in day-to-day decisions? Which is the most powerful? Which one commands people's deepest loyalties? To which one should we hold in case of conflict?

These questions are as old as humanity's systematic thinking about politics and law, about loyalty and ethics, about society and history. But although the questions have been perennial, the answers have varied with place and time. The family, the kin group, the tribe, the war band of a leader and his followers, the village, the city-state or polis, the kingdom, the empire, the nation, the religious community of Christendom or of Islam, the secular faiths of socialism or of communism, the regional community of all Africans or all Asians, and finally the world community of all humankind—each of these at some time and some place has held the loyalty of people in situations of social and political conflict.

Much of classic Greek political thought was centered on the politics of the city-state which were replacing the politics of tribes and tribal kings[1] Much of Roman thought was focused on the translocal politics of the Republic, and later the Empire which superseded the politics of city-states.[2] Much of the medieval thought dealt with the politics of Christendom and its two potentially universal

---

*Ronald Inglehart, *The Silent Revolution: Changing Values and Political Styles Among Western Publics* (Princeton: Princeton University Press, 1977); Charles E. Osgood *et al., Cross-Cultural Universals of Affective Meaning* (Urbana: University of Illinois Press, 1975).

[1] The changes in the Greek concepts of loyalty and virtue—*areté*—were traced by Werner Jaeger in *Paideia: The Ideals of Greek Culture,* 2d ed., trans. Gilbert Highet, Oxford University Press, Fair Lawn, N.J., 1960, vol. 1, book 1, chap. 1, pp. 3–14.

[2] See the classic presentation by Sir Ronald Syme, *The Roman Revolution,* Oxford University Press, Fair Lawn, N.J., 1960.

institutions, the Empire and the Papacy, while other medieval thinkers fixed their attention on the politics of kingdoms and the rights and duties of kings.[3] Early modern thinkers then saw the sum of politics with Machiavelli in the actions of princes unifying ever-larger territories by skill and boldness, force and fraud. They were convinced with Hobbes that such a strong princely state was needed to save the population from the dreaded anarchy of a lawless state of nature and a war of all against all.[4] Later on, however, this state is no longer seen as ruled by the absolute will of the prince. It now is seen as governed in large part by the law of nature and the reasonable needs of its citizens in the thought of John Locke; or as ruled by the exigencies of its size, environment, history, and culture, as in the view of Montesquieu; or as destined to follow the enlightened general will of the small homogeneous community of its people, as in the thought of Rousseau; or finally, as subject to the slow accumulation of practical experience, hallowed by tradition and emotion, as in the thought of Edmund Burke.[5]

Only in the nineteenth and twentieth centuries, finally, does political thought come to focus fully on the nation and the nation-state, from the days of Hegel and Mazzini to those of Max Weber and of the nationalists of our own time.[6] At the same time, however, another current of thought increasingly saw humanity itself as a focus of political organization, from the ideas of Kant and Marx to the founders of the League of Nations and the United Nations, and to the propo-

[3] Cf. Dante Alighieri, *De Monarchia,* excerpts cited in Francis W. Coker, *Readings in Political Philosophy,* rev. and enlarged ed., The Macmillan Company, New York, 1958, pp. 226–242; Gerald G. Walsh, S.J., *Dante Alighieri, Citizen of Christendom,* The Bruce Publishing Company, Milwaukee, 1946; John of Salisbury, *Statesman's Book of John of Salisbury,* trans. John Dickinson, Russell & Russell, Inc., New York, 1963.

[4] Cf. Niccolo Machiavelli, *The Prince,* in *The Prince and the Discourses,* trans. Luigi Ricci, with intro. by Max Lerner, Modern Library, Inc., New York, 1950; Jacques Maritain, "The End of Machiavellianism," *Review of Politics,* vol. 4, no. 1, 1942, pp. 1–33; Thomas Hobbes, *Leviathan,* in M. Oakeshott (ed.), Barnes & Noble, Inc., New York, 1966.

[5] Cf. John Locke, *Two Treatises of Government,* in Peter Laslett (ed.), Cambridge University Press. New York, 1960; "Montesquieu, The Spirit of the Laws," in *Complete Montesquieu,* The Macmillan Company, New York, 1964, J. J. Rousseau, *The Social Contract,* in C. Frankel (ed.), Hafner Publishing Company, Inc., New York, 1960; Edmund Burke, *Reflections on the French Revolution,* Dutton Everyman Paperbacks, E. P. Dutton & Co., Inc. New York, 1955; Ross J. S. Hoffmann and Paul Levack (eds.), *Burke's Politics: Selected Writings and Speeches of Edmund Burke on Reform, Revolution and War,* Alfred A. Knopf, Inc., New York, 1949.

[6] Cf. Georg W. F. Hegel, *The Philosophy of History,* with prefaces by Charles Hegel and the translator, J. Silbree, and a new introduction by C. J. Friedrich, Dover Publications, Inc., New York, 1956 (also paperback); and *The Philosophy of Right,* trans. T. M. Knox (ed.), Oxford University Press, Fair Lawn, N.J., 1962; Carl J. Friedrich (ed.), *The Philosophy of Hegel,* Random House, Inc., New York, 1953 (also paperback); Giuseppe Mazzini, *Life and Writings of Joseph Mazzini,* Smith, Elder & Co., London, 1890; Hans Kohn, in *Prophets and Peoples: Studies in Nineteenth Century Nationalism,* The Macmillan Company, New York, 1946, chap. 3, pp. 77–104. On Max Weber's nationalism and its limits, see the important paper by Raymond Aron and the discussion by Hans Paul Bahrdt, Wolfgang J. Mommsen, and Karl W. Deutsch on "Max Weber und die Machtpolitik" in *Max Weber und die Soziologie,* J. C. B. Mohr, Tübingen, 1965, pp. 103–120, 124–145.

nents of informal but growing world community or even formal federal world
government today.[7]

Much of this thought has been speculative and normative, though taking its
start most often from some observations or intuitive perception of the world of
facts as they seemed given there and then. Since then, much careful historical
work on the rise and growth of nationalism has been added, as well as a number
of major studies of federalism, constitutionalism, and supranational integration,
as in the work of Carl J. Friedrich, Kenneth C. Wheare, and Quincy Wright.[8]
More recently, modern social science also has increased our powers to observe
and compare systematically this empirical world of facts around us and to subject many of these facts and processes to quantitative measurement and logical
and mathematical analysis. At the same time, the behavioral sciences have given
us a good deal of new and partly verified information as to how people think,
feel, perceive, and act, individually and in groups.[9] What, if anything, has this
new knowledge of facts and methods added to our understanding of the old
problem of the nation and the world?

Clearly only extremely sketchy answers can be indicated here. They will be
limited mainly to questions of nationalism, touching only indirectly upon the
problems of supranational integration. The basic concepts and operational

[7]Immanuel Kant, "Essay on Universal History with a Cosmopolitan Intent" and *Perpetual
Peace,* trans. L. W. Beck, The Bobbs-Merrill Company, Inc., Indianapolis, 1957; Carl J.
Friedrich, *Inevitable Peace,* Harvard University Press, Cambridge, Mass., 1948; Quincy
Wright (ed.), *The World Community,* The University of Chicago Press, Chicago, 1948;
Grenville Clark and Louis Sohn, *World Peace through World Law: Two Alternative Plans,*
3d ed., enlarged, Harvard University Press, Cambridge, Mass., 1966.

[8]See particularly Hans Kohn, *The Idea of Nationalism,* The Macmillan Company, New
York, 1944, and *Nationalism: Its Meaning and History,* rev. ed., D. Van Nostrand Company,
Inc., Princeton, N.J., 1955, 1965; Carlton H. Hayes, *Nationalism: A New Religion,* The
Macmillan Company, New York, 1961; Boyd C. Shafer, *Nationalism: Myth and Reality,*
Harcourt, Brace & World, Inc., New York, 1955; Merle Curti, *The Roots of American
Loyalty,* Columbia University Press, New York, 1946; and for two works confronting
historical evidence with modern social science concepts, see David M. Potter, *People of
Plenty: Economic Abundance and the American Character,* The University of Chicago Press
Chicago, 1954, 1957, and Seymour Martin Lipset, *The First New Nation,* Basic Books, Inc.,
New York, 1963.

[9]For some relevant recent collections, see Richard L. Merritt and Stein Rokkan (eds.),
Comparing Nations: The Use of Quantitative Data in Cross-National Research, Yale Univer-
sity Press, New Haven, Conn., 1966; J. David Singer (ed.), *Human Behavior and International
Politics: Contributions from the Social-Psychological Sciences,* Rand McNally & Company,
Chicago, 1965, and *Quantitative International Politics,* The Macmillan Company, New York,
1966; and Herbert C. Kelman (3d.), *International Behavior: A Social-Psychological Analysis,*
Holt, Rinehart and Winston, Inc., New York, 1965. For some case studies, applying some
of the new methods, as well as some traditional ones, to specific countries and periods, see
Bruce M. Russett, *Community and Contention: Britain and America in the Twentieth
Century,* The M.I.T. Press, Cambridge, Mass., 1963; Richard L. Merritt, *Symbols of Ameri-
can Community, 1735-1775,* Yale University Press, New Haven, Conn., 1966; William J.
Foltz, *From French West Africa to the Mali Federation,* Yale University Press, New Haven,
Conn., 1964; Lucian W. Pye, *Politics, Personality and Nation-building: Burma's Search for
Identity,* Yale University Press, New Haven, Conn., 1962; Raymond A. Bauer *et al., Ameri-
can Business and Public Policy: The Politics of Foreign Trade,* Prentice-Hall, Inc., Englewood Cliffs, N.J., 1963.

definitions which I am going to use must start out from work which will be familiar to those who have read my earlier writings, but I hope to carry them here a little further than before.

A nation is a people in possession of a state. To take possession of a state, some members of this people must constitute the bulk of the directing personnel of this state, and a larger number of members of this people must have some sense of identification with this state and give it their support.

A people, in turn, is a large, general-purpose communication net of human beings. It is a collection of individuals who can communicate with each other quickly and effectively over a wide range of localities and of diverse topics and situations. In order to be able to do this, they must have complementary habits of communication, including usually language and always culture as a common stock of shared meanings and memories and hence as a common probability of sharing many similar perceptions and preferences in the present and near future. Members of the same people are similar to each other in regard to some of their habits and characteristics and interlocking in regard to other habits. When a significant part of the members of a people desires to gain political power for its ethnic or linguistic group, we may call it a nationality. When such power is acquired, usually through controlling the machinery of a state, we call it a nation.[10]

The importance of such nations is quite recent in world history. Nationalism and nation-states go back at most to the Dutch and English revolutions of the sixteenth and seventeenth centuries, respectively. For most of Western Europe, nationalism grew into a mass movement and a major political force only with the French Revolution and its consequences.[11]

What is this nationalism that has so recently emerged? Nationalism is a state of mind which gives to "national" messages, memories, and images a preferred status in social communication and a greater weight in the making of decisions. A nationalist gives preference in attention, transmission, and communication to those messages which carry specific symbols of nationality, or which originate from a specific national source, or which are couched in a specific national code of language or culture. If the greater attention and the greater weight given to such messages is so large as to override all other messages, memories, or images, then we speak of nationalism as "extreme." In such cases, the messages preferred by a nationalism will outweigh and override those of humanity, prenational tradition, or world religion, despite any warnings of the latter against idolatry or blasphemy.[12]

[10] For a further discussion of these concepts, see Karl W. Deutsch, *Nationalism and Social Communication,* 2nd ed., The M.I.T. Press, Cambridge, Mass., 1966. Cf. also Carl J. Friedrich, *Man and His Government,* McGraw-Hill Book Company, New York, 1963, chap. 30, "State and Nation," pp. 547–566.

[11] See Hans Kohn, *The Idea of Nationalism,* and Shafer, *op. cit.*

[12] On the relation of nationalism to idolatry, see Hayes, *op. cit.,* and A. J. Toynbee, *A Study of History,* Oxford University Press, Fair Lawn, N. J., 1946, vol. 4, pp. 261–300. For a broader philosophical definition of idolatry, see Toynbee, *op. cit.,* vol. 7, pp. 548–550.

In the mind of the extreme nationalist, and in the communications system of any extremely nationalistic group or state, the messages preferred by nationalism also tend to outweigh most or even all messages from the world of fact and to drown out or override all feedback information about the consequences of the nationalist's own current behavior. Extreme nationalism is thus an epistemological disaster. It produces cognitive deprivation or paralysis. Like other forms of ideological extremism, it prefers ideologically encoded messages, even if they are in error, to any messages in other codes or symbols, even if those messages should happen to be true. The extreme nationalists, like the adherents to any other extreme ideology, thus become like blind people with very short white sticks. They ignore reality until it hits them, and those few events or things that cannot be ignored, to them, as to all the blind, are sudden.

From the viewpoint of communications, it is possible to define operationally just when and to just what extent nationalism or any other ideology has become "extreme."[13] It is *extreme* to exactly that extent to which urgent and relevant messages from reality are overridden by unrealistic or irrelevant messages which this ideology prefers. Conversely, nationalism or any other ideology is moderate within a given network of social communication to the extent that realistic messages are still transmitted within it and still have a significant effect on the making of actual decisions.

Can we do market research for nationalism? When, where, and under what conditions are nationalistic ideas, policies, and leaders accepted by large numbers in a population? Nationalistic ideas must be invented and proposed by national prophets and leaders, and they must be spread actively by large groups or parties of their adherents and by at least one of the mass media of communications, such as the pulpit, the school, the printing press, radio, the cinema, or television. But above all else, they must encounter some audience that is susceptible to them and likely to respond by adopting them eventually as its own. What makes a population thus susceptible to nationalism, and which groups in it become susceptible first?

There is much evidence to suggest that susceptibility to nationalism increases sharply with *social mobilization*, that is, with the shift of people away from a subsistence economy and local isolation into exposure to the demonstration effects of more modern technology and practices, to exposure to mass media of communication, to the use of money, to trading with relative strangers, to greater dependence on distant markets, and eventually to literacy, nonagricultural occupations, wage labor, urban residence, membership interest groups or organizations, voting, and other forms of political participation. Not all of these changes occur at the same time, but in most populations they tend to go together

[13] For a discussion of the importance of the distinction between "nationalism" and "extreme nationalism" in modern Catholic social thought, see Don Luigi Sturzo, *Nationalism and Internationalism*, Roy Publishers, Inc., New York, 1946.

to a considerable degree which can be measured by the statistical correlations among them.[14]

Each of these changes tends to weaken or to break the crust of custom. It moves some portion of human behavior out of the sector dominated by static or slow-changing tradition, into the sphere of individual decision and of potential public regulation or public management. Thus the sector of tradition has been shrinking, most often irreversibly, wherever the commercial revolution and the monetization of economic life have entered. The sphere of private and individual decision has expanded, but the sphere of public regulation soon expanded with it, and this public sector then continued to grow thereafter.

In the course of this worldwide process, individuals can rely less and less on custom, or on the tradition-guided consensus of village, kin group, or tribe, but they must rely more on themselves as individuals and on the common language, skills, and culture which must help them to cope with strange places, with unfamiliar and uncertain patterns of work and living, and with strangers as partners in the frighteningly expanding division of labor. A national language compatible with at least some of the traditional values and childhood memories may then increase an individual's sense of identity and of belonging, and so may the membership in some new group of former strangers, now united and made more familiar by a common national language. The greater the need for people to communicate in order to make a living, the greater is the importance of language in their lives, and the greater is their potential motivation to prefer a national language of their own.

At the same time, social mobilization increases the stakes of politics. Where almost all wealth, opportunities, and values are allocated by fixed traditions, little or nothing can be reallocated by political effort. But in a mobilized society many values, such as wealth, status, and power, are allocated by the unstable and changing outcomes of the interplay of many uncoordinated individual decisions in the marketplace and potentially also by public decisions about some reallocation by law or government. Here political action can make a difference.

If some people are attracted into politics by opportunity, others are driven there by need. To many city dwellers, housing, water, health, and care in old age are no longer furnished by the village or the family. Streets, sewers, water mains, hospitals, farm prices and food prices, wage rates and levels of employment—all these are subject to political decisions. Those who need these services have a strong incentive to take an interest in the political process by which many of these services are allocated and sometimes produced. Social mobilization thus means potential politicization, and quite likely it means politicization along the lines of language and ethnic culture, that is, nationalism intermingled with and

---

[14] Cf. Chapter 5, pp. 90–129. For additional data, see Bruce M. Russett *et al.*, *World Handbook of Political and Social Indicators,* Yale University Press, New Haven, Conn., 1964, pp. 261–292, and Statistical Series nos. 9–10, 24, 31–38, 50–53, 63–65.

reinforced by elements of rising expectations and frustrations and of social discontent.

Social mobilization of this kind has been progressing in recent decades in many countries at an average yearly rate of shift of between 0.5 and 1.0 percent of the total population from the predominantly non-mobilized into the predominantly mobilized sector.[15] This seems to be about twice as fast as was the case in the mid-nineteenth century in those European countries such as Norway, Ireland, Italy, or Germany, where similar processes were then still under way. Moreover, in nineteenth-century continental Europe, a 1.0 percent increase in the share of literates among the total population was associated on the average with an increase of perhaps no more than 0.5 percent in the share of persons among the adult population voting or otherwise taking part in politics. In the mid-twentieth century, these proportions may have become reversed. Since both processes—the spread of literacy and the growth of voting—may have become, at the same time, twice as fast as they used to be, the process of political mobilization in some countries today may be about four times as fast as it was in some of the European countries 100 years ago. At the higher speeds of the mid-twentieth century, social mobilization can shift the political balance in many countries within the lifetime of a generation.

Social mobilization makes people potentially more nationalistic and more likely to assert their differences from other peoples, and it does so at the fast median rate of shift of roughly 0.75 percent of the total population per year into the mobilized sector of their society. In theory, this relatively rapid shift could be balanced by processes of linguistic and cultural *assimilation* which tend to make people more alike, to make minority groups learn the majority's language and culture, and often to make them abandon their old language and culture.

Assimilation, however, is usually a much slower process. If we measure it in terms of the average annual percentage shift of the total population to the adoption of the dominant language and culture, it seems to occur most often at the average rates of 0.1 or 0.2 percent of the total population per year. Social mobilization, in other words, often is about five times as fast as linguistic assimi-

---

[15] This rate is computed or estimated by taking for each country the *median* of the several distinct but not unconnected indicators of social mobilization, such as the average annual percentage shifts of the relevant age group of the total population from nonexposure to demonstration effects of modernity to exposure to them; from nonexposure to mass media to media exposure; from subsistence economy to the money economy; from nonvoting to voting; from illiteracy to literacy; from agricultural to nonagricultural occupations; from rural to urban residence; from self-employment to wage labor or salaried employment, etc. These computations or estimates can be carried out with the help of such data as are given in the sources listed in note 14 above, and as are currently being collected by the Yale Political Data program. As more and better data become available, our assessment of rates of social mobilization will become increasingly based on computation, and less on estimates, but the order of magnitude of such rates can be assessed with some confidence for a considerable number of countries. For a recent discussion of various problems inherent in the use of quantitative indicators of this kind, see also the essays in Raymond A. Bauer (ed.), *Social Indicators,* The M.I.T. Press, Cambridge, Mass. 1966.

lation. This means that on the average, for every five persons mobilized, only one becomes assimilated by the predominant national or international language or culture, while four become potential supporters or potential recruits for some self-assertive nationalist movement of some mobilized but unassimilated language group. The recent increase in seemingly indigestible minorities such as Flemings in Belgium, French Canadians in Canada, Dravidians, Sikhs, Bengalis, and Maharashtrians in India, Turks and Greeks in Cyprus, and the vast rise of anticolonial nationalisms in the world—where assimilation was reduced still more by contrasts of race—may attest to the ubiquity and strength of the process. Nor has it run its course. This is not the place to present any more complex mathematical models. Suffice it to say that the assimilation of positive political loyalties may not be much faster than the assimilation of language and that at the present rates at least another half-century, and perhaps one whole century, of national tensions and conflicts may be expected.

Even this forecast may be optimistic. At an assimilation rate of a shift of less than 0.1 percent of the total population per year, the assimilation of a large linguistic minority or rather politically disfavored language group—say, 70 percent of the population of the region, and numbering at least half a million people in compact settlement—should take about 700 years, whereas at the rate of 0.2 percent, about 350 years would be required. Both these figures accord well with assimilation periods known from history.[16] There seems to be no

[16] Thus in Finland average annual assimilation rates of this kind have remained below 0.1 percent during the last two centuries. In 1750, the Swedish-speaking minority predominated in that country politically, socially, and economically. This Swedish minority appears to have amounted to 16.9 percent of the population in 1750, and to 13.2 percent in 1900 when its political privileges, but not many of its economic and social ones, had disappeared. This decline in the Swedish percentage of the population corresponds to a shift to the Finnish language of 3.7 percent of the population in 150 years, or an average rate of shift of 0.025 percent per year. At this rate, it would have taken more than 500 years to assimilate the last Swedish-speakers to Finnish speech and culture. (During the same period, the Finnish shift to Swedish was, of course, negative by the same amounts, so that if the 1750-1900 trends had continued, the Finns would not have been turned into Swedish-speakers at any foreseeable time.) In the period 1900-1940, the proportion of Swedish-speakers declined further to 9.7 percent of the population, corresponding to an accelerated—but still very low—average annual rate of assimilation of 0.09 percent of the population. (The rate of urbanization alone, which usually is less than one-half of the median rate of overall social mobilization, amounted in Finland between 1900 and 1940 to about three times as much per year, or to 0.27; for the years 1940 to 1958 the shift to urbanization accelerated further to 0.57 per year.) At this recent assimilation rate, however, the remaining Swedish minority may be completely absorbed by the Finns within little more than a century, but a majority would have moved into cities much earlier, within not much more than 30 years.

Such rates of shift are, of course, all rather crude devices. They do not separate the effects of differential fertility of the different ethnic or language groups from the effects of genuine conversion of persons from the preferred or predominant use of one language to that of another. For a variety of reasons, however, such rates of shift are convenient tools for first-stage analysis and for crude projections from highly imperfect historical data. The figures given in this note were calculated from data in Karl W. Deutsch, *Nationalism and Social Communication*, Appendix I, "Finland," pp. 196-208, and Russett *et al.*, *World Handbook*, p. 54.

reason to think that assimilation in a common culture, so strong and homogeneous as to produce an integrated nation, would occur much faster.

The more hopeful view of only 50 to 100 years of national tensions is based on another line of reasoning. In recent decades, net rates of assimilation of 0.1 percent have been observed in cases of minority groups which at the same time had a natural population increase of about 2.0 percent per year. This suggests the possibility that the gross assimilation rate may have been as high as 2.1 percent in the extreme case, in which the disfavored, submerged, or "minority" language group should in fact have made up the large majority or indeed the bulk of the entire population. Most of this increase would then have been compensated by the natural increase of the minority concerned, leaving only 0.1 percent of net assimilation. We may expect, however, that population growth will decline in the future to 1.0 percent per year or less, as it has in many countries after the spread of industrialization, literacy, and some form of birth control, physical or social. If, then, in our extreme example, the gross assimilation rate should still continue at 2.1 percent per annum, the net assimilation might then proceed at 1.1 percent per year, that is, at a faster rate than the mobilization process, and after about 70 years, many minorities might become cut in half by assimilation. If assimilation in the age of mass media and mass education could be accelerated further, or if people could be assimilated much faster in a common civic loyalty while retaining their diversity of language and culture, and if furthermore assimilation among nations—e.g., within larger regional political communities—could be made to proceed at similar rates, then the outlook for soon overcoming the age of nationalism would improve still further.

Against these more favorable prospects of internationalism, however, an opposite developmental possibility must be considered. We may think of any code of communication, such as any language, any culture, and any ideology, as exposed to the impact of many small variations arising in the usage of some individual member or small subgroup within it. If communication—that is, the flow of messages—within the smaller group is much more frequent and much more relevant than is communication across its boundaries, many of the new usages will become part of the communication code within the group. The group, that is to say, will develop its own dialect, or its own language, or ideology, or code of measurements, different from the corresponding codes of other groups outside it. If, on the contrary, the flow of messages across group boundaries is much larger or more salient than the communications flow within the group, then a larger code, common to both this group and its outside partners, is likely to prevail and to be maintained more or less uniformly for at least as long a time as this prevalence of cross-boundary communications lasts.

In essence, this is a mathematical sketch of the story of the Tower of Babel. If the number of persons in a communication network increases, and if the frequency of communications is in any way unevenly distributed—for instance, if communication falls off with geographic, social, or cultural distance—then the entire set of communicators in the large net will become divided sooner or later into at least three different subsets. The first of these subsets will be that of those users of the common code or language among whom translocal or cross-group messages are so frequent and so salient that they constitute the effective signals among the members of this translocal set, whereas the local messages, or those exchanged within the smaller groups, amount to no more than noise. The prevalence of translocal over local communications, in other words, must amount to some effective signal-to-noise ratio, according to this reasoning, if a trans-local language, culture, or people is to be maintained.

The second subset would consist of those persons for whom the opposite conditions hold. Within each of the several groups of these relatively local or intra-subgroup communicators, communications within the group would predominate as signals, whereas outside or cross-group messages would constitute no more than background noise.

These two groups—the "cosmopolitans" and the "locals," to adapt here from another context Robert Merton's and David Riesman's vivid terms[17]—are likely to be more stable the higher the signal-to-noise ratio by which their character is maintained.

The third subset, unlike the first two, is likely to be unstable, and its population often may be small. It is the subset of those communicators for whom the ratio between in-group and cross-group communications, either by frequency or salience, is *not* steep enough to permit effective signal-to-noise discrimination. Its members will be neither clear-cut "locals" nor clear-cut "cosmopolitans." They will be using a mixture of both evolving communication codes, or else alternate between using each code, as each code becomes more sharply standardized and different from the other. They will be marginal, therefore, to each group of users. They will be under great social pressures to abandon marginality and under great technical and cultural pressures to accept the economies and advantages of standardization on a clear-cut single code and of synchronization to the rhythm and timing of a single group. Many of them are likely, therefore, to try to imitate or join either the uniform group of translocal communicators or any one of the diverse local groups with its own code of communication, language, or culture. Nonetheless, new marginal communicators will be produced whenever and wherever in-group and cross-group communications remain so evenly balanced for a longer time that no stable and effective signal-to-noise ratio can be formed by means of which either pattern of communications could prevail.

What follows from these considerations? As long as there are any substantial effects of unevenness and distance upon communication, the splitting up of very

[17]Cf. Robert K. Merton, "Patterns of Influence: A Study of Interpersonal Influence of Communications Behavior in a Local Community," in Paul F. Lazarsfeld and Frank Stanton (eds), *Communication Research, 1948–1949,* Harper & Row, Publishers, Incorporated, New York, 1949, pp. 180–219; and David Riesman, *Constraint and Variety in American Education,* with a new preface, Doubleday & Company, Inc., Garden City, N.Y., 1958.

large networks of communicators into smaller sub-groups with their communication codes, languages, cultures, or variations of ideology is highly probable. It
becomes more probable with increasing numbers of communicators, with increasing frequency of communication, with increasing risk of communication
overload and sharper competition among messages, and with increasing unevenness or variance in the distribution of communications. This process of splitting
will stop, according to this reasoning, at those group sizes where local and translocal communications will be equally frequent and salient, but these equilibrium
points are likely to fall far short of all humanity. Although some nations and
nation-states may in time yield to assimilation or merger with their neighbors,
the general cultural, ideological, and perhaps national diversity of humankind
thus has powerful and continuing processes of probability behind it.

By contrast, the probabilities favoring a uniform and stable translocal or
transnational regional or worldwide language or culture are much weaker, and
they are likely to remain so for a time. Decisive here is not that modern technology has made it possible to telephone or telecast some messages around the
globe within a few seconds. What counts is how many people spend how large
a proportion of their total time and attention on such globe-girdling messages,
against the time and attention they are spending on national or local ones. Under
these conditions, if the common tower of humanity is to be built much higher,
it will require not only a great deal of simultaneous translation but also a growing
set of expert cultural and political negotiators to maintain at least minimal
cooperation among humankind's perhaps irreducibly diverse components.

None of these lines of reasoning has yet been carried to its end. From the
viewpoint of communications alone, a vast amount of work remains to be done,
analytical, empirical, and statistical, before the processes of national and international assimilation and differentiation will be more adequately understood.
But if this research work should be undertaken, it may be expected that its
results will not be trivial.

Nation-states, however, and the division of the world's peoples among them,
are maintained by more than just communication. What do nations do for their
members, and what can their members do through them? What functions do
they perform? How well and at what cost, in comparison to what alternative
agencies that could perform them?

Putting it in the most simple terms, a nation-state does mainly seven things:

1. The nation-state *coordinates*, or keeps order; that is, it maintains recognizable rules and commands backed by some limited probability of credible enforcement; thus it coordinates the expectations of its population, and it partly steers
their learning of old and new habits of social teamwork and cooperation at a
tolerable level of tension and conflict.

2. The nation-state *responds* to at least some specific popular needs: It maintains its limited capacities for enforcement of its commands and rules upon a
basis of widespread habits of popular compliance and support, which alone

make this enforcement practicable; and it maintains this compliance by acting with at least a minimal degree of responsiveness to popular needs and desires.

3. The modern nation-state *accepts* a general role of *responsibility* for responding to many diverse needs of its people. As an institution it is, therefore, in Talcott Parsons' terms, diffuse, particular, and ascriptive. It must be, in principle, available for almost everything that is urgently needed or desired; it is thus available only to its citizens or people, and they have a claim on it by right of birth or right of what they are, rather than of anything they did or do to earn this right. The nation-state thus offers some psychological security and an ever-widening scope of services. In advanced non-Communist countries today, total government spending at all levels—national, state, and local—amounts to roughly 35 percent of the gross national product, in contrast to all international organizations taken together, which are spending less than 1.0 percent of the income of the people. This 35 percent proportion of government spending is approximated by the United States, and it rises to over 40 percent for West Germany and to over 50 percent for Sweden. In all these advanced countries, peacetime expenses for the machinery of enforcement, repression, or defense, that is, for armed forces, prisons, and police, amount to far less than one-half of the total.[18]

4. The nation-state *protects*, because it reduces, albeit imperfectly, the transmission of international shocks, price fluctuations, economic depressions, and economic or political disturbances; and it is usually the first and chief agency called upon to cope with their impact on its people.

5. The nation-state *preserves group privileges;* it is the chief tool for maintaining international differences in income, living standards, and cultural and economic opportunities among the peoples of the world. In the world arena, these international income differences show a range of over 60:1, and they may still be growing. They are higher than they are within any but the very worst governed and most backward and unstable nation-states.[19] The more rich and relatively privileged a people is in comparison to other peoples, the potentially more important is this function of the nation-state to its members and the more intense are the fears and emotions which can be channeled behind national separateness—if not apartheid—from humanity. In this sense, the richest countries of the world, Communist and non-Communist alike, are facing political and emotional problems vis-à-vis the poorer nations of the world which are in some ways comparable to the problems of the respectable white middle-class suburb of Cicero, Illinois, at the edge of the black slums of Chicago.

6. Within its secluded territory and economy, the nation-state *enhances social mobility upward.* It offers a higher chance of rising in society—that is, of vertical social mobility—to more of its people than would any wider, more open, and more competitive supranational system. This is true, of course, only so long as

[18] Russett *et al., World Handbook*, Table 15, p. 63.
[19] Cf. *ibid.*, Tables 44, 69, 71, and 72, pp. 149-151, 155-157, 237-247. The worst governed and most backward countries, however, do not often publish statistics on this topic.

no more effective supranational facilities for sustained social mobility upward—and hence for opening and broadening the entire social structure—have been developed; but up to now this has not been the case.

7. Finally, the nation-state *offers psychic orientation and security* by being so often more generally responsible and responsive to its population than any other large-scale social institution. It offers to most of its members a stronger sense of security, belonging, or affiliation, and even personal identity, than does any alternative large group. The greater the need of the people for such affiliation and identity under the strains and shocks of social mobilization and alienation from earlier familiar environments, the greater becomes the potential power of the nation-state to channel both their longings and resentments and to direct their love and hate.

It is perhaps clearer now why during the last three generations, and even more the last twenty years, the nation-states have become so much stronger and more numerous, and why the international organizations, despite their impressive growth, thus far have remained so much weaker.

Yet despite its flourishing, the nation-state has failed. It is the most powerful human instrument ever developed in the course of history for getting things done—so many things, so effectively, and for so many people. But it has failed in what has seemed to John Locke and to the founding fathers of the American Republic the most natural and basic task of government: to safeguard the lives of its people. In case of all-out war, no country can defend its capital, its chief cities, and the families of its elite members living near them. In case of nuclear war, the United States cannot defend New York City or Washington, D.C.; the Soviet Union cannot defend Leningrad or Moscow; Communist China cannot defend Peking or Shanghai. All the nation-state can do now is to risk or spend the lives of its soldiers and its cities as gambling stakes on the gaming tables of power, strategy, or ideology, in games which none of the players control or fully understand. The nation-state is thus in danger of becoming for its people a cognitive trap in times of peace and a death trap in the event of war.

Most of us wish to keep this failure of nationalism *not* at the center but at the margins of our consciousness, like a pain in the lungs after twenty years' smoking. Nation-states are habit-forming, and nationalism has become an addiction for millions of people. Not all of them know it, but those who are least aware of their habit may find it most difficult to change.

Yet the feeling has grown that nationalism is ceasing to be legitimate. That is, it is becoming increasingly difficult to pursue the values of nationalism without inflicting intolerable damage or danger upon other of our basic values, such as the values of religion, of humanity, of truth, and of survival.

The dilemma is familiar. People cannot live, it seems to most of them, without the nation-state; but in a world of proliferating nuclear weapons, they are unlikely to survive long within it. And to many of the more thoughtful among them, the legitimacy of either so living or so dying is becoming ever more doubtful.

What prospects do we have for working ourselves out of this dilemma? Six perspectives seem relevant to me here.

1. The support and service functions of the nation-state—economic, social, educational, medical, scientific, and cultural—may well continue to increase for the next half century or more to some extent regardless of the ideologies professed.

2. With the increase of social mobilization, and with its attendant increases of the social and political needs and expectations, and of the political participation of large masses of people, almost all countries in the world will become much harder to govern, and they will be particularly hard to govern from abroad. *We are entering an age of rising costs of foreign intervention.* In every year, on the average, a billion dollars of foreign aid will buy less political influence for us, or for any other foreign donor, than it would have bought the year before. Every 10,000 soldiers shipped abroad this year will purchase with their time or with their blood less political control for the country that sent them than they might have so purchased in the past, but their sacrifices will purchase even less political control abroad for their homeland in the future. For the next half-century at least, the world is becoming irremediably pluralistic. It can be destroyed by violence, but it cannot be controlled by it.

3. The functions of international organizations may increase at the same or at a faster rate, so that the gap between national and supranational services and powers may become less wide. This would require new, larger, and more direct channels of communication, feedback, and responsiveness between the international agencies and the people they are meant to serve. This would not solve the problem, but it might help to keep it manageable.

4. One of the basic problems is still that of *economic growth*. The average annual per capita income of the world's population was roughly $600 at 1966 prices. There is no way in which such a low income could be redistributed so as to ensure peace and contentment among all. At this low income, a marginal addition of another $100 would seem large enough and desirable enough to many people to risk or initiate violence or war—international or civil war—to get it. If there is any truth to the theory of marginal utility, however, there are higher levels of income at which further increments of income are not worth, to most people, the cost of violence. At these levels of wealth, violence would still be resorted to, e.g., for psychological reasons, but the powerful, steady, and coordinating reinforcement from economics would be gone. We do not know what such a "peace level" of income might be. But we recall that when the per capita income in the United States averaged, in the early 1930s, below $1,500 in today's money, there was still frequent loss of life in labor conflicts. Today, at an average 1966 income of $3,000, wage disputes have ceased to be a killing matter, although fear for real estate values in half-poor neighborhoods—but not in rich ones—sometimes still reinforces the propensity to bloodshed. It seems not implausible, however, that much of the economic drive to nationalism, racism, and violence would abate at an average world-income level 50 or 60 percent

above that of the United States today. The higher of these figures would suggest a real world-income of \$4,800 per capita, or eight times the amount of 1966.

This potential peace level could be reached in about seventy-two years, by means of a net annual economic growth rate of per capita income of about 3 percent, which is almost exactly the average economic growth rate of sixty-eight countries in the 1950s. Since the average rate of population growth in the world during those years was close to 2 percent, the gross growth rate of income was close to 5 percent. If this modest performance of the 1950s is maintained—better still, of course, if it is improved even to a modest degree—a 3 percent per capita growth rate will double real per capita income every twenty-four years, or double it three times, that is, multiply it by 8, in seventy-two years. By that time, if present rates of population growth should not decline, there should be four times as many people in the world, or between 12 and 14 billion, just about as much as could be accommodated tolerably well, according to Professors Harrison Brown and Kirtley Mather, on this planet at present-day levels of technology and tolerable density of settlement.[20]

We could get there, then, in just about the seventy-two years which we are

[20] See Harrison Brown, *The Next Hundred Years: A Discussion Prepared for Leaders of American Industry,* The Viking Press, Inc., New York, 1957, 1963, p. 164; also pp. 67, 80–81. Other writers present a picture compatible with Brown's. According to O. E. Baker, of the 6.4 billion acres of land that are "ultimately arable," only about 3.7 billion were actually in use, with 2.4 billion of these cultivated and 1.3 billion used as pasture, leaving another 2.7 billion still available for future utilization. Accordingly, the world's arable land still could be expanded by about 73 percent. At the same time, it is widely held that if the average current methods of agriculture were brought up to the level of the most efficient ones practiced today, the world output per acre could be doubled or more, even without any further progress in agricultural science and technology. Since at least some such progress must be expected for the next seventy-odd years, it seems likely that the food output of the world from agriculture—without major recourse to photosynthesis or to the more intensive exploitation of the oceans—could be raised by a factor of four or five, sufficient to feed at least poorly four to five times the present world population. This reasoning would suggest a limiting world population of 12 to 14 billion by the mid-twenty-first century, with a limiting density of world population of about 100 per square kilometer, or four times the world average in 1961, somewhere near the current levels of Pennsylvania (90), Poland (96), Denmark (107), and Hungary (108), etc., and well below the present levels of New York (119), Switzerland (133), India (138), and Italy (164). Such a state of affairs might not be particularly comfortable or desirable, but it seems neither hellish nor impossible. Given a well-developed and applied technology, even at the mid-twentieth-century level, such settlement densities seem quite compatible with a wide range of institutions and ways of life, including the democratic institutions of the West. The oft-cited "Standing Room Only" theory would apply to much higher population levels and later periods than the ones envisaged here. Cf. W. S. Woytinsky and E. S. Woytinsky, *World Population and Production: Trends and Outlook,* The Twentieth Century Fund, New York, 1953, pp. 48–50, 322–324, 534–537; Russett *et al., World Handbook,* Tables 1, 40–42, pp. 18, 139–148; O. E. Baker, "Land Utilization in the United States," *Geographical Review,* January, 1923; Lester R. Brown, *Man, Land and Food: Looking Ahead at World Food Needs,* Foreign Agricultural Economic Report no. 11, U.S. Department of Agriculture, November, 1963, pp. 83–90, 100–132. For an earlier optimistic estimate, based on a much smaller rate and extent of population growth, see Kirtley Mather, *Enough and to Spare,* Harper & Row, Publishers, Incorporated, New York, 1944, pp. 49–54, 67–70; and for a study of current needs and capabilities, see *The World Food Budget,* 1962–1966, Foreign Agricultural Economic Report no. 4, U.S. Department of Agriculture, October, 1961.

likely to have available for the job. We would then get to a humankind which would be much richer, on the average, than is the richest country, the United States, now. But could this wealth also be tolerably well distributed?

5. The fifth point is the *eventual acceptance of an international income tax.* Today's nation-states are dedicated to the opposite purpose: to keep their wealth as much as possible in the hands of their own people. Nonetheless, even now some rich countries have been spending up to 1 percent of their gross national product on economic aid to poorer countries. Should it not be possible to increase this rate in time to 5 percent of the income of the rich countries and hence to about 2 or 3 percent of the world total? In 1962, this world total was close to $1,800 billion and such an international income tax would have yielded between $36 and $54 billion, more than most of the serious plans for world economic development require. This may even become politically possible. Early in this century, when the United States was a much poorer country, the resistance of its rich citizens against any Federal income tax was intense. Now that the United States is rich, a very steep income tax is universally accepted. As the world becomes as rich as the United States is now, will not its people also become more tolerant of international income taxes? And would not this whole political and economic problem by worthy of far more sustained research than it has had so far?

6. All this, of course, depends on peace, or at least on avoiding all-out war. It would be useless to discuss rising living standards for the dead. This leads us to the sixth and last of our prospects for the next decade, and hopefully, the next half-century. It is the prospect of perhaps splitting the atom of sovereignty—of separating sovereignty over national regulation, welfare, and service, which is likely to persist for several decades, from the sovereignty over the right to escalate war, which must be curbed quickly. Here again, one first step might be vital: *the renunciation of the national right to initiate or escalate warfare without an international mandate.* No one is a good judge of his or her own cause, and neither is any nation. Self-defense must be redefined so as to exclude escalation. In past centuries, this condition, that no member may initiate or substantially enlarge a war without the prior permission of the other allies, has been basic in the success story of the Swiss Confederation. It is a basic condition, of course, in any federal union, such as the United States. The same condition today could do much to restore our threatened Atlantic Alliance. It would oblige us not to initiate or escalate war without the prior mandate of our allies; and it would oblige us to deescalate it, so far as anything in our power was concerned, if escalation had occurred but no specific positive mandate for it from our allies was forthcoming within a reasonably short time. Without this condition, no strong supranational alliance among equals can be maintained among the vast risks of today's world.

We cannot build a supranational alliance around the United States, much less move toward a federation of the Western countries, so long as we ourselves in the United States refuse to give up our sovereign right to make war in Asia, or to enlarge war in Asia—or anywhere else—whenever and however our own national government alone sees fit. The overt insistence of many French leaders, far beyond the ranks of the "Gaullists," on greater equality in the Western alliance is symptomatic also of at least some latent feelings among our other European allies,[21] and there seems little doubt that in time similar demands for greater equality will come from our allies in Latin America and Japan. We can build an Atlantic community and a world community, but only on conditions that we, too, as a nation, will share its disciplines as loyal citizens.

[21] For some elite interview data bearing on this point, see Karl W. Deutsch *et al., France, Germany and the Western Alliance,* Charles Scribner's & Sons, New York, 1967; Karl W. Deutsch, *Arms Control and European Unity,* John Wiley & Sons, Inc., New York, 1967; Karl W. Deutsch, "Integration and Arms Control in the European Political Environment: A Summary Report," *American Political Science Review,* vol. 60, no. 2, pp. 354–365, June, 1966. For a different view on this point, see the chapter by Ithiel de Sola Pool in I. de S. Pool, ed., *Contemporary Political Science: Toward Empirical Theory,* McGraw-Hill, New York, 1967.

17 | Limited Growth and Continuing Inequality: Some World Political Effects

A first version of this chapter was presented on October 15, 1974, in West Berlin at the annual meeting of the Club of Rome. It was an early response to the coming of computer models of the present and future of the world. At that time the computer world model by Mesarovic and Pestel (1974) had appeared, superseding in many ways the earlier much-publicized model by Forrester and Meadows (1972). Since then, important contributions have appeared by Cole (1973), Fritsch (1976), Herrera (1976), and Leontief (1977).

A somewhat revised version of the 1974 text was published under the title "On Inequality and Limited Growth."

As will be seen, this chapter deals mainly with some of the expectable psychological consequences of the images of future scarcity, if such images should come to be widely accepted. Some broader material conditions and consequences of a possible stopping of economic growth in the near future are discussed in the concluding chapter that follows.

During the years 1972-1975, major changes have occurred in the images of world politics and world economics that once prevailed in the mass media, affecting public opinion in the world of the private-enterprise countries. Images of future scarcity have replaced the expectation of abundance; pictures of continuing growth and progress have given way to images of long-term stagnation, poverty, and exhaustion of resources. The acceptance of these new images was promoted by large campaigns of publicity and education, and by now a considerable literature, much of it of very serious quality, has sprung up around them.

What degree of realism can these new images claim? And what might be the consequences of their widespread adoption at the present time? As regards the first of these two questions, the realism or unrealism of the images of future scarcity will be discussed for a long time. In any case, the new literature has

"On Inequality and Limited Growth: Some World Political Effects," by Karl W. Deutsch, is reprinted from *International Studies Quarterly*, vol. 19, no. 4 (December 1975): 381-398, by permission of the Publisher, Sage Publications, Inc. With only minor changes, this article forms the present chapter.

drawn public attention to many real and important problems for the next ten to thirty years, even though not always in a balanced manner. For the longer future, however, perhaps for a span of fifty to eighty years from now, the one-sidedness of its perspective may be more critical, and its predictive power may well prove a great deal weaker.

This possibility in turn makes the second question crucial. For the images we now accept as those of our long-run future have at least some limited power to shape or distort that future itself within the limits of the political and economic pathways and choices offered to us by reality. It is therefore mainly with this second question—the impact of "limited growth" images on the politics of the real world—that the rest of this chapter will deal.

What are some of the critical aspects of this real world in which we live?

Today's world is in many ways interdependent, in many respects unequal and nationally self-preoccupied, and to a great extent ungovernable. These three conditions are linked in a self-aggravating cycle. Interdependence has a stronger potential for creating damage than for creating remedies, making the consequences of inequality more dangerous. Inequality in both economic and cultural areas, and national self-preoccupation, make the world more ungovernable, for they make it harder to maintain among nations that level of international communication, and of cognitive and evaluative consonance, necessary for sustained and flexible cooperation or acceptance of common laws or governmental institutions. Lack of international cooperation and governability in turn aggravates the dangerous joint effects of uncontrolled interdependence and unrelieved inequality (for other discussions of interdependence, see Brown, 1972, 1973; Kindleberger, 1973; Cooper, 1968; Myrdal, 1957).

INTERDEPENDENCE

The world's economic interdependence is strong in regard to some commodities, but not to others. As a hypothesis that seems to fit the evidence, we may conjecture that interdependence tends to be strong in regard to that class of commodities which fulfill the following conditions:

1. They are greatly in demand and highly transportable.
2. A major part of the demand for them comes from regions and countries other than those which are major sources of their supply or their processing.
3. A significant part of the demand for them is relatively inelastic, at least in the short run.
4. There are no large stockpiles or readily mobilizable reserves on hand.
5. There are no ready, short-run substitutes for them at comparable cost, nor for the current sources of their production.

Nowadays, commodities of this kind are grains, soybeans and similar basic foodstuffs, oil and petroleum products, chemical fertilizers, some nonferrous metals, and perhaps wood pulp and timber. To a lesser degree, similar conditions hold for some products of highly developed industries, such as some pharmaceuticals, and some items of highly advanced technology, such as computers, jet aircraft, intercontinental rockets, and perhaps modern geophysical and oil-drilling equipment, as well as oil tankers, oil refineries, and equipment for petrochemical plants and undersea mining.[1] Not to be included in this grouping are the nuclear fuels, such as uranium 238 and 235, and plutonium—as well as the skills and information required for their use—which fulfill the first, second, and fifth of these conditions, but not the third and fourth. Many countries can defer the decision to acquire large amounts of fissionable materials for either energy or weapons purposes, and they can delay the acquisition of the corresponding installations and trained personnel. Similarly, the nations disposing of large stockpiles or supplies of such materials have few motives at present, if any, to make them available to others. Other goods that contribute to the peacetime image of international interdependence are sugar, coffee, tea, citrus fruits, bananas, and other tropical fruits. While these play an important role in the consumption patterns of most of the highly industrialized countries, demand for them is elastic. In times of war blockade or other emergencies, people can go without them or find more or less imperfect substitutes.

The trading of commodities meeting these conditions creates considerable opportunities for the use of nationalistic power politics and oligopolistic exploitation. In the absence of countervailing political processes and institutions, any increase in the share of such commodities, or any increase in the relatively inelastic portion of the demand for them, will lead to situations in which these types of political behavior will offer short-term rewards and hence, their occurrence will increase. The introduction of substitutes for these commodities, new sources of supply, the reduction of monopolistic practices, and the growth of stockpiles should have the opposite effect. Further, the effects of interdependence are enhanced, and demand tends to become less elastic for those commodities that are economically crucial, in that they are necessary prerequisites for the production of still other goods or services, such as artificial fertilizers for intensive food production, or energy, indispensable at many stages for producing a very wide array of goods and services.

The strategic interdependence of the world is as large as, or larger than, the economic one. Intercontinental ballistic missiles with nuclear warheads can reach any target on earth within forty minutes. Even "conventional" transport planes can move troops and weapons to any theater of war or confrontation within one or two days. The world is becoming one in a community of threat and fear.

Worldwide interdependence is not limited to certain key commodities or weapons. Today's world is probably even more interdependent in regard to information than in regard to tangible goods. Scientific discoveries and tech-

---

[1] In earlier periods, coal, iron, and aluminum played a similar role, but these have now become more widely available.

nological advances are quickly communicated, or else duplicated by parallel discoveries, across many countries. Trends in art, architecture, painting, music, poetry, and fashion all quickly spread among many peoples, often first among a vanguard of specialists or intellectuals, but soon also to the level of mass culture, such as new styles in popular music or the wearing of blue jeans. To a lesser but still significant degree, something similar holds for the spread of financial and monetary changes, and of political movements and ideologies.

Many governments consider the demand of their subjects for such information to be highly elastic: they can shut it off by censorship and other measures, or so they think. In fact, popular demand for a wide variety of information about culture, art, music, literature, life styles, as even more than about politics and economics, may be relatively inelastic in the long run, and people then will go to considerable lengths to get the information they desire. Something similar holds for information about science and technology. Scientists and industry need it, and their work will be noticeably retarded if it is denied to them. Some dictatorships may be willing to pay this price, but it is a real one.

In some other respects, however, world interdependence is distinctly smaller, and in part it may be on the decline. In 1871, it has been estimated, a larger proportion of savings was invested abroad than was the case a hundred years later (Morse, 1971: 386). In most countries in our own time, a rising share of national income and employment is being taken up by services, construction, and maintenance, that is, by activities that tend to remain largely within the national territory of each country. During the twentieth century so far, international commodity trade in the long run has tended to account for a declining share of income within many nations and in the world at large. World trade amounted to about 30% of the world gross national product in 1913, but only to about 22% in the late 1950s and 18% in the late 1960s.[2] There is reason to think that the proportion of people employed directly in the international sector may have declined correspondingly. Insofar as persons directly employed in this international sphere form a potential basis of political support for internationally oriented rather than domestically oriented politics, the relative political support basis for such policies may have similarly shrunk (see Lerner, 1956: 220; Deutsch and Eckstein, 1961).

In other aspects, too, the interdependence of the world is limited. Airplanes can carry letters swiftly over land and sea, but the vast majority of mail is exchanged within the national frontiers of each country. About 1965, this domestic portion was 89% in Sweden and West Germany, 91% in Britain, 96% in the United States and 98% in Japan (Taylor and Hudson, 1975: 373–376). A great deal of news spread by the mass media through many countries, but to a much lesser degree to that one-third of the people who live in fourteen

[2] I am indebted to Professor Simon Kuznets for the estimates. Data for 124 countries (42 comprise over 98% of world GNP) in 1965 show a trade-to-GNP ratio of 17.6%. (Unpublished calculation by Brita Widaier, Science Center Berlin, August 1978).

Communist-ruled countries, and also to those many millions who live in countries subject to the national censorship practices of various non-Communist regimes. Even without formal censorship, a significant portion is eliminated from transmission or reception by the differences in the interests and attention of mass audiences in different countries and cultures, which tend to concentrate heavily on domestic affairs, leaving little time and thought for "foreign" problems and events. A study in the 1950s showed that the average American newspaper then devoted only about one-twelfth of its nonadvertising space to events outside the United States, but that their readers gave only one-fourteenth of their reading time to such items (International Press Institute, 1953). Elite papers, such as the New York *Times* and the Washington *Post*, paid more attention to world events, and a still smaller subelite among their readers who paid attention to editorials could find 40% of the latter dealing with international affairs (Chapter 8, above; Sola Pool et al., 1970). This evidence confirms a familiar picture. Elites may have some interest in world problems, but the focus of attention of the masses, even in a democratic and highly educated nation, is predominantly national and local. What is true of their attention holds no less of their experiences and memories or of the actions which they expect their leaders to take, and which they are willing to support.

The world today is thus most interdependent in regard to some critical commodities in short supply, in its vulnerability to weapons of mass destruction, and perhaps, in the long run, also in regard to the preservation of our common environment, the biosphere of our planet. But it is perhaps least interdependent in its political systems, and particularly in its conditions for mass acceptance and mass support for innovative, habit-changing policies that would appear to benefit other groups more directly and quickly than one's own.

INEQUALITY

Today's world is largely poor, partly hungry, and generally very unequal. Its inequality makes poverty harder to bear, an effect seen to be increasingly more terrible as one moves toward the unfavorable end of its distributions, down to those hungry 800 million—about one-fifth of the world's population—who live in acute poverty, at the edge of starvation, and sometimes below it.

In 1972, for example, the world was poor and unequal. Its average gross national product per capita was close to $1,075 (for 132 countries at 1972 prices), and the median per capita income was well below $400 (Sivard, 1974). A standard indicator of income inequality, the Gini index, which in the 1960s had registered for the *domestic* income inequality within each of 12 developed countries a median value of 40%, out of a possible 100, showed in the same decade an ominous reading of 64% for the world as a whole, if one were weighting each country by its population; and a staggering inequality index of 84%

for the world treated as an ensemble of those 120 of its nations for which data were available, and weighting each nation equally so as to treat it as a separate experiment or case (see Deutsch, 1966: 240-241; Deutsch, 1974: 140-141).

This degree of inequality among the world's countries has not diminished in the early 1970s; it is close to, or perhaps larger than, the inequality among the incomes of individuals, and of social classes, in most of the world's most ill-governed and unstable countries. While rising oil prices reduced the poverty of a few small developing countries, they increased the poverty of more and larger ones, and thus added to the problem of inequality in the world as a whole.

But the degree of inequality among countries, large as it is, does not sum up the total extent of income inequality in the world. For here one must also take into account the way in which the lack of equality among nations is conjoined to that among the classes and strata within each of them. The total range of world inequality and of consumption patterns thus stretches from the richest strata in the rich countries to the poorest persons in the poor ones.

Further, inequality exists within other dimensions than that of income. Economic inequality is closely linked to, though not identical with, inequalities of power. It is unequal power that makes it often possible for the marginal tastes and desires of the strong and rich to prevail over some vital needs of the weak and poor. A country well supplied with grain, oil, fertilizer, or fertile acreage would need considerable military power in order to be able to withhold supplies from other countries whose people are hungry or starving. Military power would also be required if such supplies were not to be withheld, that is, stored, destroyed, or not produced (deliberately or by drift and accident), but if they were instead to be doled out in return for payments or concessions which otherwise would not have been forthcoming. Such a price demanded in exchange for food may concern economic, monetary, or legal concessions or changes in military, political, cultural or population policy. By the same token, it would also take considerable power, political, economic, or military, for the government of a country in urgent need of supplies to be able to demand and obtain their prompt delivery on less onerous or uncongenial terms.

Where inequality and scarcity meet, they may thus create an increased demand for military power, both in the advantaged and the disadvantaged countries. And, if this domestic political demand for more arms and forces should become explicit and successful, it would divert needed capital from productive investment that in time might reduce the original scarcity. Consequently, military and armament competition is likely to make the food or oil shortages worse, and the deepening economic crises may further enhance the pressure to increase military capabilities in a potentially amplifying feedback sequence.

On the other hand, inequality among nations may have been declining during the last two decades in regard to literacy; elementary, secondary, and higher education; infant death rates; life expectancy; and perhaps in the per capita number of newspaper copies and radios. In regard to all of these, the rate of

Figure 17-1

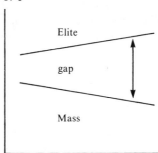

growth in highly developed countries tends to slow down as they approach a saturation level, while it may still be accelerating in developing countries. (For some projections 1959-1975, see Russett et al., 1964; for more recent data, see Taylor and Hudson, 1972; Sivard, 1974 and 1977). But by contrast, disparity in regard to income and to military power may have increased in some respects in comparison to the 1920s and 1930s, even though it probably has declined from its short-lived peak in 1945-1946. As many countries recovered from the devastations of World War II and acquired more modern technology, they tended to move the world toward technological and economic equality, and this trend may have been strong enough to outweigh the opposite effects of more rapid economic growth in the world's most advanced countries and regions.

Traced in their development across time, inequality and privilege may follow the pattern of an elite or that of a vanguard. An elite within a country is a group which enjoys a significantly higher amount of some value or values than does the rest of the population, and which does so in relative permanence. The trend lines of elite and mass in regard to some value thus look like a slab or like a wedge (see Figure 17-1). A vanguard is a group which does or has today what others will do or have tomorrow. The trend lines of vanguard and mass in respect to their shares of some value may resemble a rhomboid pattern (see Figure 17-2):

Figure 17-2

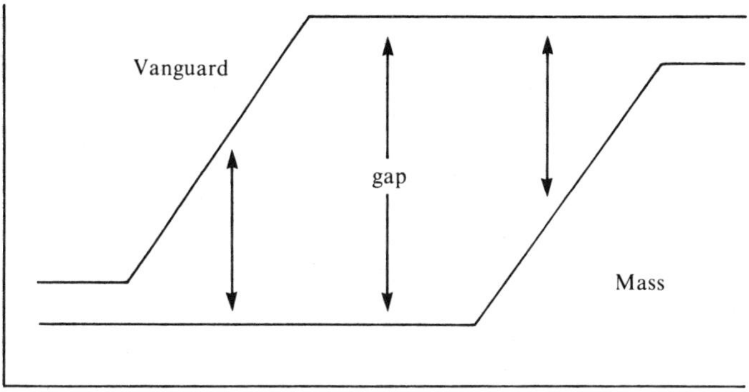

the gap between the two levels may be small or nonexistent at the start, may increase with the rise of the vanguard, reach a maximum and perhaps retain it for a span of time, decline again as the mass catches up, and end, perhaps, with no significant gap or a small one. Whether this is in fact what happens, empirical research must show. But in order to make the best use of whatever empirical data we might find, it will be necessary to examine closely some of the different renderings of the concept of inequality, and the operational meanings of the terms itself.

Inequality of income, for instance, can be measured in absolute or relative terms. Measured absolutely, it is the difference between the average incomes of a rich and a poor country (or class, or individual). Measured relatively, it is their ratio. Thus, an absolute gap of, say, $100 in the average per capita income of two countries means a great deal if both are poor, but is close to trivial if both are rich; the absolute measurement alone gives no clue as to its context. Similarly, if one country has twice the average per capita income of another, this ratio can continue to be accurate at a great number of income levels, even if both countries become richer and the absolute income gap between them increases. In fact, if two countries become richer, it is even possible for the ratio between their average incomes to decrease somewhat, but for the absolute income gap between them to increase. In that case, observers who wished to assert that inequality was growing would stress the absolute income gap while those who wanted to show that inequality had lessened would emphasize the income ratio. Such are the uses of statistics when employed in a search not for discovery but for persuasion.

To such different selections of statistical measures there correspond different notions of human behavior. If human beings are moved mainly by envy, or by the desire to imitate some reference group closely, then absolute income gaps will always tend to provoke indignation and resentment in the relatively poorer country or group, even if both groups or countries should be in fact quite rich, and even if their relative inequality of income should have declined.[3] If, on the contrary, people are motivated mainly by felt needs—that is, by desires for inputs which, if lacking, are followed by observable damage—then these needs should have thresholds of saturation. Increasing riches then should be followed by satiety with material goods, and income gaps and even income ratios should eventually become irrelevant for peoples living at a sufficiently high level of abundance. This second argument—that of gradual saturation—has a familiar look. It is the argument of the declining marginal utility of any good or class of goods, and in this form it is an argument which has been at the basis of a great deal of Western economic theory during the last hundred years.

Which of these two presumed responses to inequality prevails in the real world—constant envy or declining marginal utility—cannot be deduced from

[3]The view that a widening gap in incomes is always bad, even when both parties are getting richer, is espoused by Galtung (1971). For an interesting discussion of some related issues, see Høivik (1971).

theory alone. It is largely a question of empirical fact, accessible to empirical research. Yet it seems strange that so little of this empirical research has been carried out, for our appraisal of world politics and the chances for world peace during the next one hundred years may well hinge on the answer. And, if we are facing such large questions in regard to the responses of the poorer partners in a relationship of inequality, what about the probable responses of the richer ones?

Here, four variables may be decisive:

1. the absolute level of perceived or felt scarcity and need,

2. the degree of cultural and moral sympathy and solidarity among the two groups, and particularly of the more favored one toward its disfavored counterpart,

3. the amount of effective communication between the two groups or countries, facilitating the coordination of their behavior, and

4. the timing, frequency, and magnitude of the rewards experienced by the members of the favored group for such solidarity and coordinated actions.

When scarcity becomes extreme, as in cases of thirst or famine, or in a struggle for lifeboats in a shipwreck, human behavior tends to become more frequently and more intensely competitive. When our disfavored competitors seem alien to us in language, culture, class, or race, or in any combination of these, then solidarity declines; we are more likely to become callous toward their misfortune and generally more distrustful, fearful, and hostile toward them. When there is little effective communication with them, and that little still marred in large part by mistrust and deceit, then most behavior will remain uncoordinated and often mutually damaging, and such lack of coordination will often be interpreted as deliberate hostility (see Rapoport and Chammah, 1965). Finally, when effective communication and coordinated behavior are not reinforced by rewards of sufficient salience, frequency, and timeliness, they will not be learned reliably and will not become habits of thought and action on which policies may be based. And to some extent, the same four conditions will have similar effects also on the members of disfavored groups and the peoples of poor countries. Increased scarcity will tend to enhance their distress and resentment. Greater ethnic or cultural distance and alienation will make their hostility more frequent and more ruthless. Lack of effective communication and coordination will have the same effects. And if hostile behavior appears to be rewarded by experience, it will be reinforced and may become habitual.

Furthermore, there is a last condition, which is ambiguous in its effects: the sense of human power, acquired from demonstration effects and personal experience in our age of vastly enhanced technology.[4] Power lends confidence

[4]For empirical evidence on the psychological and the sociological impact of modernizing, see Inkeles and Smith (1974). A philosophic discussion of the consequences of an increased sense of power is sketched by Russell (1945: 728–729): "The most important effect of machine production on the imaginative picture of the world is an immense increase in the sense of human power . . . . To frame a philosophy capable of coping with men intoxicated with the prospect of almost unlimited power and also with the apathy of the powerless is the most pressing task of our time."

to friendship and confidence to hate. It may make us expect success in cooperation or success in conflict. It is an amplifier of attitudes. During the last one-and-
a-half centuries, the sense of human power has been growing and gradually
spreading throughout the world. Faster transport and communication have
brought many more peoples, cultures, and races into superficial contact, but
have left them, in large part, still alien to each other. Increased interdependence
has enhanced the need for effective communication and coordination, but often
without in fact providing them. And experience thus far has provided as many or
more short-run rewards and reinforcements for competition and hostility than
for international and interracial solidarity and sympathy.

Of the factors which tend to promote competition and hostility, only scarcity
has been declining, if not for all of humanity, at least for its majority. Today
one-fifth of humankind is counted as poor; four-fifths or nine-tenths would have
had to be so counted 150 years ago. In the intervening years, as scarcity receded,
albeit often with heartbreaking slowness, hope grew that it would soon recede
still more. Rising expectations of eventual abundance thus became joined to
rising expectations of greater future international cooperation and solidarity.
Together with the relative inefficiency of earlier weapons systems, this hope for
peaceful improvements may have helped until now to keep international conflicts from being even more ubiquitous and devastating than they have been.

But what is the probable effect if the world is now told to expect more
scarcity, not less, and not for a short period but for a long one, and perhaps even
in permanence? Such a message comes at a time when hundreds of millions live
at the edge of subsistence, where needs are most intense, when the gulf of alienation between a great many of the world's peoples is still wide, when coordination among nations is still rare and poor, and when short-term, day-to-day
rewards for nationalistic and intensively competitive behavior have often been
greater and more frequent than those for international brotherhood. To plunge
such a world into a "revolution of declining expectations" is to risk a new age of
international conflicts that in the end may prove fatal to all of us. At a time
when people need to accept vast and rapid changes in outlook and behavior,
only credible expectations of significant material improvements can make such
changes palatable for many millions.

UNGOVERNABILITY

Here we enter the dimension in which international interdependence is weakest
and least dependable: the dimension of habitual mass compliance with laws and
the commands of government, and of mass support for governments and political
systems when they are challenged or threatened. Poverty and inequality, cultural
and ethnic alienation, lack of systemwide coordination, and the paucity of
quick and adequate rewards for behavior patterns of civil solidarity all combine
to make many modern nations increasingly hard to govern. Even more formi-

dable are the difficulties which similar conditions still are putting in the way of world government, and of lesser, or more specialized international institutions with quasi-governmental powers.

In today's world, only local or national governments have a good chance of being accepted and obeyed by the masses of the population. Neither ship nor state, Aristotle suggested, should be made so big that they would not obey the rudder (Aristotle, 1948: V, 4–6). In most regions of the world during the next half century, even at best only the nation-state will be sufficiently small, homogeneous, and popular to steer its own behavior.

Dynamic processes will reinforce this fact. In 1900, perhaps only 15% or 20% of all people had been able to read and write. But in 1972, as much as 65% of the people of the world was literate; and by 2010 A.D., 90% may be so. In every developing country, *social mobilization*—the spread of money, markets, demonstration effects, mass media, literacy, migrations, wage labor, industrialization, and urbanization—puts, on the average every decade, another 7% of the population into contact with relative strangers, making a national language and culture a necessary substitute for the old tradition, familiarity, and childhood memories that no longer can be relied on as predictors of the future and guides to action in their new environments. The same process, at about the same average speed, puts people into situations where they need public services and political tradition (Chapters 5 and 16, above; Kuhnle, 1975; Kothary, 1973; Pašić, 1973; Flora, 1973; Zapf and Flora, 1973).

But the *assimilation* of people into a new common language, culture, and a new ethnic unity, through the general prevalence of intermarriage and the probability of some common family ties, moves much more slowly: on the average, at only 1% per decade among populations that remain rooted in their original areas of residence. Today, perhaps less than 10% of the world's population speaks English. To make 90% adopt this language would take about 800 years, if past trends are a guide (Chapter 16, above: esp. pp. 304–306; and fns. 15, 16; see also Werbos, 1974; Kuhnle, 1975).

It seems most likely, therefore, that world developments in the next half century will continue to be characterized by the importance of national languages, states, and most often loyalties. The rise of mass participation and mass politics is most likely to enhance this trend. In such a world, nations will need to be reassured that scarcity will not become extreme in their lifetime and in that of their children. Without this assurance, fear and greed may join to drive nations into wars for supposedly dwindling resources. When World War I was accompanied and followed by increasingly pessimistic expectations among the German middle classes, the widespread acceptance of the warlike ideas of Oswald Spengler's *The Decline of the West* and of Adolf Hitler's *Mein Kampf* was a part of their response. Could such a tragic and destructive development be repeated on a worldwide scale?

To prevent such a drift toward catastrophe, many measures will have to be taken now or in the next few years. National and international stockpiling, an

international system of reserves of food and fuel, the opening up of new agricultural acreages and mineral deposits, the improvement of technologies, the
development of substitute materials and energy sources, the transition to less
heavy but more sophisticated equipment (e.g., to transistors and printed electronic microcircuits)—all these may help to stave off a "revolution of falling
expectations" and thus to buy more time for the world to become truly joined
"for better or worse, for richer or poorer" in the unity of the human race.

REFERENCES

Aristotle (1948) Politics, Book V. (Sir Ernest Barker, trans.). Oxford: Clarendon
    Press.

Brown, L. R. (1973) World Without Borders. New York: Vintage.

—— (1972) Interdependence of Nations. Development Paper 10, October. Wash-
    ington, D.C.: Overseas Development Council.

Cole, H. et al., 1973. Models of Doom: A Critique of the Limits to Growth.
    New York: Universe Books.

Cooper, R. N. (1968) The Economics of Interdependence. New York: McGraw-
    Hill.

Deutsch, K. W. (1974) Politics and Government. Boston: Houghton Mifflin.

—— (1967) "Nation and world." Ch. 16, pp. 297–314.

—— (1966) Nationalism and Social Communication. Cambridge: MIT Press.

—— (1961) "Social mobilization and political development." Ch. 5, pp. 90–
    129.

—— (1956) "Shifts in the balance of communication flows: a problem of
    measurement in international relations." Ch. 8, pp. 153–170.

—— and A. Eckstein (1961) "National industrialization and the declining shares
    of the international economic sector." World Politics (January): 267–299.

Flora, P. (1973) "Historical processes of social mobilization, urbanization and
    literacy, 1850-1965," in S. N. Eisenstadt and S. Rokkan (eds.) Building
    States and Nations: Models and Data Resources. Beverly Hills: Sage.

Forrester, J. W. and D. Meadows (1972) Limits to Growth. New York: Universe
    Books.

Fritsch, B. (1976) Limited Growth and Political Power. Cambridge, Mass.:
    Ballinger

Galtung, J. (1971) "A structural theory of imperialism." Journal of Peace
    Research 2:81-117.

Herrera, A. O., et al., (1976) Catastrophe or New Society? A Latin American
    Model. Ottawa: International Development Research Center.

Høivik, T. (1971) "Social inequality." Journal of Peace Research 2: 119-142.

Inkeles, A. and G. Smith (1974) Becoming Modern. Cambridge: Harvard Univ.
    Press.

International Press Institute (1953) Flow of the News.

Kindleberger, C. P. (1973) International Economics. Homewood, Ill.: R. D. Irwin.

Kothary, R. (1973) "The confrontation of theories with national realities," in S. N. Eisenstadt and S. Rokkan (eds.) Building States and Nations: Models and Data Resources. Beverly Hills: Sage.

Kuhnle, S. (1975) Patterns of Social and Political Mobilization: A Historical Analysis of the Nordic Countries. Beverly Hills: Sage.

Lerner, D. (1956) "French business leaders look at EDC: a preliminary report." Public Opinion Quarterly 20 (Spring).

Leontief, W. (1977) The Future of the World Economy: A United Nations Study. New York: Oxford University Press.

Mesarovic, M. and E. Pestel (1974) Mankind at the Turning Point. New York: E. P. Dutton/Reader's Digest Press.

Morse, E. L. (1971) "Transnational economic processes," in J. S. Nye, Jr. and R. O. Keohane (eds.) Transnational Relations and World Politics. International Organization 25 (Summer): 386.

Myrdal, G. (1957) Rich Lands and Poor. New York: Harper.

O'Neill, G. K. (1974) "The colonization of space." Physics Today (September): 32–40

Pašić N. (1973) "Varieties of nation-building in the Balkans and among the southern Slavs," in S. N. Eisenstadt and S. Rokkan (eds.) Building States and Nations: Models and Data Resources. Beverly Hills: Sage.

Pool, I. de S., et al., (1970) Prestige Press: A Comparative Study of Political Symbols. Cambridge, Mass.: MIT Press.

Rapoport, A. and A. Chammah (1965) Prisoners' Dilemma. Ann Arbor: Univ. of Michigan Press.

Russell, B. (1945) The History of Western Philosophy. New York: Simon & Schuster.

Russett, B. M., H. R. Alker, Jr., K. W. Deutsch, and H. D. Lasswell (1964) World Handbook of Political and Social Indicators. New Haven: Yale Univ. Press.

Sivard, R. (1974) World Military and Social Expenditures 1974. New York: Institute for World Order.

—— (1977) World Military and Social Expenditures 1976. New York: Institute for World Order.

Taylor, C. L. and M. C. Hudson (1975) World Handbook of Political and Social Indicators. 2nd ed. New Haven: Yale Univ. Press.

Werbos, P. (1974) "Beyond regression: new tools for prediction and analysis in the behavioral sciences." Ph.D. dissertation. Harvard University.

Zapf, W. and P. Flora (1973) "Differences in path development: an analysis for ten countries," in S. N. Eisenstadt and S. Rokkan (eds.) Building States and Nations: Models and Data Resources. Beverly Hills: Sage.

18 | Some Prospects for Today's Industrial Countries

This chapter was written for a nontechnical audience, the alumni of Harvard University, and was published in *Harvard Magazine* in 1976. This was the issue dedicated to the Bicentennial of the United States, and the title of the piece was "America in Its Third Century: Nuclear Target or World Resources."

This chapter ends the book with a look at the world which all the nations have in common. Out of about 150, only about thirty countries are highly industrialized. They comprise about one-fifth of the world's population but about four-fifths of its income and of its productive machinery. Much of the fate of these industrial countries will be influenced by what happens in the developing countries where four-fifths of all human beings live. But the world's fate—and our own fate with it—will also depend decisively on what we in the industrial countries do with the four-fifths of the world's productive hardware that we control. We can misuse them for war and mass destruction. Or we can leave them idle or only half-used in irresponsible self-indulgence, unconcerned about our poorer neighbors. Or we can seek ways to use this equipment, which we now hold in trust, for the needs of all.

Despite its popular language the technical data and projections of this chapter should be worth serious attention. Research on large-scale computer world models in the International Institute of Comparative Social Research at the Berlin Science Center is designed also to produce more precise data, projections, and simulations of world developments, such as should seem probable under particular world conditions. As of now, the provisional data offered here should suffice to start us thinking.

In the period since 1950, humanity has experienced greater change than ever before—in literacy, urbanization, population, and on countless other levels.

If we could grasp the patterns of change, we might shape the future in ways

From *Harvard Magazine* 78, no. 11 (July–August 1976): 15–18. Copyright ©1976, Harvard Magazine, Inc. Reprinted by permission of the Publisher. The present text and some figures have been brought up to date.

that assure a safer and more livable world. The grim alternative, as we are often reminded, could be our own obliteration.

Where are we now? How did we get here? We might begin by considering the period of world history that immediately preceded our own—a period that lasted from about 1500 to 1950.

During that time, intercontinental shipping and a high level of technology gave Western countries a decisive edge in power over any other population they might meet. In this period of great power differential, small numbers of Westerners could defeat forces of non-Westerners whose numerical superiority was ten- or twenty-fold greater, but whose equipment dated from the Bronze or Stone Age.

The rise of countries, regions, and peoples can be seen as a step-function of the transportation and technological competencies of the West. Diagrams of such historical development look like rhomboids. One group progresses rapidly, and then levels out on a higher plateau. Another group goes on as before, leaving a great gap between itself and the first group. After some time—a generation, or even centuries—the laggards begin to catch up. As they rise, the rhomboid closes, until the two groups are nearly equal in political strength, technology, or whatever else is being compared. The gap is now very small, and it is a gap on a higher level.

This sounds like an exercise in geometry, but it happens in human history. By 1950, a rhomboid had closed. On the battlefields of Korea, a Chinese army, recruited from one of the world's most underdeveloped countries, fought to a standstill against the army of the United States, raised in one of the world's most technologically advanced countries. When the shooting was over, and 800,000 Koreans were dead—400,000 from North Korea and 400,000 from South Korea—the new boundary dividing Korea was pretty much where the old one had been.

After that came the nonvictory of the French at Dien Bien Phu, the nonsuccess of French weapons in Algeria, and our own tragic experience in Vietnam. By now the evidence is overwhelming: there is no decisive Western superiority any longer. Nor is there Russian or Chinese superiority. There is no longer a question of who shall succeed Britain as leader of the world; the job has been eliminated. There will be no more hegemonic powers. The single greatest power in the world today is the power of change.

Consider the changes in literacy, urbanization, and population over the past quarter-century. In 1955, for the first time, the majority of people over ten years of age were literate. Today two-thirds of the world's population is literate. If literacy continues to grow at 7 percent per decade, the world will be about 85-percent literate by the end of this century.

We are now crossing the line into an urban world. Humankind is acquiring a majority of city dwellers, and in the future, peasants will be in the minority.

World population in 1976 was four billion. At a growth rate of 2 percent per year, it will double by the year 2010. After that it may grow at a slower rate. As

great epidemics and childhood diseases come under control, the next generation
of parents will adapt to the idea that their children will survive in larger numbers. They may then decide to have fewer children and get better acquainted
with the ones they have. And as old-age pensions become better established,
there will be less incentive to have many children as a form of old-age insurance,
a traditional practice in Asia and Africa. From 2010 to 2050, then, population
growth could slow to a rate of 1 percent per year, and after 2050, to one-half of
1 percent. After 2100, we might actually reach zero population growth.

These are not very optimistic assumptions. More detailed estimates point to a
stopping of world population growth by about 2075 and a global population of
12 billion people by 2100. Such a number can just be accommodated: the
population density would be comparable to Switzerland today, but that's not a
bad place to live.

What other predictions can be made for the next three generations—the people
who will live out the 21st century, barring total catastrophe?

We can expect a certain shift in international power. Worldwide oligopoly
seems a likelihood, with an accompanying trend toward increased militarism,
and an almost certain proliferation of nuclear weaponry.

In the short run, over the next ten or twenty years, the terms of trade may be
less advantageous to small countries that now have high technology and capital,
but little in the way of primary materials or energy sources. Conversely, the
terms of trade for prime-raw-material countries will improve.

The experience of American farmers offers a paradigm. In the Thirties, an
American farmer had to trade fourteen hogs to purchase one electric refrigerator.
By the late Fifties, he could get a slightly better refrigerator for the equivalent
of four hogs. The hogs are still the same basic model. The farmer's terms of
trade vis-à-vis the industrial sector have improved by a factor of three or more.

We can look for continued price increases from producers of prime raw materials. Over the past three years, the Organization of Petroleum Exporting
Countries (OPEC) has raised oil prices by a factor of three or four. Eventually,
we will confront similar increases for tin, copper, and other substances. In the
short run, we can fight off such increases by keeping stockpiles and shifting our
use to other materials. But on the whole we will find that the producing countries charge more, and some of the highly industrialized countries will keep a
little less of the profit of the transaction.

None of this will be decisive, however. Many spokesmen of the Third World
overestimate their bargaining power. There is an OPEC, true, but there is also
an OFEC: an invisible but nevertheless real organization of food-exporting
countries. These countries are the world's most highly developed. It is not the
nonindustrial countries that produce the world's food surpluses, but the countries of big factories, assembly lines, and engineers—the United States, Canada,
Australia, and in certain good years, Argentina and the Soviet Union.

Someday we will realize that there is also an invisible OTEC: an organization of technology-exporting countries. In many effective ways, the prices of high technology (oil-drilling equipment, geophysical instruments, the services of skilled drilling or prospecting teams) have been controlled for a much longer time than oil prices.

Another ten or twenty years, then, could bring worldwide oligopoly. Oligopoly means that several sellers seem to compete against one another, but are tacitly or explicitly agreed not to undercut one another in price. They compete in the same way that the Chase Manhattan Bank competes with the First National City: you get a teddy bear for opening a modest account in one bank, or a barbecue grill for opening a slightly larger account in the other. What you don't get is a higher interest rate. Banks charge a low interest rate for depositors and a high interest rate for borrowers, and on that they agree.

In a world of universal oligopoly, everyone organizes to overcharge everyone else. You offer a little less in the market than you used to, and charge a little more. Then you repeat the process until it's no longer a little. Ultimately, something has to give. A worldwide situation of oligopoly would create tremendous political and military pressure to destroy the organizations of the weakest competitors.

There could be strange reversals. Formerly unorganized groups might turn out to have the greatest strength and resilience, once they were organized. Groups that were once strongly organized might turn out to be weaker than they thought. To cope with new economic pressures, many countries will be tempted to increase their military potential.

This pressure toward militarization will come at a time when weapons systems are generally alike, and generally available.

What happens when you militarize? In domestic politics, there are those who think that increasing the size and weight of the military sector makes for stability. But the armies of Peru, Portugal, and Greece have demonstrated that military establishments are not necessarily more stable, and that military leaders are no more unbuyable than any other bunch of bureaucrats or politicians. They may be more heavily armed, but that does not make them wiser. The more militarization, the more tyranny and risk of error.

The most recklessly irresponsible thing we could do in the future would be to go on exactly as we have in the past ten or twenty years. It is hard to imagine a more dangerous policy than the conservatism that exists today. It puts me in mind of the man who fell from the top of the Empire State Building, and remarked as he passed the second floor, "So far experience shows that everything has been going well." All too soon did he learn what was really happening.

What, then, can Americans and other industrialized peoples do to make life safer and more livable for at least three more generations? What are our most pressing needs, and how best can we respond to them?

One urgent need will be greater capital accumulation. Roughly speaking the world will need about eight times as much capital for the decade between 2000 and 2010 as we need now.

If we have twice as many people, we will need twice as much capital to produce food; and twice as much capital will be needed to produce the energy that produces the food. Creating babies is a labor-intensive but low-capital process, while creating the food that babies need is capital-intensive.

Because much of the world's land reserve has largely been used up, we are moving from extensive to intensive cultivation—that is, from low to high fertilizer levels. This movement began in European agriculture, and is now becoming worldwide. But fertilizers alone don't make crops grow; water is needed. In many parts of the world, rainfall is scarce or unreliable. To get water to where it is needed, countries like India and Pakistan would require an invasion by armies of plumbers, setting up pipelines and pumping plants. That means capital. Storage and transport of food means capital. And capital, like machinery, requires energy.

For much of this century, we have been swimming on a wave of cheap energy produced by cheap oil. Since oil was cheap, we adopted petroleum-based fertilizers in place of nitrogen fixation from the air. We shifted from hydroelectric stations to thermal power stations, to some extent, because although hydroelectric plants get water for free, the capital required for the dam is greater than the capital needed for the pipes and kettles of a thermal power station burning oil or coal.

Liquefied coal may provide the solution to a future oil shortgage, but it would require much more capital (not to mention the cost of repairing damage to the landscape). One way to avoid burning either oil or coal would be to shift to nuclear power. But a nuclear power station costs at least three times as much capital per kilowatt-hour as a thermal power station. This does not take into account the cost of disposing of the poisonous by-products of fission. Someday, we will probably shift back from fission to fusion. It involves containing materials at temperatures of millions of degrees, and the material for doing so will again involve more capital. In any event, it is probably safe to say that we are likely to need twice as much capital per kilowatt-hour by the year 2010 as we need currently.

In addition to meeting the requirements of food and energy production, we need capital to help reduce inequality in the world. At the moment, conditions are flagrantly unequal: the range of inequality between richest and poorest, in terms of per capita income, is as great as 100 to 1 in some countries.

Suppose we determine to double the median income in the world—$1,000 per capita in 1976—equivalent to about $650 in 1967 dollars. This is going to take a major economic effort to double it, especially if most of the improvement is to be felt in poorer countries. It will put a tremendous demand on our output of energy and our use of prime raw materials.

Where will we find all the capital we require? We could begin by looking at armaments. At present, we sterilize about 6 percent of the world's annual income in armaments—more in the richer countries, less in the poorer ones. I use the word sterilize because when we put iron into a machine tool, it produces other machines. When we put it into a tank, the only thing it produces is rust—or death.

Perhaps there are ways to scare each other for half of what we spend today. Robert McNamara used to talk about getting a bigger bang for our buck. If we can get more corpses for a dollar than we used to, we may be able to threaten humanity with equal effectiveness for about half the capital we now expend.

Another approach to capital formation would be research. In 1965, we spent 3 percent of our gross national product on research; by the Seventies, we had cut that back to about 2 percent. If we went back to 3 percent, or even 4, we could do two very important things.

We could pursue urgently needed lines of research, such as developing better food plants and more effective ways to use solar energy. We could also develop technologies that save capital rather than use it, and reduce our plundering of the world's resources. Printed circuits use less copper than wire-and-solder ones; miniaturization techniques like microdot or microfilm can save forests, if used on a sufficiently wide scale.

We could also find ways to share information more extensively with other countries. Information, after all, is the kind of good you can give another without impoverishing yourself. It is a kind of invisible capital.

We will have to choose. We can try to monopolize our technology, dole it out with an eyedropper to a few deserving client states, and have them pay through the nose for it. Or we can be generous with it, recognizing that there are masses of people to be fed and that only scientific and technological knowledge will break the bottlenecks of hunger and poverty.

If we make the second choice, we may all end up in a world that is more cooperative, that can share its achievements, and is less threatened by its insufficiencies.

The United States has tremendous technological resources. In the short run, we could use them to build up food reserves for the world, since the first and most dangerous threat to the world is mass famine in certain countries.

Imagine the possible consequences of such famines. Some large countries, such as India, still have reasonably rational governments, as governments go these days. Indira Gandhi, like her successor Morarji Desai, and before them Indira's father Jawaharlal Nehru and Mohandas Gandhi all were products of the liberal Western educational system. But if India should have mass famines, Morarji Desai will no longer be prime minister. India's future leader might be a fundamentalist with a profound belief in Kali, the goddess of death, or Shiva, who Hindu tradition says will destroy the world in a fiery dance, so that new life will rise from the ruins of the incinerated globe.

Nearly every country has memories of suicidal heroism, some of which could be developed into death cults. The Japanese recall the Kamikaze pilots of World War II. Israelis remember the suicide of the defendants of Masada. The Arabs have the tradition of the Hashishim, which gives us the word assassin.

This kind of emotional dynamite, exacerbated by the pressures of famine and despair, could find the technological and physical equipment to initiate policies and processes of large-scale destruction. If we sit back and let it happen, we will be numbered among the victims.

If, on the other hand, we find ways to prevent great famines, we will have done more for world stability than we could in any other way.

At the moment, we are threatened by the fact that national states distort the perceptive and reporting systems of the world. They hide the joint threat of death, hunger, and catastrophe. They underreport the gains we make against these dangers, insofar as we make them, and overreport advances that are relatively picayune. Compared with a nuclear war in the Mediterranean, what is the difference between having 25 or 40 percent of Cyprus?

When Egypt and Israel decided to adjust their frontier rather than war again in the Sinai, they won a joint victory: a victory over death. They saved the lives of at least 2,600 young Israelis, the number that were killed in the October War, and at least an equal number of Egyptian lives.

National states tell the electorate what it supposedly wants to know: how far the state is ahead of its rivals. We concentrate on scoring points against each other—Israelis against Arabs, the United States against the Soviet Union, the Soviet Union against the Chinese, the Turks against the Greeks. We are so busy scoring these little points that we fail to notice how we play our games in canoes that float smoothly in the waters above Niagara Falls. We had better pay attention and start paddling.

We need to begin to change our thinking, our perceiving, and the way we report the world to ourselves and allow it to be reported to us. In the end, humanity will have to change its patterns of action greatly; but the change must begin with a change in patterns of thinking and feeling. To an important degree, many private groups around the world are searching for strategies of reorientation, and are well ahead of national governments in their search. Eventually, with luck, I think reorientation will come. Humanity will be able to take its own fate into its own hands, and see to it that our children, and our children's children, shall have life and have it more abundantly.

Index

Abstract symbols, 213
Activity process, 283
Admission system, 82
Agriculture, 83, 234, 332
Alfieri, Vittorio, 58
Amalgamated security community, 182, 185, 189, 190, 197, 247
American Business and Public Policy (Bauer, Pool, and Dexter), 200
Anderson, Russel F., 157
Anti-Semitism, 61
Aristotle, 284, 325
Arms control, 86, 249–268
  attitudes of European press on, 262–263
  decline of proposals for (1960–1964), 263–264
  multilateral nuclear force, 265–266, 267
  national nuclear deterrent, 264–266, 267
  nuclear proliferation, fear of, 264
Arms Control and Disarmament Agency (ACDA), 249
Arms race, 2, 86
Arndt, Ernst, 61
Articles of Confederation, 186, 191
Aspirations
  assimilation of, 286
  equalization of, 70, 71
Assimilation, 304–306, 325
  cultural, 15, 16, 23, 136, 282–283, 304
  dimensions of, 286–287
  linguistic, 138, 304–306
Atlantic Alliance, 253, 260–261, 313
Atlantic Community, 261
Atlantic Union, 149
Attainments, assimilation of, 286–287
Austro-Prussian War, 220
Automatic discrimination, 51–52

Backwash effect, 276
Balance of power, 189, 190
Barker, Sir Ernest, 5
Barnave, Antoine, 281

Baruch Plan of 1946, 262
Bauer, R., 200
Becoming Modern (Inkeles and Smith), 283, 286
Behavioral loyalty, 273
Benedict, Ruth, 24
Berlin Handbook of World Political and Social Indicators (ed. Taylor), 6
Beyond Conjecture: Data-Based Research in International Relations (Jones and Singer), 200
Beyond Regression: New Tools for Prediction and Analysis in the Behavioral Sciences (Werbos), 4
Bidault, Georges, 237
Bipolarity, 204, 206, 256, 258
Bismarck, Otto von, 61, 192
Black Muslims, 84
Blacks: *see also* Discrimination
  agriculture, 83
  education, 82, 84
  intelligence, 88
  voting, 81
Bolívar, Simón, 28
Boundaries, 271–272
Brewer, T., 200
Bridgman, P. W., 13
Brown, Harrison, 312
Brown, L. R., 316
Buchanan, William, 205
Bunche, Ralph, 79
Bureaucracy, 100
Burke, Edmund, 53, 281, 299
Burrell, Sidney, 182

Cairnes, E. J., 72, 73, 76
Canning, George, 61
Cantril, Hadley, 205
Capabilities, assimilation of, 286
Capital
  accumulation of, 332–333
  differential concentration of, 17, 21–23
  scarcity of, 276–277

Castlereagh, Viscount (Robert Stewart), 61
Casualties-to-prisoners ratio, 273–274
Catholics, 57
Censorship, 319, 320
Center for Research on World Political Institutions, Princeton University, 180, 212
Chamberlain, Joseph, 61
Chamberlin, Edward H., 45
Chammah, A., 323
Chenery, Hollis, 239
Chinese Exclusion Act, 61
Chinese Revolution, 90
Christianity, 32
Churchill, Sir Winston, 235
City-states, 298
Civil service, 101, 223
Civil War (American), 195, 273
Classic economic theory, 59
Classification of individuals, 55
Cleaver, Eldridge, 79
Club of Rome, 298, 315
Cobden Treaty of 1860, 59
Coercion, 189–190
Cognitive consonance and dissonance, 269, 281
Cold war, 2, 261
Cole, H., 315
Colonies, 7, 184, 186, 191, 194, 203, 212, 237–238
Commercial revolution, 57
Common Market: see European Community (EC)
Communications, 15, 70, 71, 101, 307–308
    distance and, 171
    growth of grids, 17, 19–20
    nationalism and, 302, 306–308
    shifts in balance of international flows, 153–170
Communications Program of the Center of International Studies, M.I.T., 156
Communism, 225, 227, 236, 261
Community, defined, 14
Community and Contention: Britain and America in the Twentieth Century (Russett), 179
Competition, 24–25, 45, 50–52, 54, 58–60, 70, 71, 229
Compliance habits, 278
Conditioning, 71
Conscription, 195, 222
Conservatism, 331
Consociation, 288
Consolidation, 286
Consonance process, 282
Constitution of the United States, 191

Cooper, R. N., 316
Cooper, Thomas, 58
Coordination, 323–324
Core areas, 17, 18–19
Corn Laws, 59
Cosmopolitans, 307
Council of Europe, 243
Country
    defined, 14
    integration and, 274–276
Criticality, threshold of, 97–98
Crouching Future, The (Hilsman), 200
Cultural assimilation, 15, 16, 23, 136, 282–283, 306
Culture, 78–87, 221
Curley, James Michael, 81
Customs Cooperation Council, 243
Cybernetics, 13
Cymrodorian Society, 58

Dano-Norwegian language, 41
de Gaulle, Charles, 250, 251, 257, 258, 260, 261, 265
de Tocqueville, Alexis, 69
Declaration of Independence, 215
Decline of the West, The (Spengler), 325
Desai, Morarji, 333
Détente, 217
Deutsch, Karl W., 3, 35, 179, 276, 284, 318, 320
Dexter, Lewis, 156, 200
Dictatorship, 218, 225, 230, 290, 318
Dien Bien Phu, 329
Disarmament: see Arms control
Discrimination, 4–5, 44–45, 65–89; see also Intolerance
    economic theories and, 71–78
    in education, 52
    in employment, 46–50, 72–75
    ethnicity and culture, 78–87
    multiplier effect and, 76–78
    in real estate, 76
    against women, 55, 56, 74, 76
Disintegration of populations, 80–81
Disjoined Partners: Austria and Germany Since 1815 (Katzenstein), 179
Distance, 171–175
Distribution costs, 62
Dodd, Thomas, 82
Doeblin, Alfred, 286
Dollfuss, Engelbert, 42
Dominance, loss of, 195–196
Dominguez, Jorge, 4, 91, 275
DuPont, Victor, 281

East-Central European integration, 8, 217–233
Eckstein, A., 318

Economic distance, 171
Economic growth and development, 220–221, 238–242, 297–298, 311–312
Economic stagnation, 195
Economic theories, 44–52, 59, 229–230
  discrimination and, 71–78
Edinger, L. J., 179
Education, 29, 81, 82, 84, 166–168, 222, 223
  admission system, 82
  blacks and, 82, 84
  discrimination in, 52
Einstein, Albert, 215
Eisenhower, Dwight D., 233
Eisenstadt, Samuel, 280
Elites, 101, 142–143, 256–261
  broadening of, 192
  closure of, 195
Emerson, Rupert, 2, 13, 141–142
Eminent domain, law of, 87
Empire, 277, 298, 299
Employment, discrimination in, 46–50, 72–75
Energy, 330, 332, 333
Englis, Karel, 62
Enlightenment, 63
Erhard, Ludwig, 258, 259
Essence, 269, 273–274
Ethnic awareness, 17, 27–31
Ethnic solidarity, 80
Ethnicity, 78–87
Ethnie, concept of, 277–278
European Civil Aviation Conference, 243
European Coal and Steel Community (ECSC), 237, 239, 243–245
European Community (EC), 234, 239, 260, 276
European Defense Community (EDC), 187, 206, 235, 243, 259
European Economic Community: *see* European Community (EC)
European Energy Authority, 235
European Monetary Union, 235
European Parliament, 235
European Political Community, 243
Evaluation, political integration and, 270, 284–285
Exchange economies, shift to, 17–18
Existence, 269, 271–273
Expectations, mass, 193–194

Famines, 333–334
Farm labor, 46–47, 53
Farmers' organizations, 62
Fascism, 2, 225
Federal World Government, 149
Federalism, 218
Feedback, 92

Festinger, Leon, 269, 281
Feudalism, 16, 57
Flora, Peter, 279, 325
Folkemaal, 41
Foltz, William J., 5, 141, 142, 143, 179
Food production, 9, 332–334
Force de frappe, 251, 265
Ford, Franklin, 287
Foreign aid, 311
Foreign policy, 85–86
Foreign trade, 72, 77, 78, 103, 206, 210, 246, 252, 253
Forrester, J. W., 315
France, Germany and the Western Alliance (Deutsch, Edinger, Macridis, and Merritt), 179
Frankfurter Allgemeine Zeitung, 253
Franklin, Benjamin, 214
Free trade, 59, 77, 229–230
Freedom, 284
Fremdheitserlebnis, 26–27
French Community, 244
French Revolution, 90, 301
Friedrich, Carl J., 139, 140, 300
Fritsch, B., 315
From French West Africa to the Mali Federation (Foltz), 5, 179
Fundamental democratization, 13, 92, 151

"G.I. Bill of Rights," 63
Gaelic, 38, 41, 58
Galtung, Johan, 275
Games, 23–24
Gandhi, Indira, 333
Gandhi, Mahatma, 215, 333
Garibaldi, Giuseppe, 61
Gemeinschaft, 242–243
General Inquirer, The (Stone), 200
Genesis of political integration, 270, 274–284
Gesellschaft, 243
Gettysburg Address, 215
Gini index, 319
Gladstone, William, 61
Glazer, Nathan, 277
Gleim, Johann, 58
Greer, Donald, 287
Gross national product (GNP), 94, 96, 100, 297, 318
Group awareness, 17, 27–31
Group organization, 61
Guilds, 56, 57, 62
Guyot, Dorothy Hess, 6

Haberler, Gottfried von, 72
Habsburg Empire, The (Kann), 179
Hanson, B., 200

Harris, Chauney, 171
Haug, Marie, 71
Hayes, Carlton, 3, 283
Hebrew language, 41
Hegel, Georg, 299
Henry VII, King of England, 186
Herrera, A. O., 315
Hibbs, Douglas A., Jr., 4, 91
Highlighting process, 282, 283
Hilsman, R., 200
Hitler, Adolf, 54, 290, 325
Hitlerism, 53
Hobbes, Thomas, 299
Holmes, Oliver Wendell, 88
Hudson, Michael E., 5, 6, 271, 276, 318, 321

Ibo tribe, 81, 83
Immigration, 62
Impersonality, 70, 71
Income, 100, 108–109, 188, 210, 220, 275–276, 311–312, 319, 321–322, 332
Income tax, international, 315
Independence, 202–203, 284, 285
Indicators, interchangeability of, 94–96
Industrial Revolution, 22, 57, 90
Inequality, 319–324, 332
Infant mortality, 320
Information: see Communications
Inglehart, Ronald, 298
Inheritance, 66
Inkeles, Alex, 283
Innovation rates, 229–230
Insecurity, 24–25, 51, 69, 71
Inspection arrangement, 264
Intake-output ratio, concept of, 156–157
Integration: see International integration; Interregional integration; National integration; Political integration; Political symbols; Regional integration, large and small states in
Intellectual life, 223
Intelligence, 88
Interdependence, 316–319
Interest and Ideology (Hanson), 200
Intermarriage, 80, 277, 325
International income tax, 313
International Institute of Comparative Social Research, Berlin Science Center, 328
International integration, 148–152
tentative scale of, 146–147
International organization, 284, 311
International population transfer, 86–87
International Press Institute, 205, 208, 319
International Red Cross, 215

International trade: see Foreign trade
International transactions
distance and, 171–175
propensity to, 144–152
shifts in balance of, 153–170
Internationalism, 2
Interregional integration, 150, 152
tentative scale of, 146–147
Intolerance, 44–45; see also Discrimination
basic conditions for, 54–55
defined, 51
economic practice, 50–52
as irrational habit, 53–54
patterns of, 55–62
in pre-industrial age, 55–57
Introjection process, 283
Investment patterns, 229–230
Irvin, William, 6
Isard, Walter, 7
Islam, 26
Isolationism, 209–211
Izvestia, 209, 210

James I, King of England, 186
Jingoism, 61
Johnson, Lyndon B., 258
Jones, Susan, 200
Judaism, 32
Jünger, Ernst, 92

Kann, Robert A., 179, 182
Kant, Immanuel, 299
Katzenstein, Peter, 8, 179
Kennedy family, 81
Kenworthy, Eldon C., 6
Keynes, John Maynard, 76, 110
Khrushchev, Nikita, 262
Kindleberger, Charles P., 275, 316
Kingdoms, 299
Klingberg, Frank L., 205
Kohn, Hans, 3, 283
Kollar, Jan, 41
Korean War, 229
Kosinski, Jerzy, 67
Kothary, R., 325
Kuhnle, S., 325

Labor Unions, 49, 62, 223
Laissez-faire, 24, 44, 59, 99, 229, 244, 276
Land ownership, 87
Land reforms, 222
Landsmaal, 41
Language, 15, 19, 20, 28–29, 35–43, 57–58, 80, 101, 221, 277, 278, 287, 303–305
Laubach, Frank, 215

Law enforcement, 189
Lazarsfeld, Paul, 94
Le Monde, 253
League of Nations, 2, 299
Learning capacity, 289-290
Lee, Maurice, 182
Leontief, W., 315
Lerner, Daniel, 283, 318
Lerner, Max, 35
Liberalism, 99
Liberation, 284
Lichterman, Martin, 182
Life expectancy, 320
Limited growth, 315-326
Lincoln, Abraham, 215
Lincoln-Douglas debates, 215
Lindgren, R., 179, 182
Linguistic assimilation, 138, 304-306
Literacy, 38-39, 95, 97-98, 142, 304, 320, 325, 328, 329
Localism, 15, 16
Locals, 307
Locke, John, 299, 310
Loewenheim, Francis, 182
Logical empiricism, 13
London *Times*, 209, 210, 253
Loos, Adolph, 221

Machiavelli, Niccolò, 25, 299
Maclaurin, W. Rupert, 275
Macridis, R. C., 179
Maerlant, Jacob van, 39
Mail: *see* Postal correspondence
Malthus, Robert, 54
Manin, Daniele, 186
Mannheim, Karl, 13, 92, 93, 151
Manteuffel, von, 192
Margaret Tudor, 186
Marginal utility, 311, 322
Marijuana laws, 278
Market size, 239-242
Marshall, Sir Alfred, 59
Marshall Plan, 237
Marx, Karl, 281, 299
Marxism-Leninism, 217
Masaryk, T. G., 64
Mass media: *see* Media
Mass Political Violence (Hibbs, Jr.), 4
Mather, Kirtley, 312
Mazzini, Giuseppe, 299
McAlister, John T., 5
McNamara, Robert, 333
McWilliams, Carey, 53
Meadows, D., 315
Measurement, defined, 154-156
Media, 29, 93, 94, 101, 102, 107, 302
Meier, Richard, 75
Mein Kampf (Hitler), 54, 325

Mendès-France, Pierre, 263
Mercantilism, 58
Merritt, Richard L., 35, 102, 138, 140, 179, 283
Merton, Robert, 307
Mesarovic, M., 315
Metternich, Prince Klemens von, 110
Middle long run, 53-54
Migration, 145, 150, 151, 166-168, 188
Military commitments, effect of excessive, 194-195
Mobilization, 285-286; *see also* Social mobilization
Moch, Jules, 263
Modernization, 91-92, 282, 285-286
Monopolies, 5, 45, 50, 59, 61-62, 73
Monopsony, 46-49
Montesquieu, Baron de La Brède et de, 299
Moravec, Emanuel, 274
Morse, E. L., 318
Moynihan, Patrick, 277
Multi-functional market, 275
Multilateral nuclear force (MLF), 265-266, 267
Multiplier effect, 76-78
Multipolarity, 256, 258
Mussolini, Benito, 290
Myrdal, Gunner, 275, 276, 316

Namenwirth, Zvi, 200
Napoleon I, 290
Nation, defined, 14, 140, 301
Nation-building: *see* National development
Nation-states, 307-313
National Consciousness in Divided Germany (Schweigler), 179
National development, 6, 133-143
National growth: *see* National development
National integration, 14, 136, 139
National nuclear deterrent, 264-266, 267
National resurgence, 22
National self-preoccupation, 208-209, 211
National symbols, 28-29; *see also* Political symbols
Nationalism, 2, 3-6, 12-129, 230, 256-257, 282, 300-302, 310; *see also* Nations, growth of; Social mobilization
assimilation and, 304-306
communications and, 302, 306-308
defined, 301
discrimination: *see* Discrimination
Eastern European, 225-226
extreme, 302
language: *see* Language
nations, growth of, 13-34
social mobilization and, 302-304

*Nationalism and National Development:
An Interdisciplinary Bibliography*
(Deutsch and Merritt), 35
Nationalism and Social Communication
(Deutsch), 3
Nationality, defined, 60
Nations, growth of, 13–34
  capital, skills, and institutions, 17, 21–
  23
  communication grids, 17, 19–20
  core areas, 17, 18–19
  ethnic awareness, 17, 27–31
  exchange economies, shift to, 17–18
  self-interest and self-awareness, 17,
  23–27
  social mobilization, 15–19
  towns, growth of, 17, 19
Nazism, 259
Needs, assimilation of, 286
Nehru, Jawaharlal, 101, 333
Neo-mercantilism, 59, 61
Neurath, Otta, 13
New York Times, 209, 210, 253–254, 319
News reporting and readership, 145, 150–
  151, 157, 207–208, 253–254, 262,
  319
Nixon, Richard M., 87
Nkrumah, Kwame, 84
North Atlantic Treaty Organization
  (NATO), 238, 243, 244, 255, 257,
  260, 265
*Norway-Sweden: Union, Disunion and
Scandinavian Integration* (Lindgren),
  179
Nuclear test-ban treaty of 1963, 262, 264
Nuclear weapons, 86–87, 317, 330; *see
also* Arms control

October War, 334
Oetlingen-Wallerstein, Count, 58
Oil prices, 330
Oligopoly, 331
Ontology, 269, 270–271
Organization for Economic Cooperation
  and Development (OECD), 244
Organization for European Economic Co-
  operation (OEEC), 244
Organization of Petroleum Exporting
  Countries (OPEC), 330
Organized labor, 49, 62, 223
Ortega y Gasset, José, 228
Osgood, Charles, 298
Overloads, 289–290

Pan-Slavism, 41
Papacy, 299
Pareto, Vilfredo, 195
Paris Agreements of 1954, 251
Parsons, Talcott, 311, 242, 243

Pašić, N., 325
Patriotism, 276
Patronage organizations, 62
Paucifunctional market, 275
Pavlovian conditioning, 71
Pearl Harbor, 290
People
  defined, 14, 301
  integration process and, 277–278
Personal symbols, 213
Personality types, 156–157
Pestel, E., 315
Piaget, Jean, 288
Pictorial symbols, 213
Plato, 26, 56, 223
Pluralism, 288–289
Pluralistic security community, 182, 185,
  196–197, 217, 246
Podhoretz, Norman, 82
Police forces, 189, 190
Political amalgamation, 231–233
*Political Community and the North Atlan-
tic Area* (Deutsch and Burrell), 179
Political compulsion, 17, 31
Political development, social mobilization
  and, 98–105
*Political Impact of the Japanese Occupa-
tion of Burma, The* (Guyot), 6
Political integration, 88, 137, 138, 142,
  269–291; *see also* Regional integration, large and small states in
  boundaries, 271–272
  East-Central European, 8, 217–233
  essence, 269, 273–274
  evaluation, 270, 284–285
  existence, 269, 271–273
  genesis, 270, 274–284
  ontology, 269, 270–271
  opportunities for intervention, 270,
  285–291
  structural correspondence, 270–271
  transaction flows, 271
  Western European: *see* Western European integration
Political participation, 193–194
Political symbols, 28–29, 154, 199–216
  independence and security as, 202–203
  as indicators, 200–202
  as instruments of political change or
  control, 211–216
  recent trends in national and international, 203–211
*Political Transformation of Tanganyika,
The* (Stephens), 5
Politics (Aristotle), 284
Pool, Ithiel de Sola, 200, 202–206, 209,
  319
Population growth, 9, 223, 312, 328, 329–
  330

Postal correspondence, 6-7, 103, 145, 146, 148-149, 188, 206, 207, 210, 246, 252
   ratio of internal to external flow, 159-166
   receiving-sending ratio of foreign, 157-159
Poverty, 51, 319
Powell, Adam Clayton, 81-82
Powell, Enoch, 85
Power, 197, 320, 323-324
Precarious Republics, The: Political Modernization in Lebanon (Hudson), 5
Preference organizations, 62
Prisoners-to-casualties ratio, 273-274
Probabilistic reinforcement sequences, 269, 280-281
Probability categories, 66-67
Production, 21, 61, 275-276
Productivity, 21, 22, 223
Prohibition, 278
Property rights, 87, 226-227
Prosperity policy, 73-74
Protectionism, 59, 77, 78, 234
Protestants, 57
Proto-integration, 287
Psychic distance, 204-205
Public opinion, 254-256

Race, defined, 65-68
Race discrimination: *see* Discrimination
Rapacki Plan of 1957, 262
Rapoport, A., 323
Real estate market, 76
Reder, M. W., 45-46
Regional integration, large and small states in, 7, 179-198
   amalgamated security communities, disintegration of, 192-196
   amalgamated security communities, establishment of, 191-192
   case studies of, 180-183
   conflict loads and adjustment capabilities, role of small states in, 184-187
   large states as cores of, 183-184
   popular beliefs on, 187-191
   relativity of large state-small state hierarchy, 184
Relevance process, 282, 283
Religious symbols, 213
Renan, Ernest, 206
Renovation schools, 84-85
Reproducible quantitative evidence, 13
Residence, change of, 94
Revolution in Vietnam (McAlister), 5
Revolutionary war, 141
Rewards, 69, 71
Rhodes, Cecil, 61
Ricasoli, Bettino, 186

Riesman, David, 156, 307
Robinson, Joan, 45, 46, 75-76
Rodrigues, John, 156
Rokkan, Stein, 280, 283
Rousseau, Jean-Jacques, 299
Royal Institute of International Affairs, 35
Russett, B. M., 8, 179, 200, 271, 276, 283, 321
Russian Revolution, 90

Salazer, Antonio de Oliveira, 290
Savings rates, 229-230
Scarcity, 9, 51, 315, 320, 323-325
Schramm, Wilbur, 207
Schumpeter, Joseph, 24
Schweigler, G., 179
Schweitzer, Albert, 215
Schwyzerdütsch, 40-41
Scott, Robert, 141
Security, 202-203
Security community, 180-182
   amalgamated, 182, 185, 189, 190, 197, 247
   pluralistic, 182, 185, 196-197, 217, 246
Self-interest, 17, 23-27
Settlement, density of, 70, 71
Shepherd, George, 71
Significance, threshold of, 96-97
Singer, J. David, 200, 271
Sivard, R., 319, 321
Skills, differential concentration of, 17, 21-23
Skinner, B. F., 71, 269, 280, 281
Slavery, 56
Small, Melvin, 271
Smith, Adam, 244, 276
Smith, David, 283, 286
Social class, 31, 281-282
Social Darwinism, 60
Social distance, 171-172
Social institutions, differential concentration of, 17, 21-23
Social mobility, 17, 19, 80
Social mobilization, 5, 15-19, 27, 28, 33, 90-129, 136, 193, 282-283, 309-311, 325
   analytical formulation, 93-98
   defined, 91-92
   nationalism and, 302-304
   political development and, 98-105
   quantitative model of, 105-110
Social Mobilization, Traditional Political Participation and Governmental Response in Early 19th Century South America (Dominguez), 4
Socialism, 24
Social-reinforcement learning, 71
Society, defined, 14

Socrates, 26
Solidarity, 9, 323, 324
Sørenson, Max, 184, 197
Spaak, Paul Henri, 237
Spengler, Oswald, 325
Spread effect, 276
Stalin, Joseph, 236, 272
Standard of living, 21, 22
State, integration process and, 278
Stephens, Hugh W., 5
Stereotyping, 79
Stevenson, Adlai, 233
Stone, Philip, 200
Stratified rewards, 69, 71
Structural correspondence, 270–271
Structuralism, 288
Studenski, Paul, 108
Students, movement of, 166–168, 252
Subsidization, agriculture and, 234
Suicidal heroism, 334
Supranational organizations, 242–246,
    311
Symbolic organizations, 213
Symbolic places, 213
Symbols: see Political symbols
Symbols of American Community, 1735–
    1775 (Merritt), 179

Taussig, Frank, 72
Taxes, 88
Taylor, Charles L., 6, 111, 153, 271, 276,
    318, 321
Teachers, 81, 82, 85
Territorial patriotism, 58
Third World Handbook of Political and
    Social Indicators (Taylor), 153
Thirty Years' War, 57
Tibbets, Frederick E., 3d, 96
Tönnies, Ferdinand, 242, 243
Towns, growth of, 17, 19, 56
Toynbee, Arnold J., 2, 15
Trade: see Foreign trade
Tradition, 303
Travel, 145, 150, 166–168, 252
Treaty of Rome, 7
Tribes, 135–138
Tweed, William Marcy, 81

Unemployment, 74, 229
Ungovernability, 324–326
United Nations, 2, 86, 87, 89, 94, 211,
    215, 299

United Nations Children's Emergency
    Fund, 215
United Nations Educational, Scientific and
    Cultural Organization (UNESCO), 215
Unity of Science, 13
Universal states, 15
Urbanization, 95–96, 298, 299

Value orientations, compatibility of, 272–
    273
Values, 63–64, 154
Van Wagenen, Richard, 180, 182
Veldeke, Heinrich von, 39
Veterans' organizations, 62
Vietnam War, 141, 250, 273
Voting participation, 102, 304

Wages, 188, 275
War, 2, 180–181
Ware, Carolyn, 73
Warsaw Pact, 217
Washington, George, 192
Washington Post, 319
Watergate affair, 290
Weber, Max, 299
Weilenmann, Alex, 111
Weilenmann, Hermann, 139, 141, 182,
    276
Weingart, M., 41
Welfare state, 24, 277
Werbos, Paul J., 4, 325
Western civilization, defined, 32
Western European Federation, 149
Western European integration, 7, 8, 234–
    248
  arms control and, 249–268
  decline in interest in, 253–261
  halting of since mid-1950's, 252–253
Western European Union, 206
What Price Vigilance? (Russett), 200
Wheare, Kenneth C., 300
White, Walter, 68
Wiener, Norbert, 13
Wilson, David A., 141
Witchcraft, 57
Women, discrimination and, 55, 56, 74, 76
World Handbook of Political and Social
    Indicators (Taylor and Hudson), 6
World Health Organization, 215
Wright, Quincy, 3, 200, 205, 302

Yom Kippur War, 274

Zapf, Wolfgang, 279, 283, 325